VAMPIRE KNIGHT

Story & Art by
Matsuri Hino

Vol. 13

The Story of VAMPIRE KNIGHT

1 Cross Academy, a private boarding school, is where the Day Class and the Night Class coexist. The Night Class—a group of beautiful elite students—are all vampires!

2 Four years ago, after turning his twin brother Ichiru against him, the pureblood Shizuka Hio bit Zero and turned him into a vampire. Kaname kills Shizuka, but the source may still exist. Meanwhile, Yuki suffers from lost memories. When Kaname sinks his fangs into her neck, her memories return!

3 Yuki is the princess of the Kuran family—and a pureblood vampire!! Ten years ago, her mother exchanged her life to seal away Yuki's vampire nature. Yuki's Uncle Rido killed her father. Rido takes over Shiki's body and arrives at the Academy. He targets Yuki for her blood, so Kaname gives his own blood to resurrect Rido. Kaname confesses that he is the progenitor of the Kurans, and that Rido is the master who awakened him!

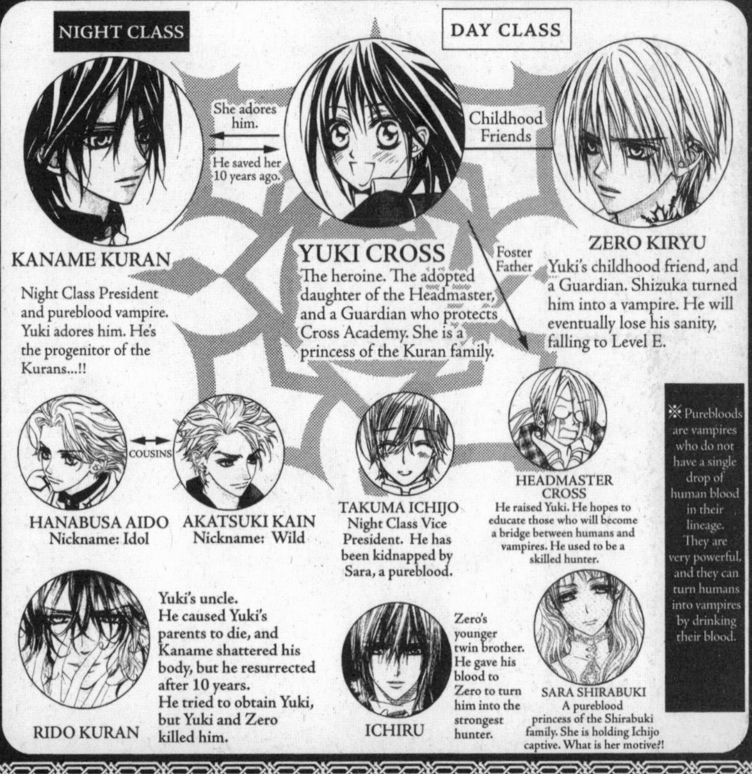

NIGHT CLASS
DAY CLASS
She adores him.
He saved her 10 years ago.
Childhood Friends
KANAME KURAN
Night Class President and pureblood vampire. Yuki adores him. He's the progenitor of the Kurans...!!
YUKI CROSS
The heroine. The adopted daughter of the Headmaster, and a Guardian who protects Cross Academy. She is a princess of the Kuran family.
Foster Father
ZERO KIRYU
Yuki's childhood friend, and a Guardian. Shizuka turned him into a vampire. He will eventually lose his sanity, falling to Level E.
COUSINS
HANABUSA AIDO
Nickname: Idol
AKATSUKI KAIN
Nickname: Wild
TAKUMA ICHIJO
Night Class Vice President. He has been kidnapped by Sara, a pureblood.
HEADMASTER CROSS
He raised Yuki. He hopes to educate those who will become a bridge between humans and vampires. He used to be a skilled hunter.
※Purebloods are vampires who do not have a single drop of human blood in their lineage. They are very powerful, and they can turn humans into vampires by drinking their blood.
RIDO KURAN
Yuki's uncle.
He caused Yuki's parents to die, and Kaname shattered his body, but he resurrected after 10 years.
He tried to obtain Yuki, but Yuki and Zero killed him.
ICHIRU
Zero's younger twin brother. He gave his blood to Zero to turn him into the strongest hunter.
SARA SHIRABUKI
A pureblood princess of the Shirabuki family. She is holding Ichijo captive. What is her motive?!

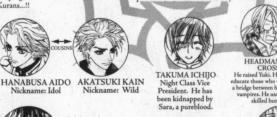

VAMPIRE KNIGHT

Contents

4 Cross Academy turns into a battlefield. After fierce fighting, Yuki and Zero succeed in defeating Rido, but right after Zero points his gun at Yuki. No matter what their feelings are, their fates will never intertwine. Zero pierces Yuki's neck with his fangs to drink her blood. The two kiss.

"The next time I meet you, I'll kill you."
"Then I'll keep running away from you..."

Yuki leaves with Kaname, and the Night Class at Cross Academy is no more.

5 A year has passed since Yuki and Zero's parting. Both the Vampire Senate and the Hunter Society have fallen apart, and Kaname and Zero have become the representatives of each group respectively. Yuki and Zero are reunited at a soirée. That night, the pureblood Ouri supposedly commits suicide, but Sara caused his death. Hoping to stop more people from becoming victims, Yuki takes Aido with her and visits Shoto, a surviving pureblood. Meanwhile, Zero is unable to hold back the destructive urges inside him...?!

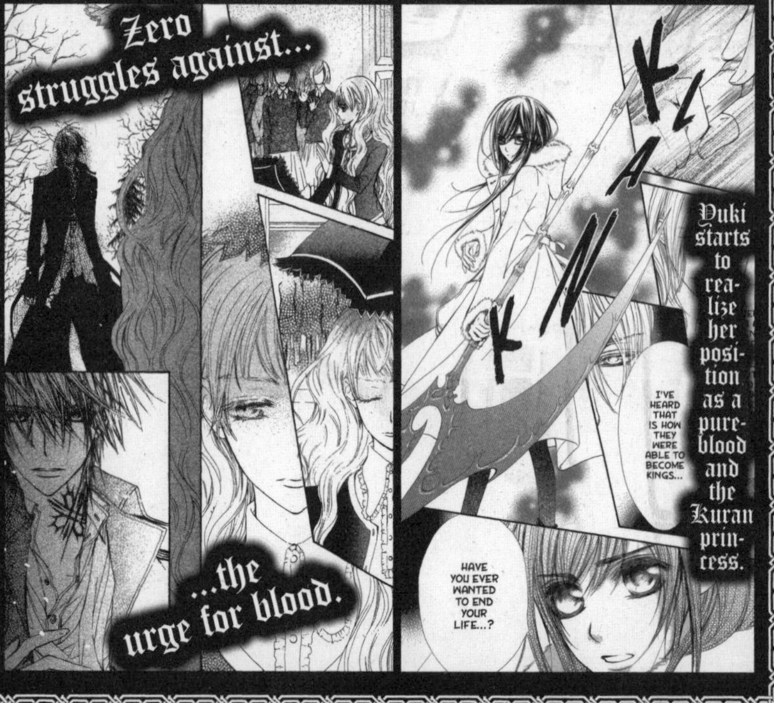
KLANK
Yuki starts to realize her position as a pureblood and the Kuran princess.
I'VE HEARD THAT IS HOW THEY WERE ABLE TO BECOME KINGS...
HAVE YOU EVER WANTED TO END YOUR LIFE...?
Zero struggles against...
...the urge for blood.

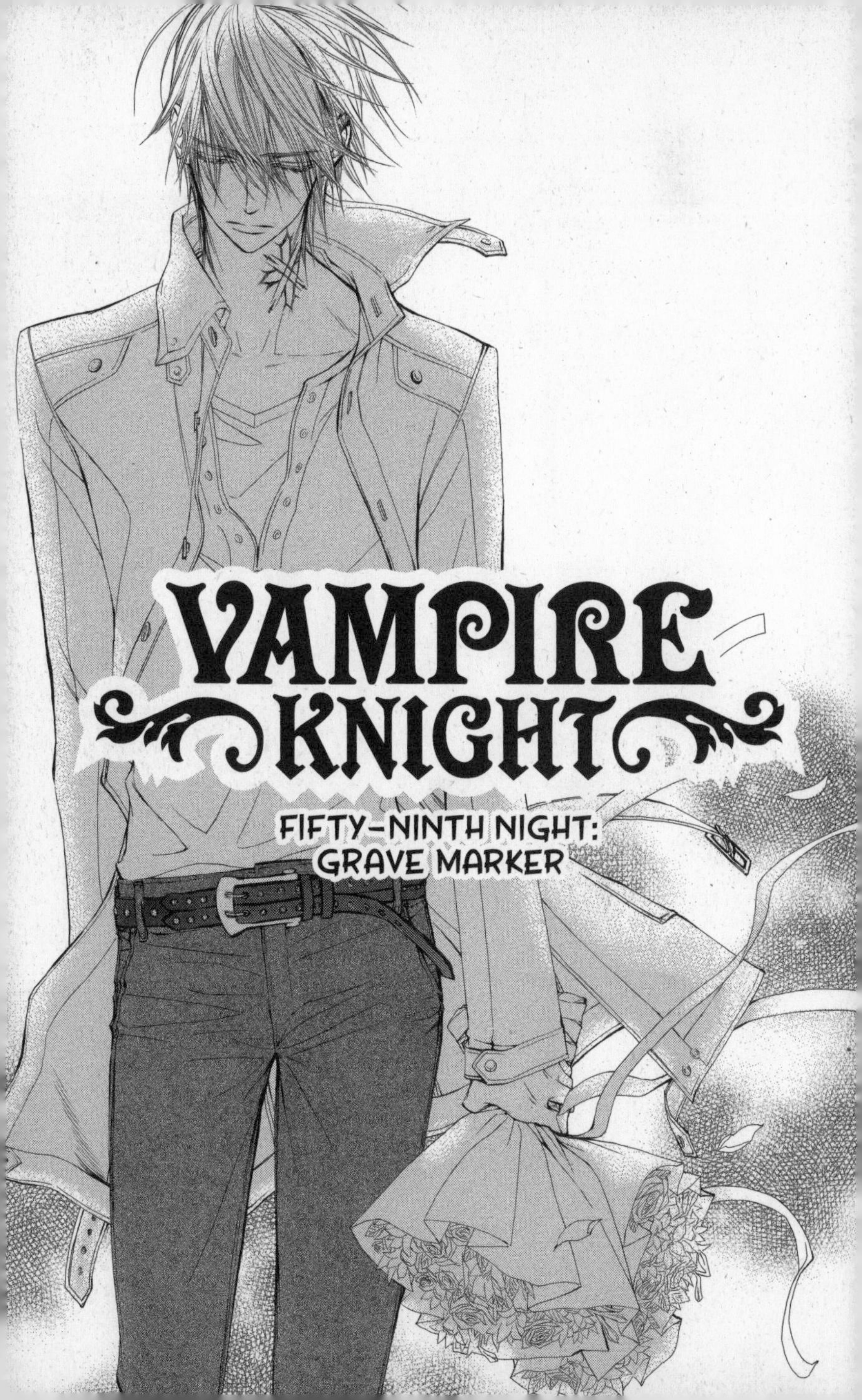
VAMPIRE KNIGHT
FIFTY-NINTH NIGHT: GRAVE MARKER

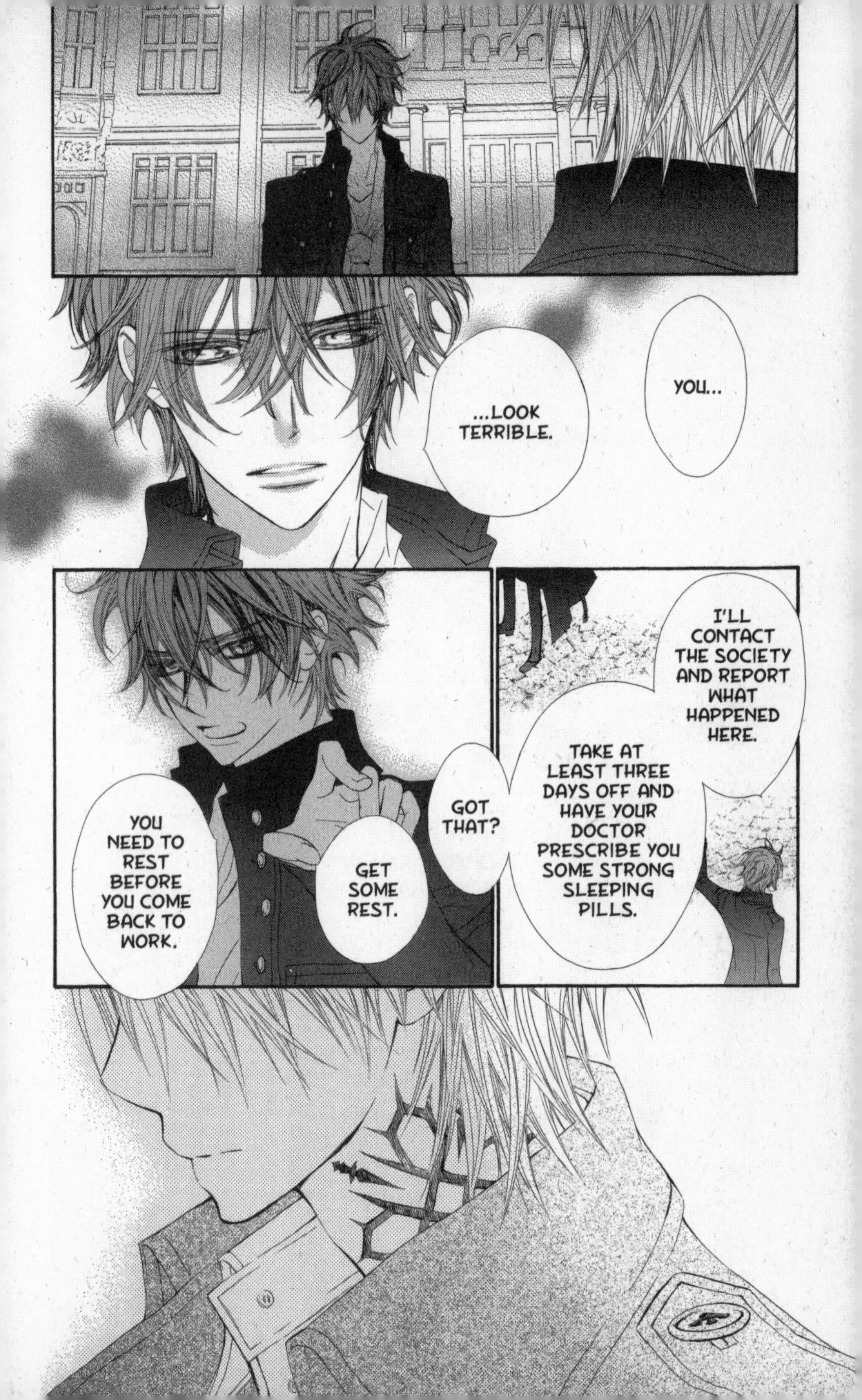
YOU...
...LOOK TERRIBLE.
I'LL CONTACT THE SOCIETY AND REPORT WHAT HAPPENED HERE.
TAKE AT LEAST THREE DAYS OFF AND HAVE YOUR DOCTOR PRESCRIBE YOU SOME STRONG SLEEPING PILLS.
GOT THAT?
GET SOME REST.
YOU NEED TO REST BEFORE YOU COME BACK TO WORK.

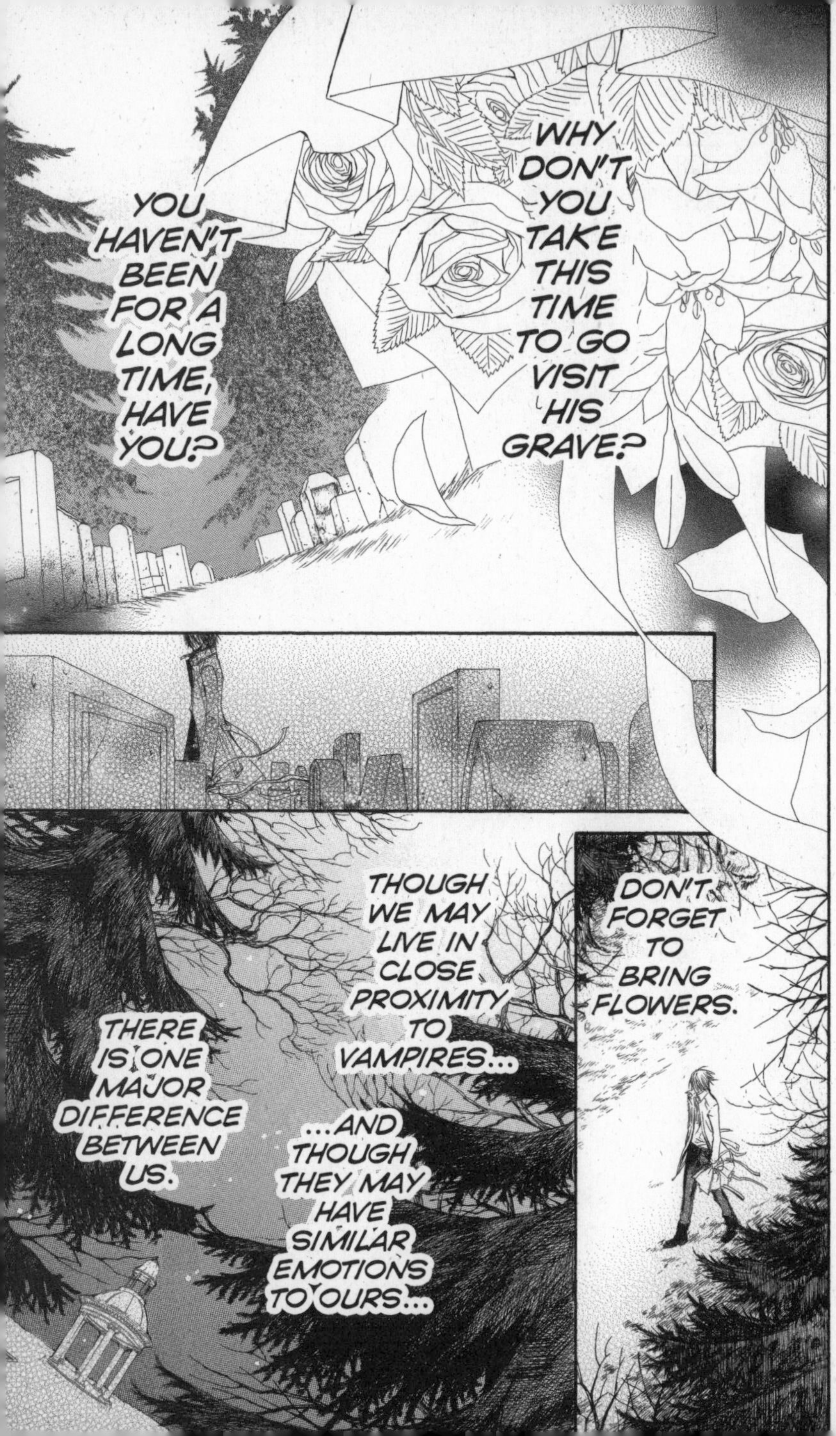
WHY DON'T YOU TAKE THIS TIME TO GO VISIT HIS GRAVE?
YOU HAVEN'T BEEN FOR A LONG TIME, HAVE YOU?
DON'T FORGET TO BRING FLOWERS.
THOUGH WE MAY LIVE IN CLOSE PROXIMITY TO VAMPIRES...
...AND THOUGH THEY MAY HAVE SIMILAR EMOTIONS TO OURS...
THERE IS ONE MAJOR DIFFERENCE BETWEEN US.

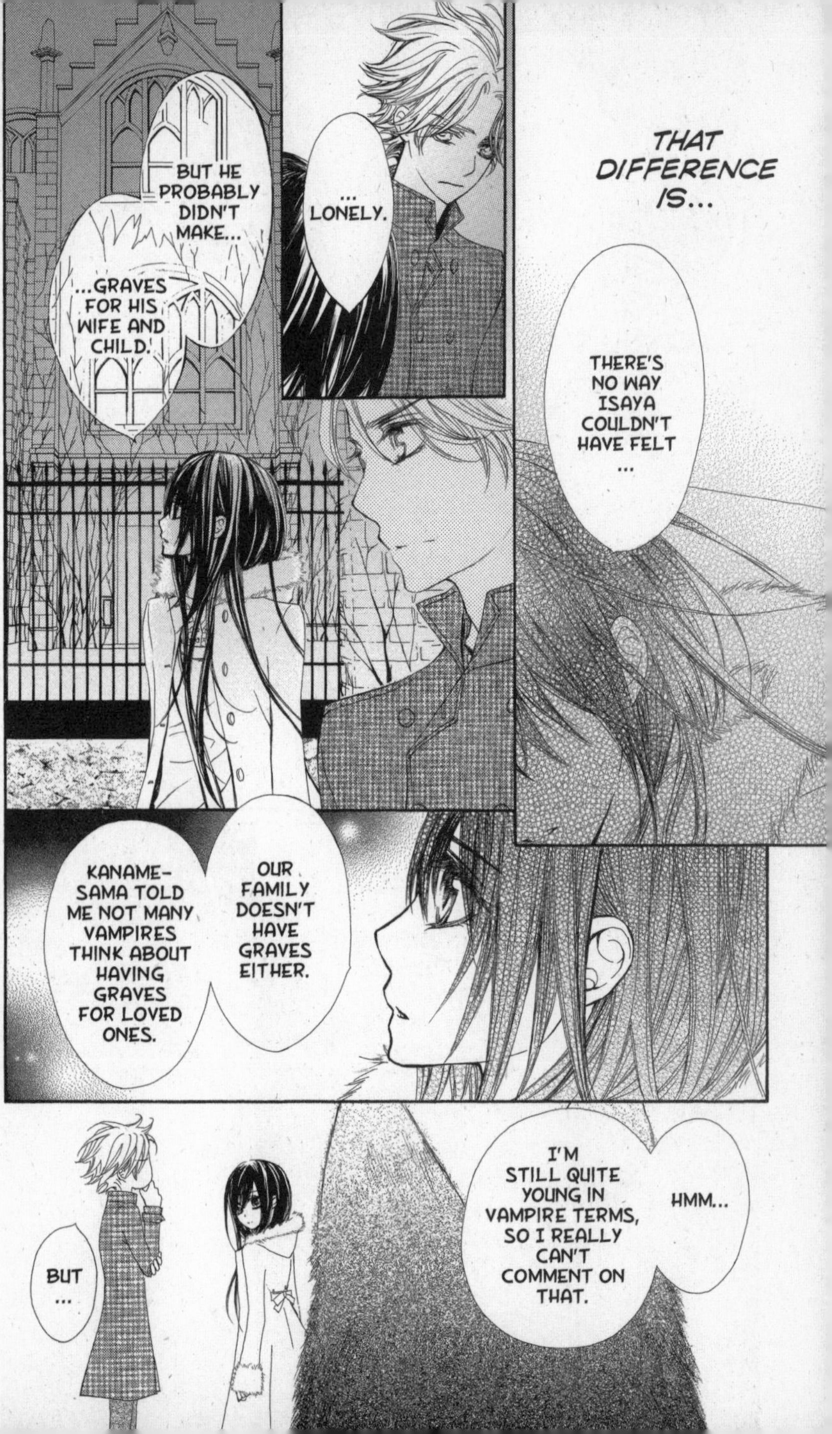
THAT DIFFERENCE IS...
THERE'S NO WAY ISAYA COULDN'T HAVE FELT ...
... LONELY.
BUT HE PROBABLY DIDN'T MAKE...
...GRAVES FOR HIS WIFE AND CHILD.
OUR FAMILY DOESN'T HAVE GRAVES EITHER.
KANAME-SAMA TOLD ME NOT MANY VAMPIRES THINK ABOUT HAVING GRAVES FOR LOVED ONES.
HMM...
I'M STILL QUITE YOUNG IN VAMPIRE TERMS, SO I REALLY CAN'T COMMENT ON THAT.
BUT ...

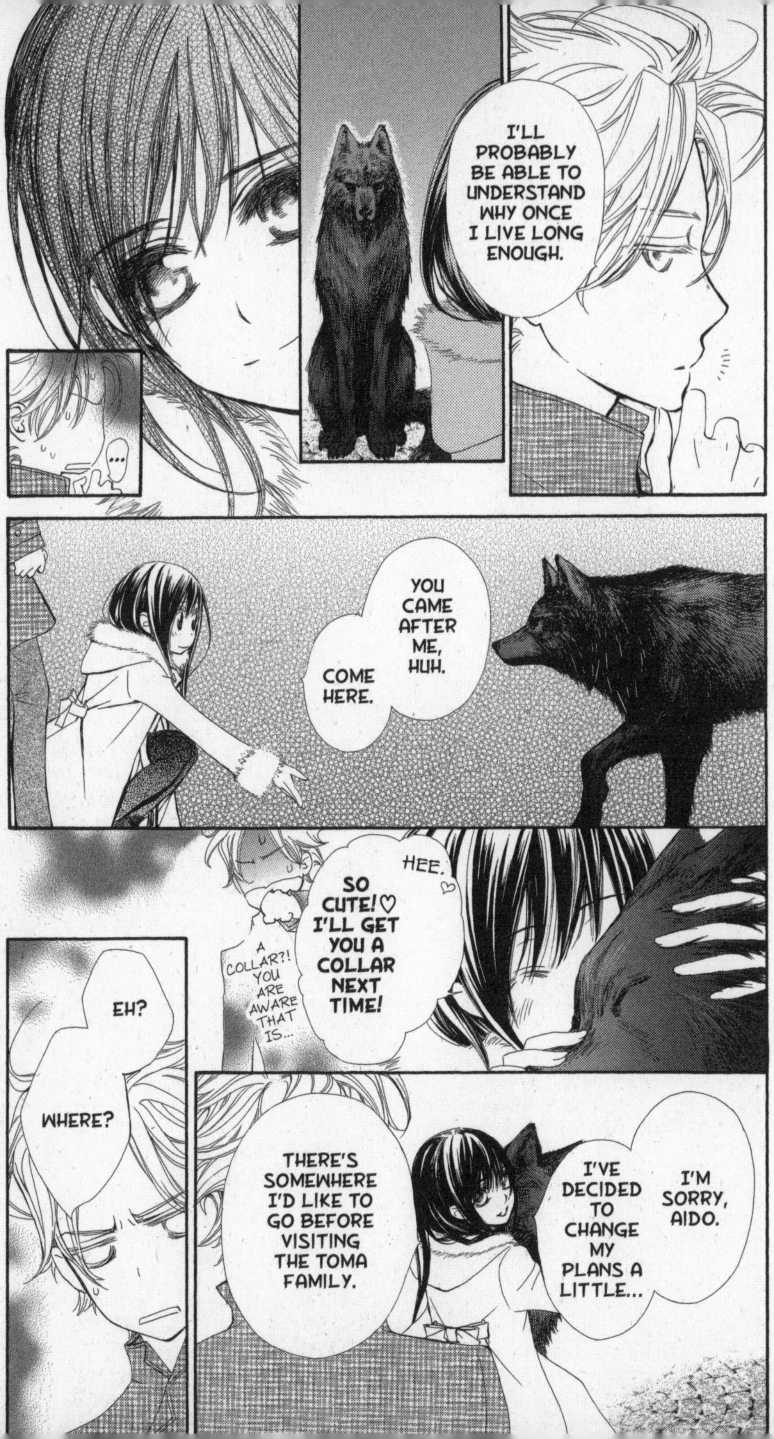

I'LL PROBABLY BE ABLE TO UNDERSTAND WHY ONCE I LIVE LONG ENOUGH.
...
YOU CAME AFTER ME, HUH.
COME HERE.
HEE.
SO CUTE!♡ I'LL GET YOU A COLLAR NEXT TIME!
A COLLAR?! YOU ARE AWARE THAT IS...
I'M SORRY, AIDO.
I'VE DECIDED TO CHANGE MY PLANS A LITTLE...
THERE'S SOMEWHERE I'D LIKE TO GO BEFORE VISITING THE TOMA FAMILY.
EH?
WHERE?

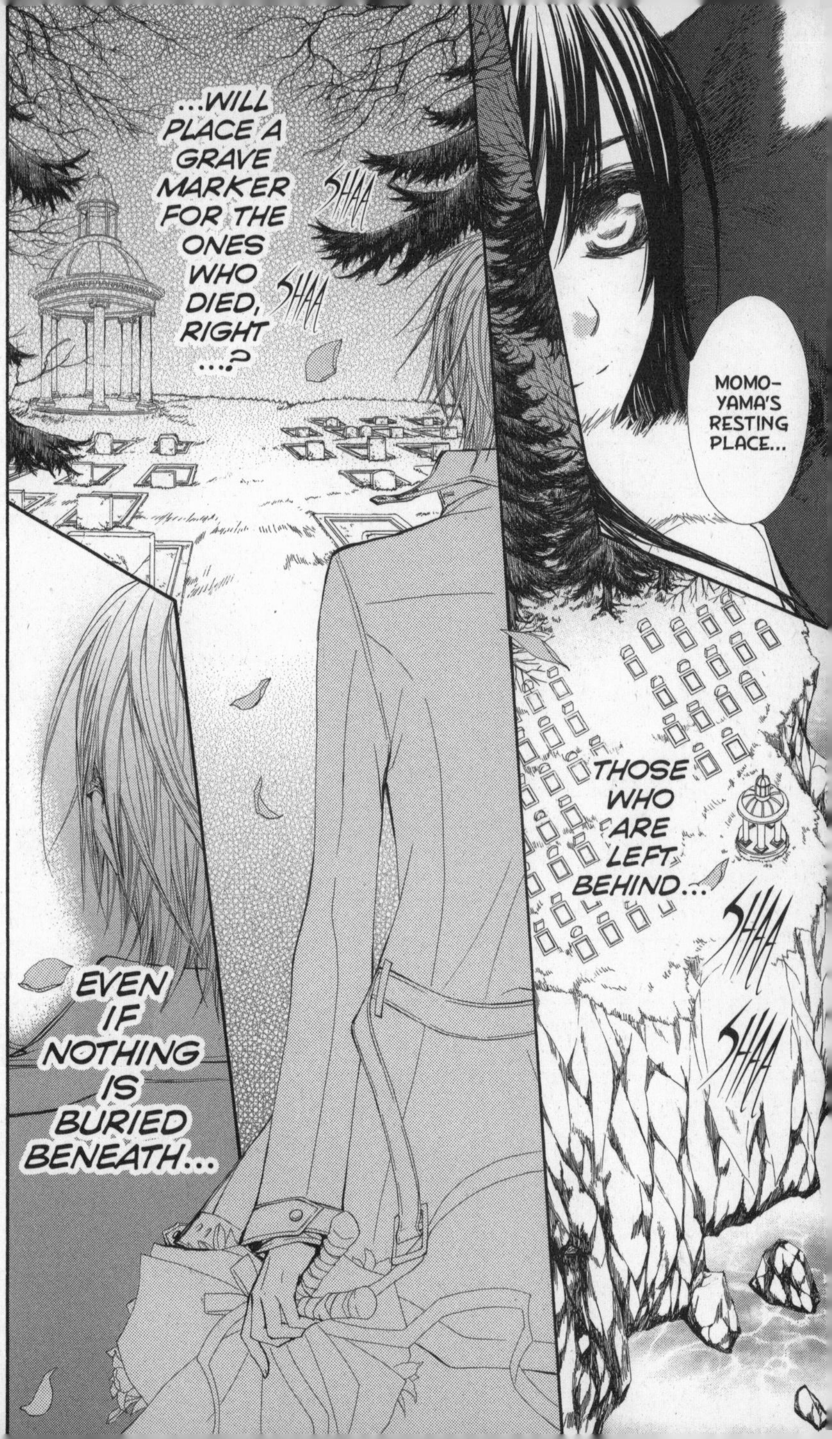
MOMO-YAMA'S RESTING PLACE...
THOSE WHO ARE LEFT BEHIND...
SHAA
SHAA
...WILL PLACE A GRAVE MARKER FOR THE ONES WHO DIED, RIGHT...?
SHAA
SHAA
EVEN IF NOTHING IS BURIED BENEATH...

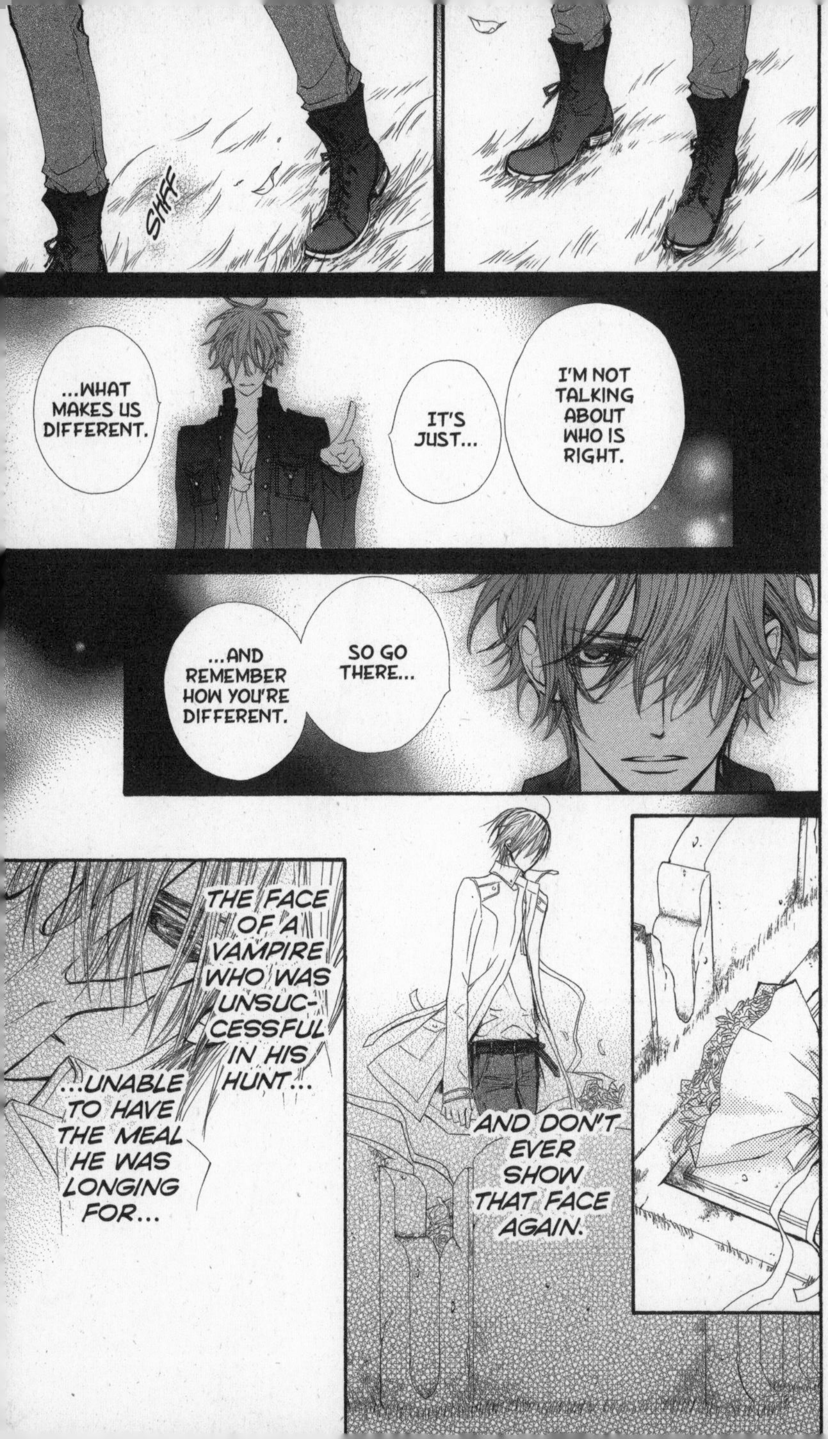
SHFF
I'M NOT TALKING ABOUT WHO IS RIGHT.
IT'S JUST...
...WHAT MAKES US DIFFERENT.
SO GO THERE...
...AND REMEMBER HOW YOU'RE DIFFERENT.
AND DON'T EVER SHOW THAT FACE AGAIN.
THE FACE OF A VAMPIRE WHO WAS UNSUCCESSFUL IN HIS HUNT...
...UNABLE TO HAVE THE MEAL HE WAS LONGING FOR...

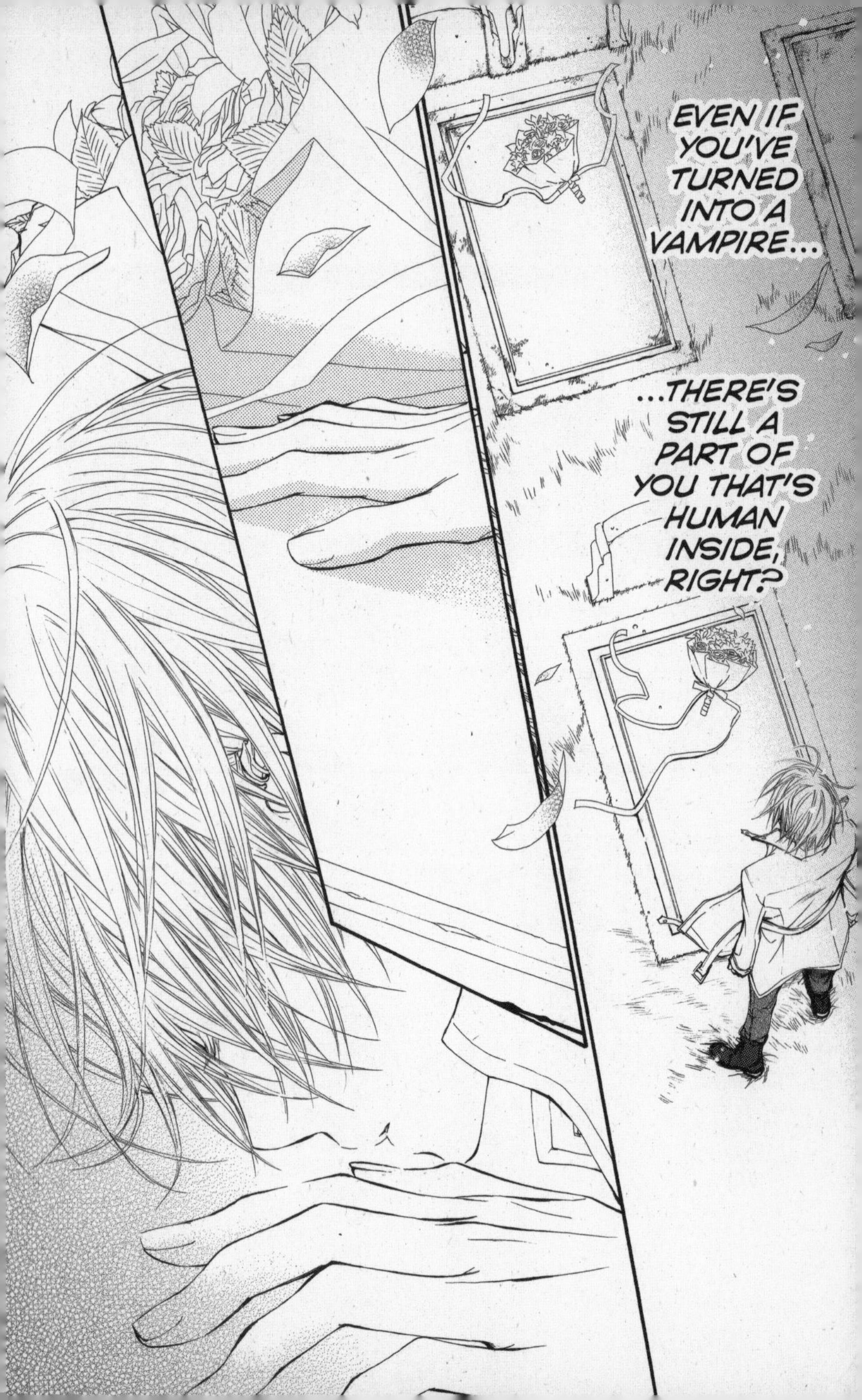
EVEN IF YOU'VE TURNED INTO A VAMPIRE...
...THERE'S STILL A PART OF YOU THAT'S HUMAN INSIDE, RIGHT?

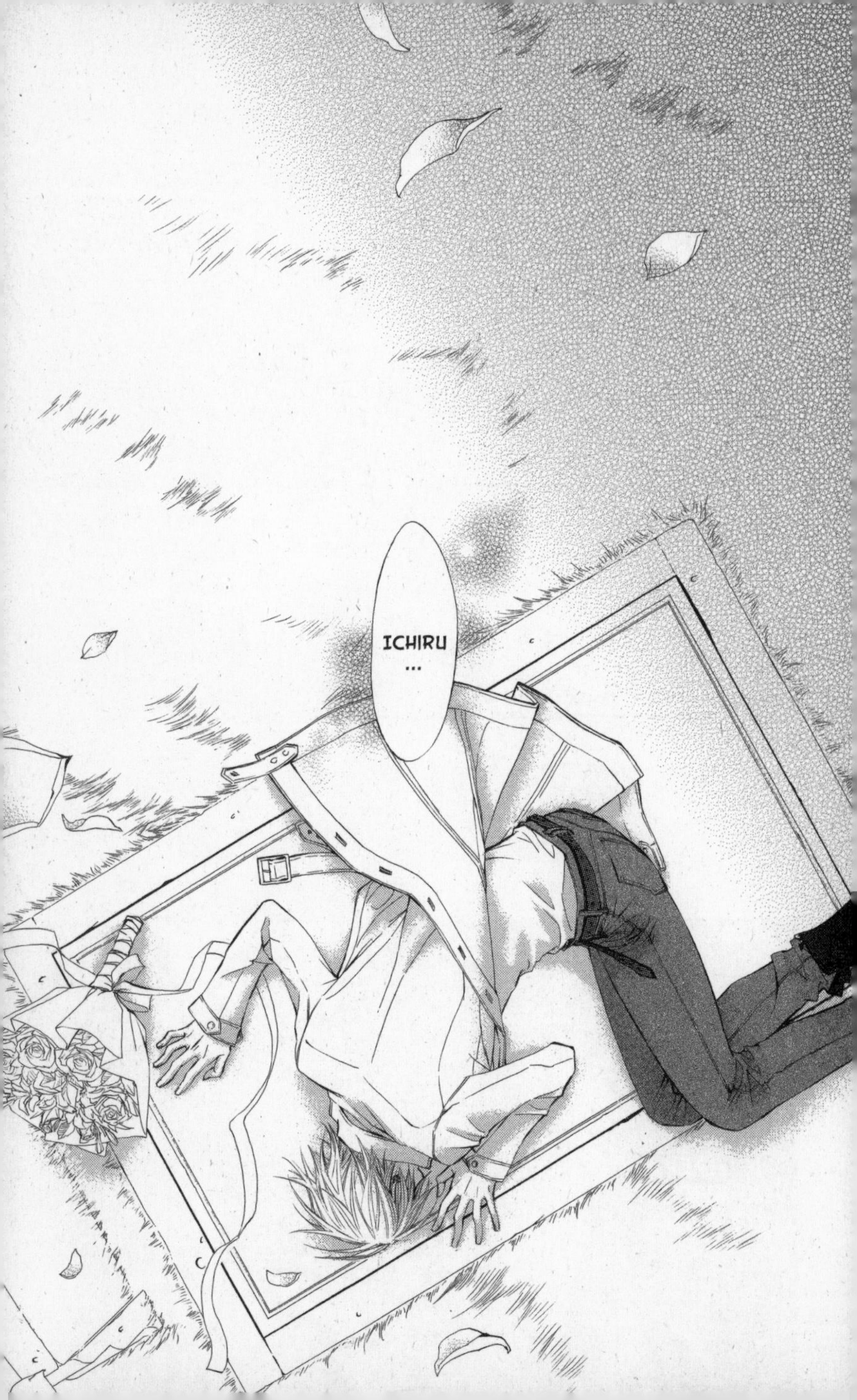
ICHIRU
...

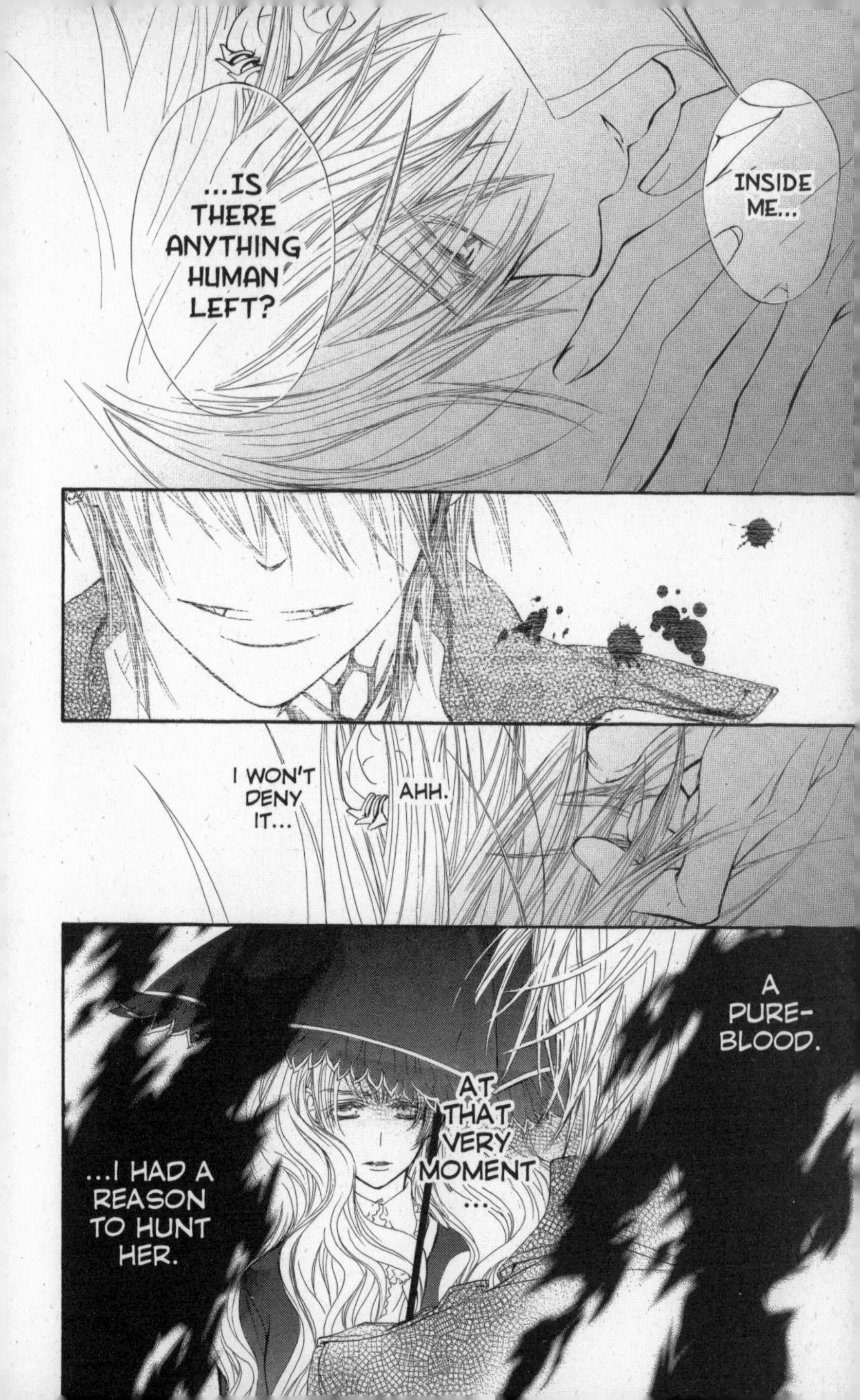
INSIDE ME...
...IS THERE ANYTHING HUMAN LEFT?
AHH.
I WON'T DENY IT...
A PURE-BLOOD.
AT THAT VERY MOMENT...
...I HAD A REASON TO HUNT HER.

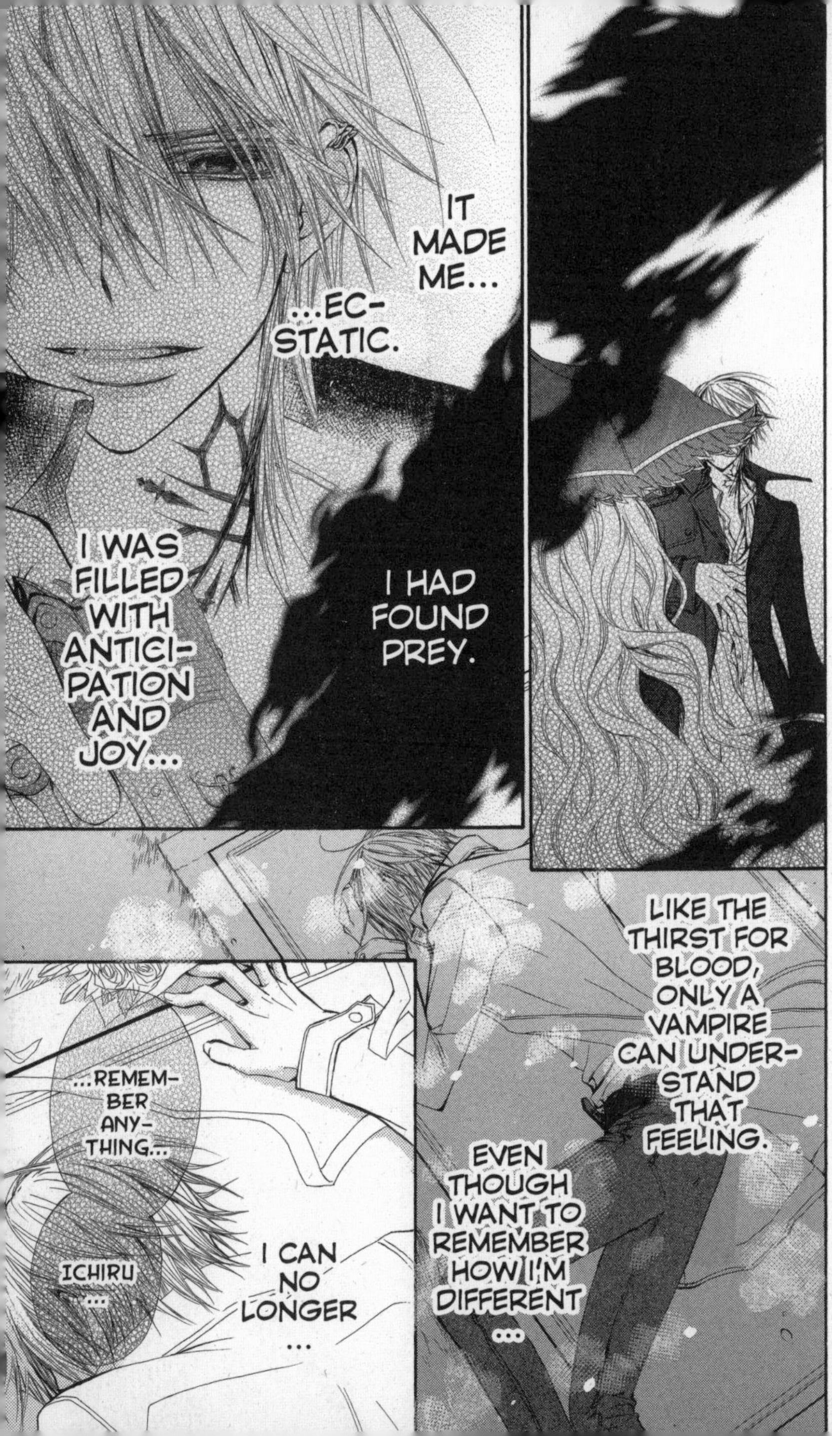
IT MADE ME...
...EC-STATIC.
I WAS FILLED WITH ANTICI-PATION AND JOY...
I HAD FOUND PREY.
LIKE THE THIRST FOR BLOOD, ONLY A VAMPIRE CAN UNDER-STAND THAT FEELING.
EVEN THOUGH I WANT TO REMEMBER HOW I'M DIFFERENT...
I CAN NO LONGER...
...REMEM-BER ANY-THING...
ICHIRU...

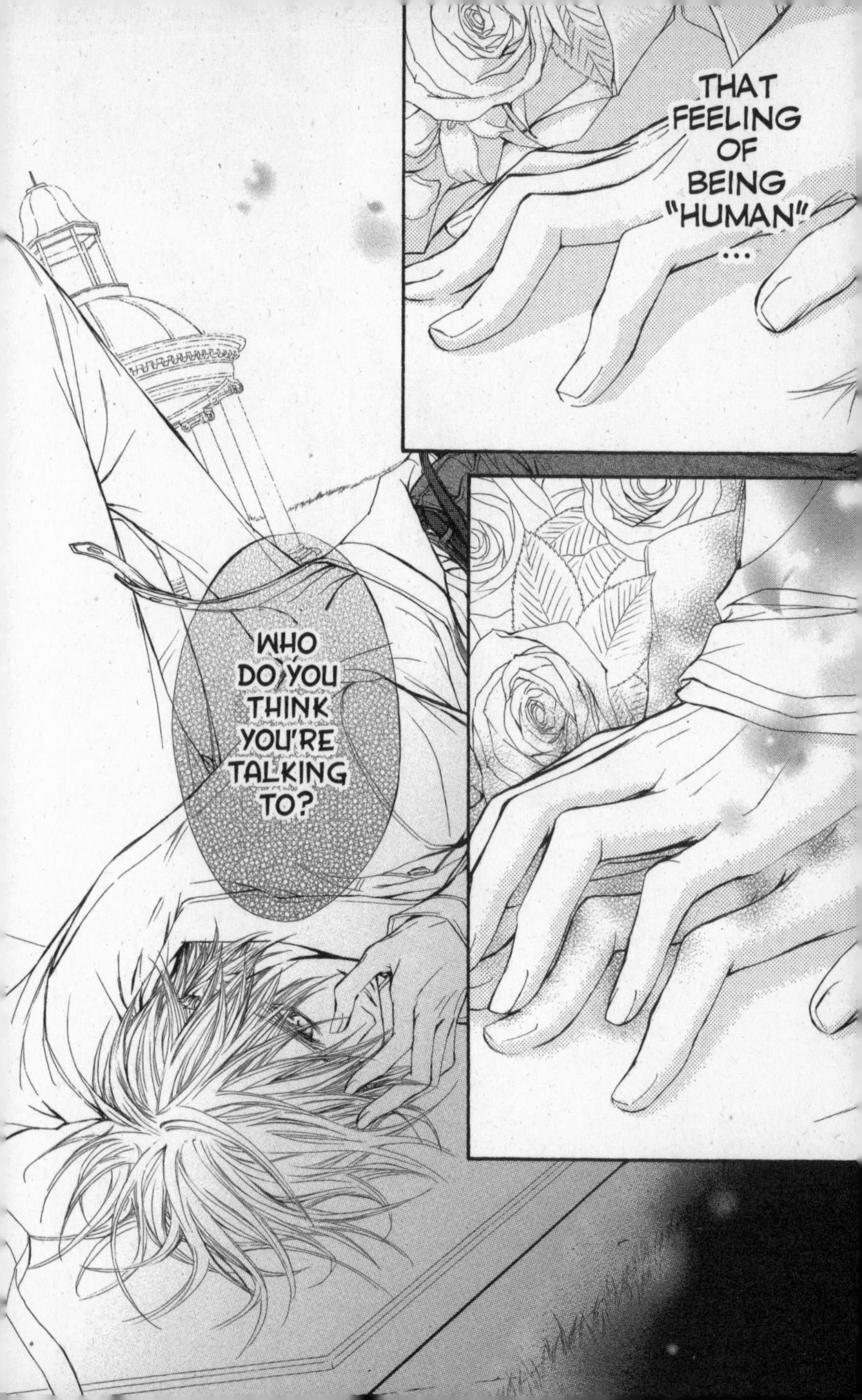
THAT FEELING OF BEING "HUMAN"...
WHO DO YOU THINK YOU'RE TALKING TO?

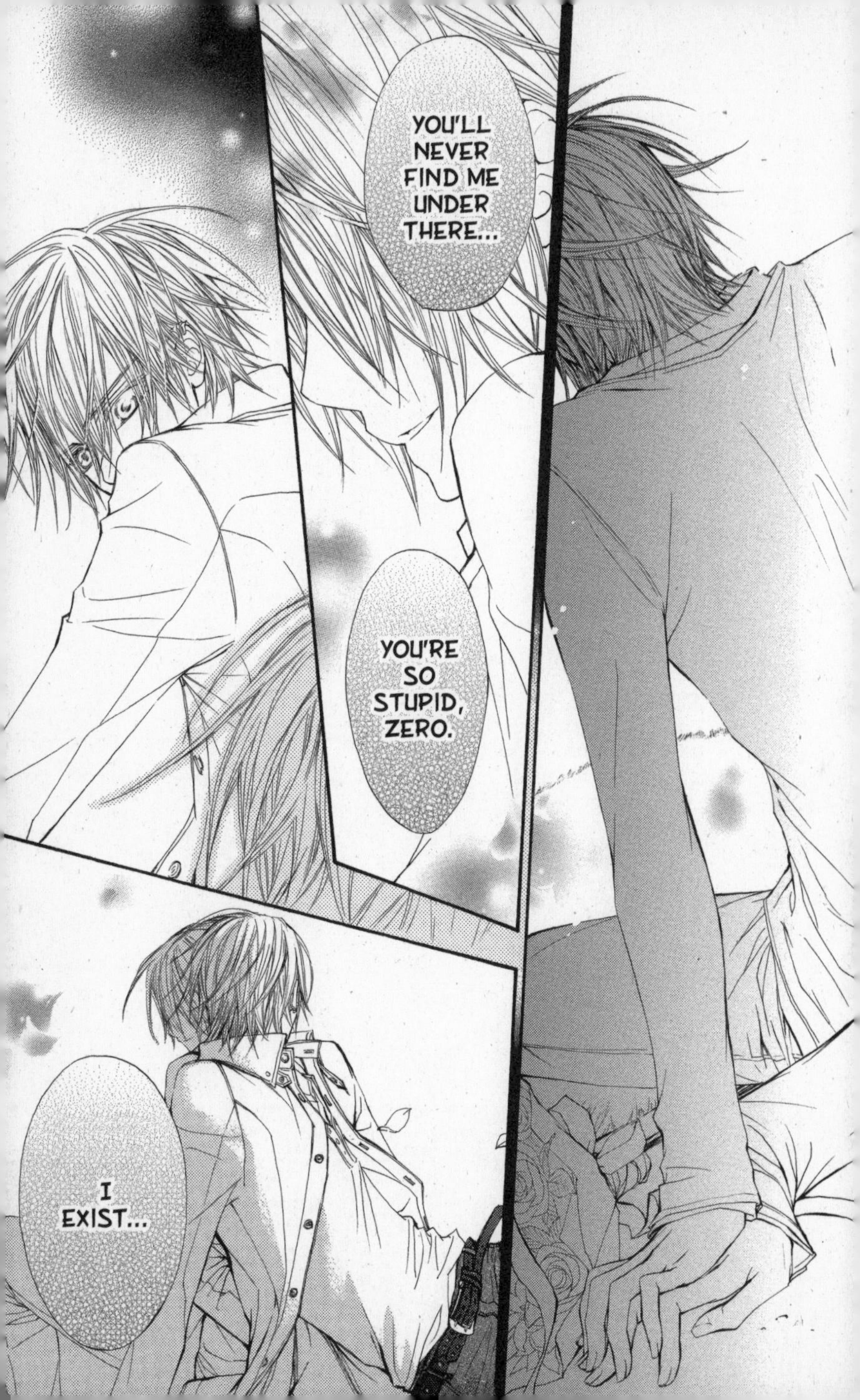
YOU'LL NEVER FIND ME UNDER THERE...
YOU'RE SO STUPID, ZERO.
I EXIST...

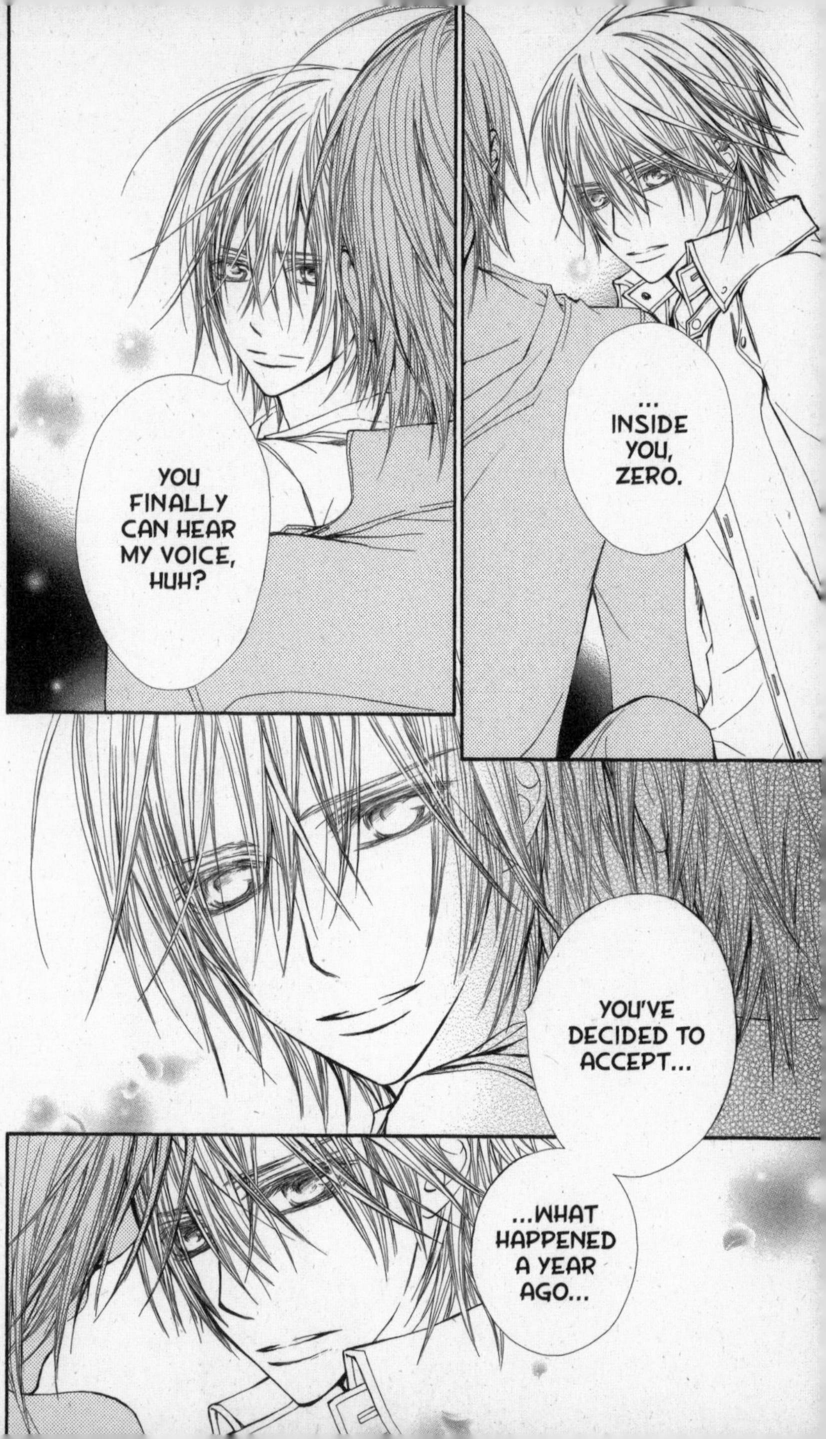
...
INSIDE YOU, ZERO.
YOU FINALLY CAN HEAR MY VOICE, HUH?
YOU'VE DECIDED TO ACCEPT...
...WHAT HAPPENED A YEAR AGO...

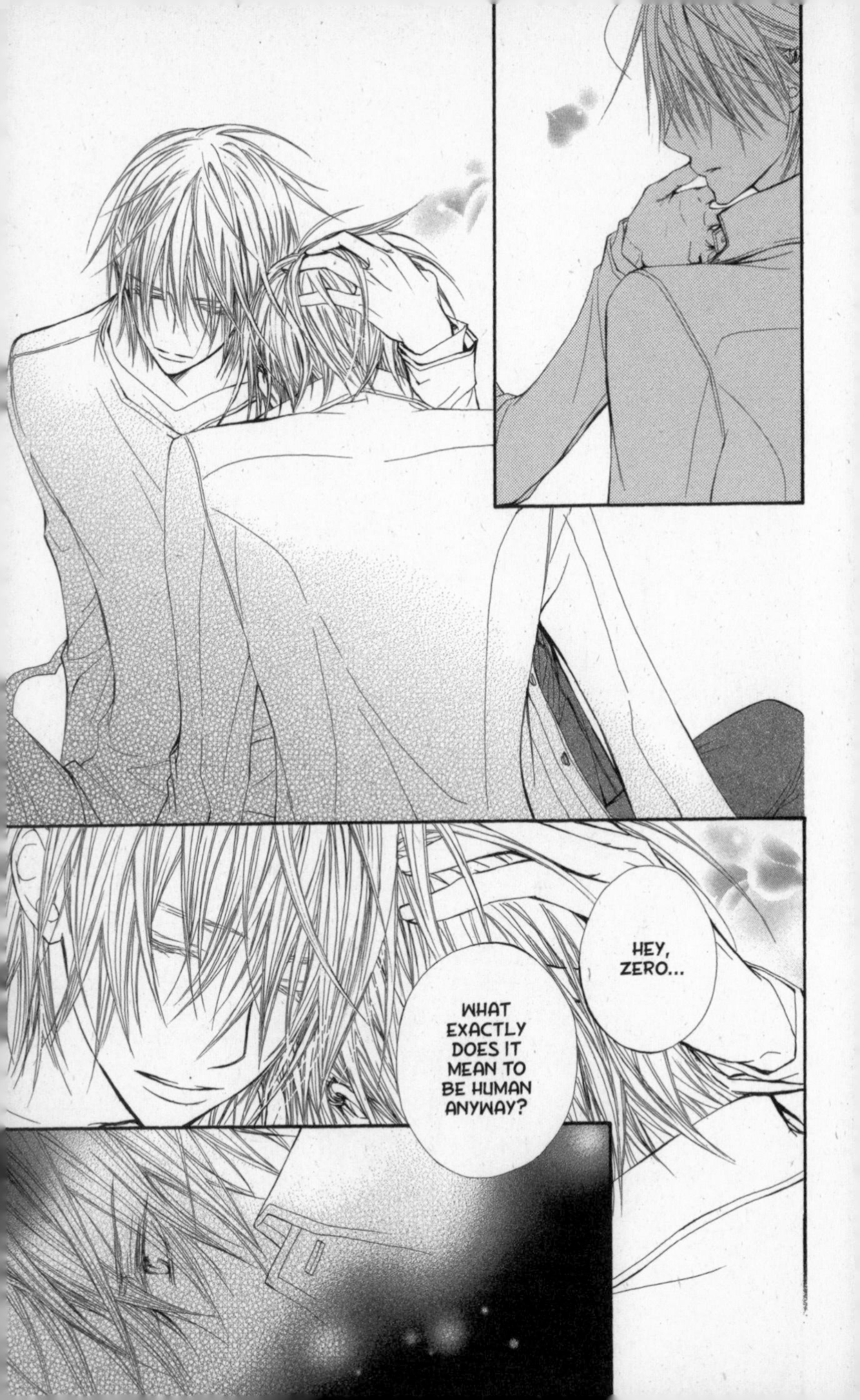
HEY, ZERO...
WHAT EXACTLY DOES IT MEAN TO BE HUMAN ANYWAY?

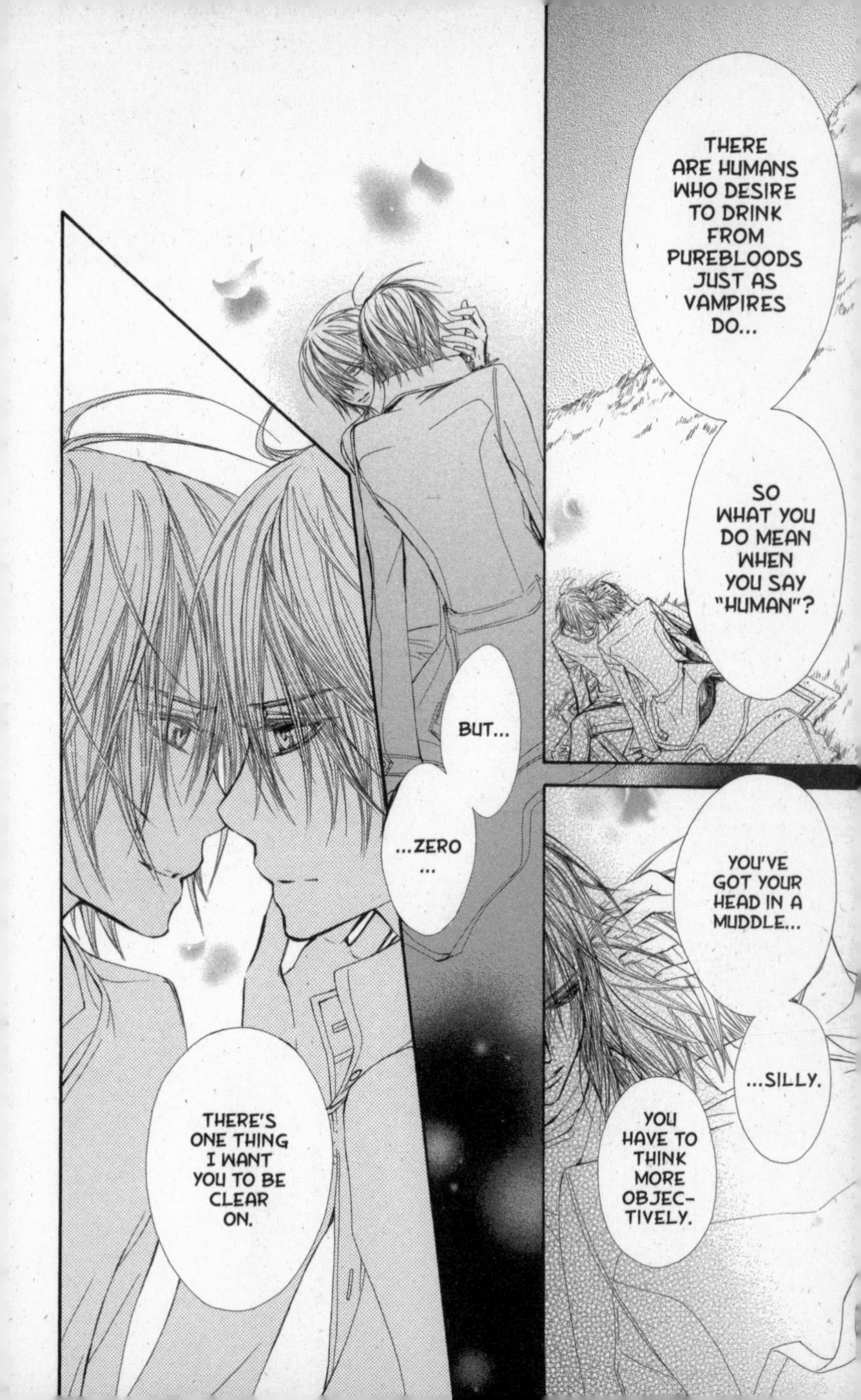
THERE ARE HUMANS WHO DESIRE TO DRINK FROM PUREBLOODS JUST AS VAMPIRES DO...
SO WHAT YOU DO MEAN WHEN YOU SAY "HUMAN"?
YOU'VE GOT YOUR HEAD IN A MUDDLE...
...SILLY.
YOU HAVE TO THINK MORE OBJEC-TIVELY.
BUT...
...ZERO...
THERE'S ONE THING I WANT YOU TO BE CLEAR ON.

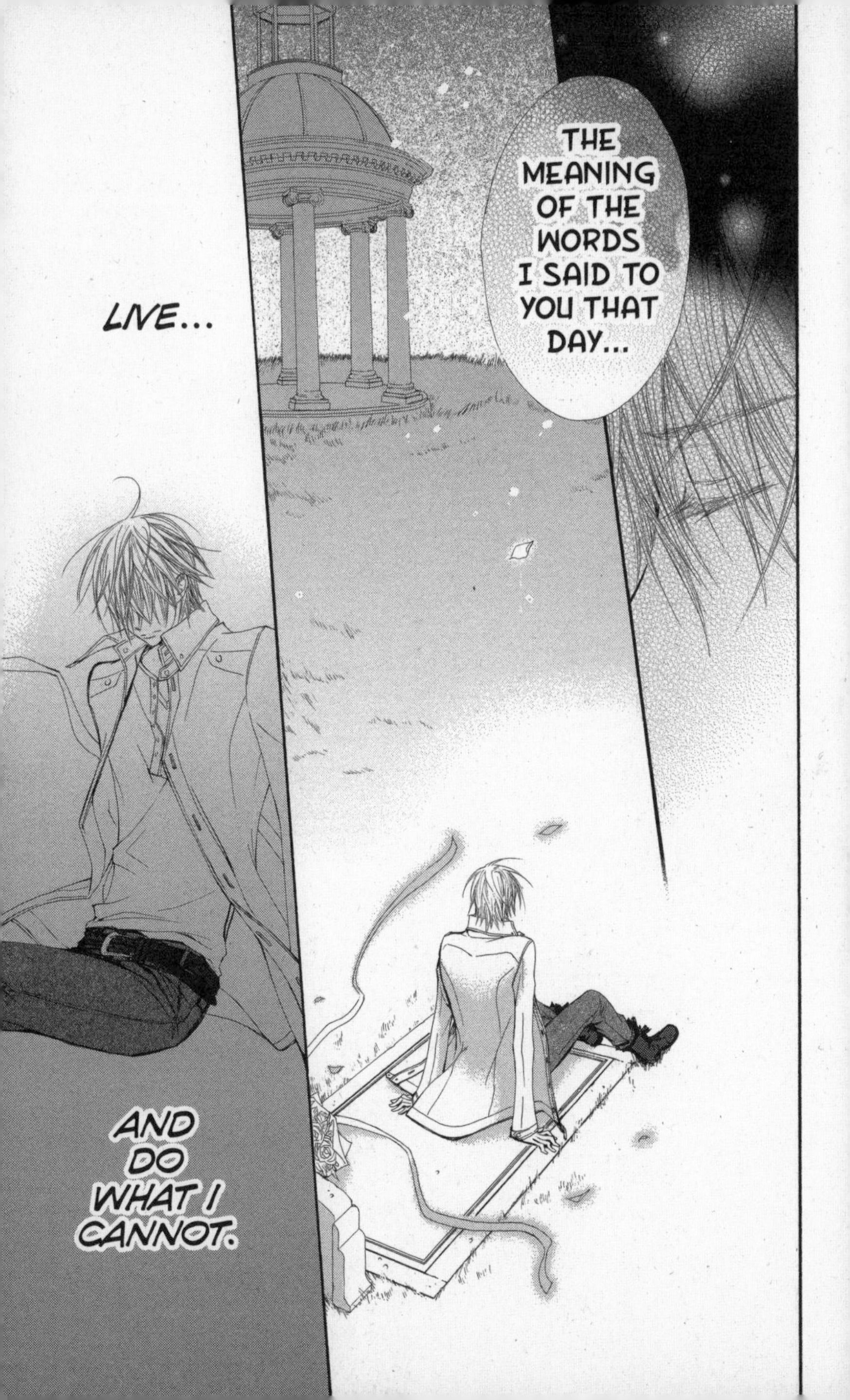
THE MEANING OF THE WORDS I SAID TO YOU THAT DAY...
LIVE...
AND DO WHAT I CANNOT.

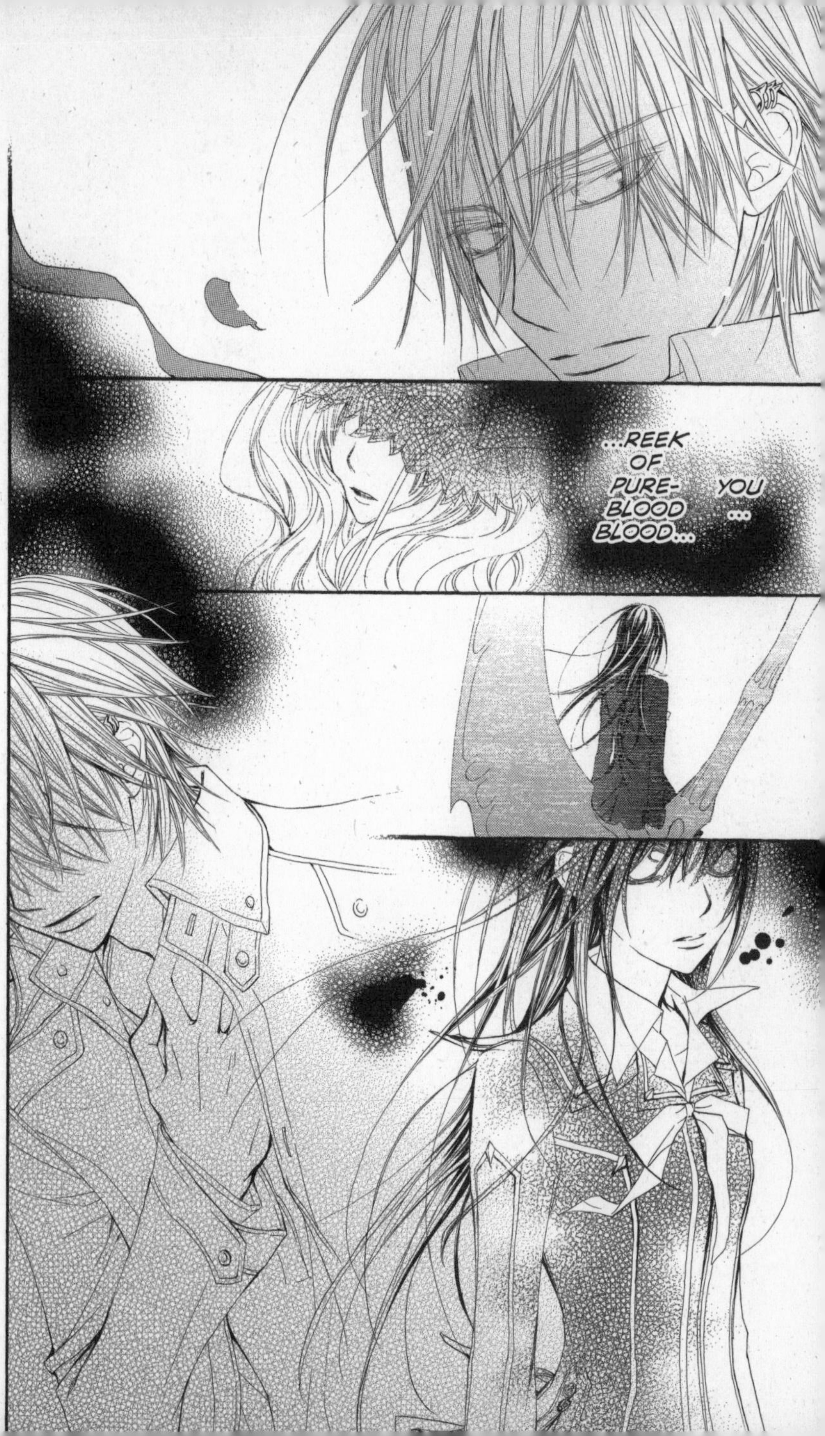
YOU ...
...REEK OF PURE-BLOOD BLOOD...

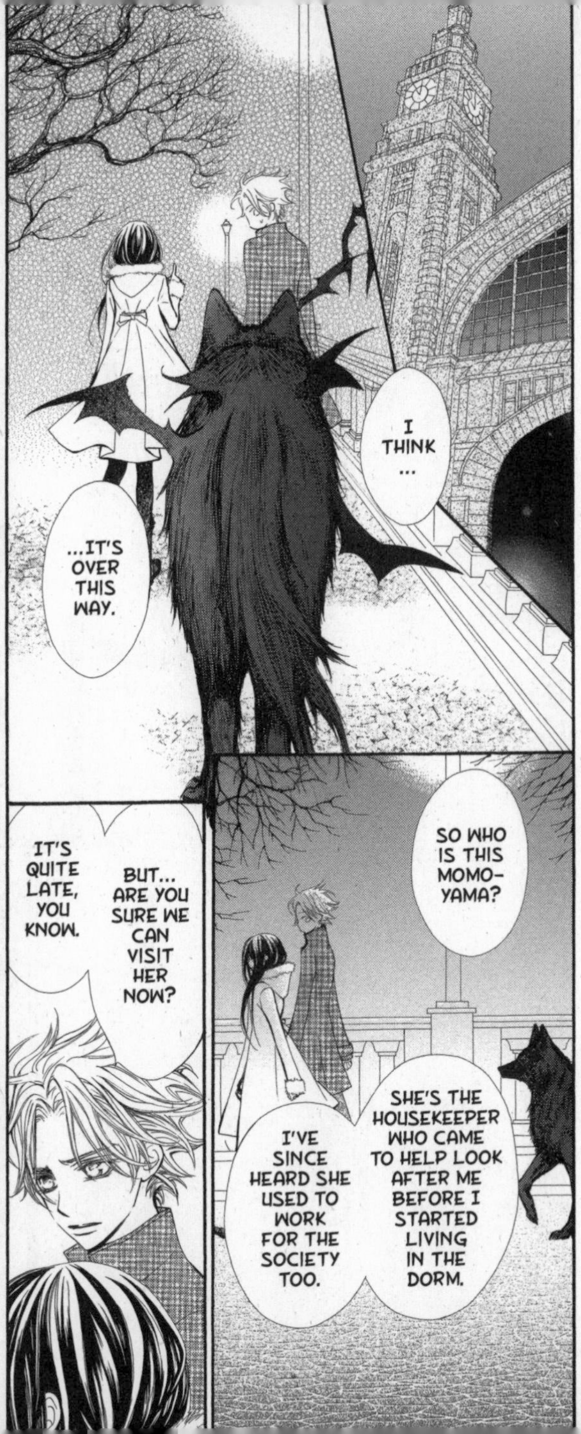
I THINK...
...IT'S OVER THIS WAY.
SO WHO IS THIS MOMO-YAMA?
SHE'S THE HOUSEKEEPER WHO CAME TO HELP LOOK AFTER ME BEFORE I STARTED LIVING IN THE DORM.
I'VE SINCE HEARD SHE USED TO WORK FOR THE SOCIETY TOO.
BUT... ARE YOU SURE WE CAN VISIT HER NOW?
IT'S QUITE LATE, YOU KNOW.

I

Thank you very much for picking up this volume! I'm Hino! And this is volume 13...! I did all I could within the given time for the covers as well as the other illustrations in this volume.

I hope you enjoy them along with the main story. I was thinking about not including the side story as it completely tears apart the usual "image" of the characters. I decided to put it in anyway after all the effort I had taken to draw it. (Um.. I'm sorry...)

The reason I'm able to continue this story is all thanks to the readers who support this series. Thank you very much. It's going to continue for a little longer, but please continue to support the series.

樋野まつり
Matsuri Hino

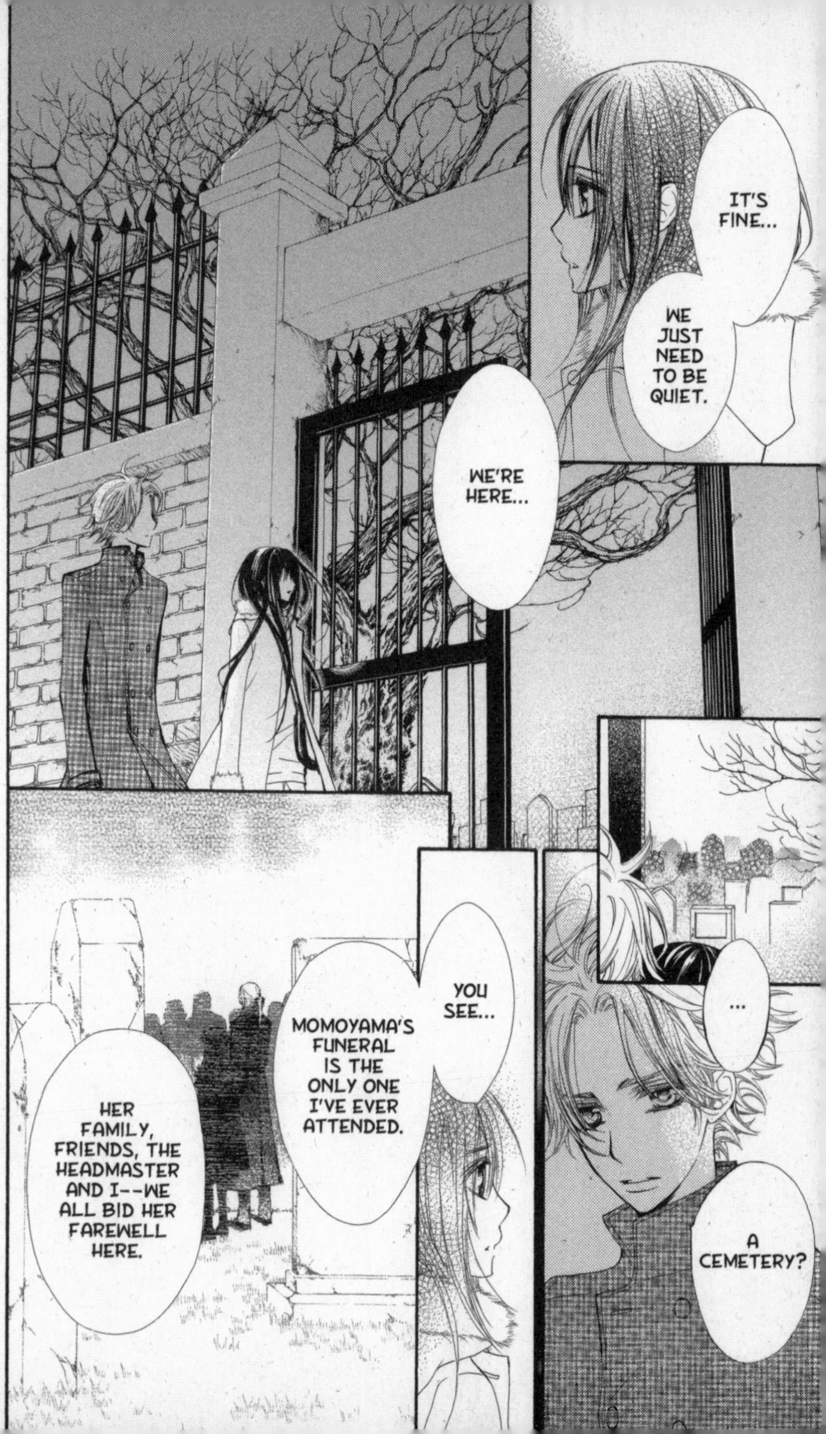
IT'S FINE...
WE JUST NEED TO BE QUIET.
WE'RE HERE...
...
A CEMETERY?
YOU SEE...
MOMOYAMA'S FUNERAL IS THE ONLY ONE I'VE EVER ATTENDED.
HER FAMILY, FRIENDS, THE HEADMASTER AND I--WE ALL BID HER FAREWELL HERE.

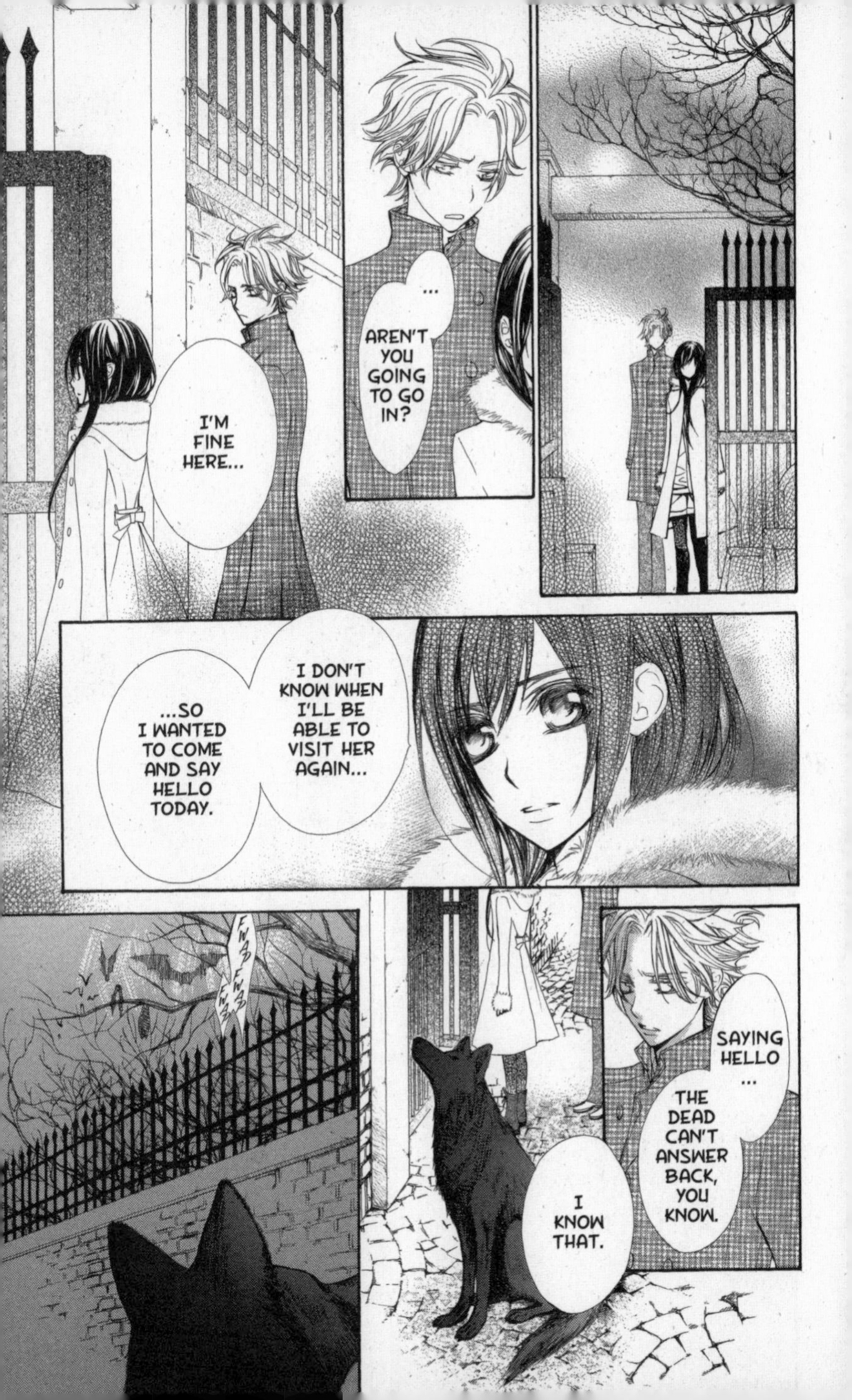
...
AREN'T YOU GOING TO GO IN?
I'M FINE HERE...
I DON'T KNOW WHEN I'LL BE ABLE TO VISIT HER AGAIN...
...SO I WANTED TO COME AND SAY HELLO TODAY.
SAYING HELLO ...
THE DEAD CAN'T ANSWER BACK, YOU KNOW.
I KNOW THAT.
FWAP FWAP FWAP

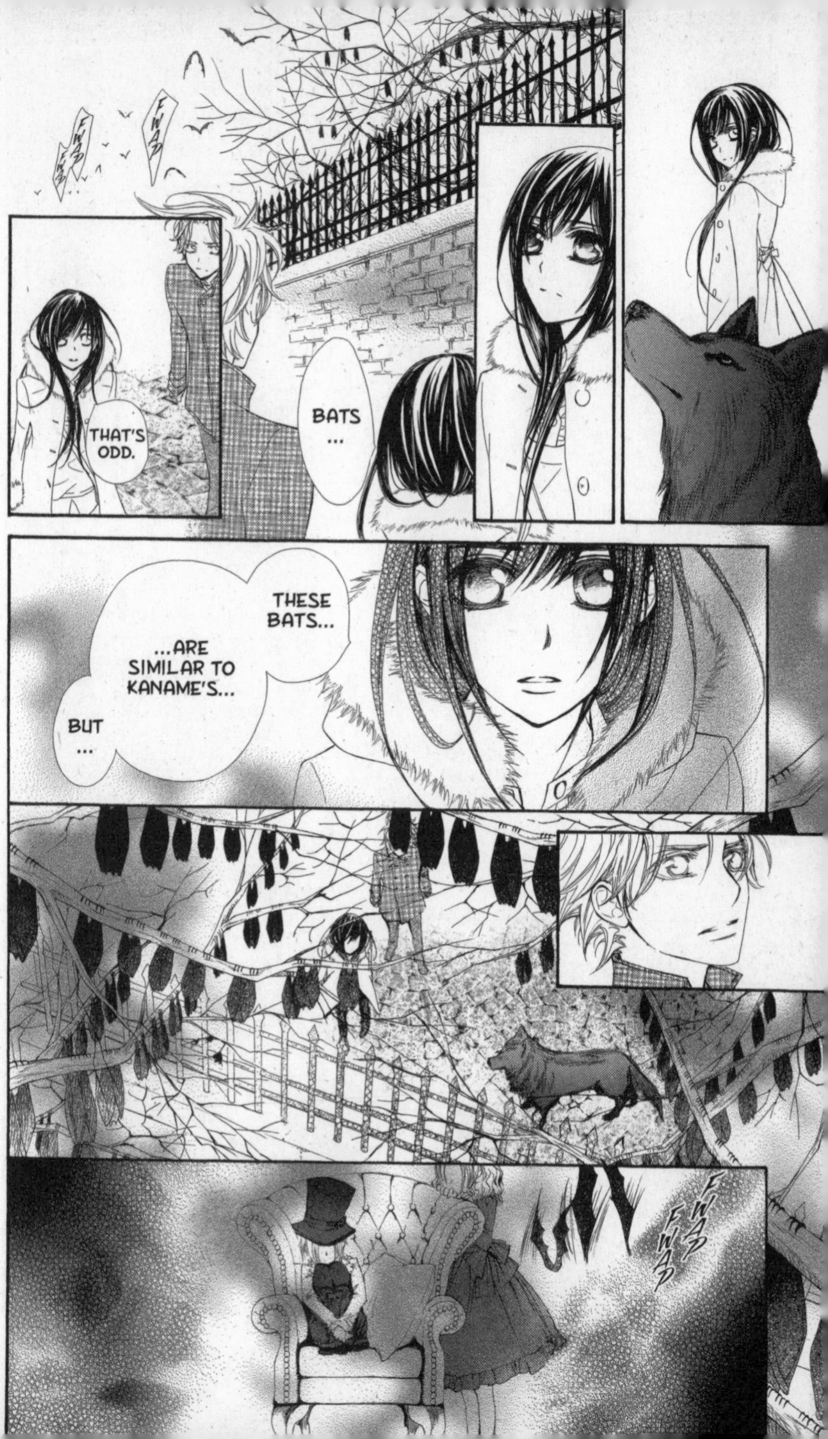
FWAP
FWAP FWAP...
BATS...
THAT'S ODD.
THESE BATS...
...ARE SIMILAR TO KANAME'S...
BUT...
FWAP FWAP

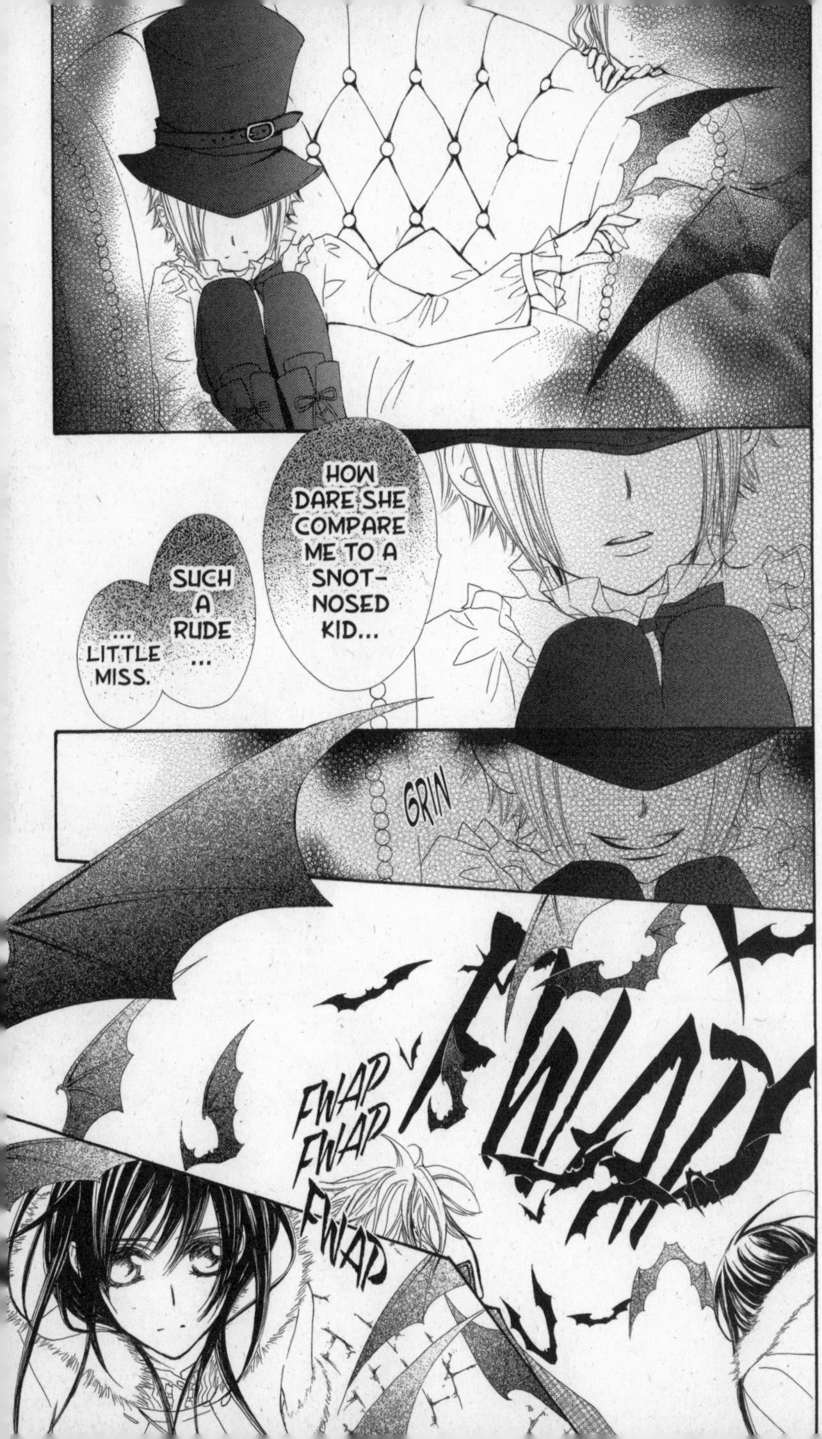
HOW DARE SHE COMPARE ME TO A SNOT-NOSED KID...
SUCH A RUDE ...
... LITTLE MISS.
GRIN
FWAP
FWAP FWAP FWAP FWAP

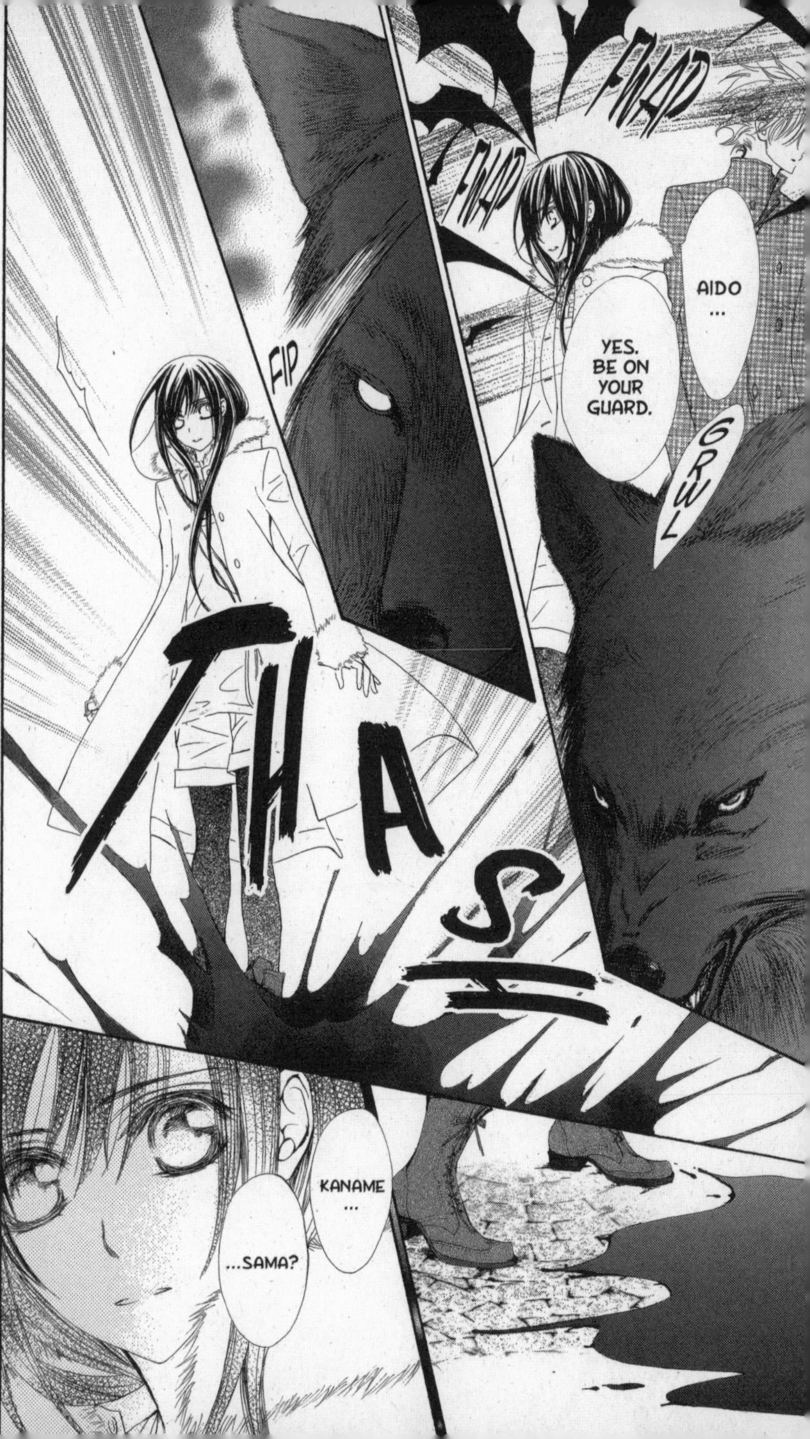
FWAP
FWAP
AIDO ...
YES. BE ON YOUR GUARD.
GRWL
FIP
THASH
KANAME ...
...SAMA?

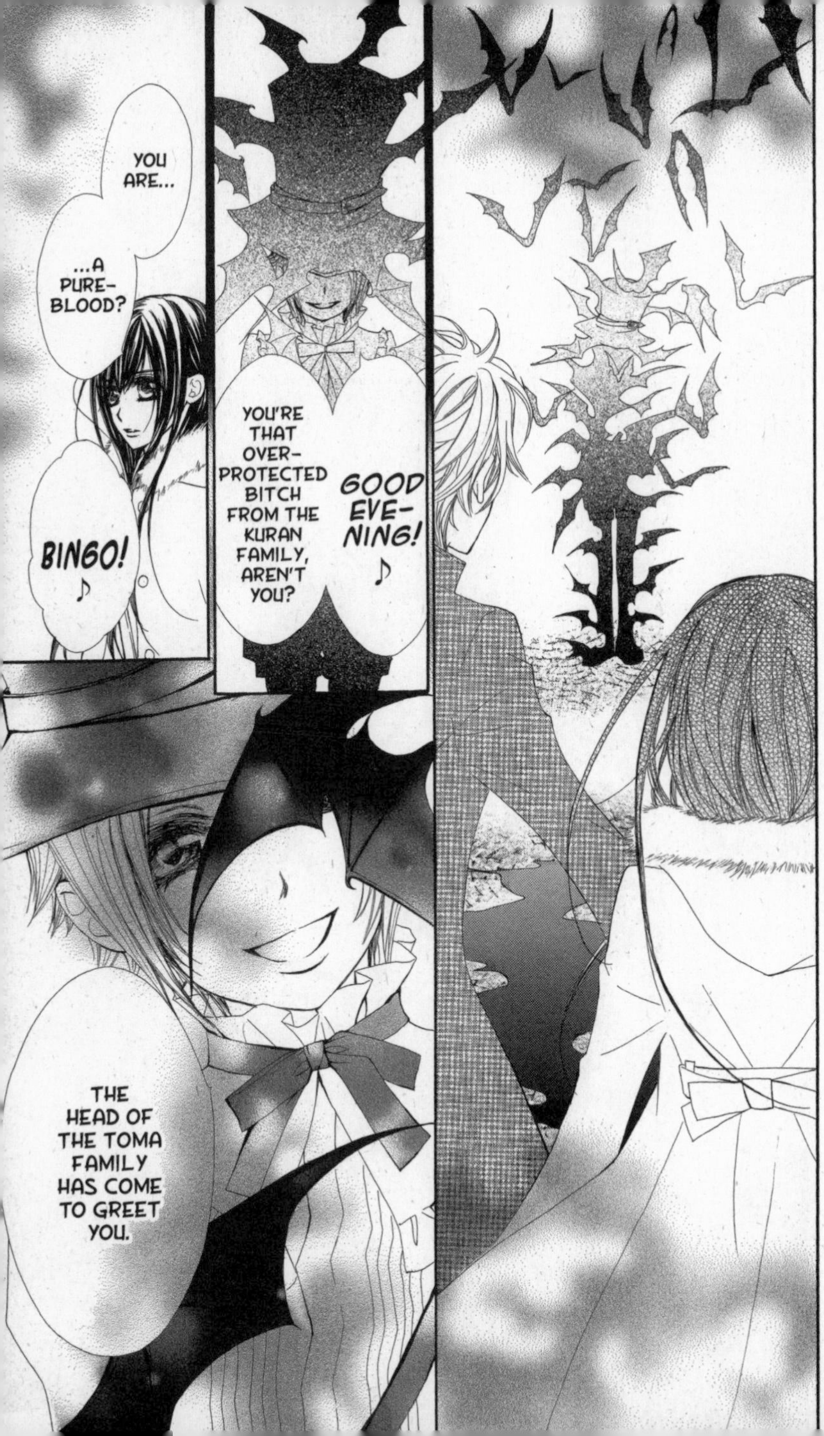
GOOD EVE-NING! ♪
YOU'RE THAT OVER-PROTECTED BITCH FROM THE KURAN FAMILY, AREN'T YOU?
YOU ARE...
...A PURE-BLOOD?
BINGO! ♪
THE HEAD OF THE TOMA FAMILY HAS COME TO GREET YOU.

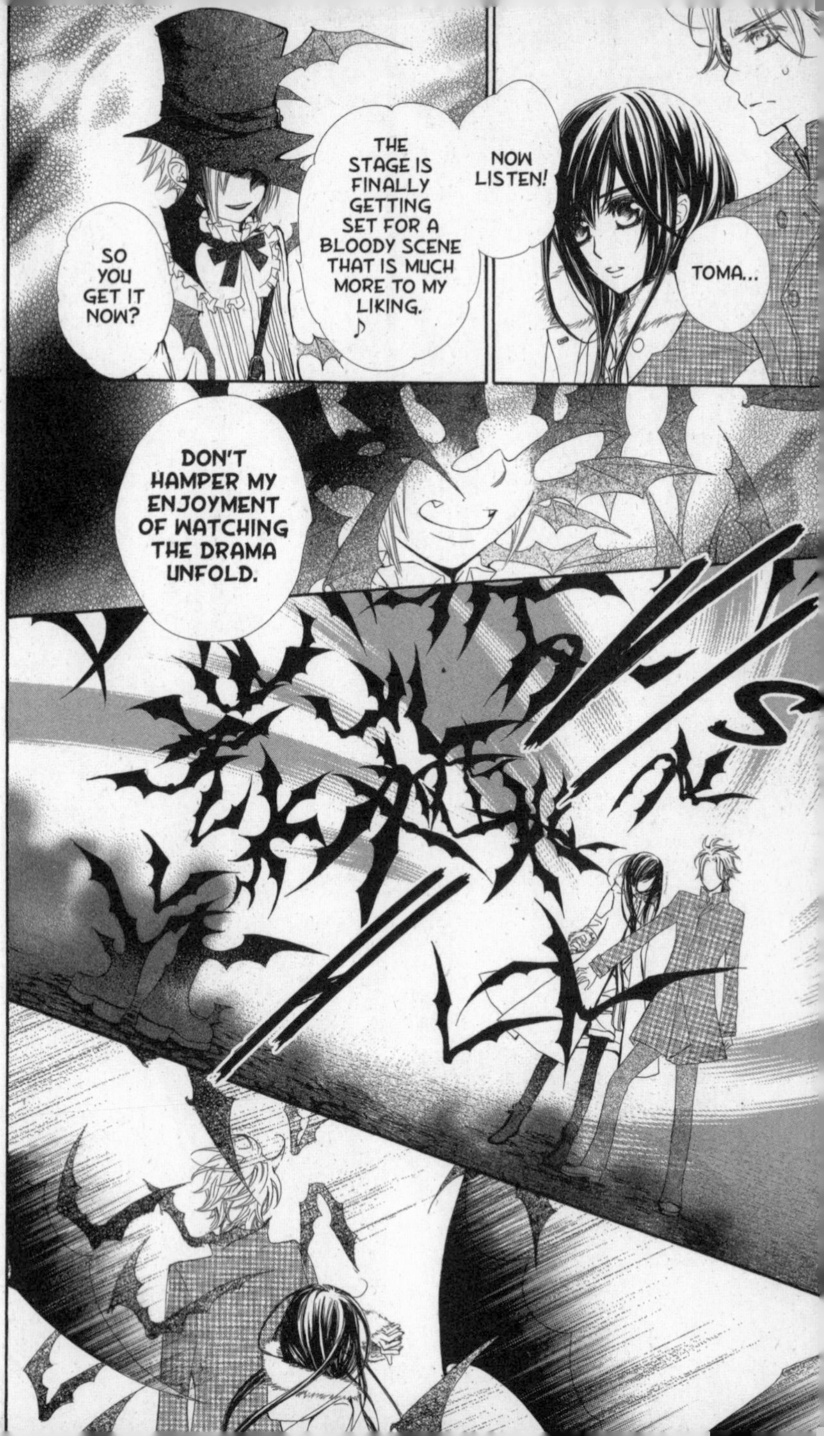
TOMA...
NOW LISTEN!
THE STAGE IS FINALLY GETTING SET FOR A BLOODY SCENE THAT IS MUCH MORE TO MY LIKING. ♪
SO YOU GET IT NOW?
DON'T HAMPER MY ENJOYMENT OF WATCHING THE DRAMA UNFOLD.

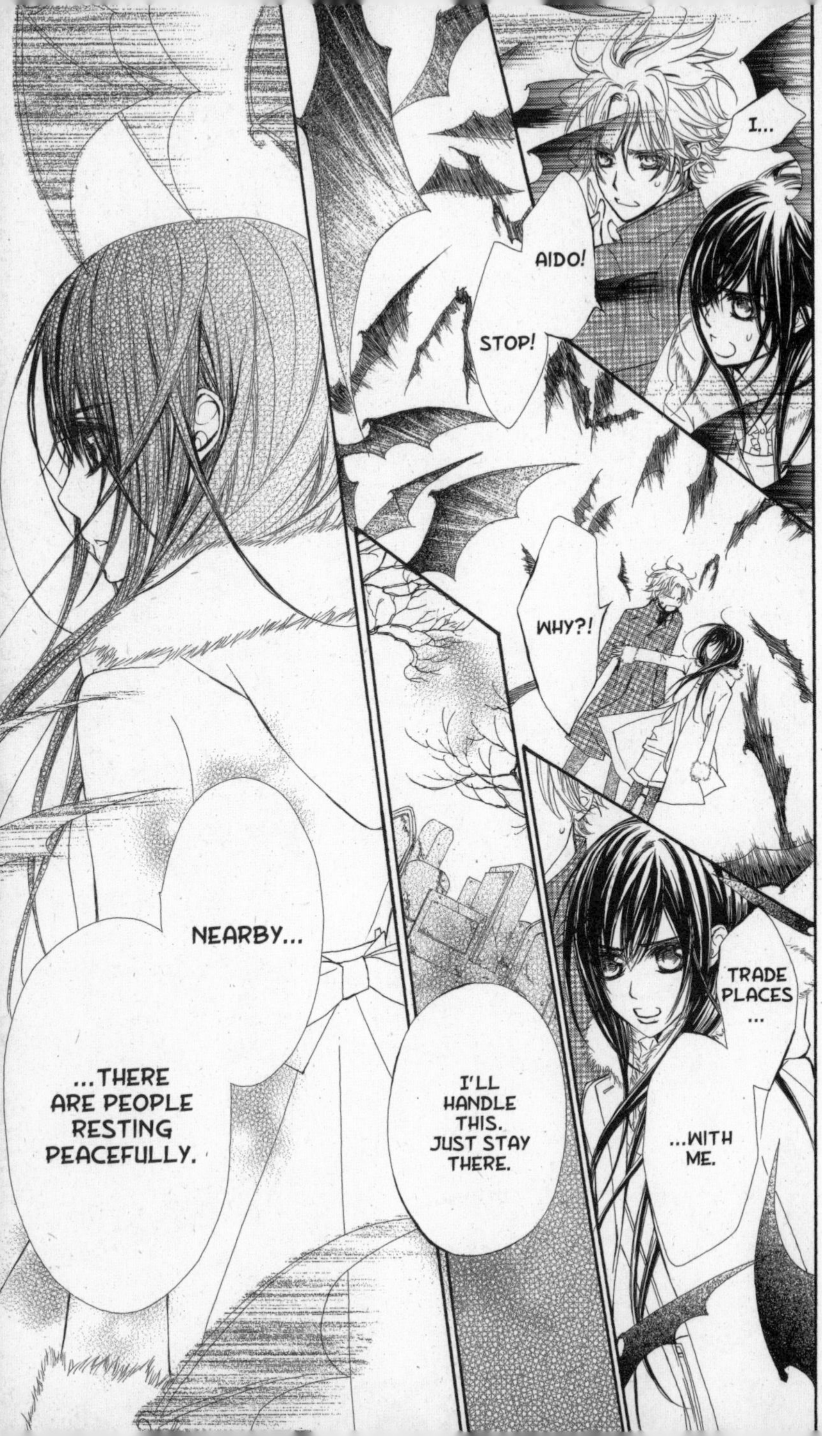
I...
AIDO!
STOP!
WHY?!
TRADE PLACES ...
...WITH ME.
I'LL HANDLE THIS. JUST STAY THERE.
NEARBY...
...THERE ARE PEOPLE RESTING PEACEFULLY.

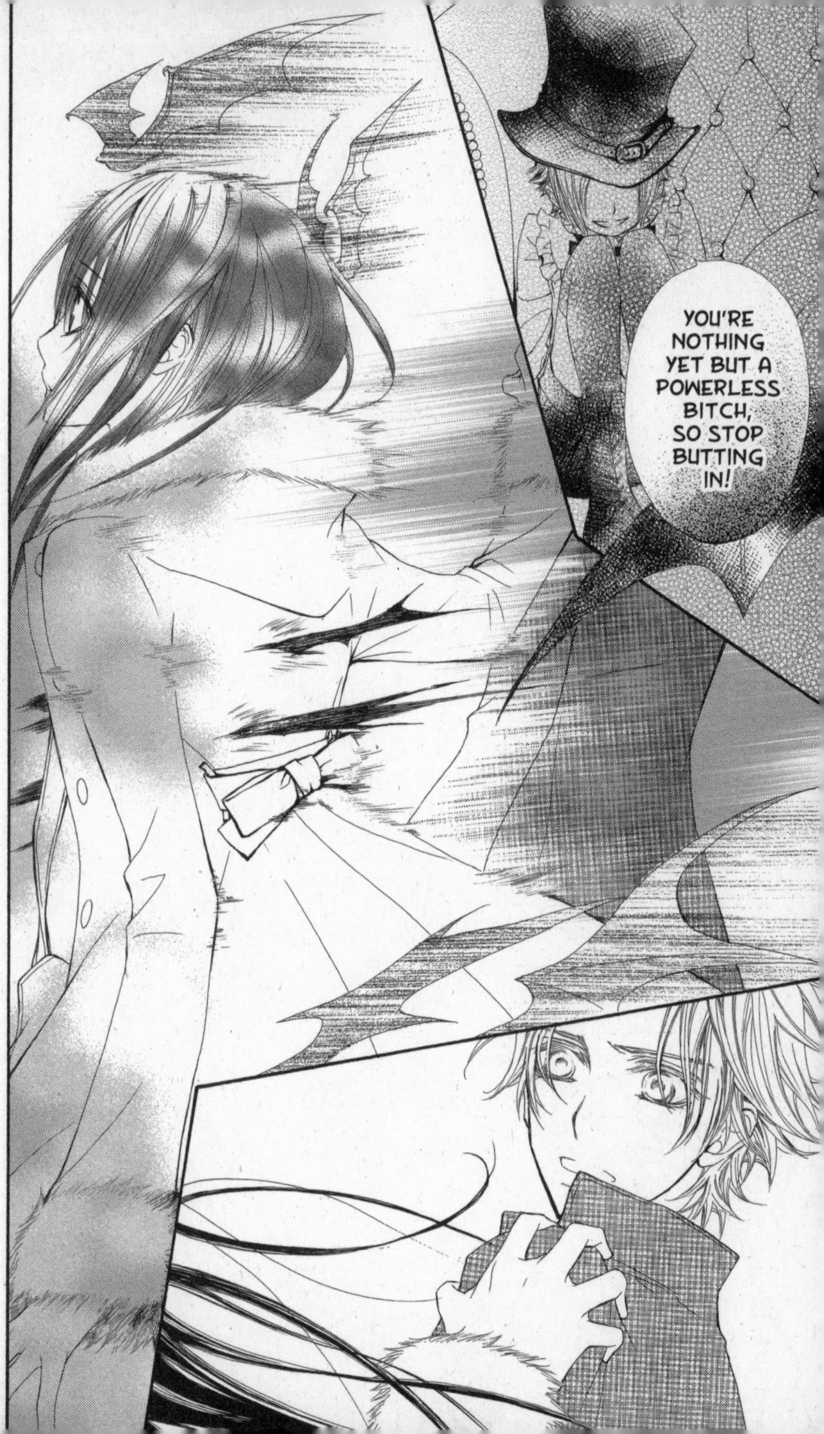
YOU'RE NOTHING YET BUT A POWERLESS BITCH, SO STOP BUTTING IN!

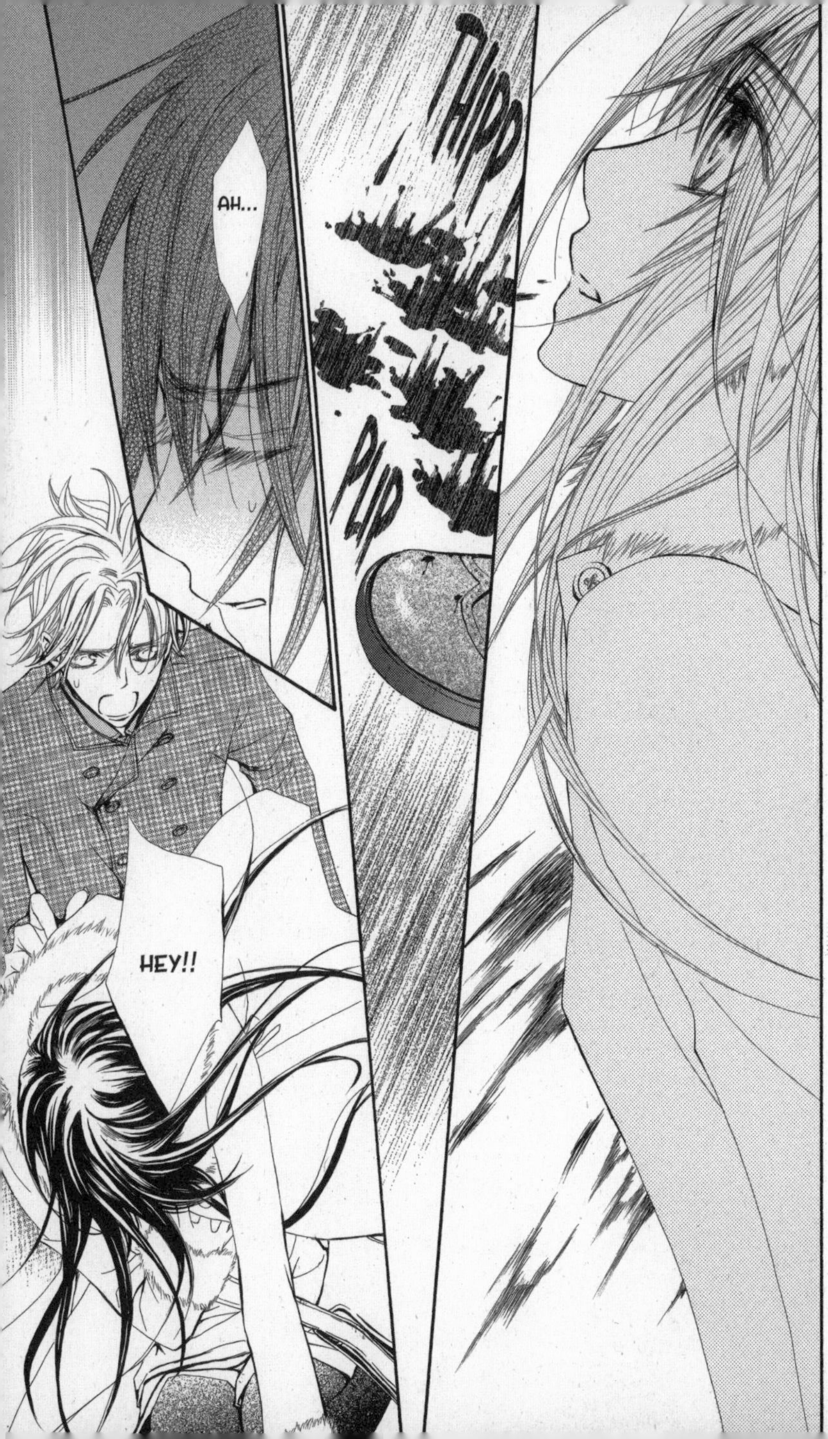
THIPP
PLIP
AH...
HEY!!

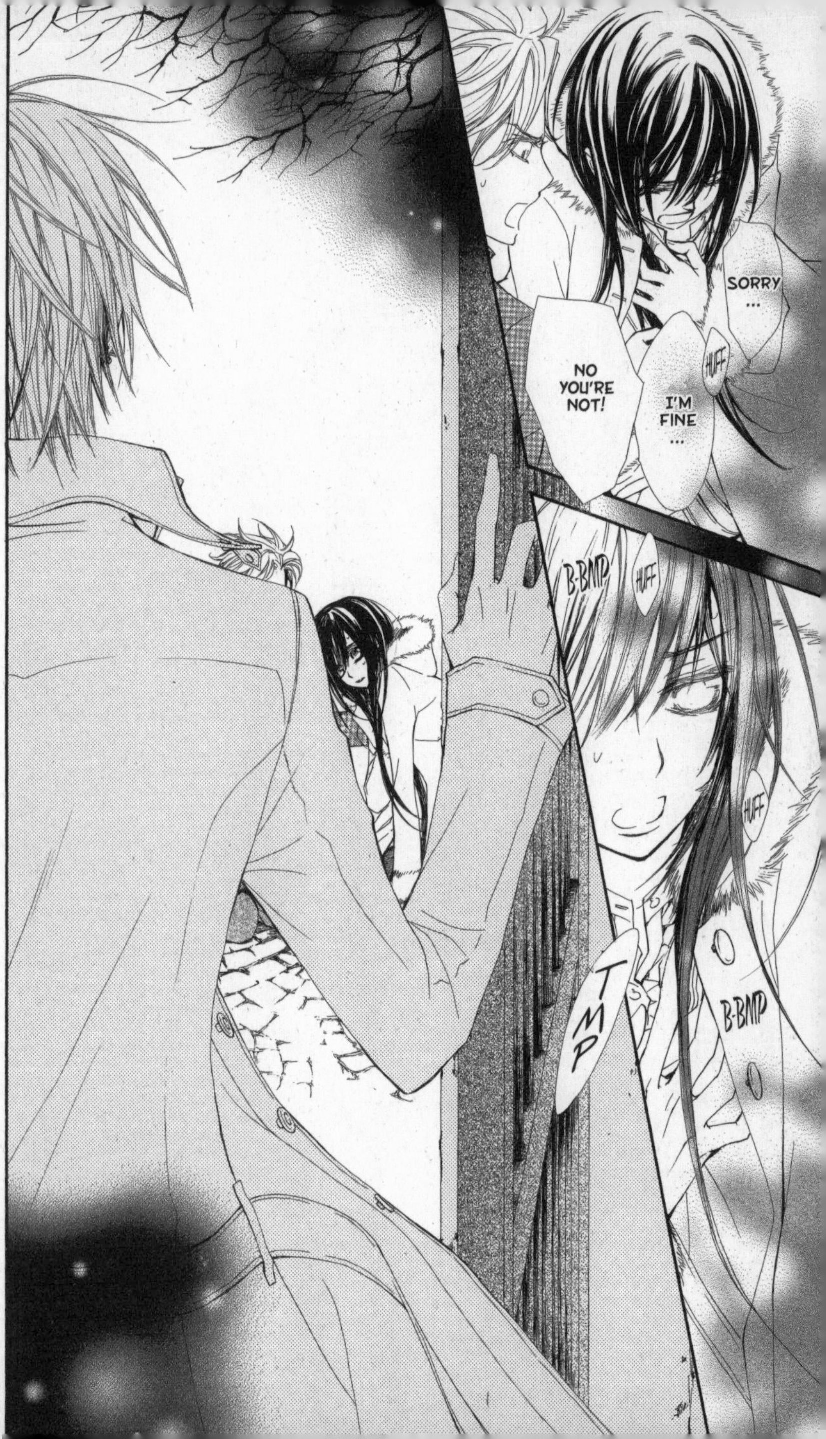
SORRY ...
HUFF
I'M FINE ...
NO YOU'RE NOT!
B-BMP
HUFF
HUFF
TMP
B-BMP

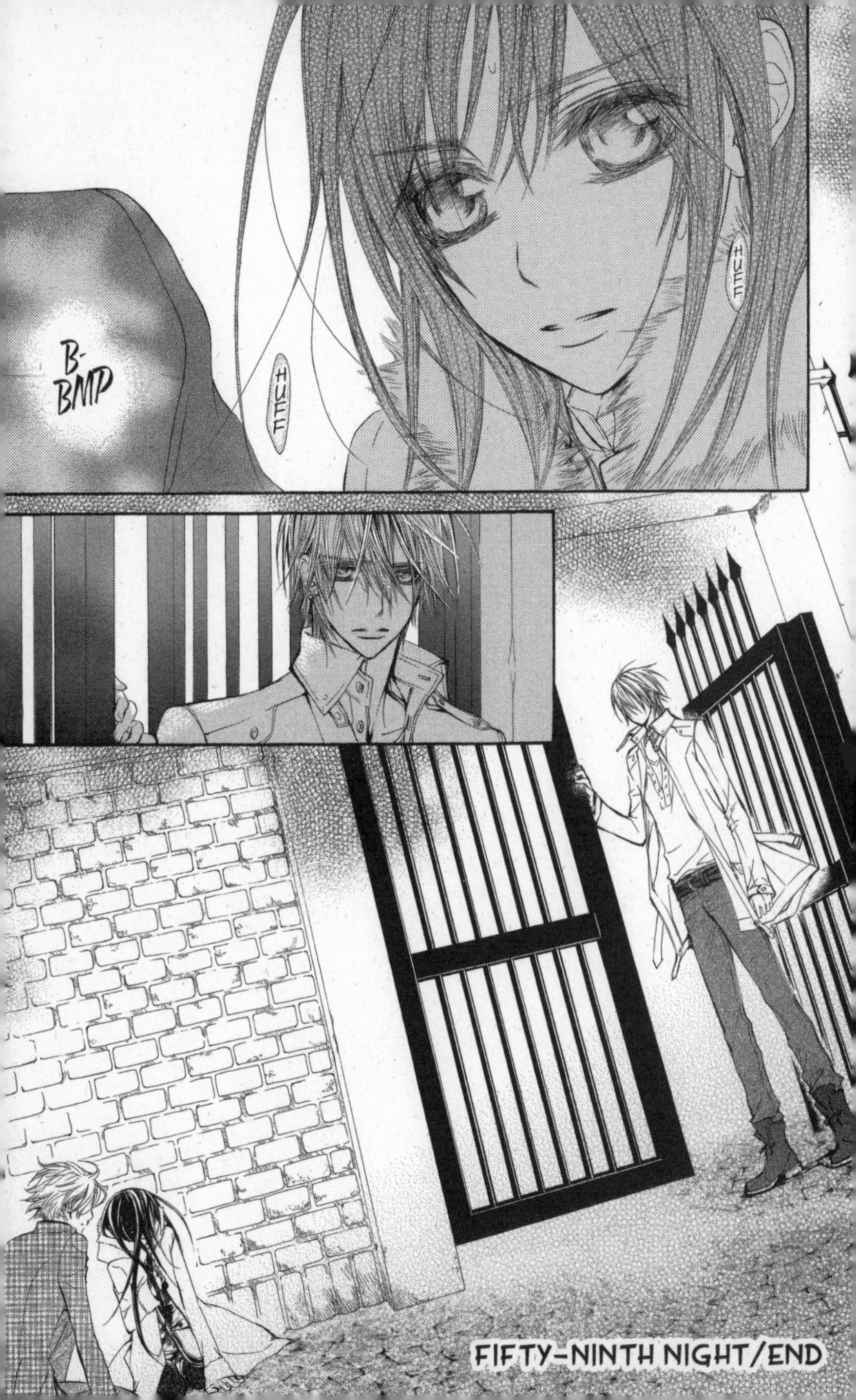
HUFF
HUFF
B-BMP
FIFTY-NINTH NIGHT/END

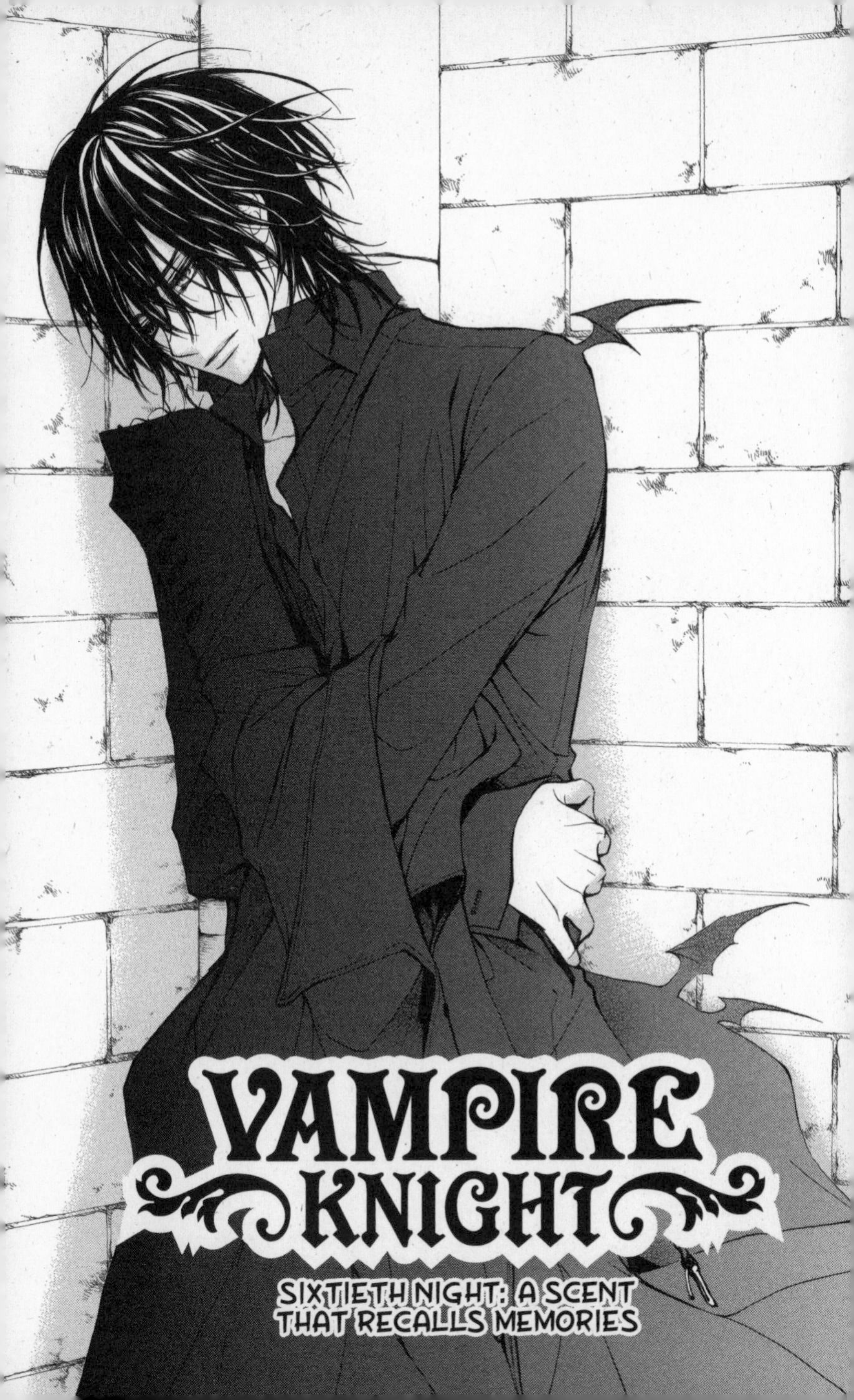
VAMPIRE KNIGHT
SIXTIETH NIGHT: A SCENT THAT RECALLS MEMORIES

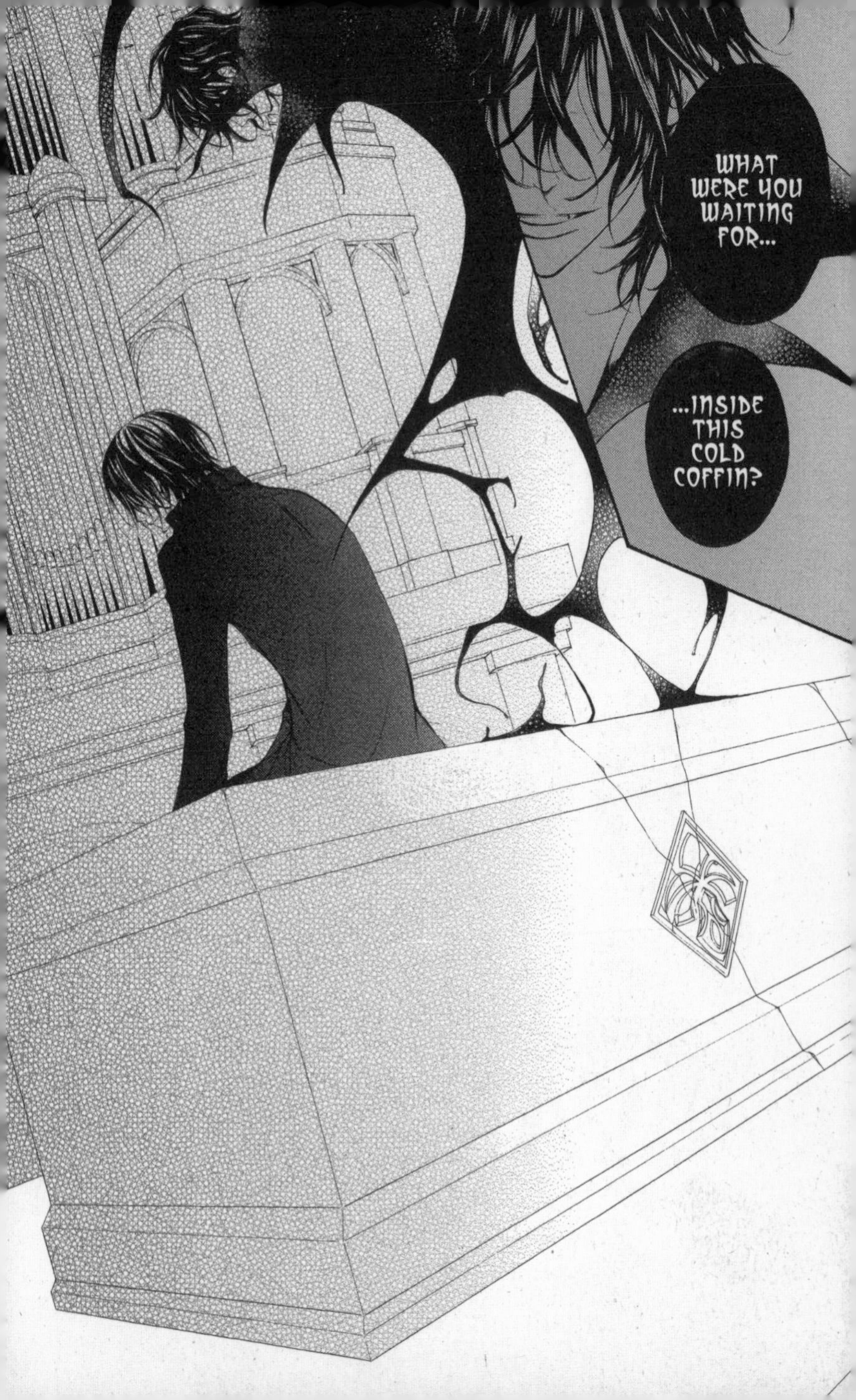
WHAT WERE YOU WAITING FOR...
...INSIDE THIS COLD COFFIN?

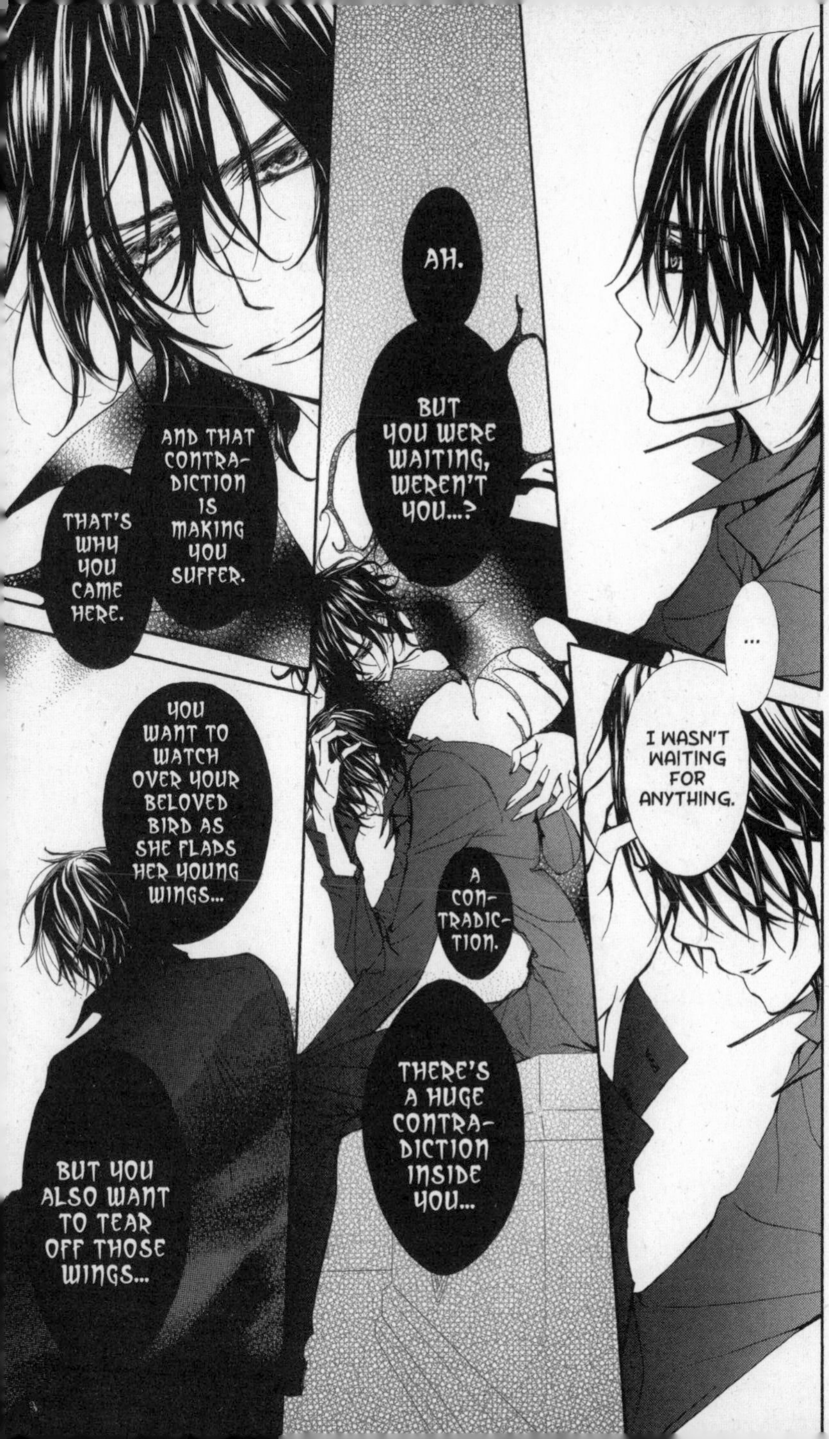
AH.
BUT YOU WERE WAITING, WEREN'T YOU...?
...
I WASN'T WAITING FOR ANYTHING.
A CONTRA-DICTION.
THERE'S A HUGE CONTRA-DICTION INSIDE YOU...
YOU WANT TO WATCH OVER YOUR BELOVED BIRD AS SHE FLAPS HER YOUNG WINGS...
BUT YOU ALSO WANT TO TEAR OFF THOSE WINGS...
AND THAT CONTRA-DICTION IS MAKING YOU SUFFER.
THAT'S WHY YOU CAME HERE.

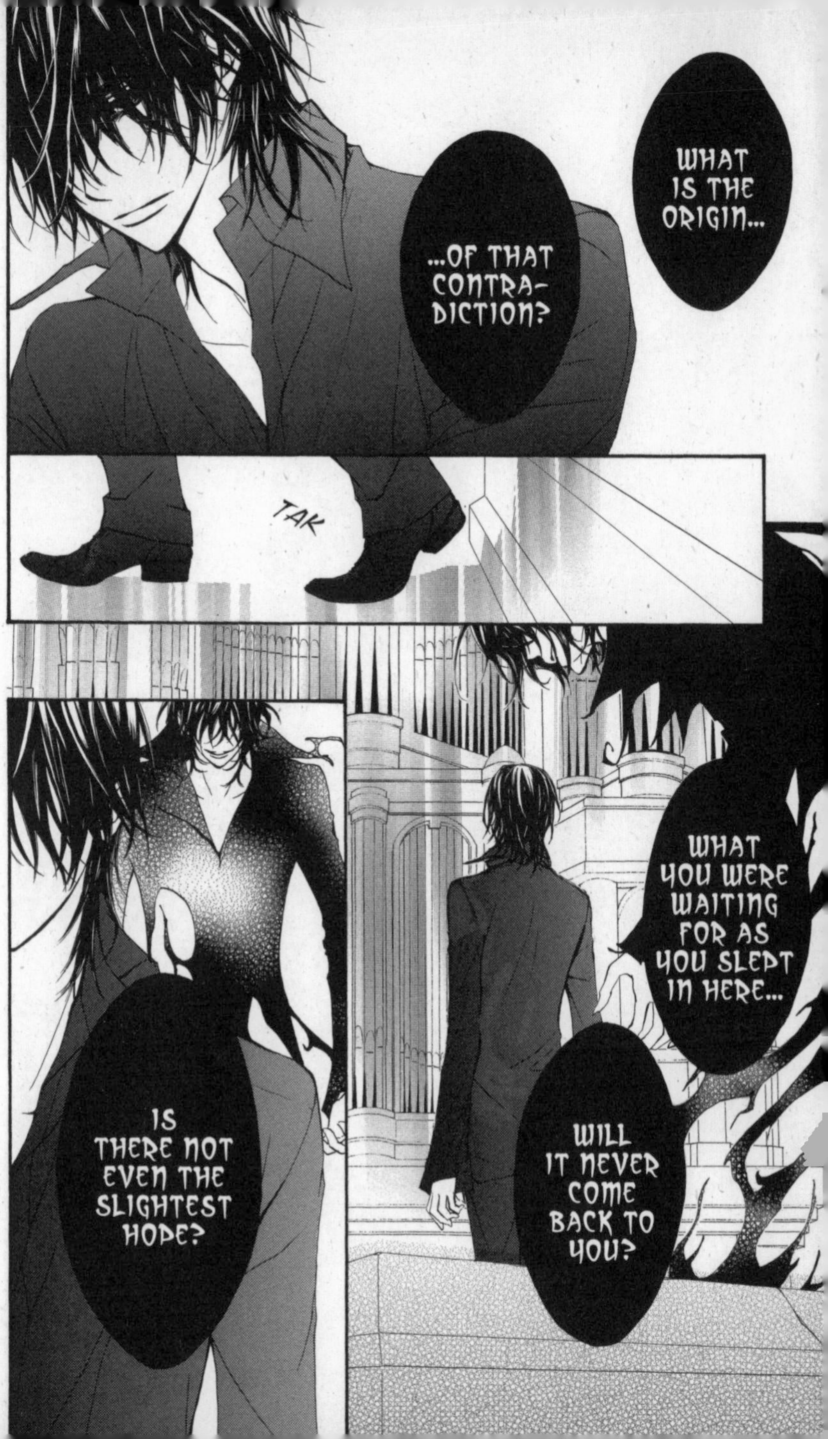
WHAT IS THE ORIGIN...
...OF THAT CONTRA-DICTION?
TAK
WHAT YOU WERE WAITING FOR AS YOU SLEPT IN HERE...
WILL IT NEVER COME BACK TO YOU?
IS THERE NOT EVEN THE SLIGHTEST HOPE?

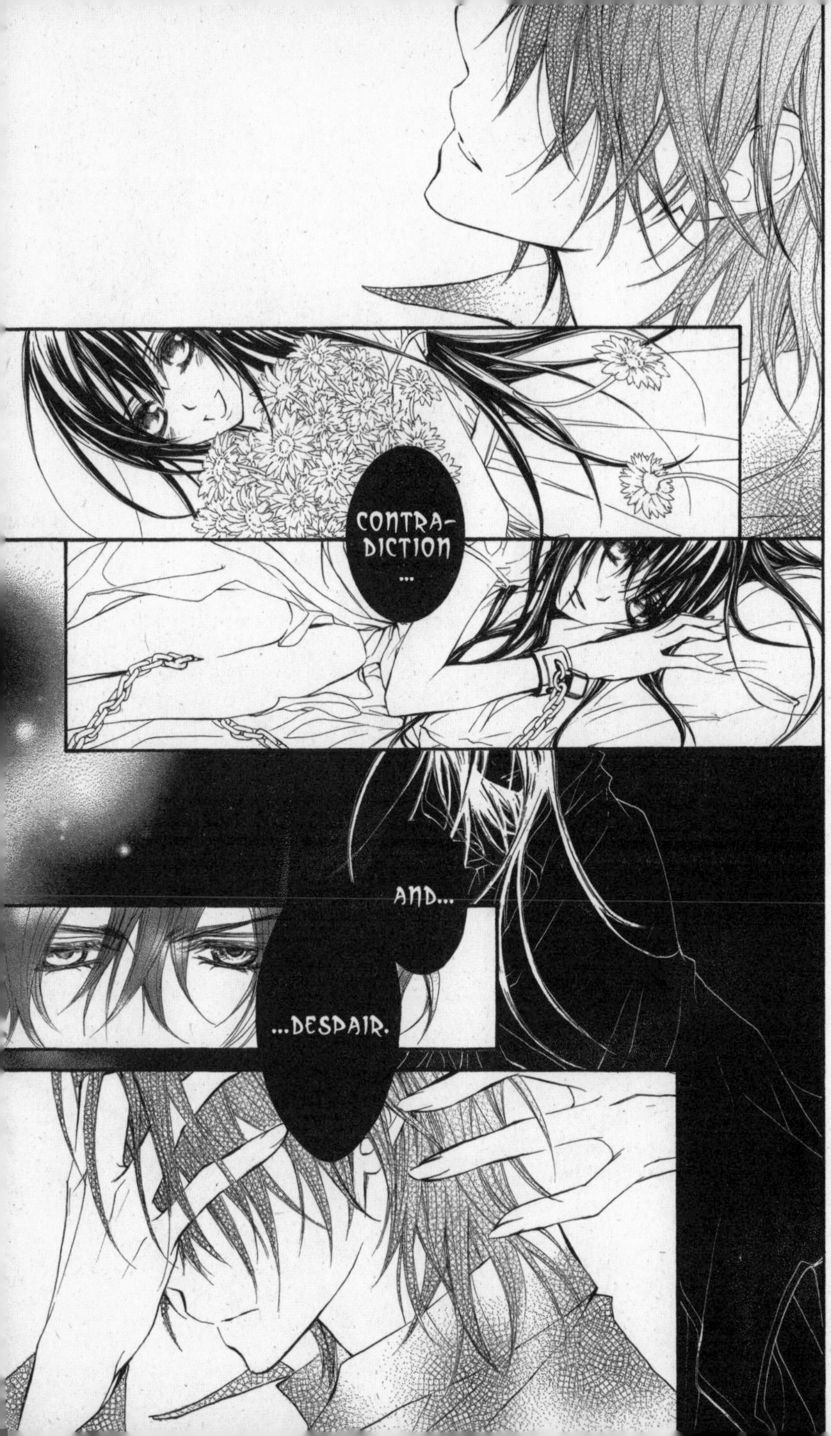
CONTRA-
DICTION
...
AND...
...DESPAIR.

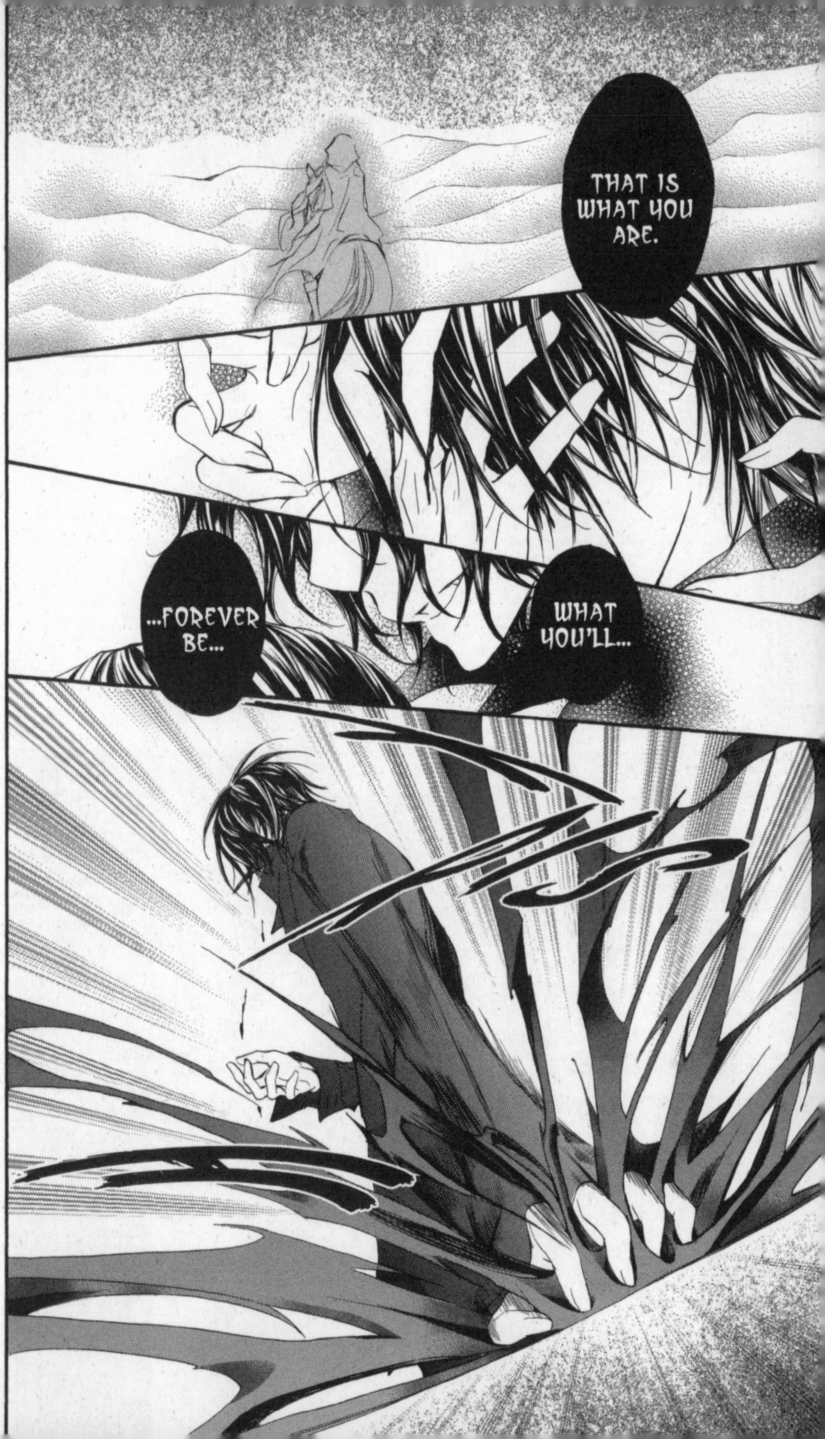
THAT IS WHAT YOU ARE.
WHAT YOU'LL...
...FOREVER BE...

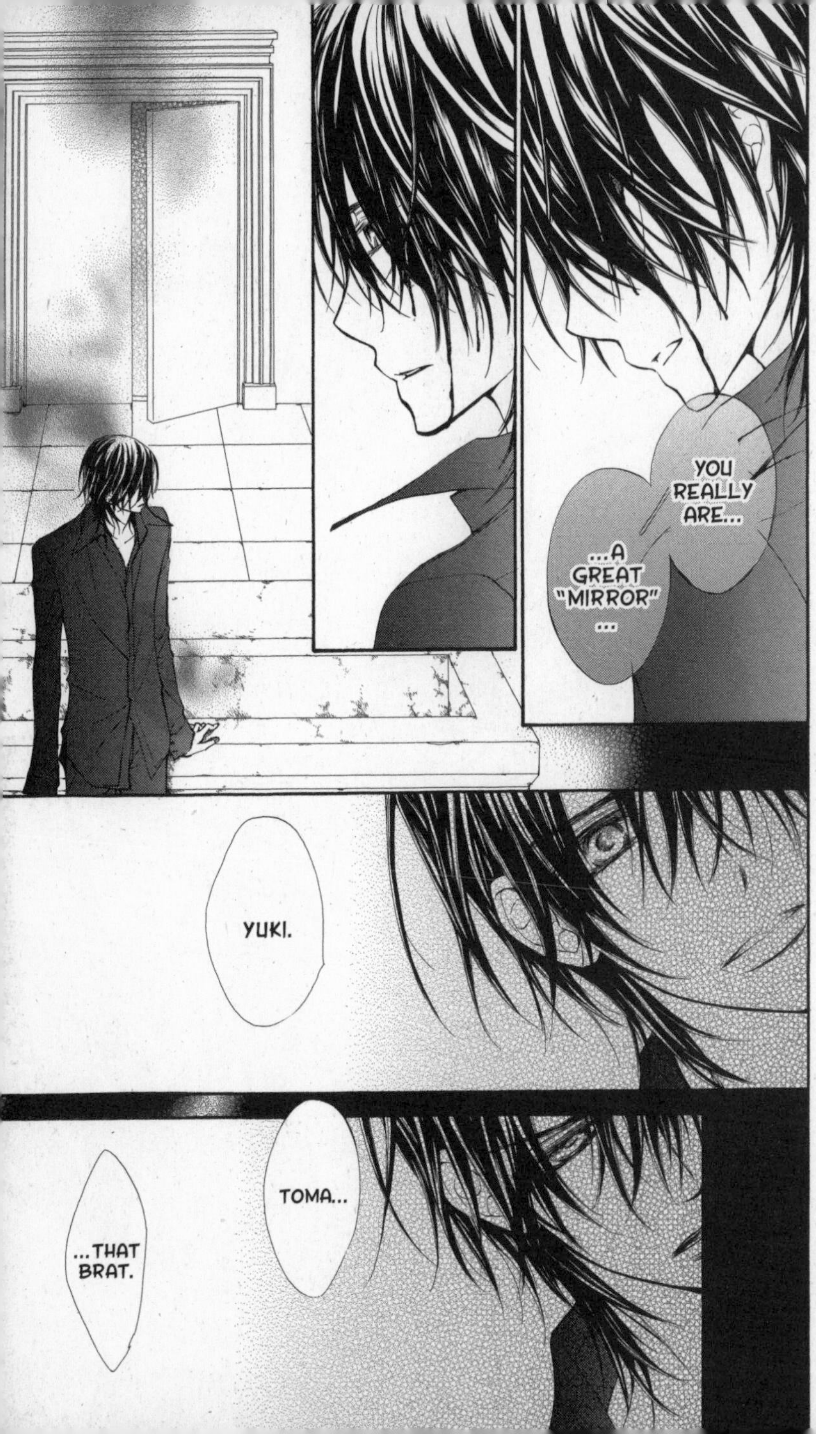
YOU REALLY ARE...
...A GREAT "MIRROR"...
YUKI.
TOMA...
...THAT BRAT.

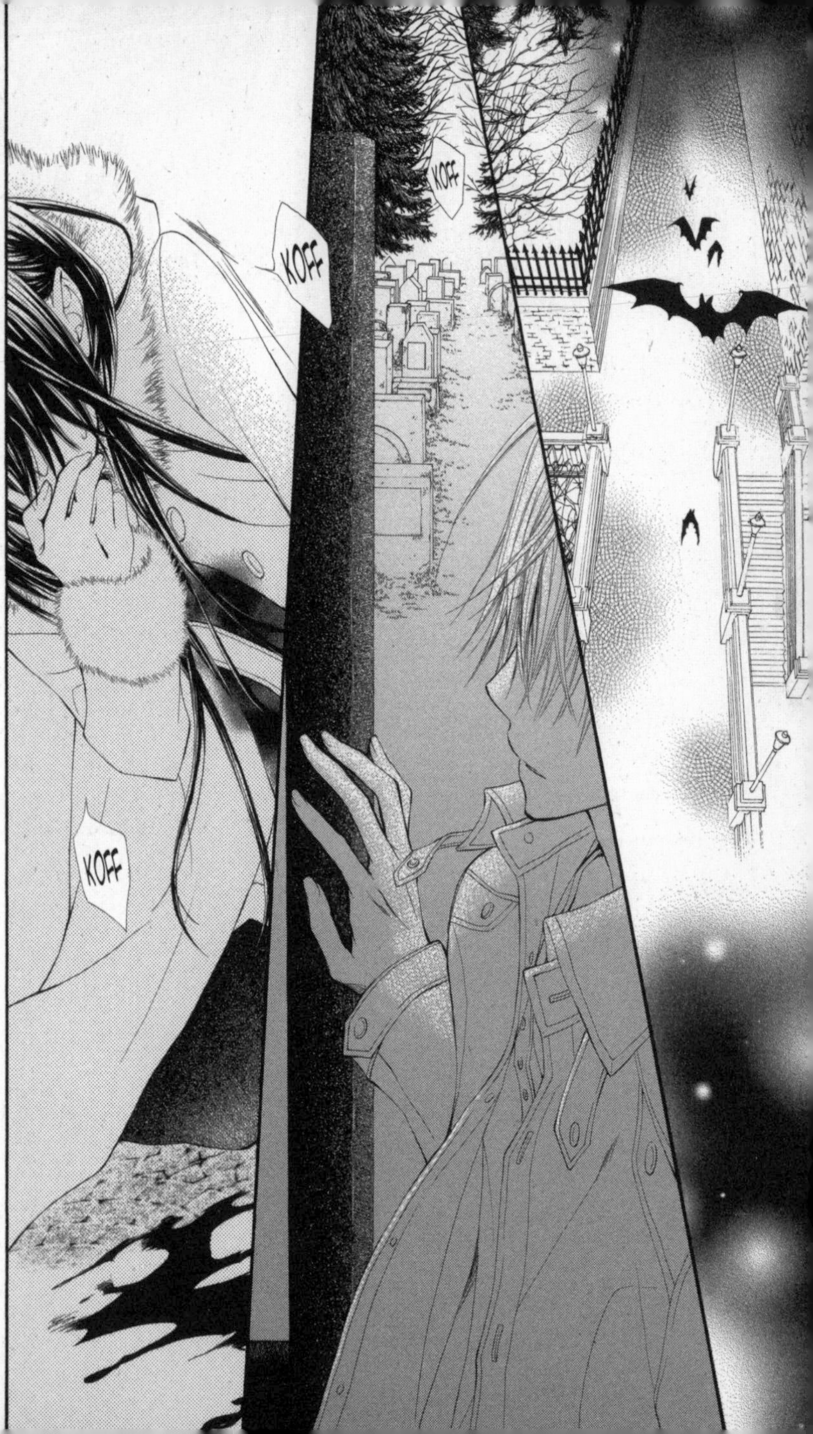
KOFF
KOFF
KOFF

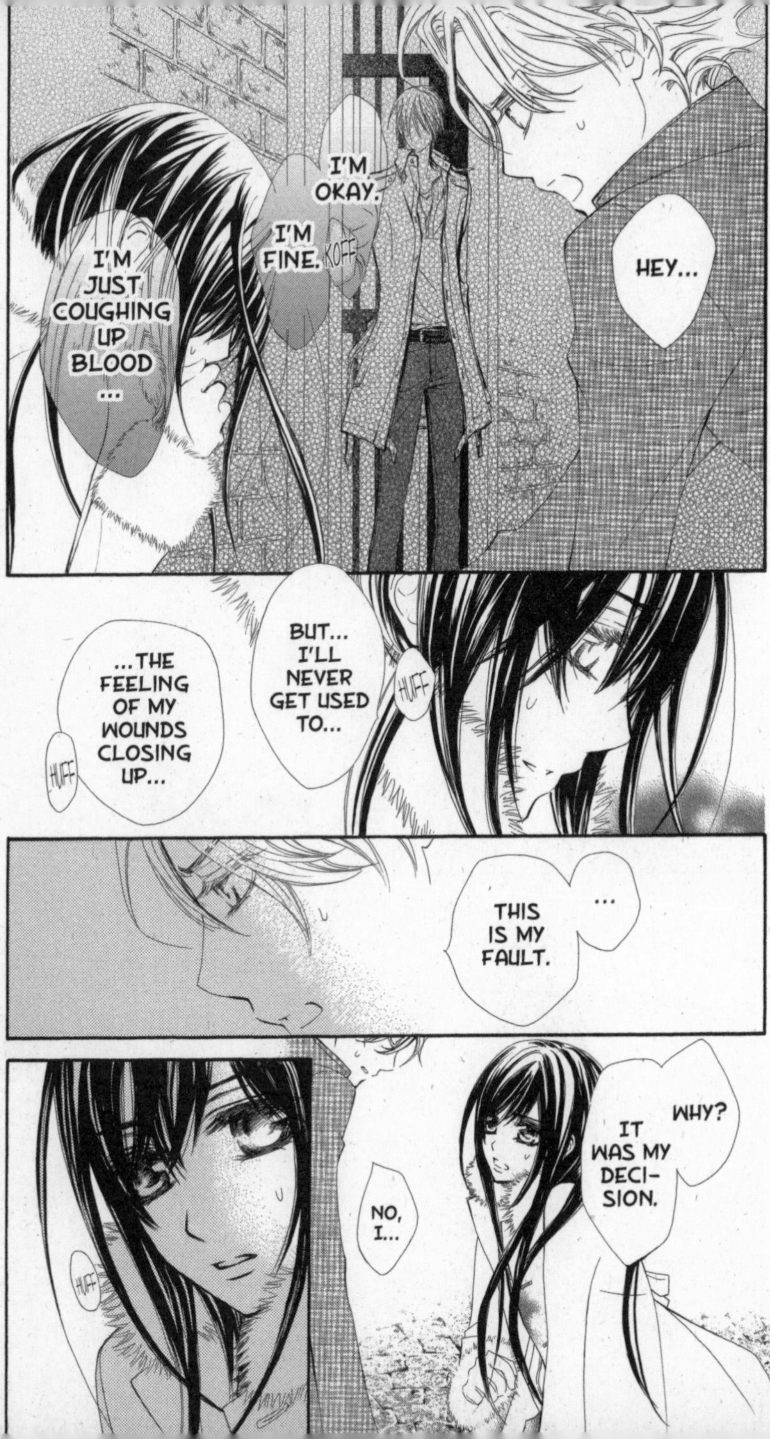
HEY...
I'M OKAY.
I'M FINE.
KOFF
I'M JUST COUGHING UP BLOOD ...
BUT... I'LL NEVER GET USED TO...
HUFF
...THE FEELING OF MY WOUNDS CLOSING UP...
HUFF
...
THIS IS MY FAULT.
WHY?
IT WAS MY DECI-SION.
NO, I...
HUFF

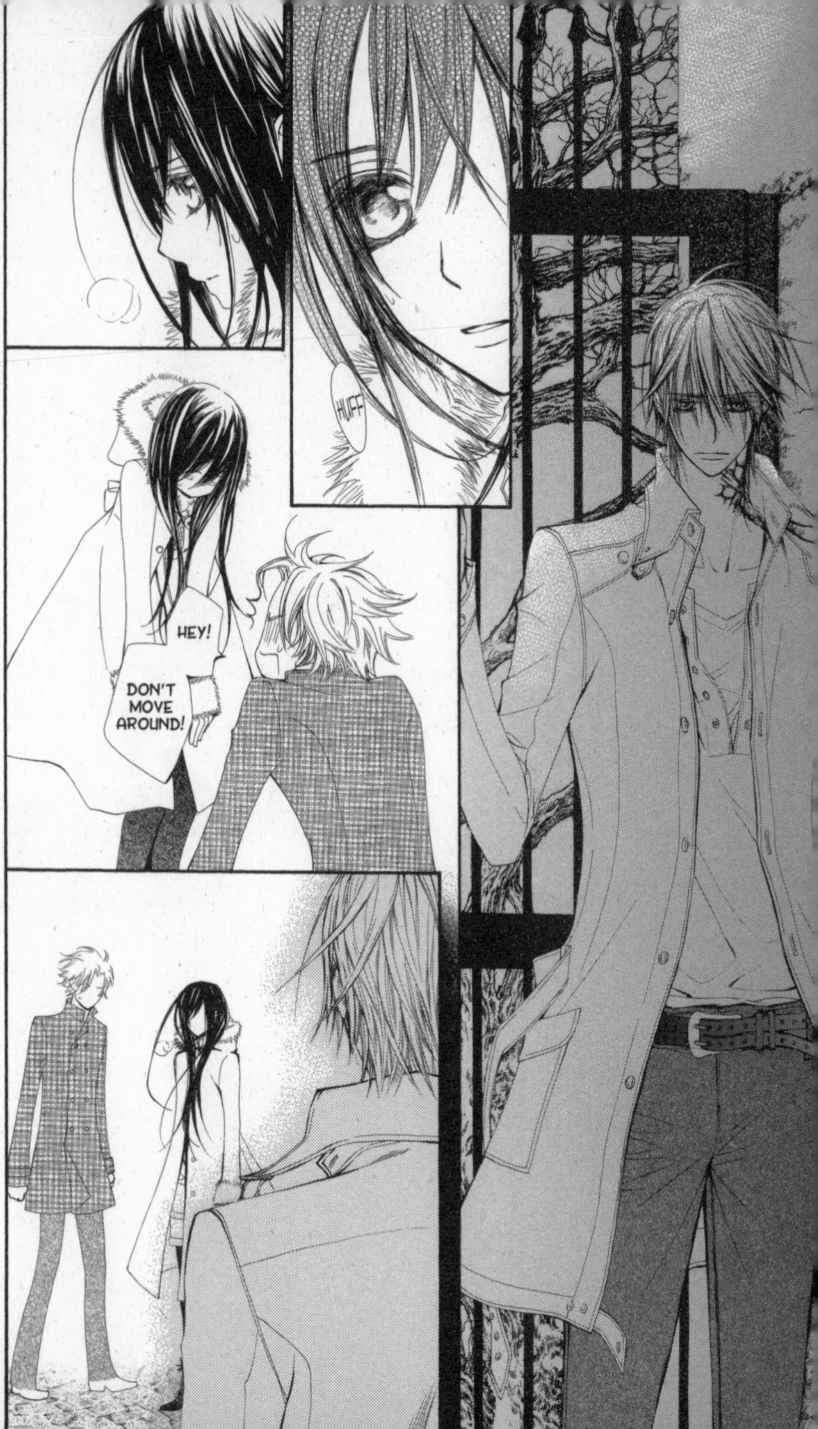
HUFF
HEY!
DON'T MOVE AROUND!

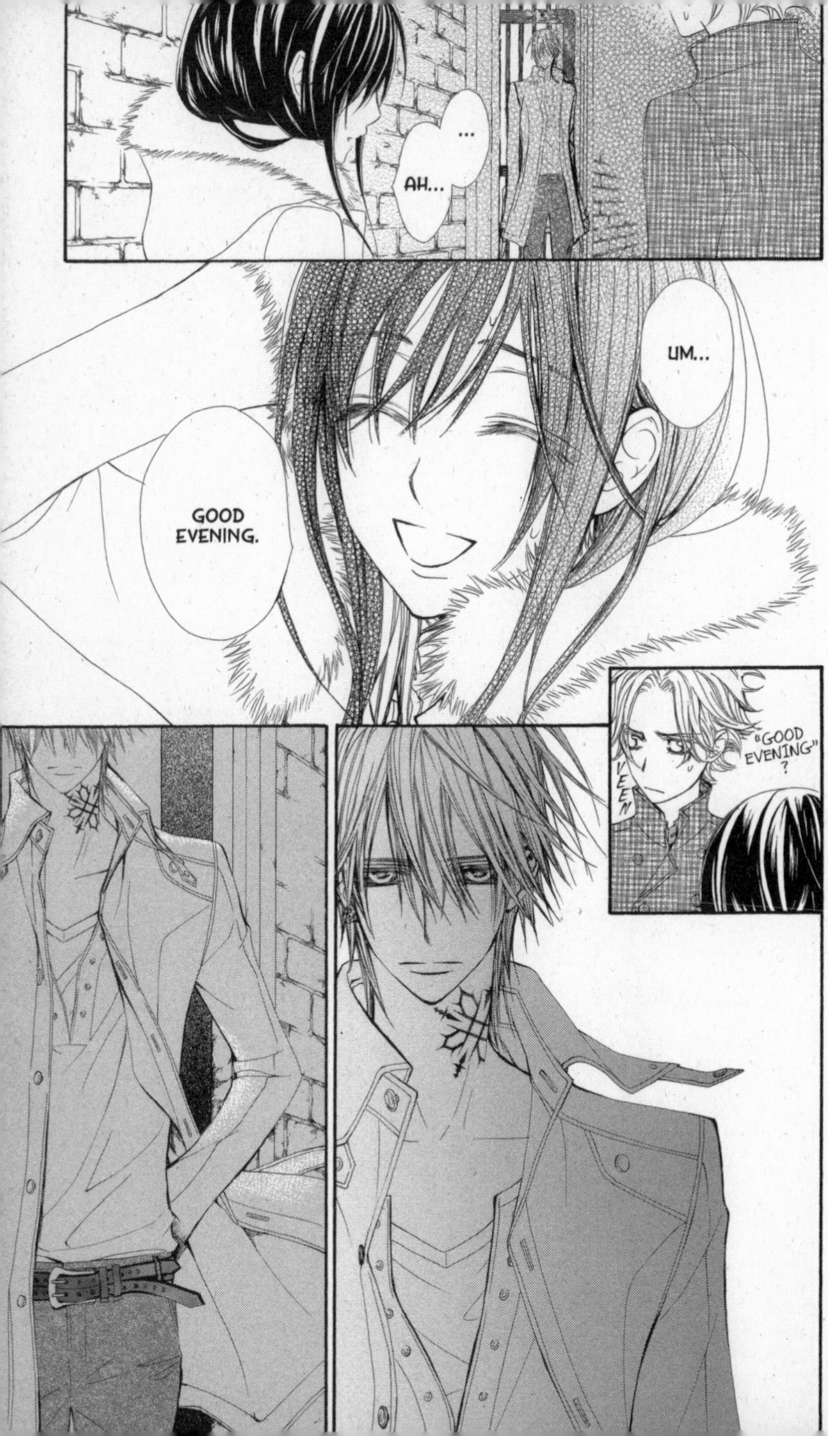
...
AH...
UM...
GOOD EVENING.
VEEN
"GOOD EVENING"?

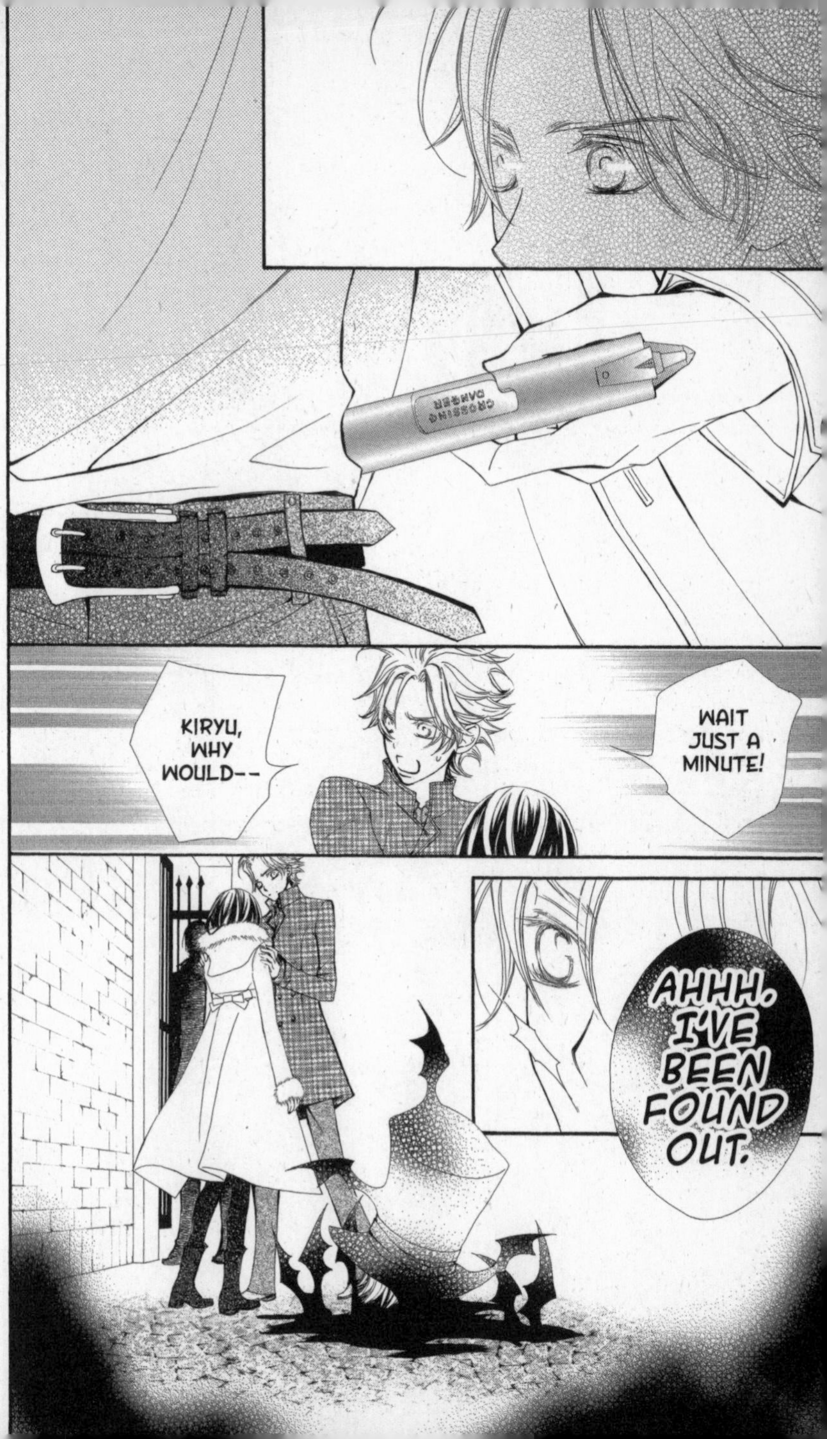
CROSSING DAGGER
WAIT JUST A MINUTE!
KIRYU, WHY WOULD--
AHHH. I'VE BEEN FOUND OUT.

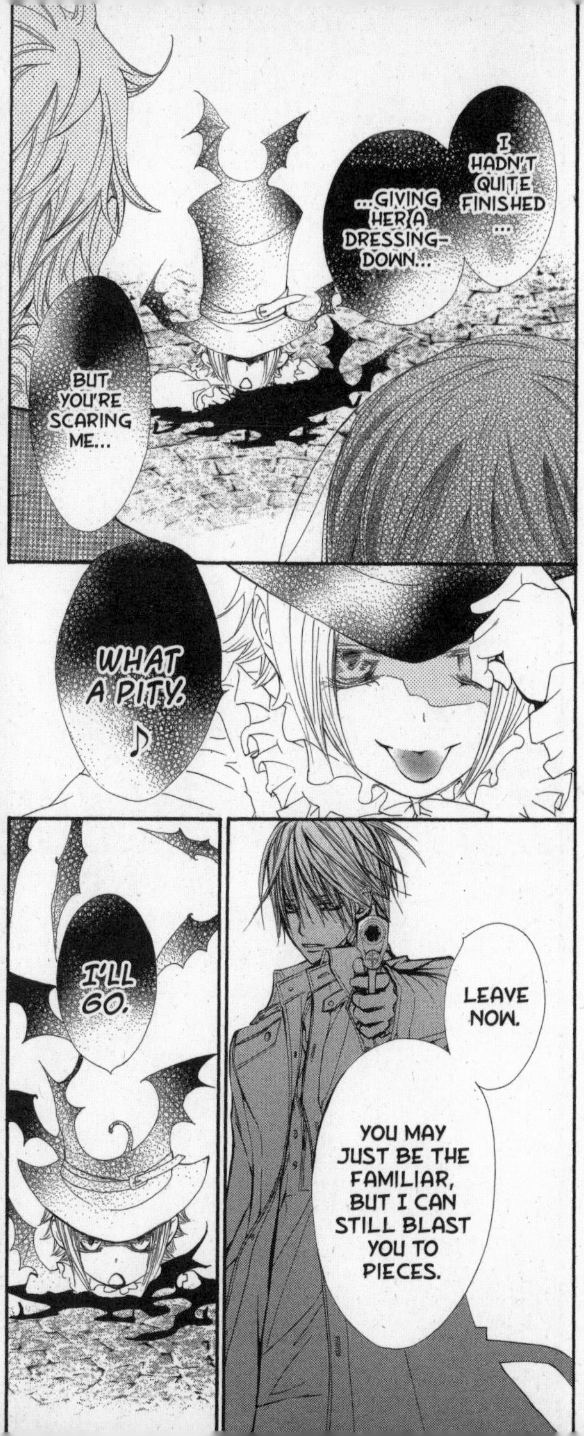
I HADN'T QUITE FINISHED...
...GIVING HER A DRESSING-DOWN...
BUT YOU'RE SCARING ME...
WHAT A PITY. ♪
LEAVE NOW.
YOU MAY JUST BE THE FAMILIAR, BUT I CAN STILL BLAST YOU TO PIECES.
I'LL GO.

II

Every month my editor comes up with a lead-in sentence for the chapter title page in the magazine. (It's usually on the first or second page of the installment.) In this space I'd like to list the recent ones I liked!

"So which one of them is really falling?" (Fifty-Third Night)

This was a lead-in to go along with the illustration for the cosplay contest results, and that lead-in made me nod my head in agreement.

"I wanted to keep holding you in my hands forever..." (Forty-Sixth Night)

This lead-in went perfectly with the two-page spread. This was exactly how I felt when I drew it. When you have the time, take a look at the title page illustrations in the manga for these lead-ins. ♡

(Continues)

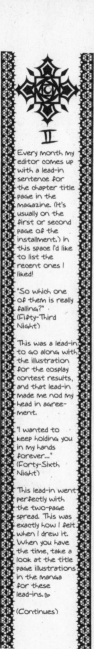

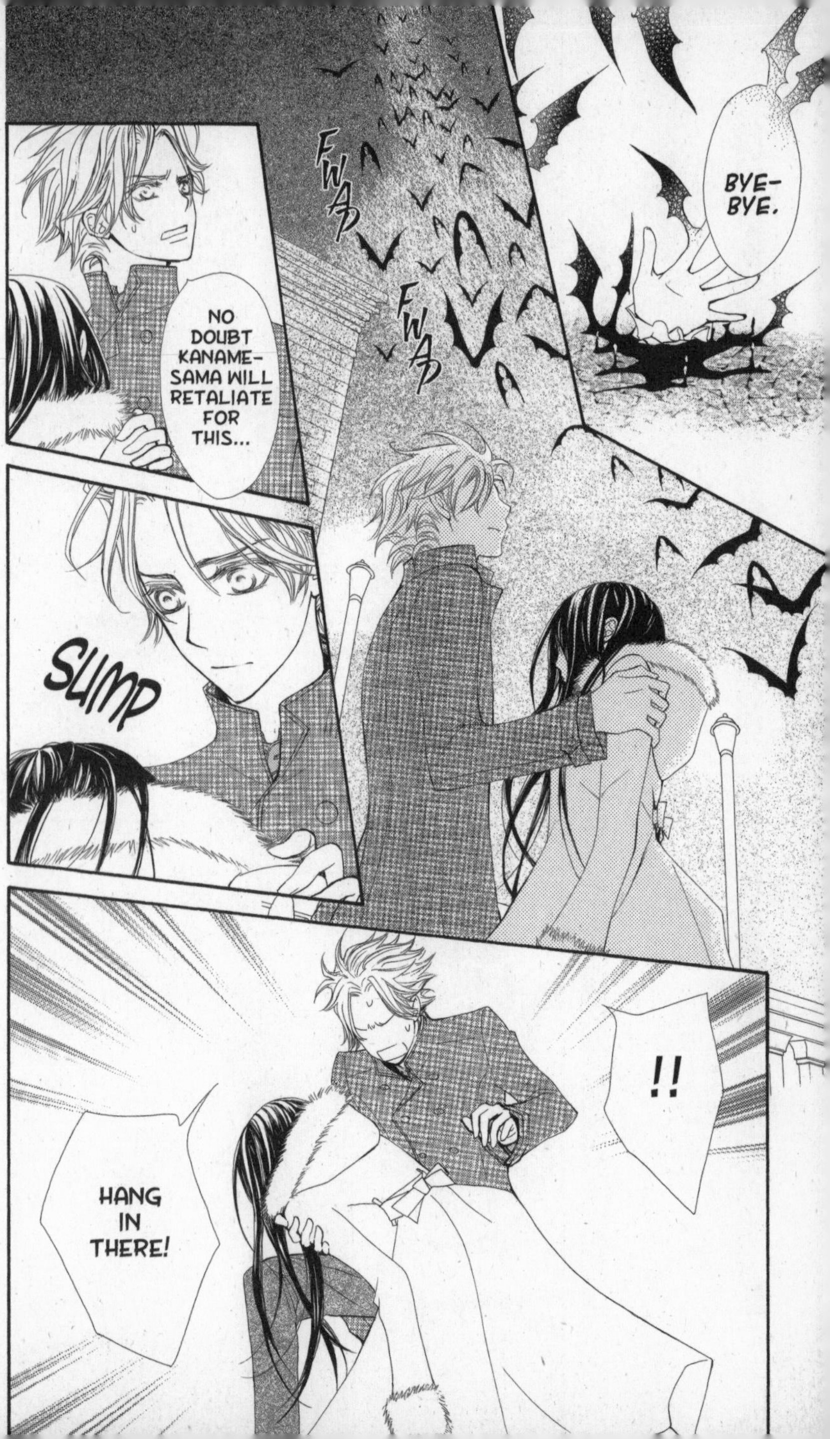
BYE-BYE.
FWAP
FWAP
NO DOUBT KANAME-SAMA WILL RETALIATE FOR THIS...
SLUMP
!!
HANG IN THERE!

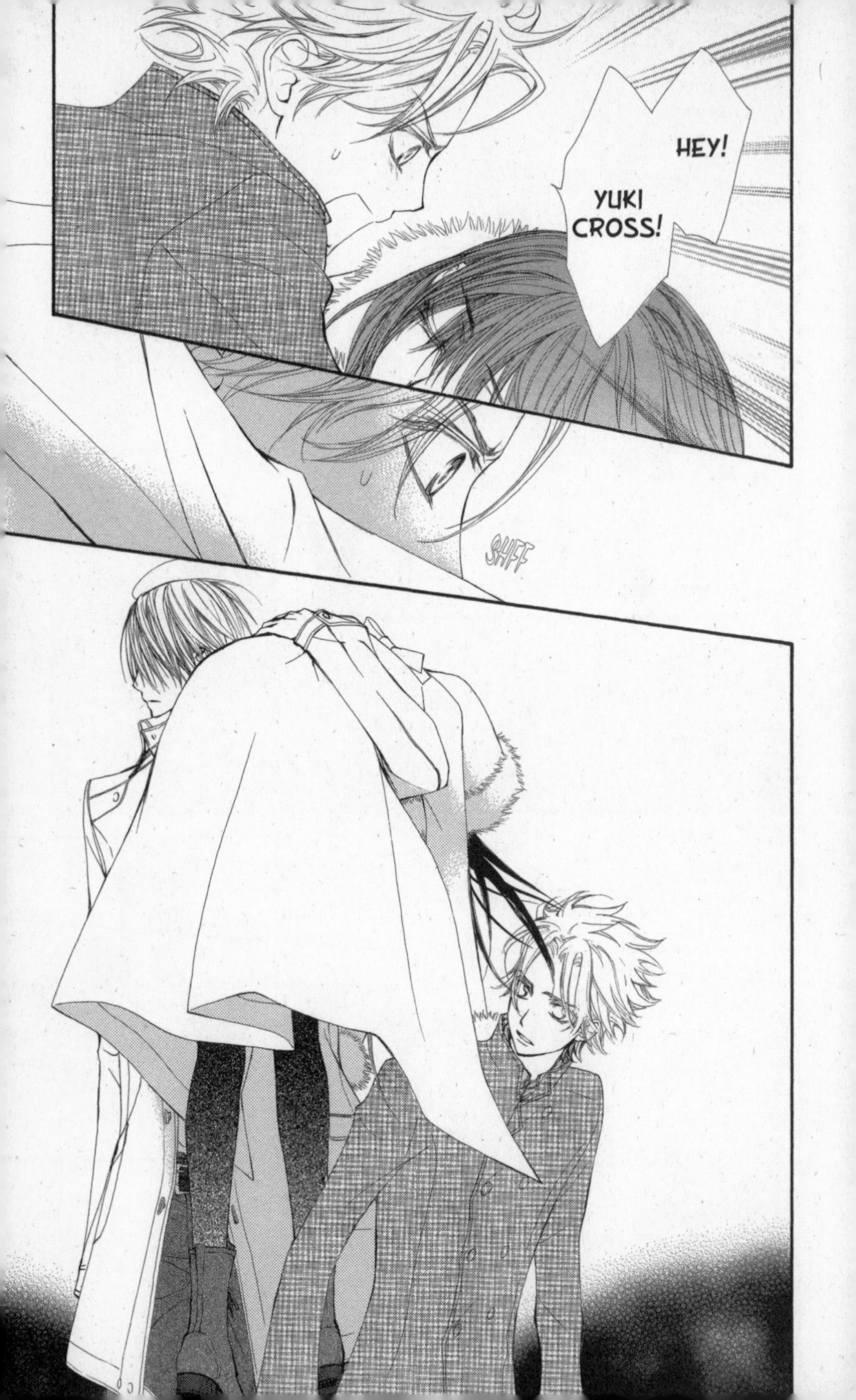
HEY!
YUKI CROSS!
SHFF

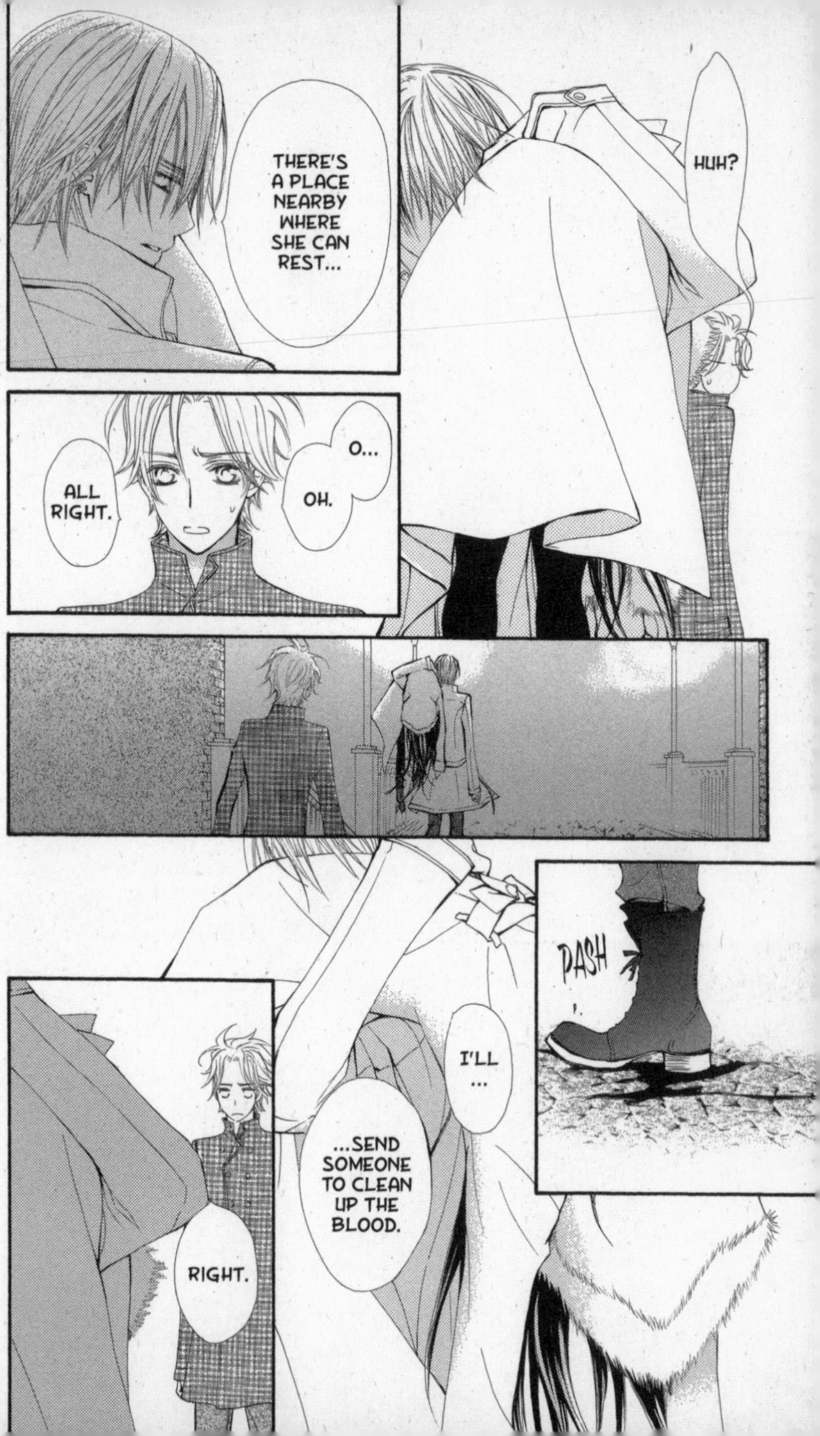
HUH?
THERE'S A PLACE NEARBY WHERE SHE CAN REST...
O... OH.
ALL RIGHT.
PASH
I'LL...
...SEND SOMEONE TO CLEAN UP THE BLOOD.
RIGHT.

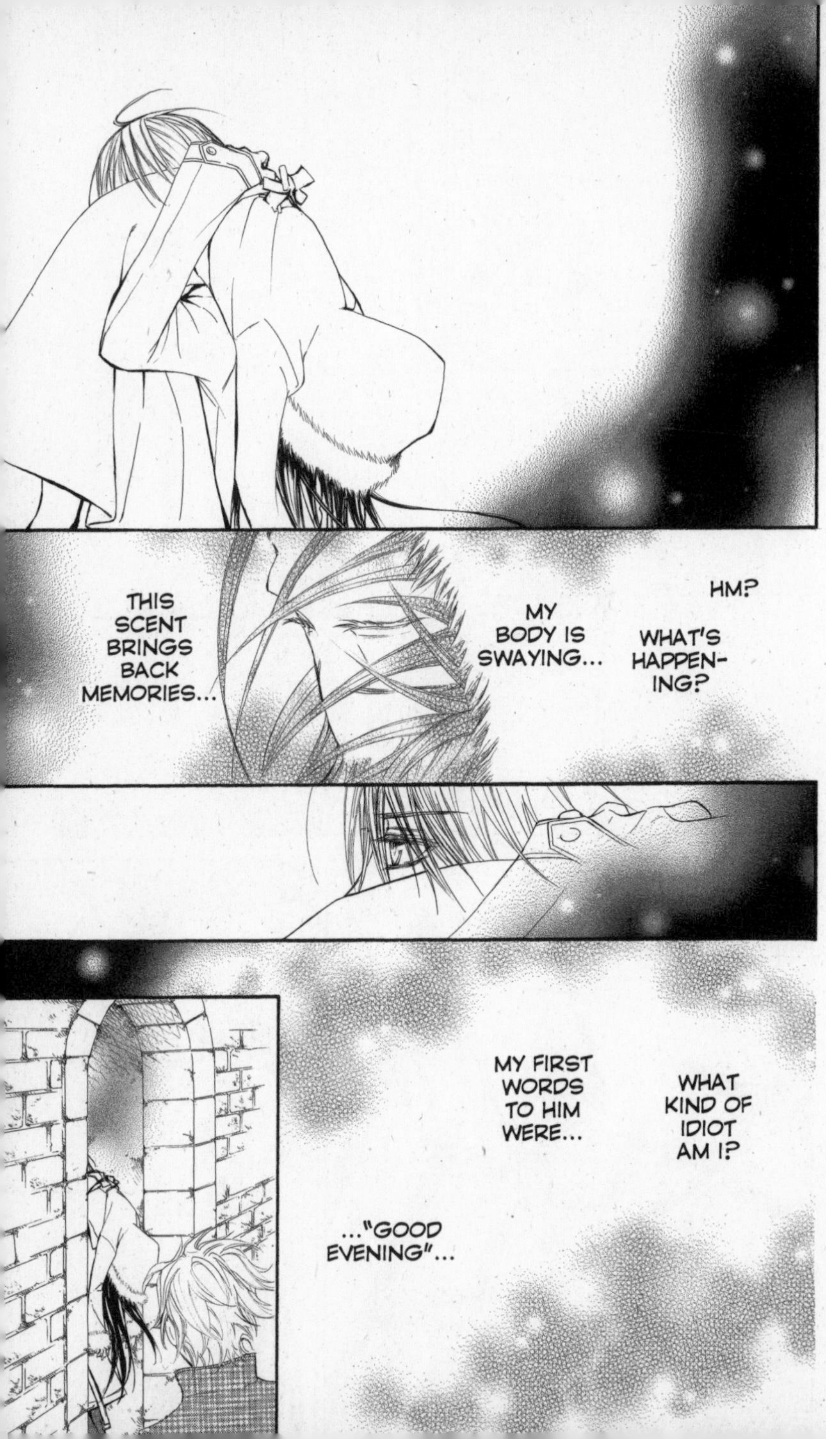
HM?
WHAT'S HAPPENING?
MY BODY IS SWAYING...
THIS SCENT BRINGS BACK MEMORIES...
WHAT KIND OF IDIOT AM I?
MY FIRST WORDS TO HIM WERE...
..."GOOD EVENING"...

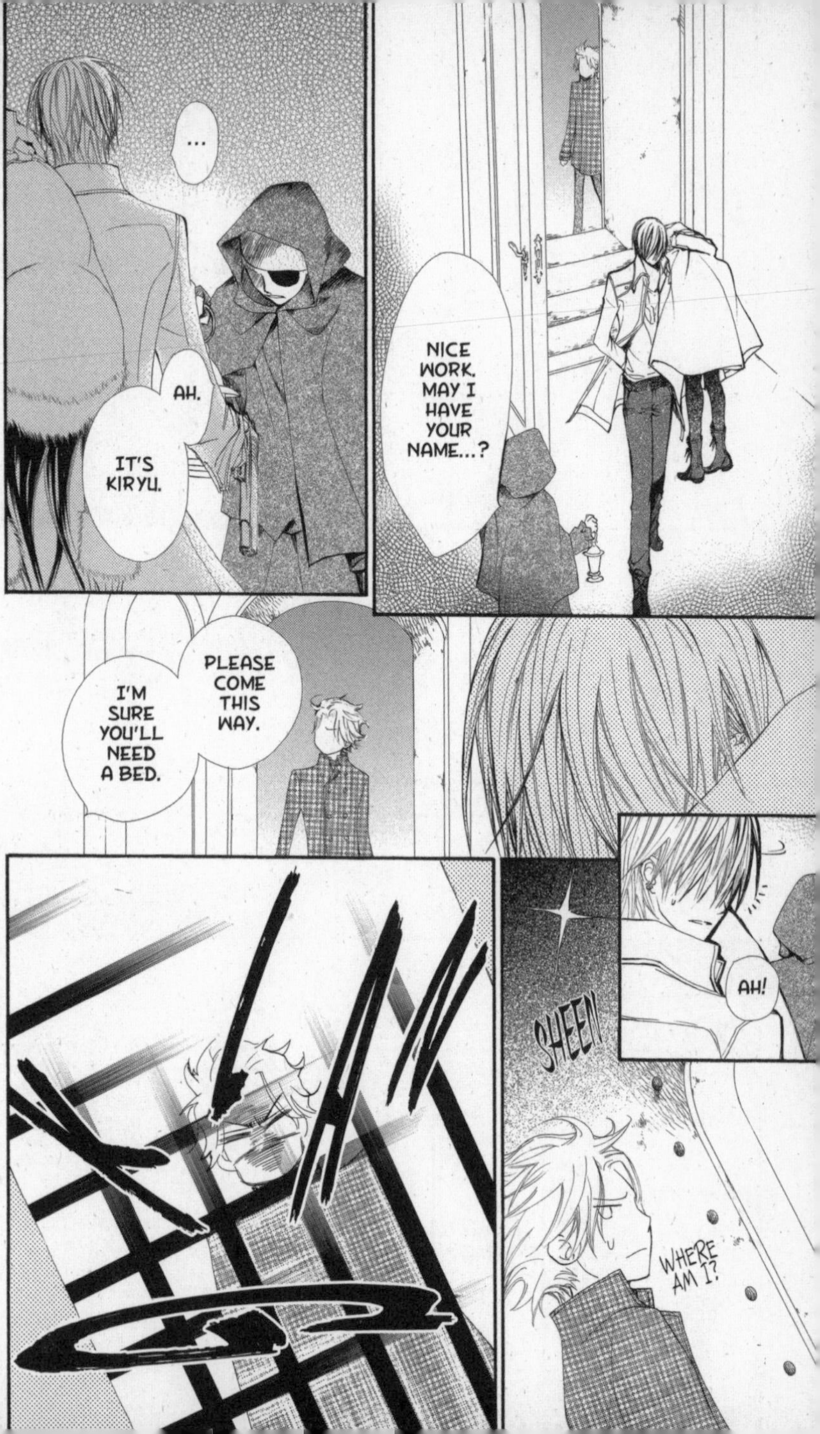
NICE WORK. MAY I HAVE YOUR NAME...?
...
AH.
IT'S KIRYU.
AH!
PLEASE COME THIS WAY.
I'M SURE YOU'LL NEED A BED.
SHEEN
WHERE AM I?

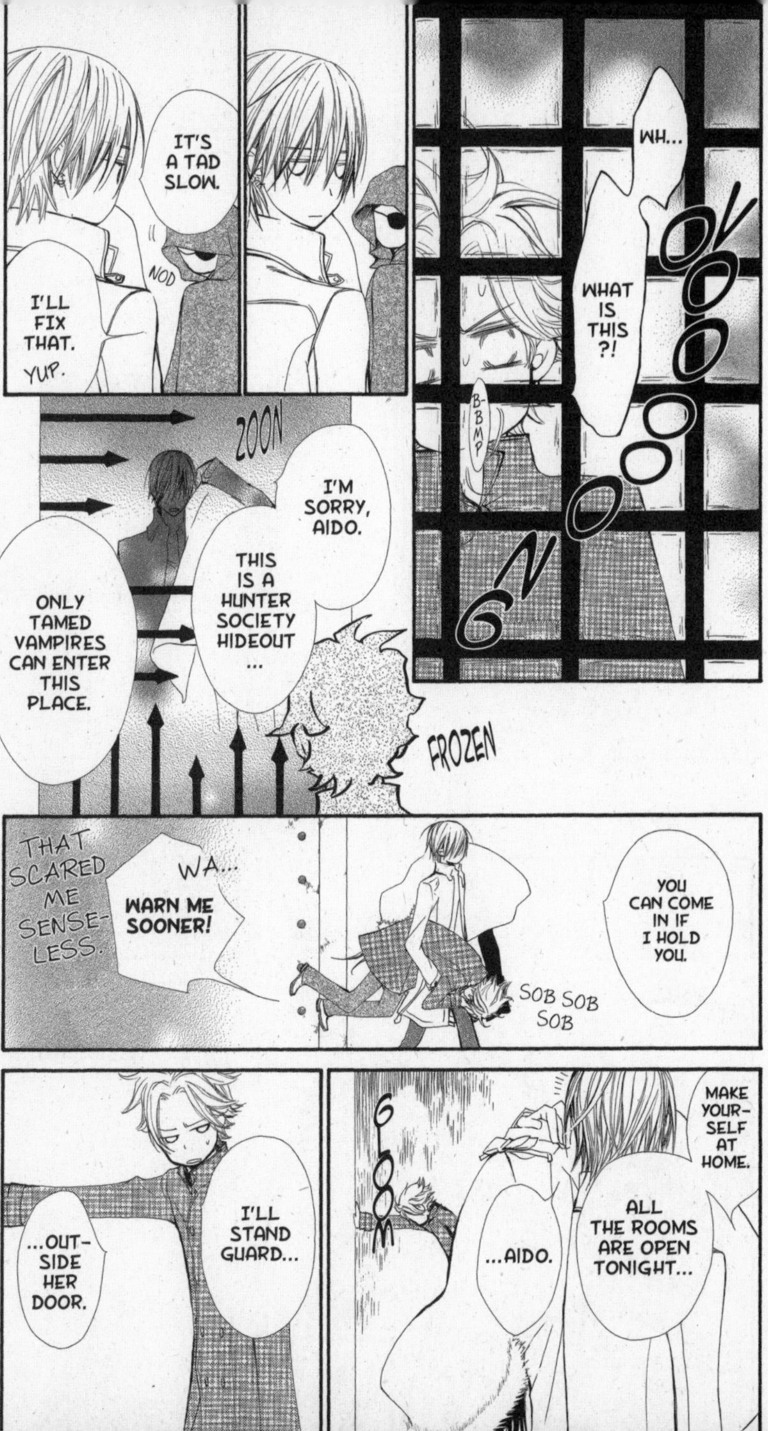
WH...
WHAT IS THIS?!
B-BBMP
IT'S A TAD SLOW.
NOD
I'LL FIX THAT.
YUP.
ZOON
I'M SORRY, AIDO.
THIS IS A HUNTER SOCIETY HIDEOUT...
ONLY TAMED VAMPIRES CAN ENTER THIS PLACE.
FROZEN
YOU CAN COME IN IF I HOLD YOU.
SOB SOB SOB
WA...
WARN ME SOONER!
THAT SCARED ME SENSE-LESS.
MAKE YOUR-SELF AT HOME.
ALL THE ROOMS ARE OPEN TONIGHT...
...AIDO.
I'LL STAND GUARD...
...OUT-SIDE HER DOOR.

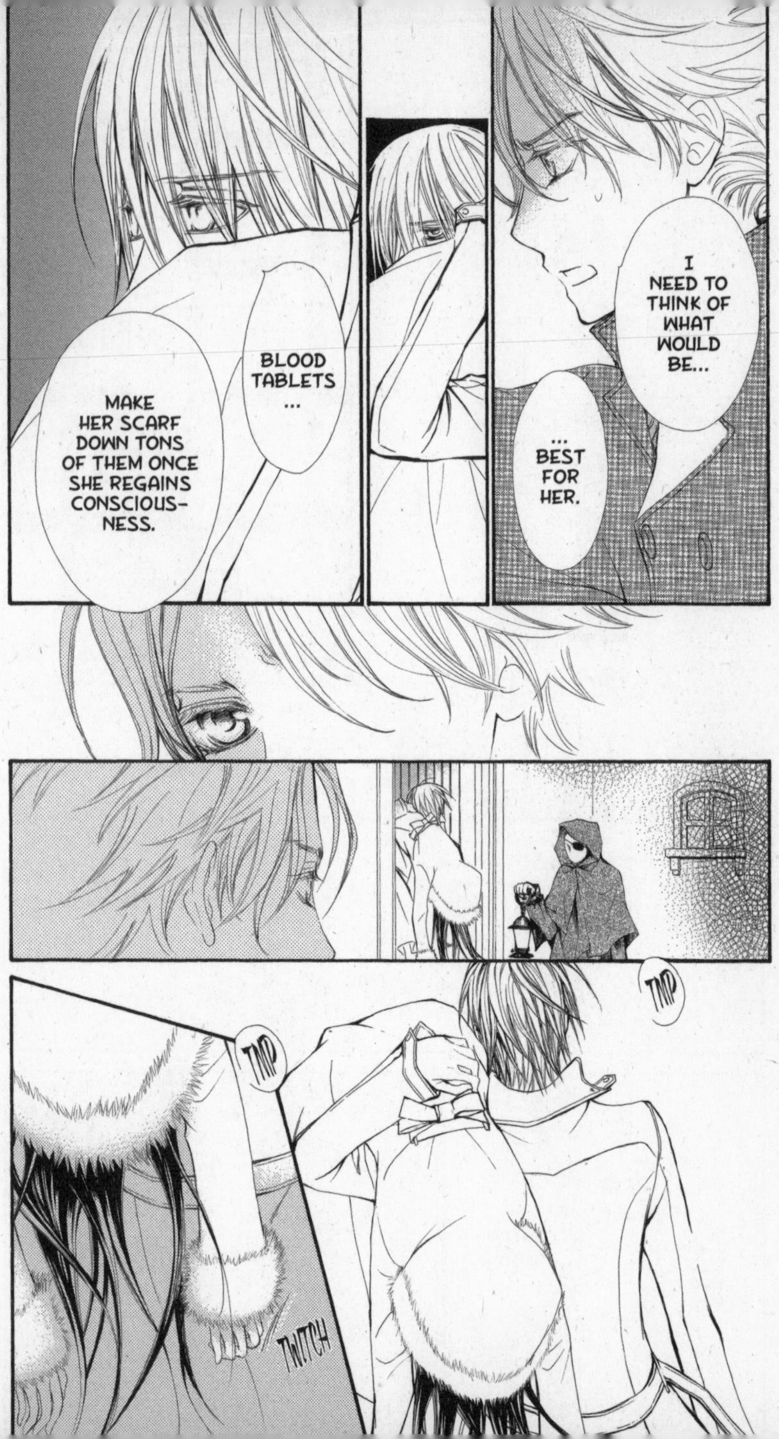
I NEED TO THINK OF WHAT WOULD BE...
... BEST FOR HER.
BLOOD TABLETS ...
MAKE HER SCARF DOWN TONS OF THEM ONCE SHE REGAINS CONSCIOUS-NESS.
TMP
TMP
TWITCH

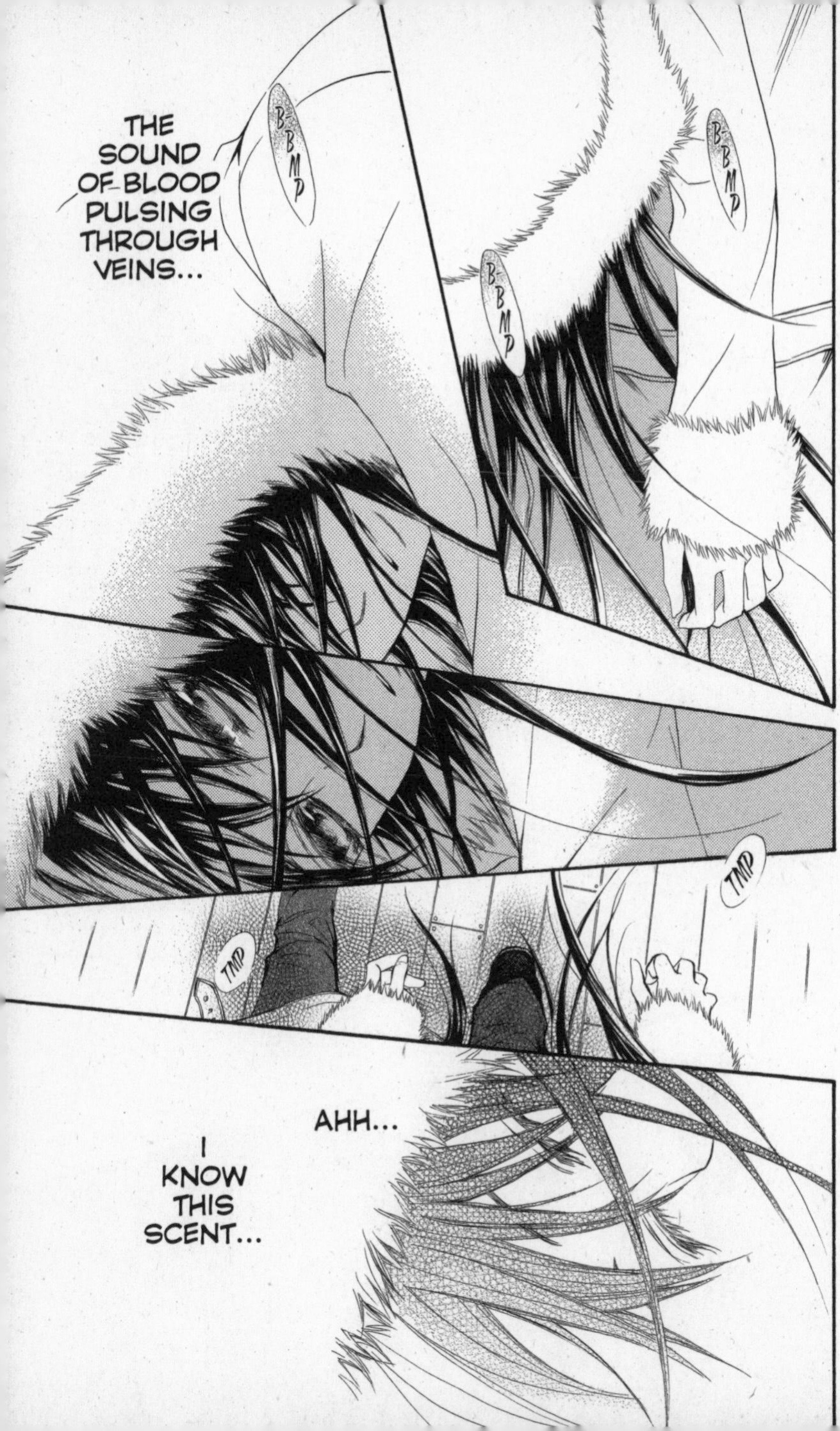
B-BMP
B-BMP
THE SOUND OF BLOOD PULSING THROUGH VEINS...
B-BMP
TMP
TMP
AHH...
I KNOW THIS SCENT...

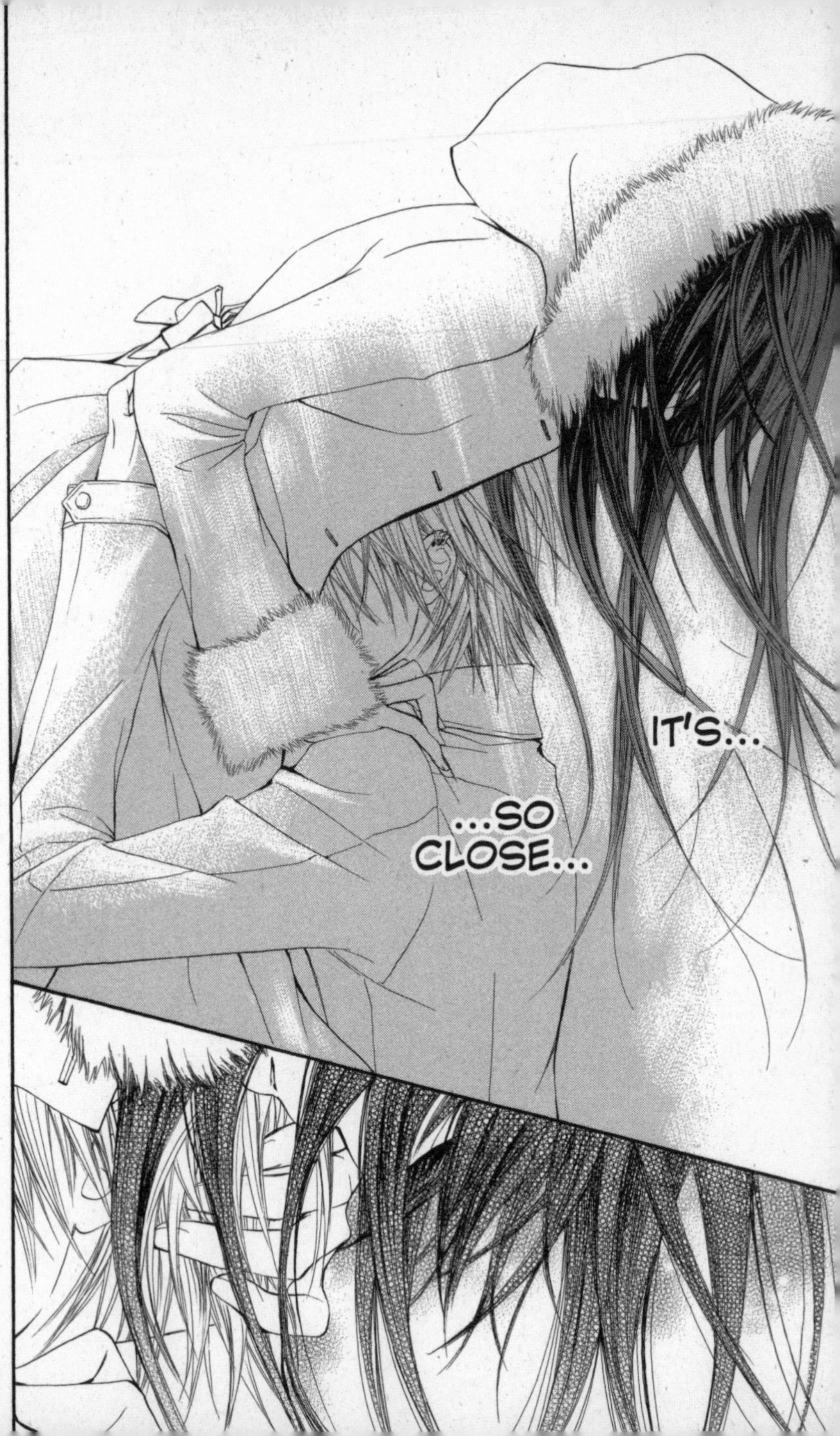
IT'S...
...SO CLOSE...

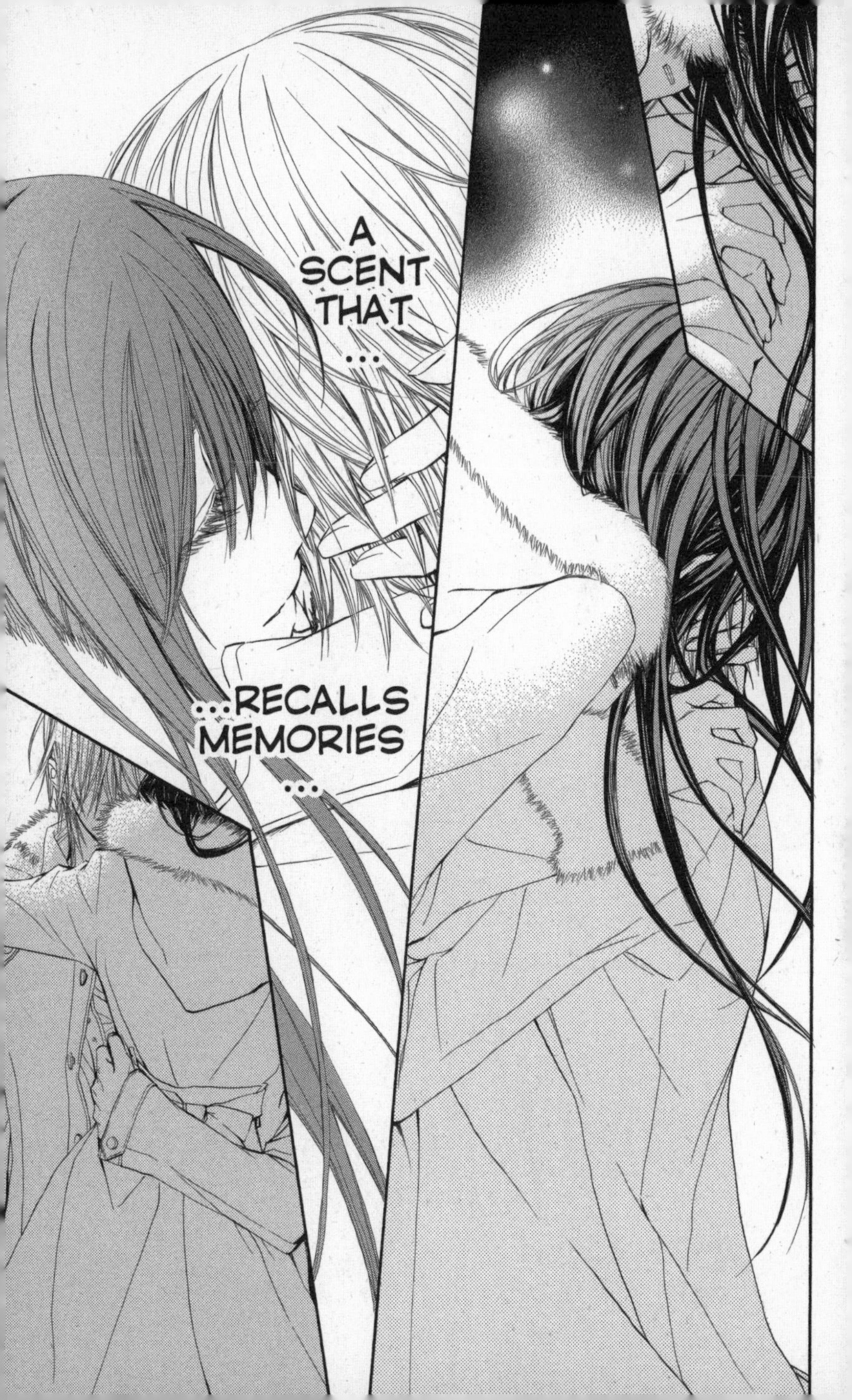
A SCENT THAT
...
...RECALLS MEMORIES
...

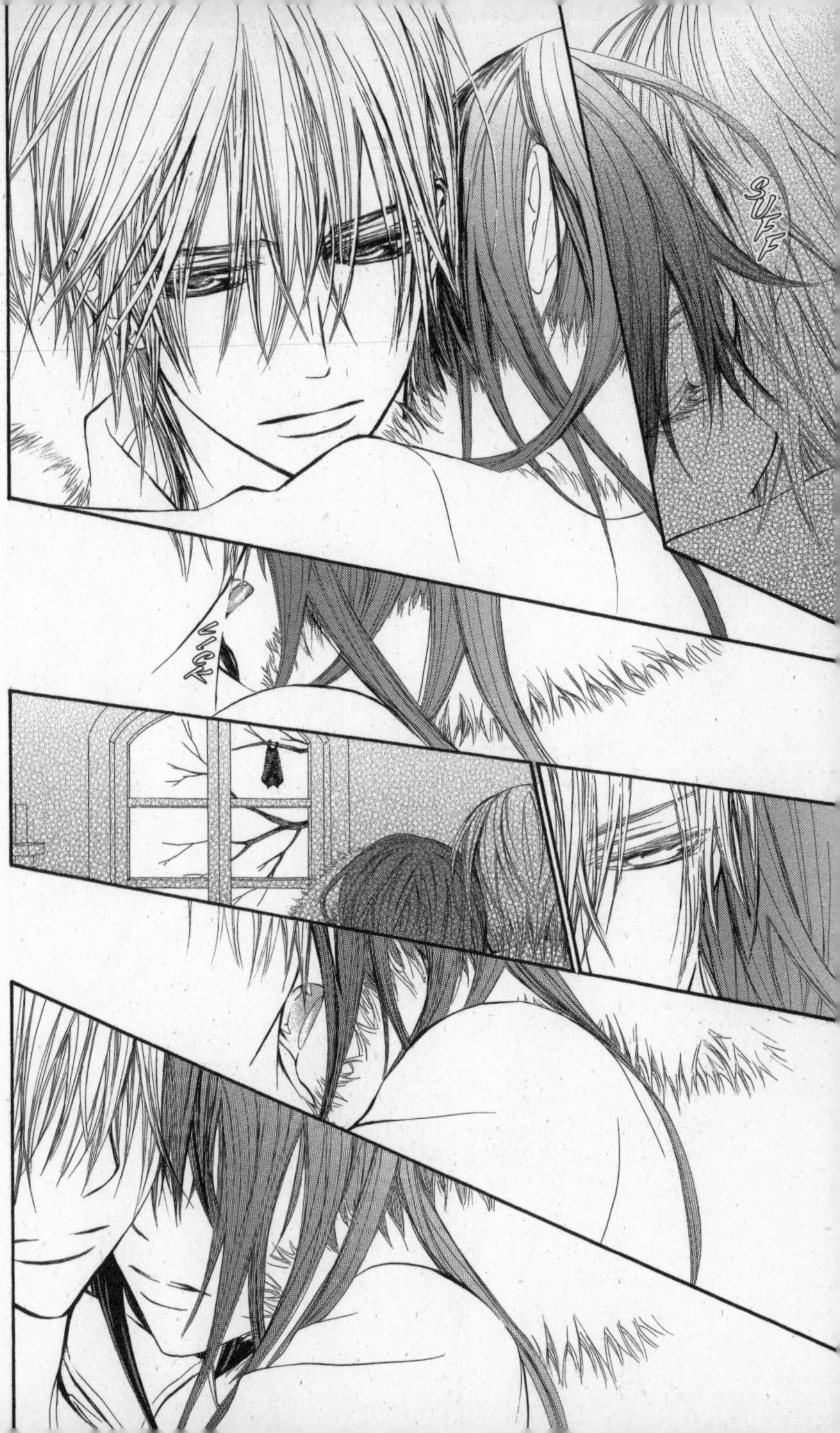
SUFF
LICK

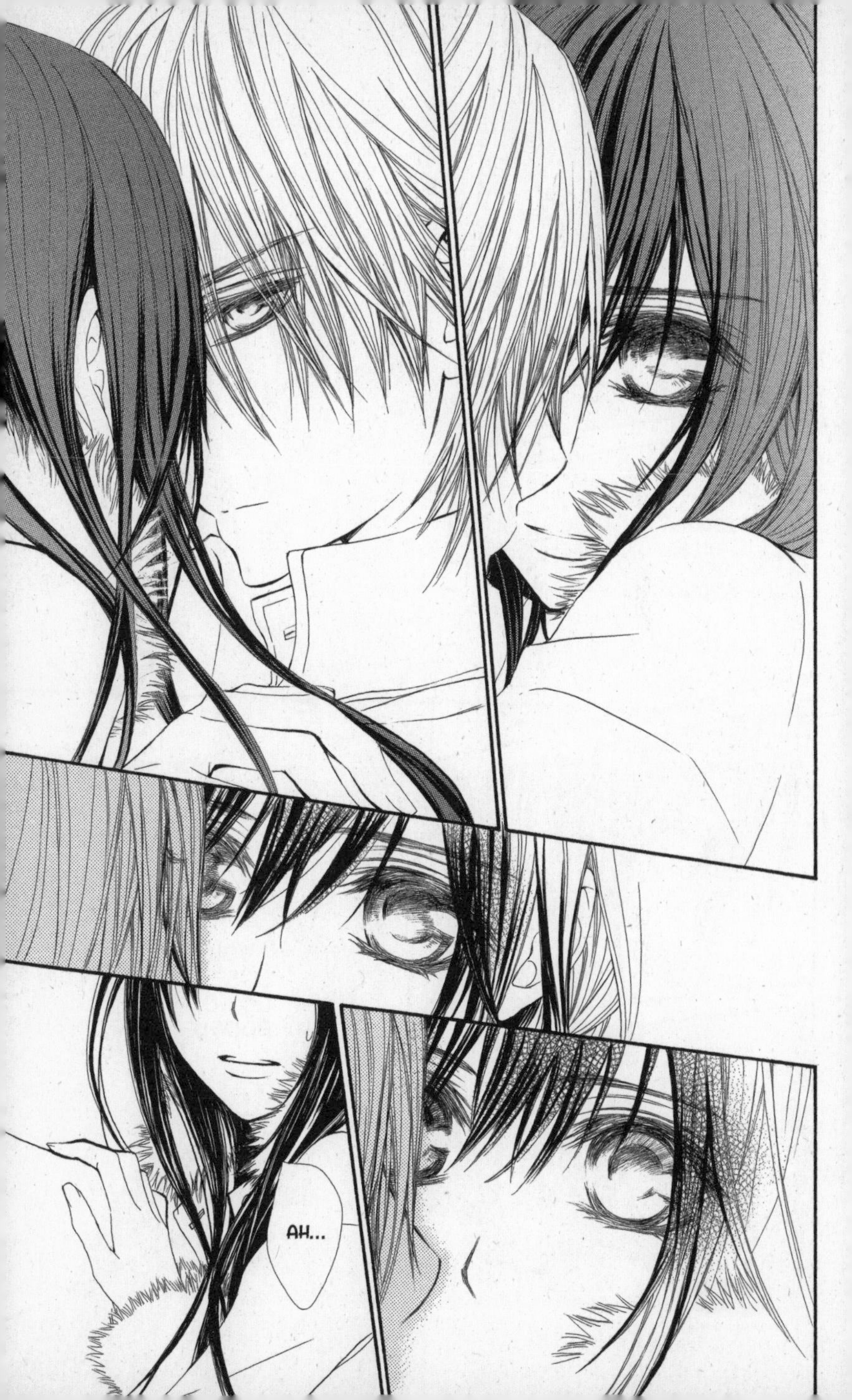
AH...

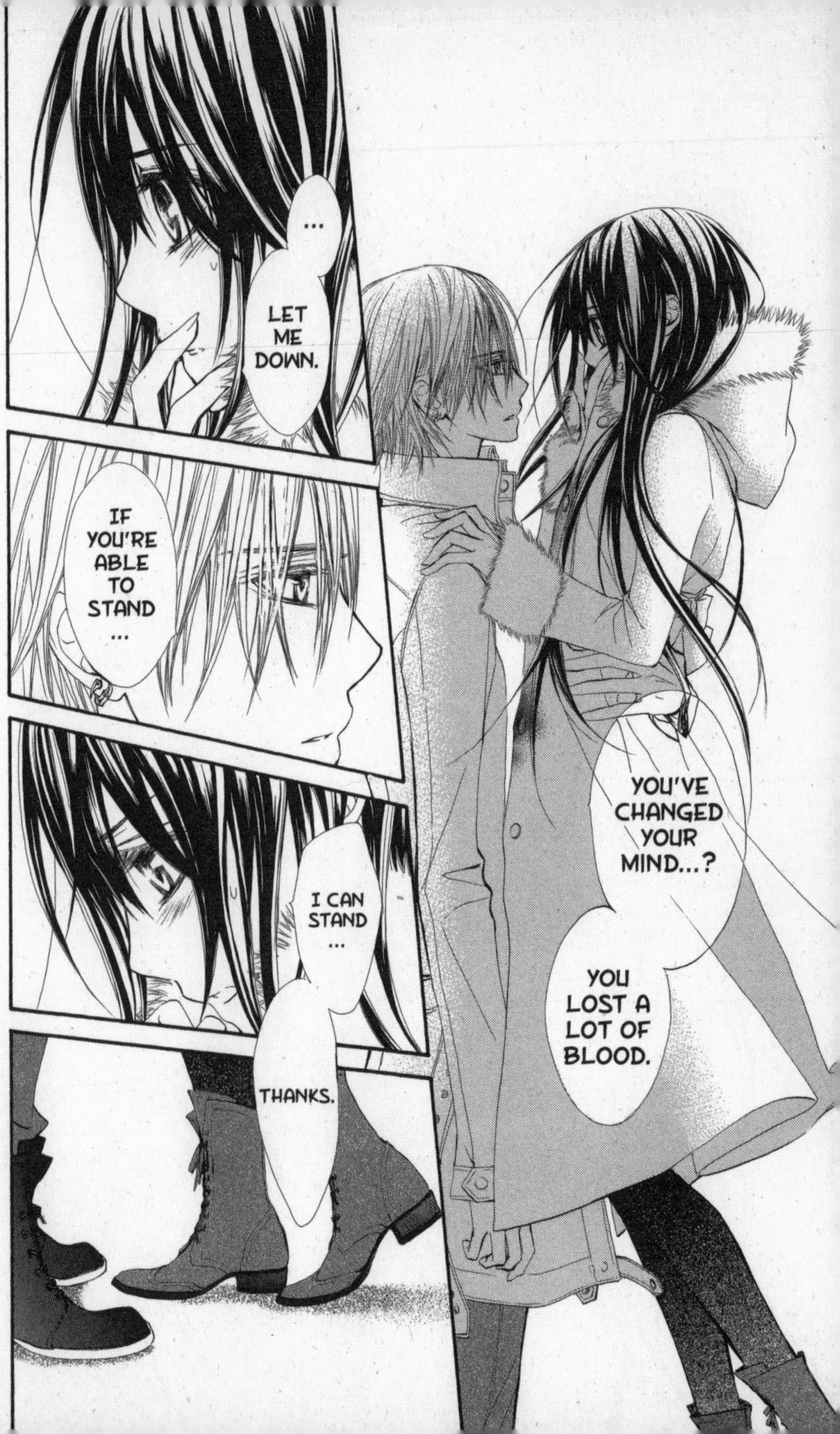
YOU'VE CHANGED YOUR MIND...?
YOU LOST A LOT OF BLOOD.
...
LET ME DOWN.
IF YOU'RE ABLE TO STAND...
I CAN STAND...
THANKS.

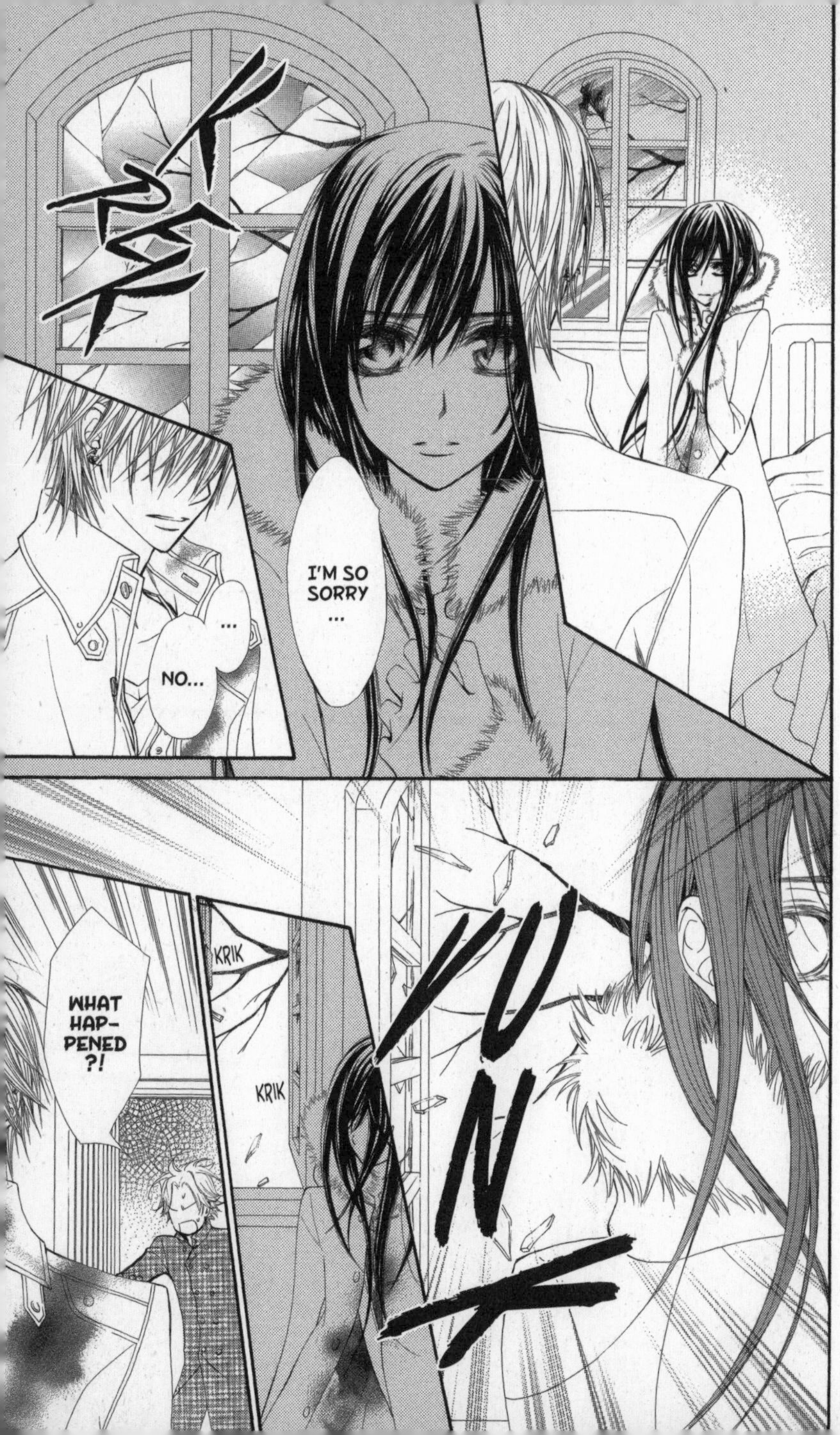
I'M SO SORRY ...
...
NO...
KRIK
KRIK
WHAT HAP-PENED ?!

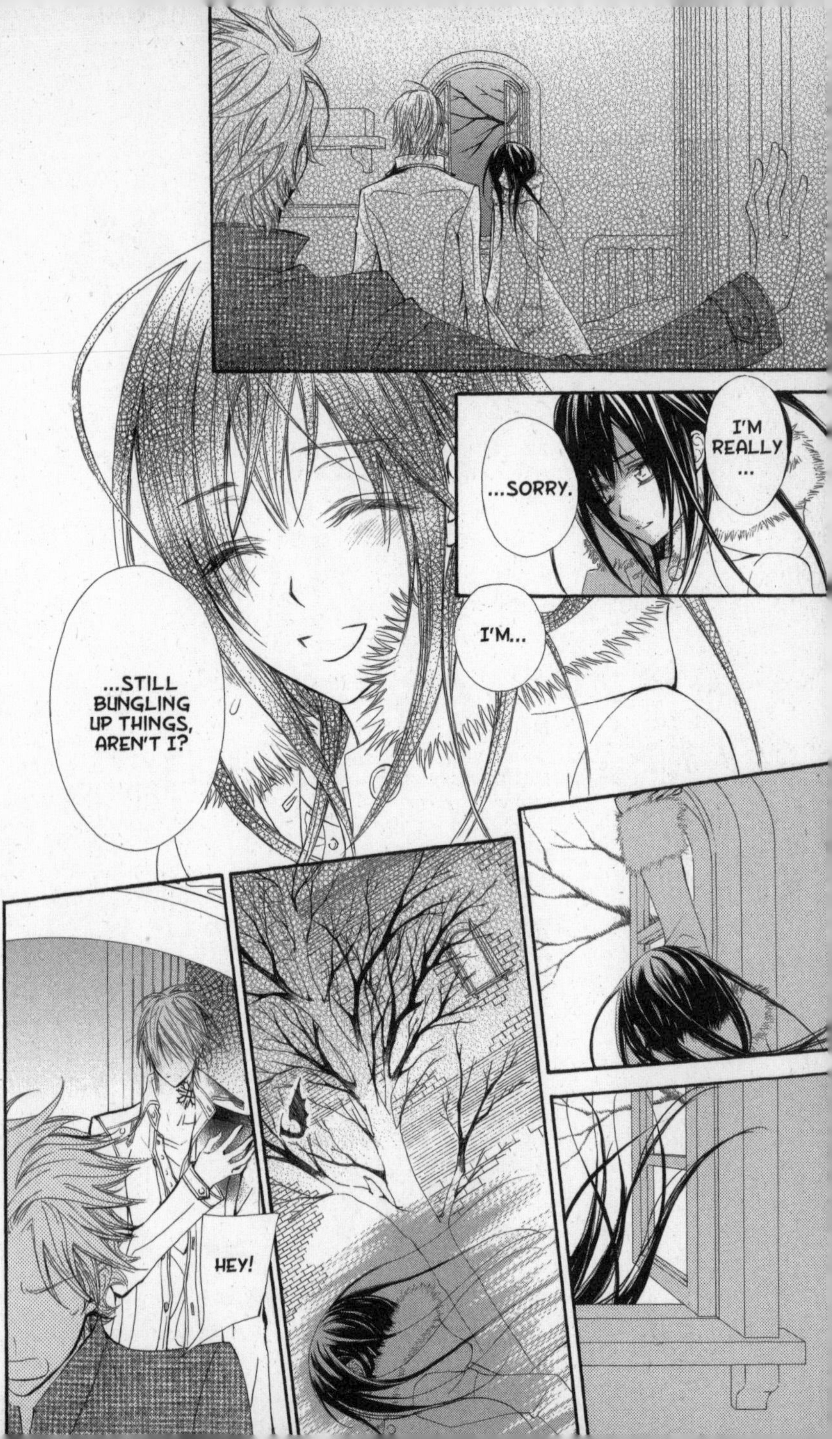
I'M REALLY...
...SORRY.
I'M...
...STILL BUNGLING UP THINGS, AREN'T I?
HEY!

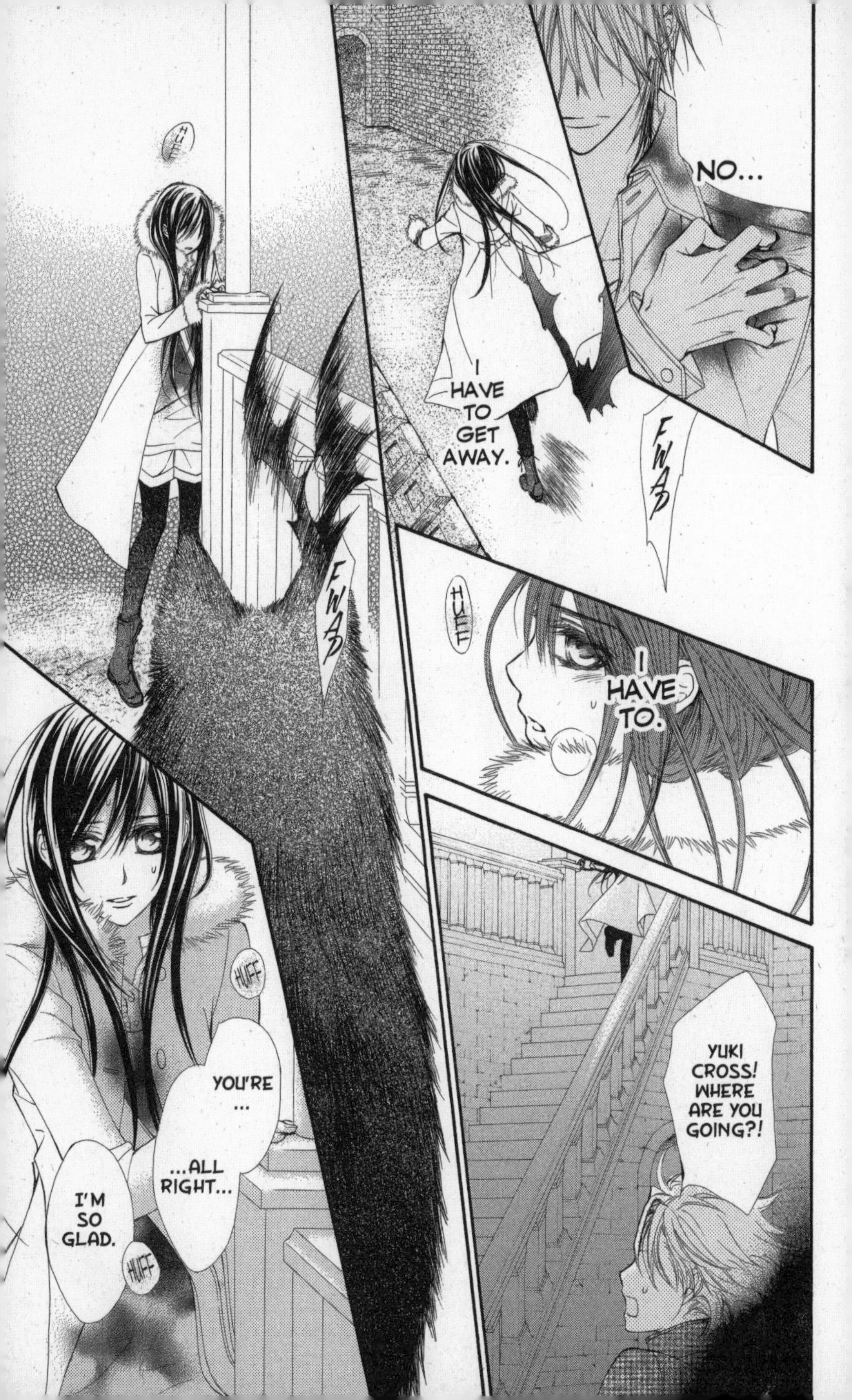
NO...
FWAP
I HAVE TO GET AWAY.
HUFF
HUFF
I HAVE TO.
FWAP
YUKI CROSS! WHERE ARE YOU GOING?!
HUFF
YOU'RE ...
...ALL RIGHT...
I'M SO GLAD.
HUFF

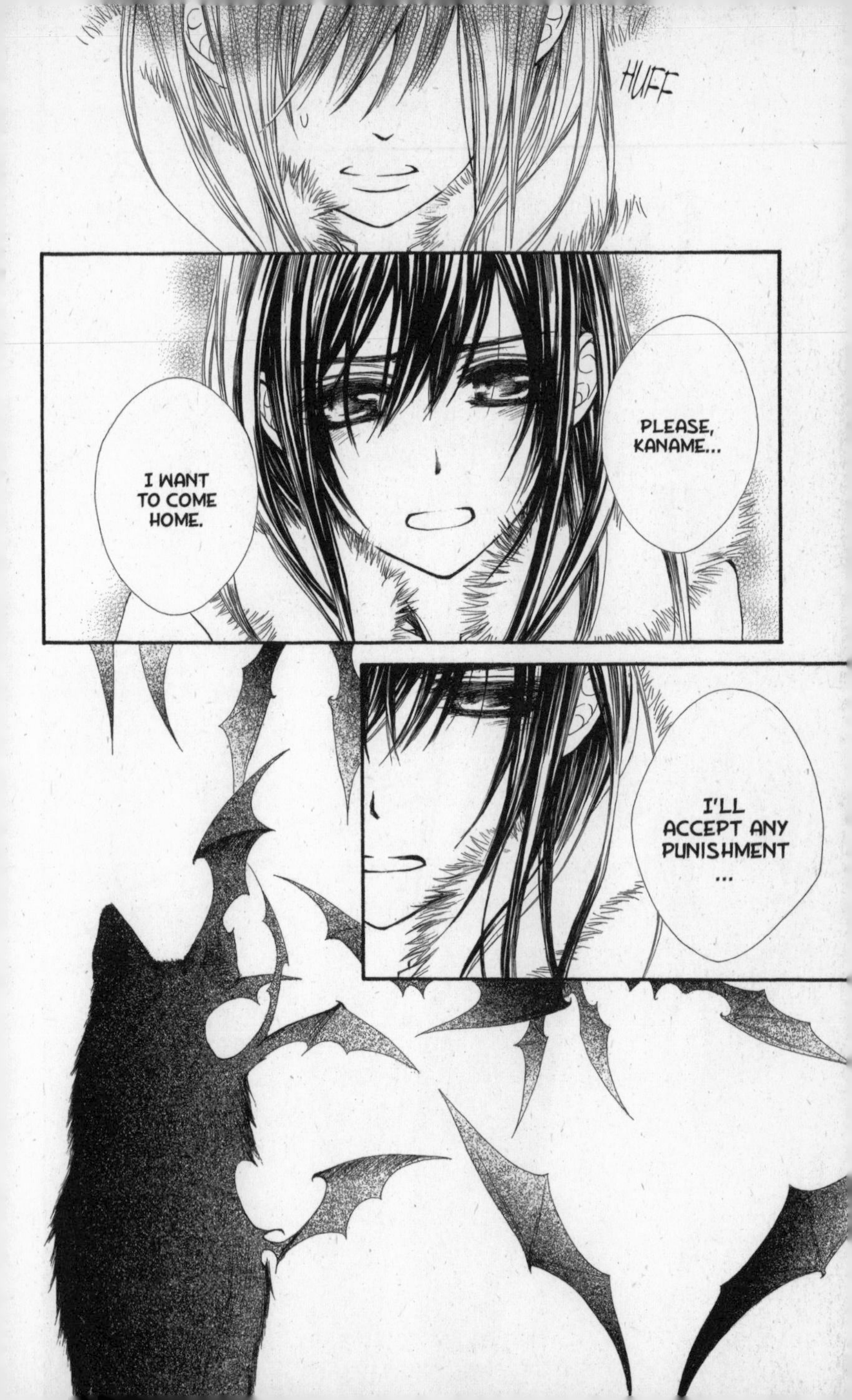
HUFF
PLEASE, KANAME...
I WANT TO COME HOME.
I'LL ACCEPT ANY PUNISHMENT ...

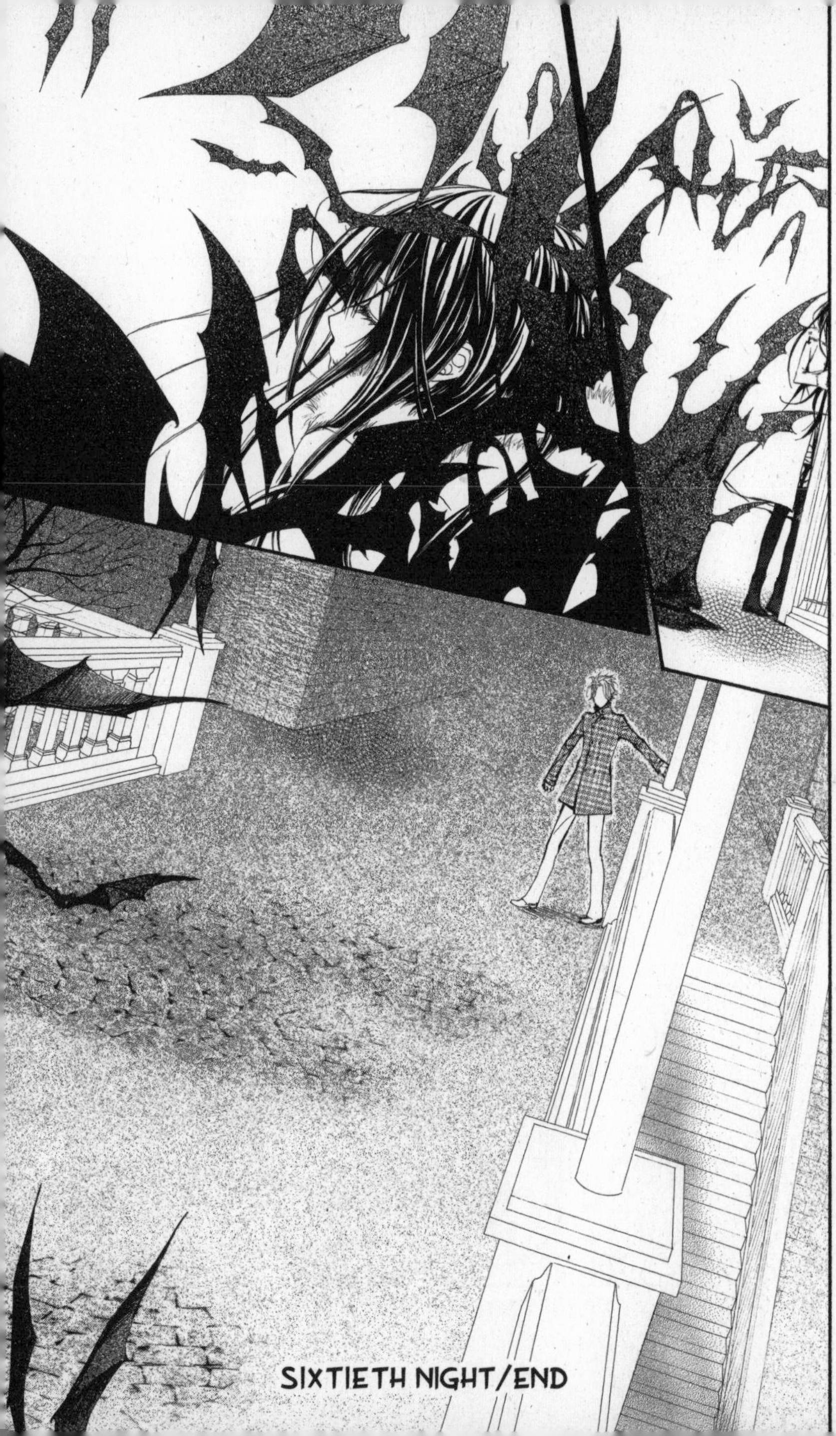
SIXTIETH NIGHT/END

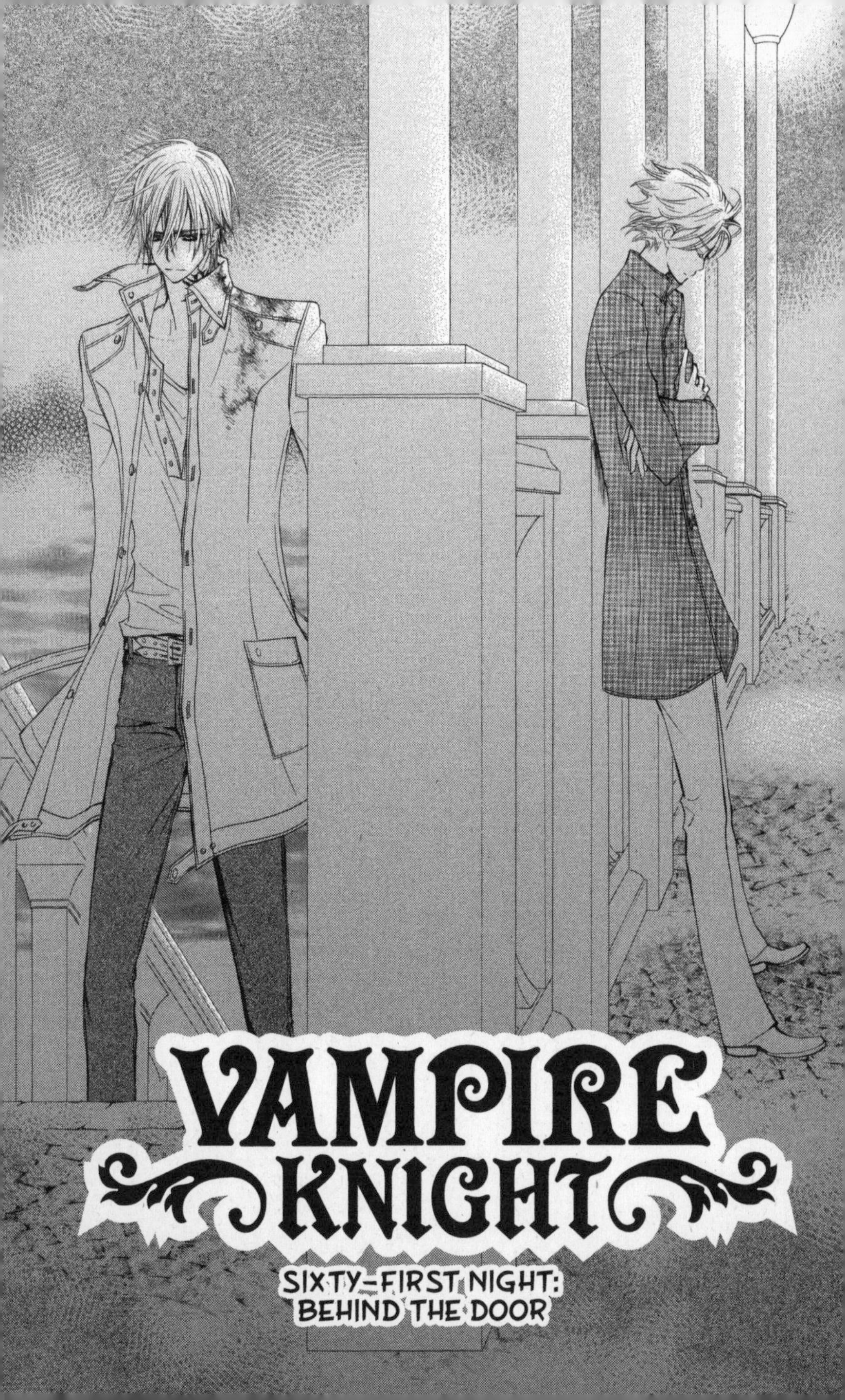
VAMPIRE KNIGHT
SIXTY-FIRST NIGHT:
BEHIND THE DOOR

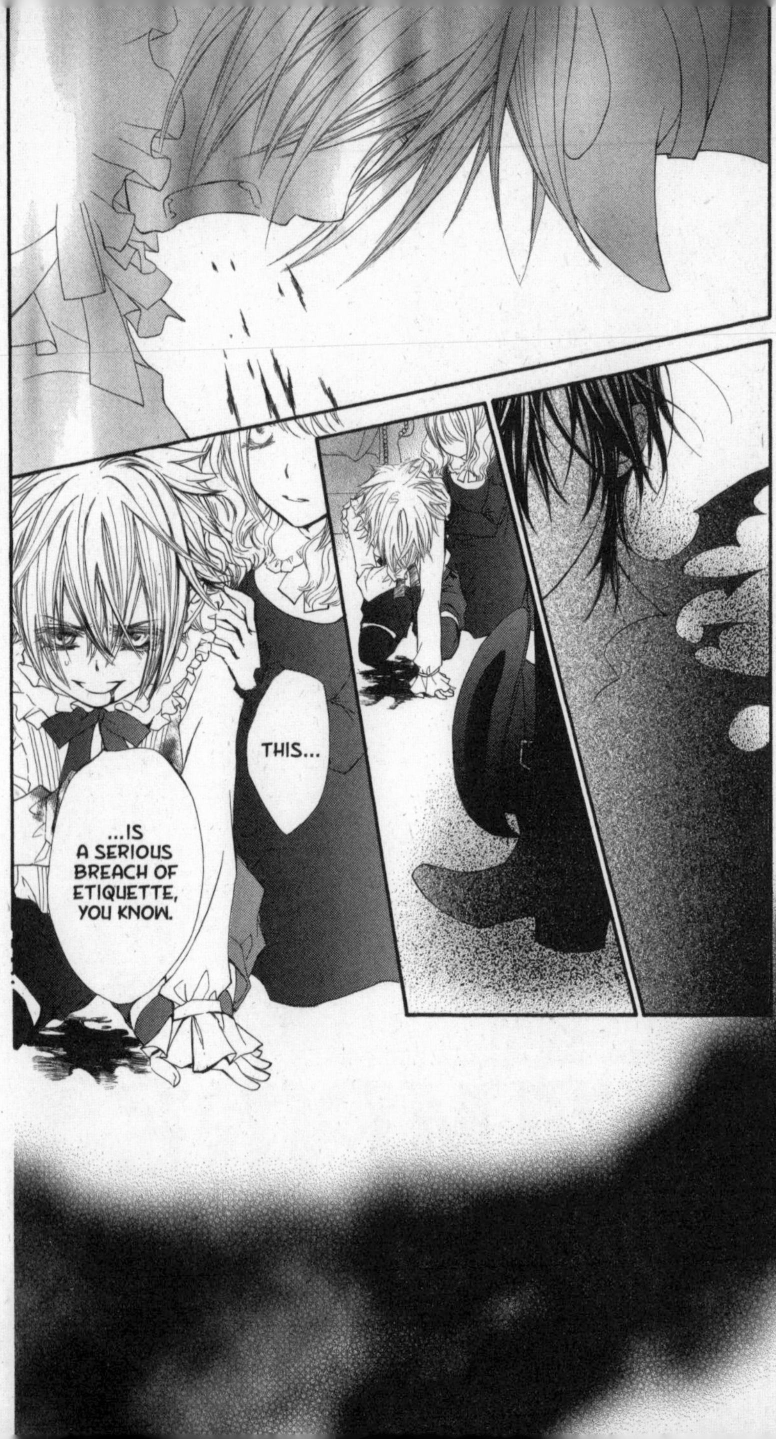
THIS...
...IS A SERIOUS BREACH OF ETIQUETTE, YOU KNOW.

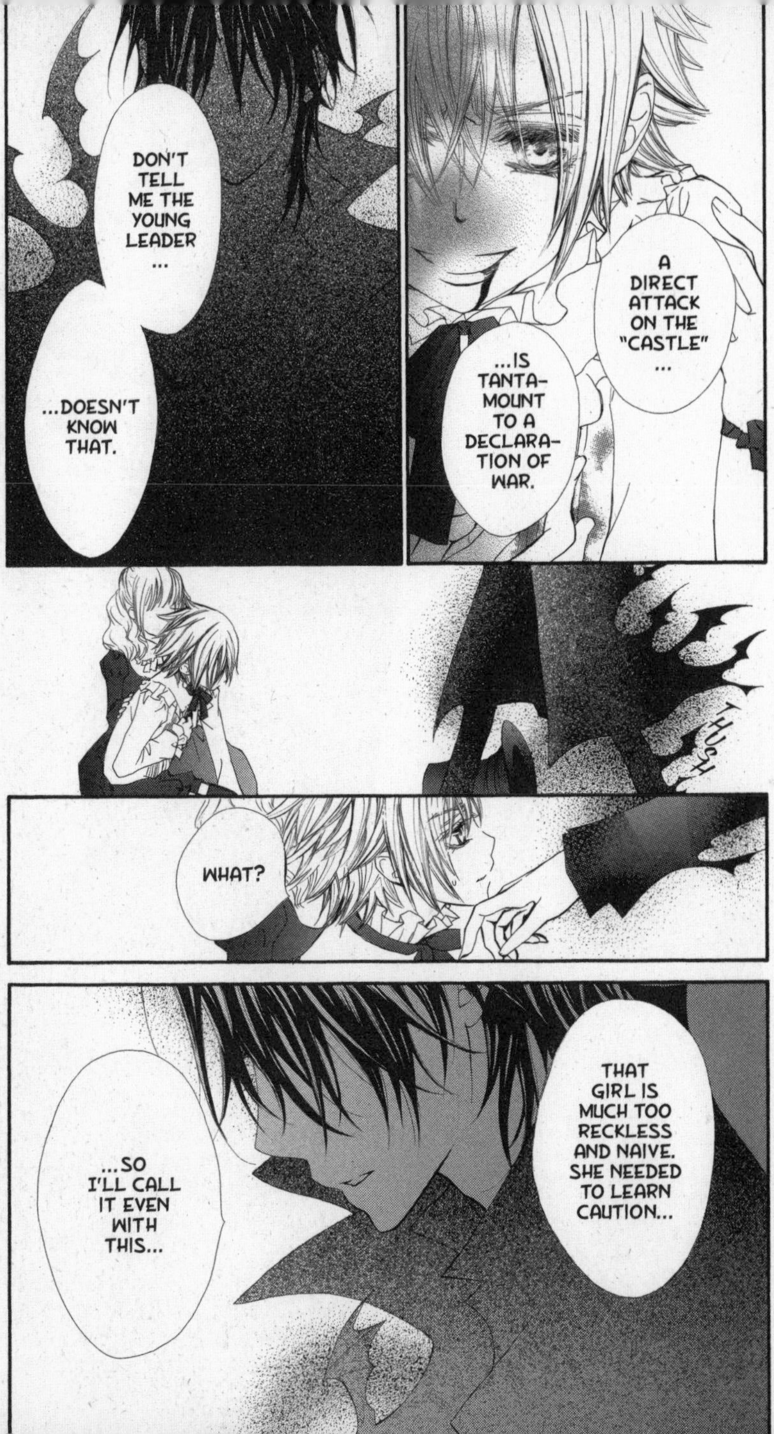
A DIRECT ATTACK ON THE "CASTLE"...
...IS TANTA-MOUNT TO A DECLARA-TION OF WAR.
DON'T TELL ME THE YOUNG LEADER...
...DOESN'T KNOW THAT.
THUSH
WHAT?
THAT GIRL IS MUCH TOO RECKLESS AND NAIVE. SHE NEEDED TO LEARN CAUTION...
...SO I'LL CALL IT EVEN WITH THIS...

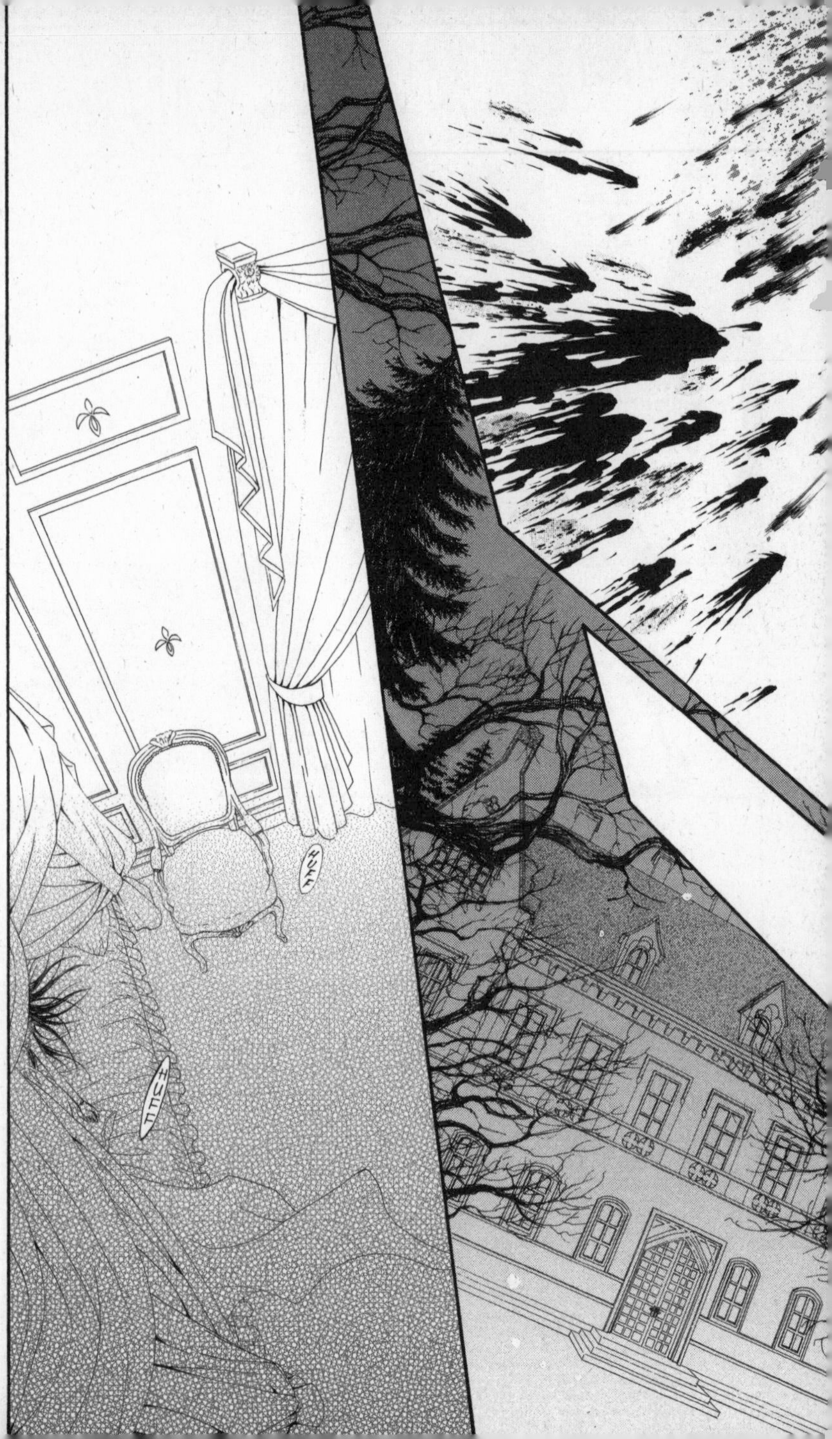
HUFF
HUFF

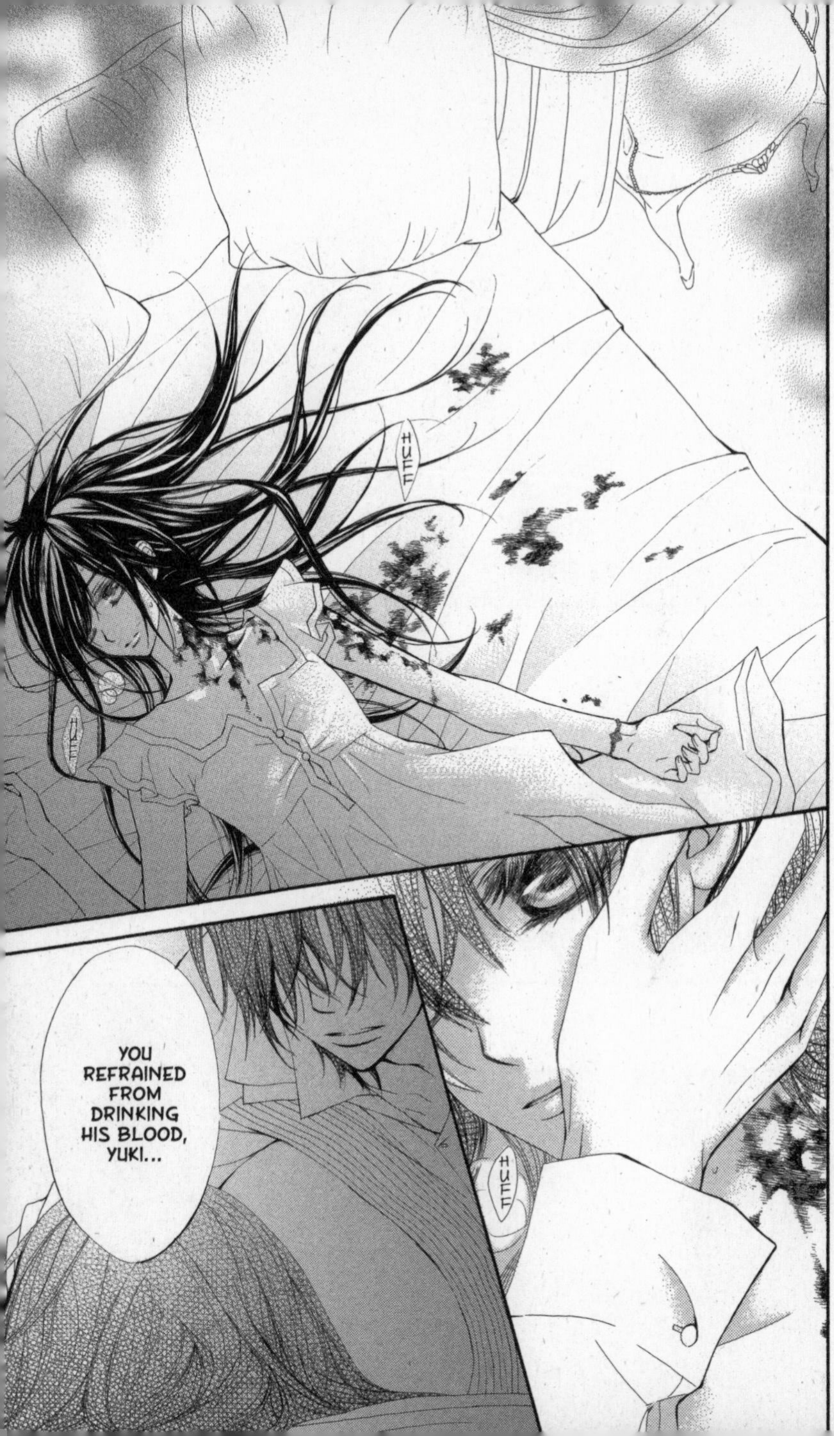
HUFF
HUFF
HUFF
YOU REFRAINED FROM DRINKING HIS BLOOD, YUKI...

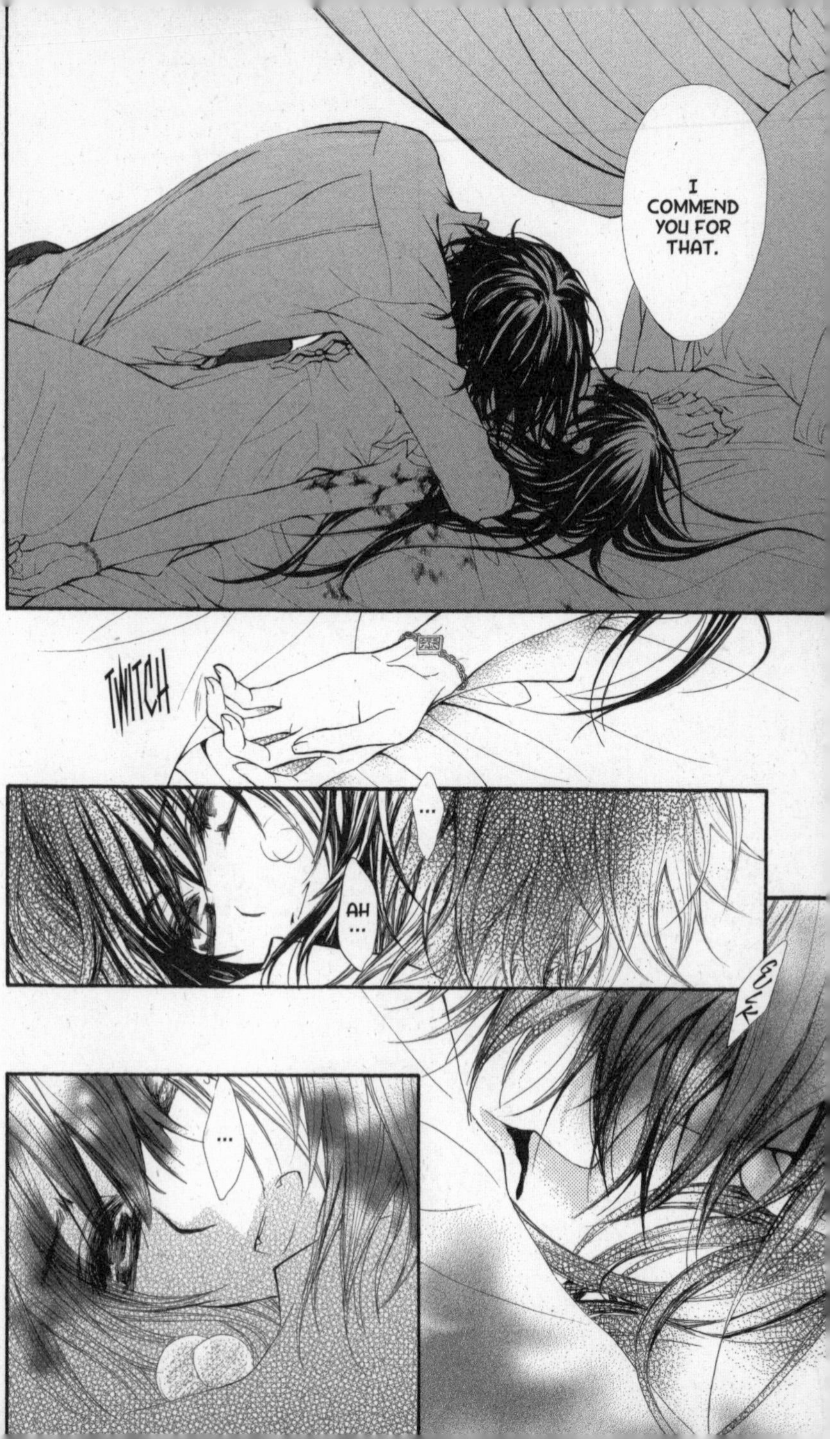
I COMMEND YOU FOR THAT.
TWITCH
...
AH ...
GULK
...

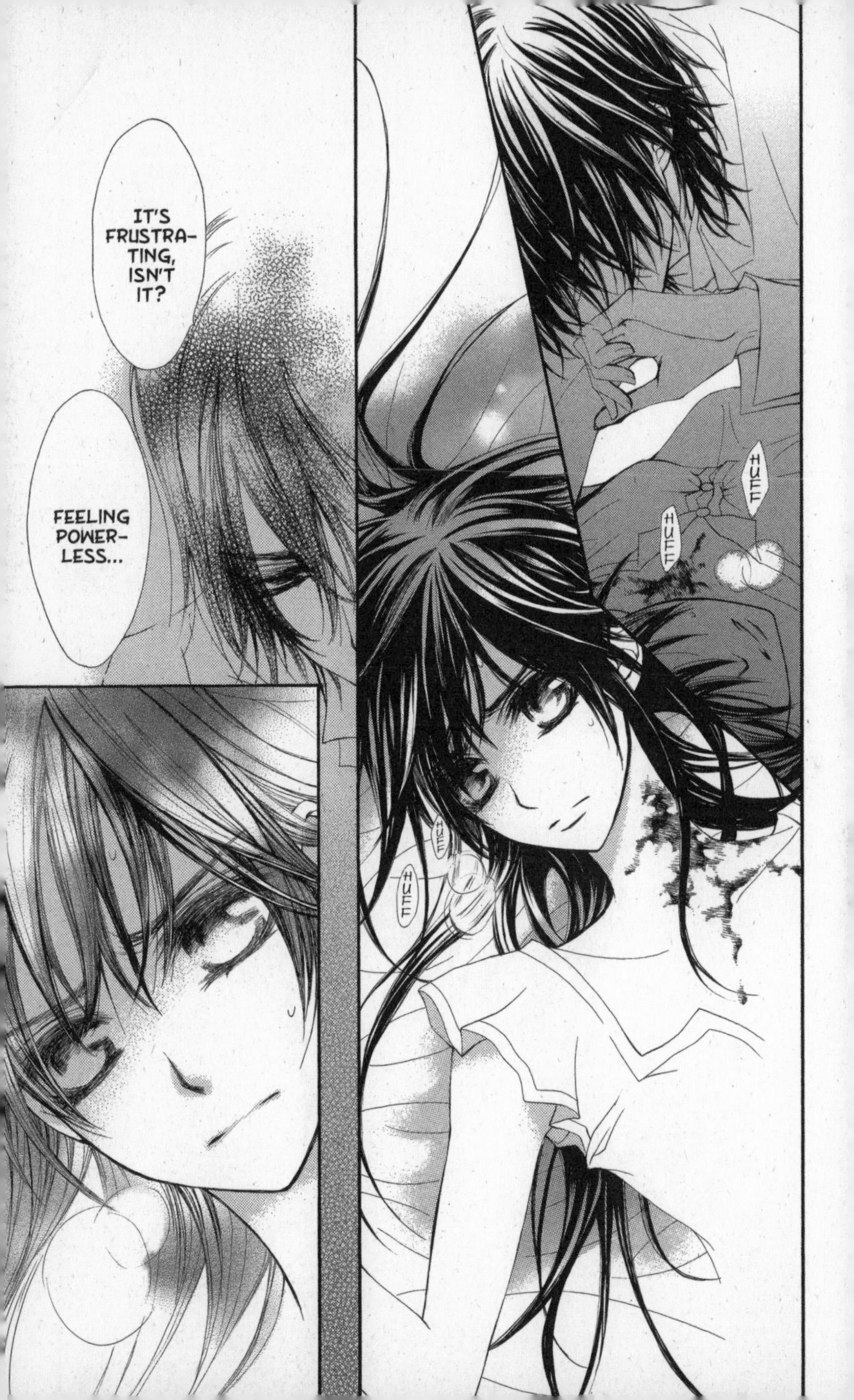
HUFF
HUFF
HUFF
HUFF
IT'S FRUSTRATING, ISN'T IT?
FEELING POWERLESS...

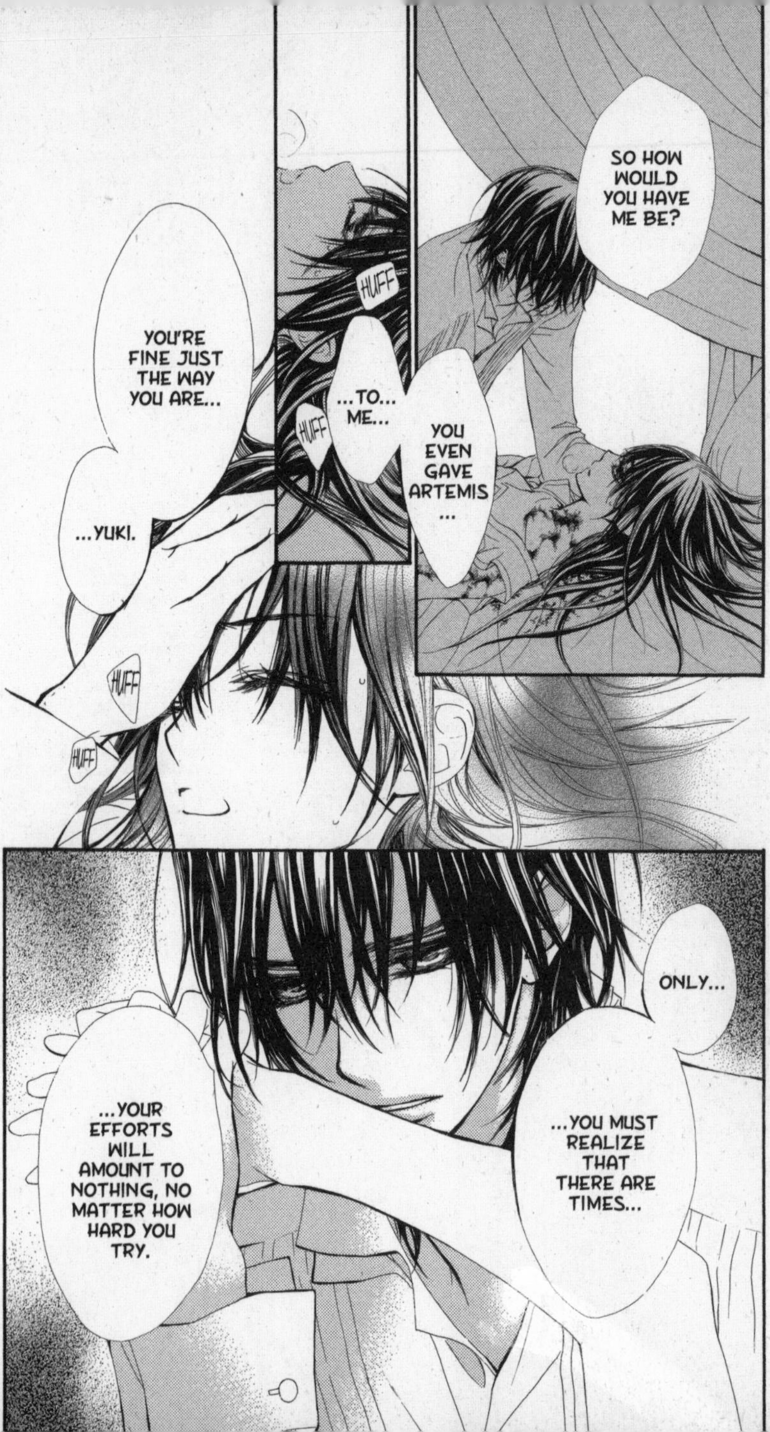
SO HOW WOULD YOU HAVE ME BE?
HUFF
YOU EVEN GAVE ARTEMIS...
...TO... ME...
HUFF
YOU'RE FINE JUST THE WAY YOU ARE...
...YUKI.
HUFF
HUFF
ONLY...
...YOU MUST REALIZE THAT THERE ARE TIMES...
...YOUR EFFORTS WILL AMOUNT TO NOTHING, NO MATTER HOW HARD YOU TRY.

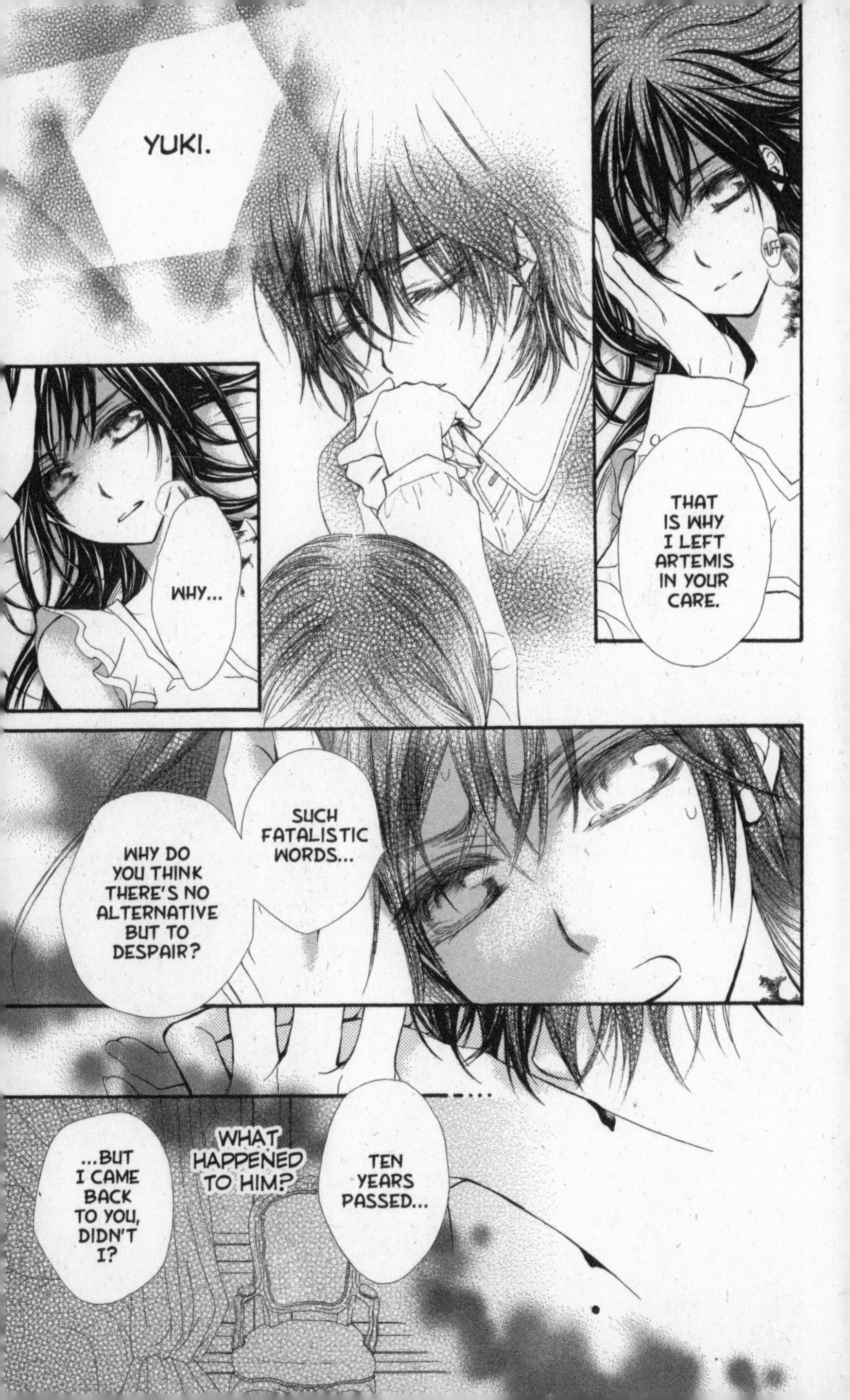
HUFF
THAT IS WHY I LEFT ARTEMIS IN YOUR CARE.
YUKI.
WHY...
SUCH FATALISTIC WORDS...
WHY DO YOU THINK THERE'S NO ALTERNATIVE BUT TO DESPAIR?
TEN YEARS PASSED...
WHAT HAPPENED TO HIM?
...BUT I CAME BACK TO YOU, DIDN'T I?

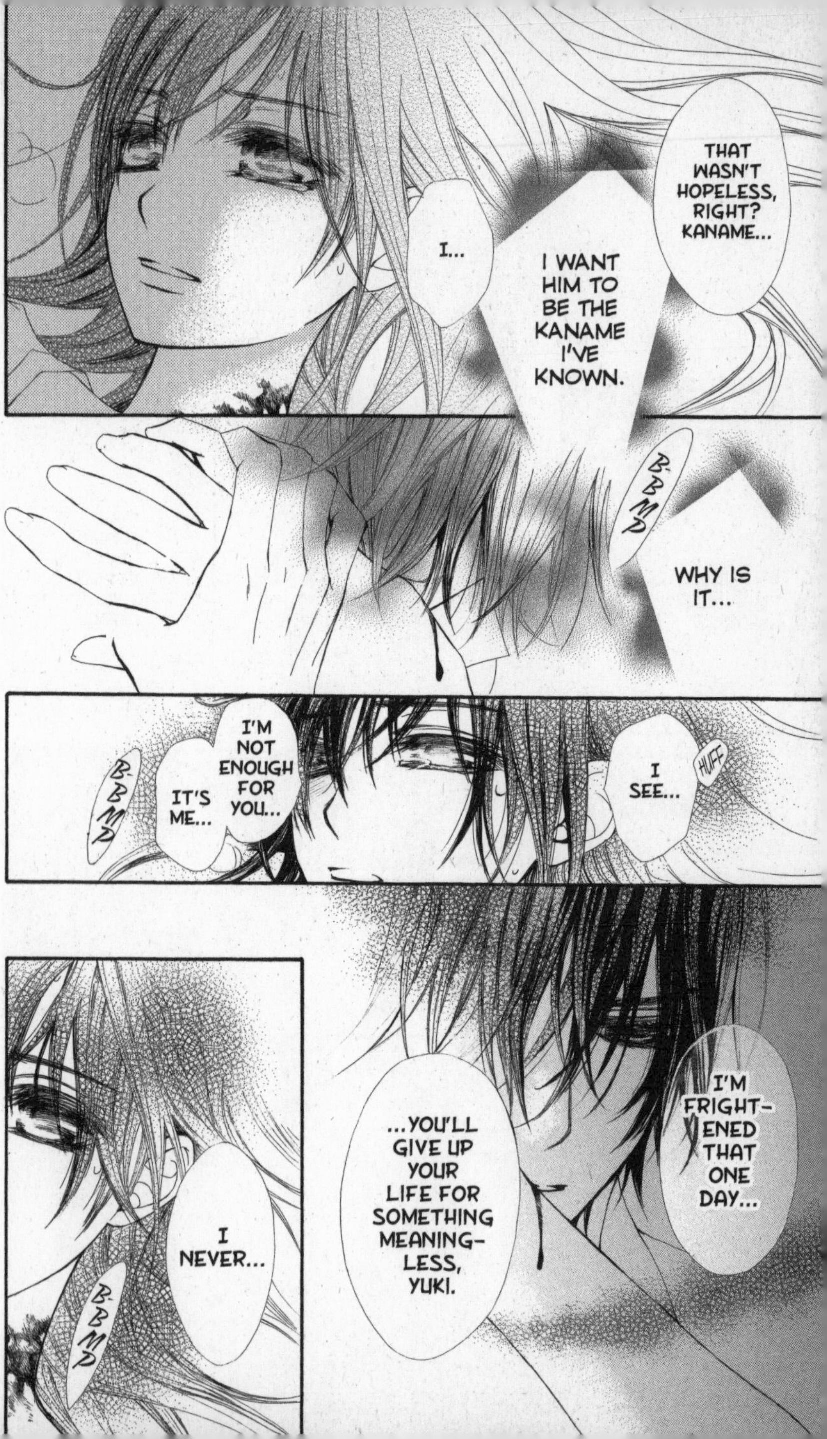
THAT WASN'T HOPELESS, RIGHT? KANAME...
I WANT HIM TO BE THE KANAME I'VE KNOWN.
I...
WHY IS IT...
B-BMP
HUFF
I SEE...
I'M NOT ENOUGH FOR YOU...
IT'S ME...
B-BMP
I'M FRIGHT-ENED THAT ONE DAY...
...YOU'LL GIVE UP YOUR LIFE FOR SOMETHING MEANING-LESS, YUKI.
I NEVER...
B-BMP

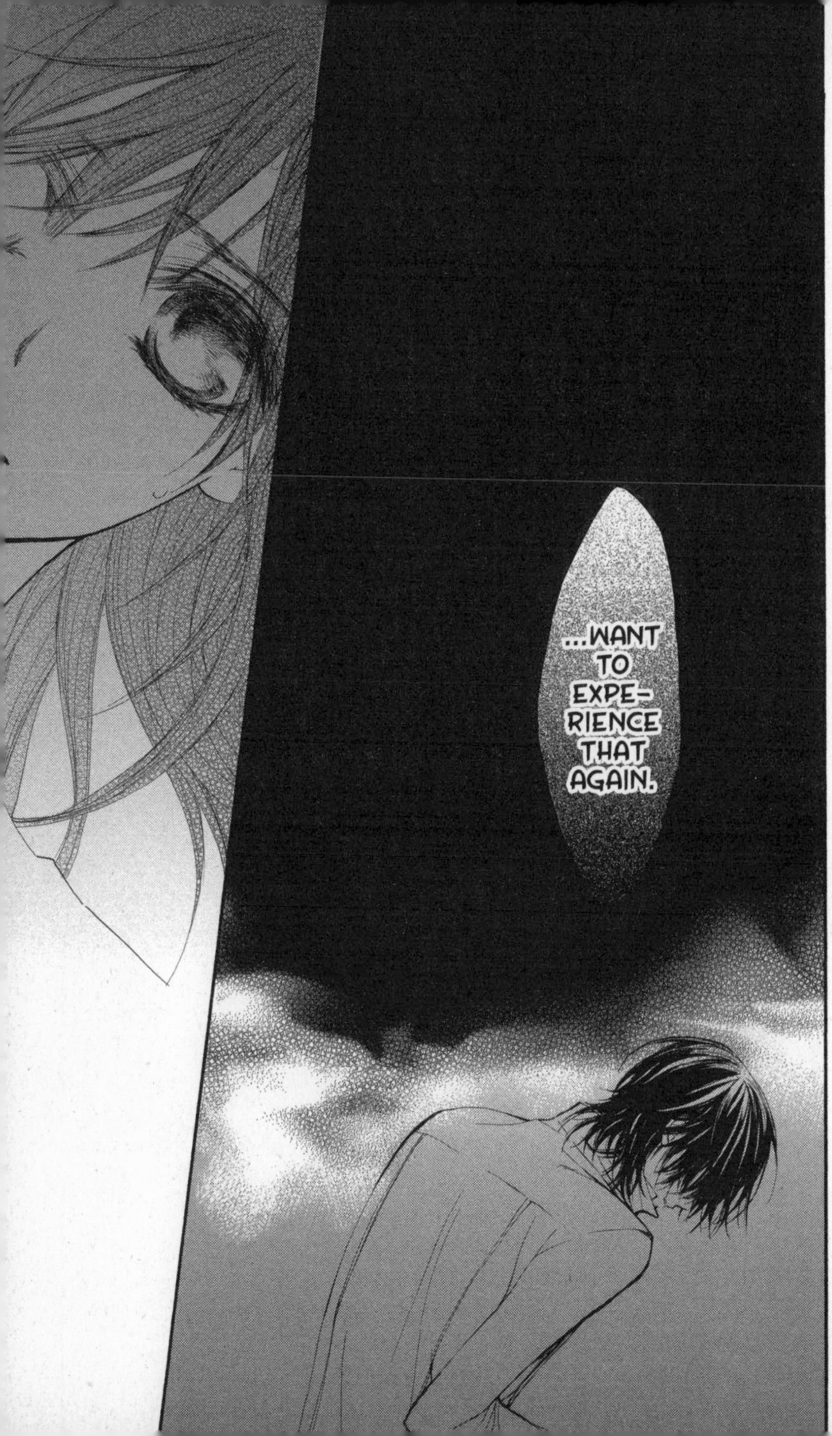
...WANT TO EXPE-RIENCE THAT AGAIN.

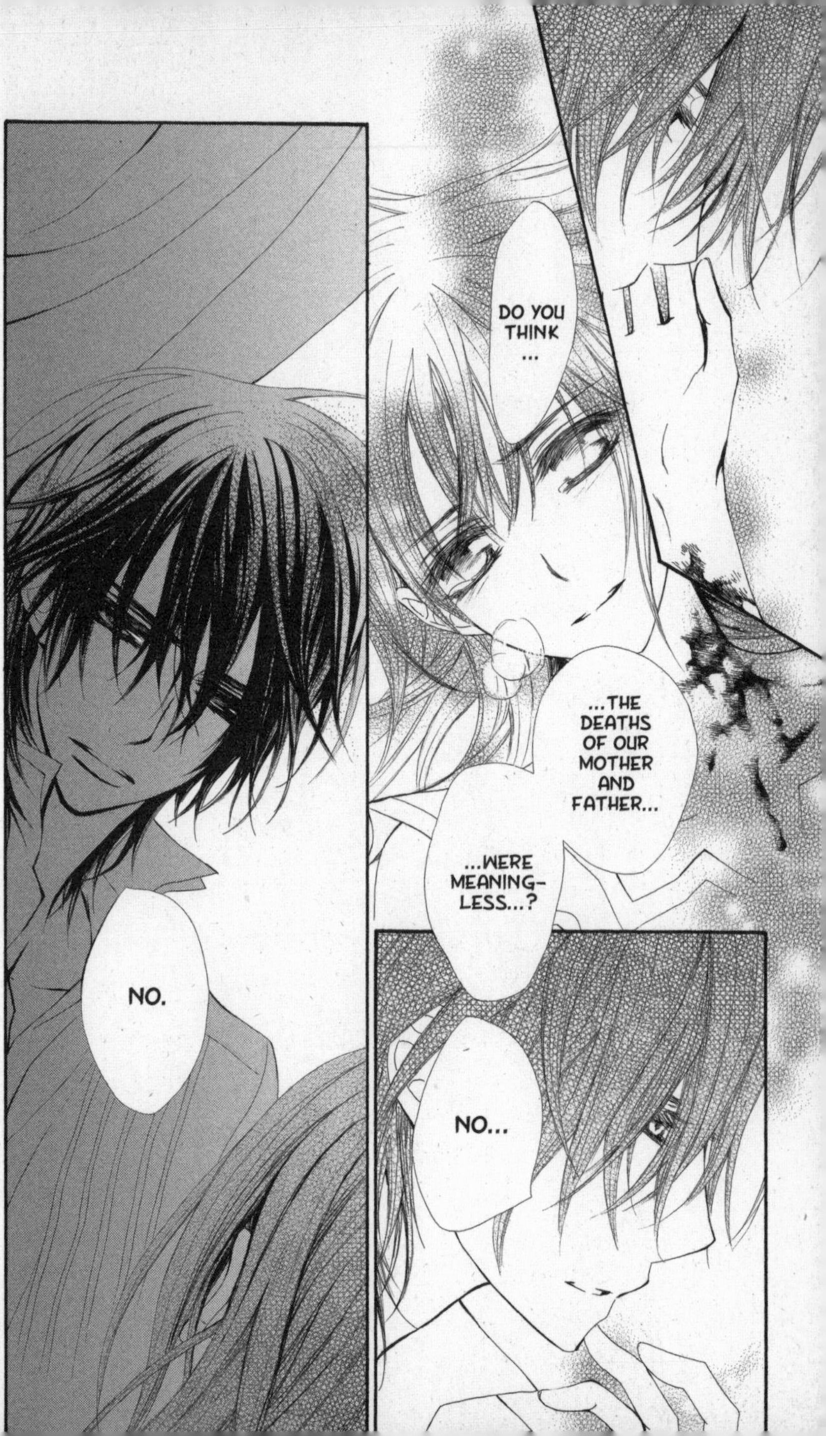
DO YOU THINK ...
...THE DEATHS OF OUR MOTHER AND FATHER...
...WERE MEANING-LESS...?
NO...
NO.

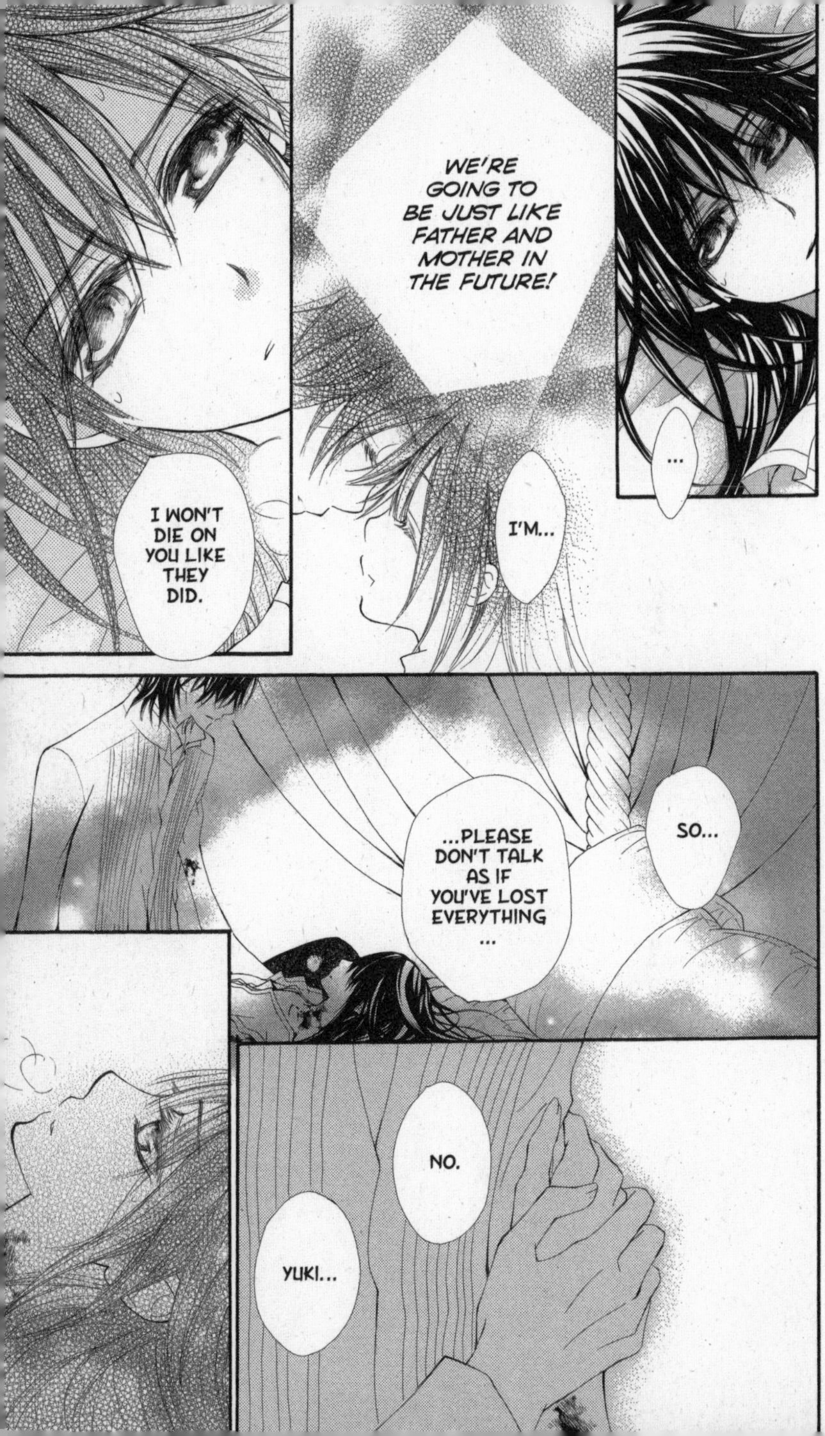
...
WE'RE GOING TO BE JUST LIKE FATHER AND MOTHER IN THE FUTURE!
I'M...
I WON'T DIE ON YOU LIKE THEY DID.
SO...
...PLEASE DON'T TALK AS IF YOU'VE LOST EVERYTHING ...
NO.
YUKI...

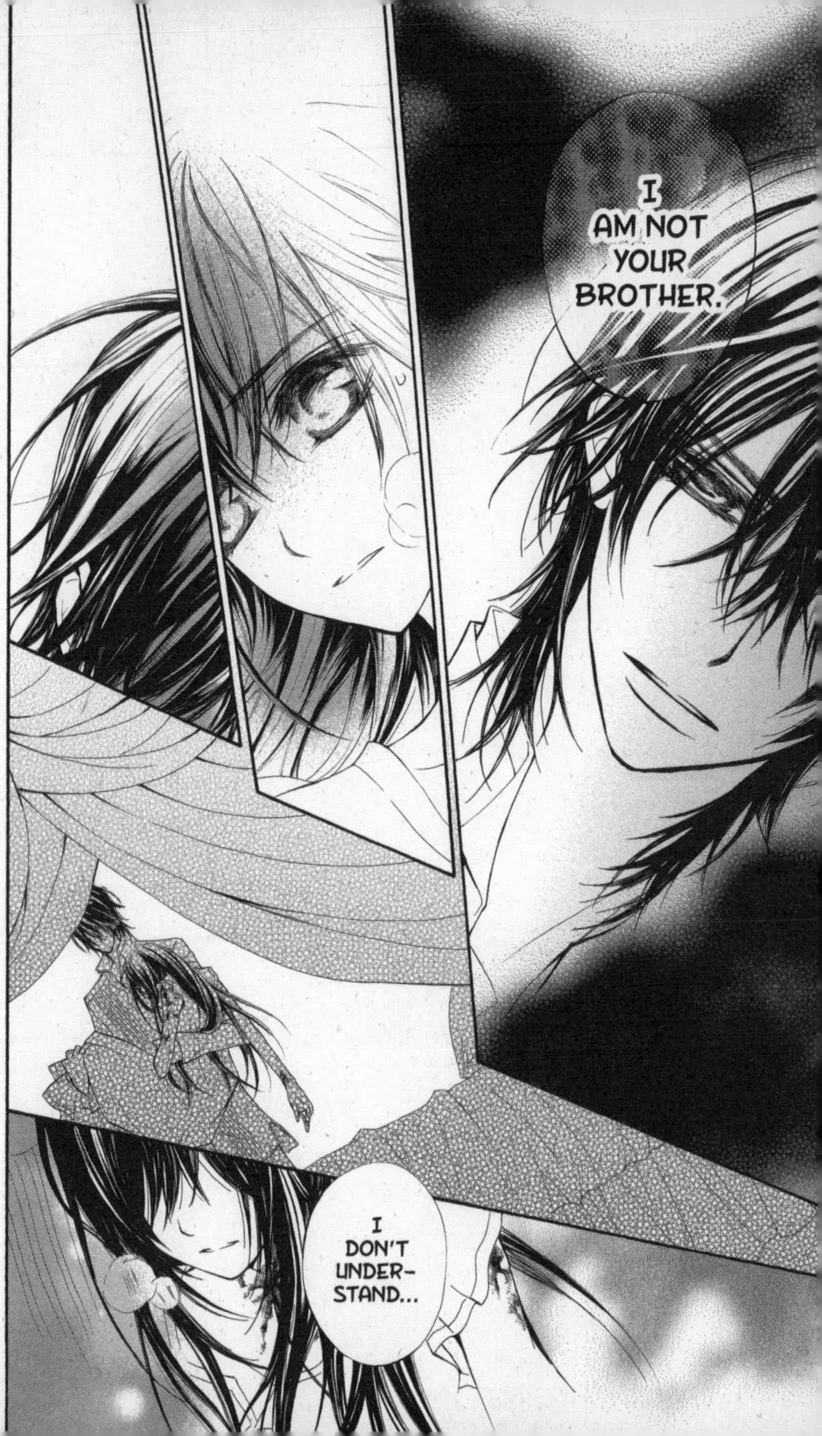
I AM NOT YOUR BROTHER.
I DON'T UNDER-STAND...

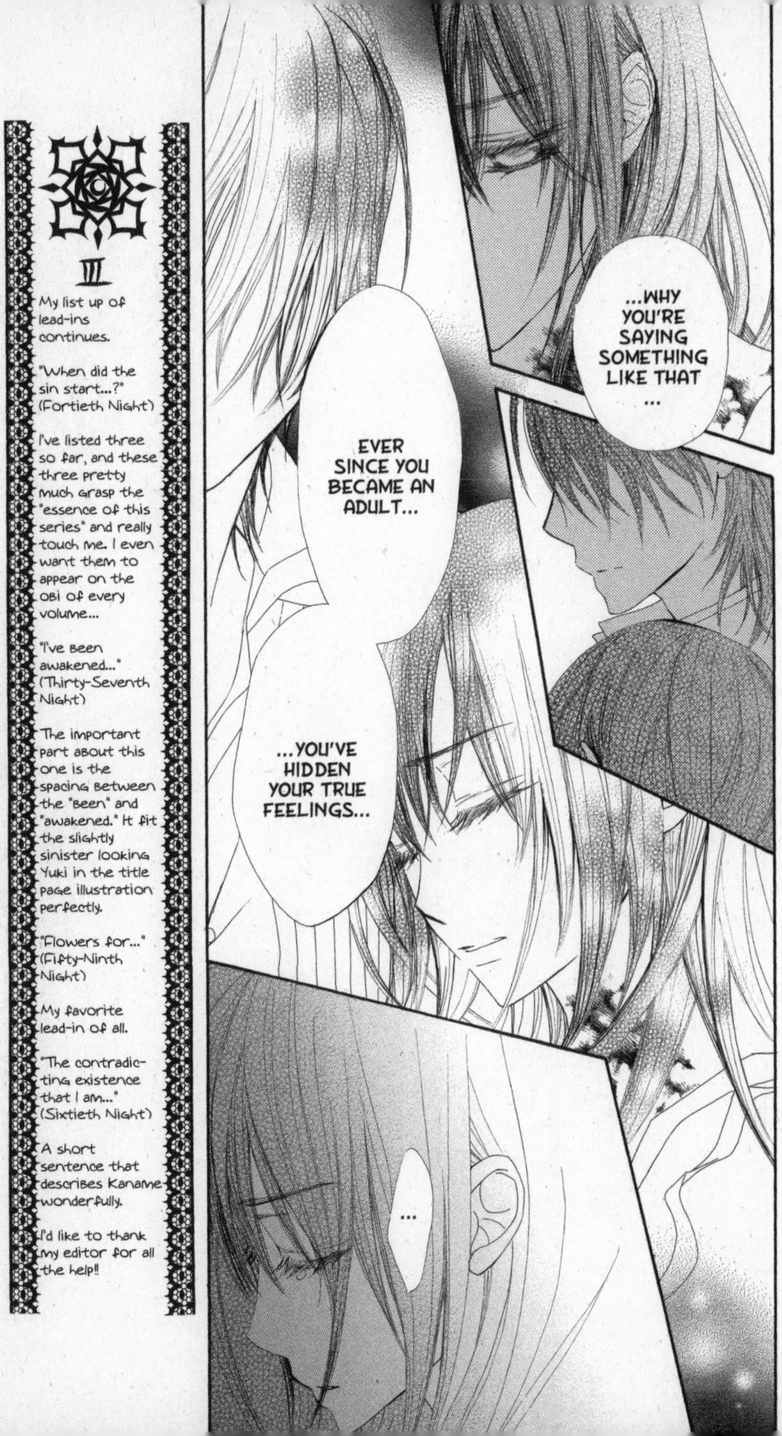
...WHY YOU'RE SAYING SOMETHING LIKE THAT ...
EVER SINCE YOU BECAME AN ADULT...
...YOU'VE HIDDEN YOUR TRUE FEELINGS...
...

III

My list up of lead-ins continues.

"When did the sin start...?" (Fortieth Night)

I've listed three so far, and these three pretty much grasp the "essence of this series" and really touch me. I even want them to appear on the obi of every volume...

"I've been awakened..." (Thirty-Seventh Night)

The important part about this one is the spacing between the "been" and "awakened." It fit the slightly sinister looking Yuki in the title page illustration perfectly.

"Flowers for..." (Fifty-Ninth Night)

My favorite lead-in of all.

"The contradicting existence that I am..." (Sixtieth Night)

A short sentence that describes Kaname wonderfully.

I'd like to thank my editor for all the help!!

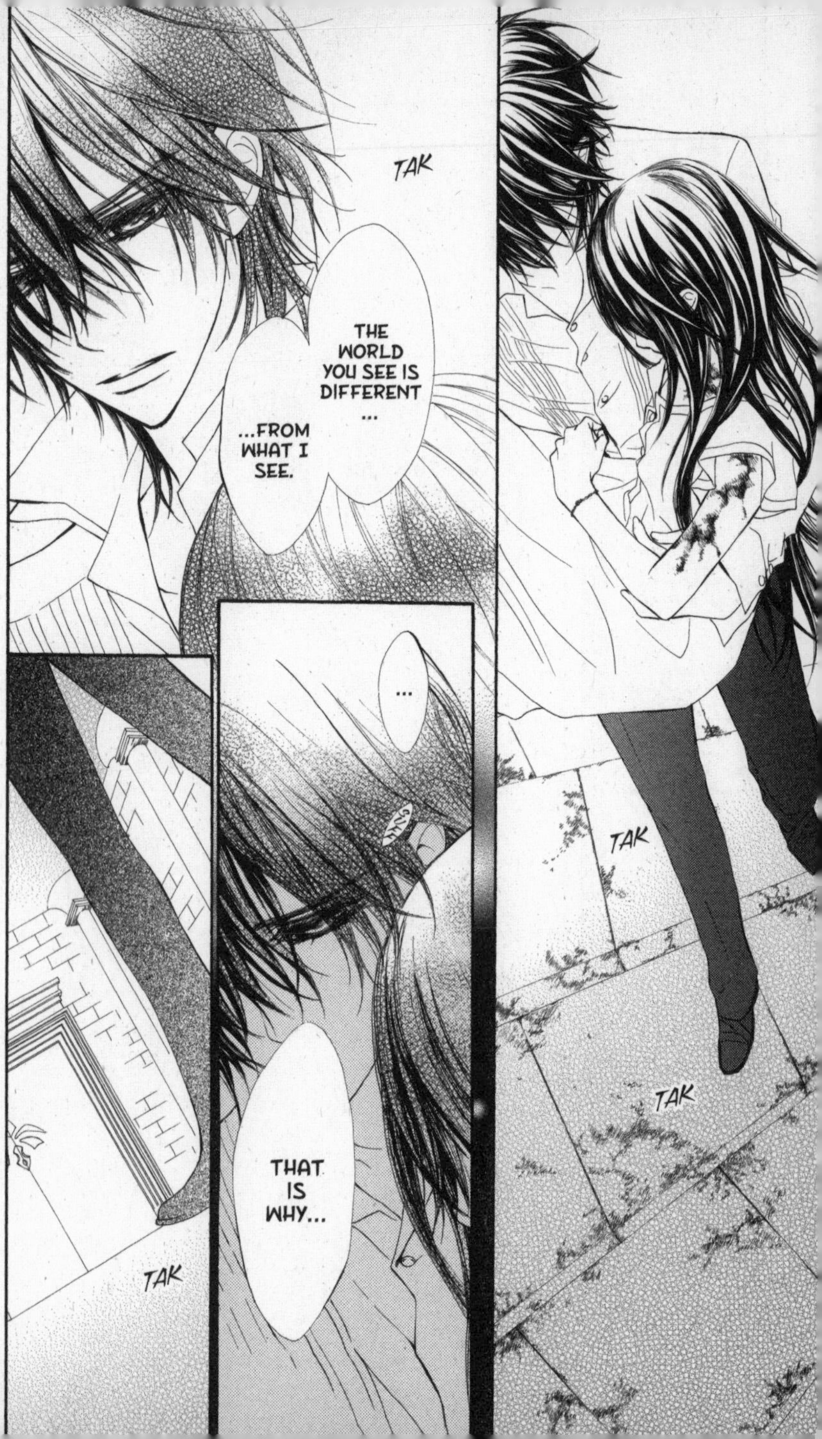
TAK
TAK
TAK
THE WORLD YOU SEE IS DIFFERENT ...
...FROM WHAT I SEE.
...
THAT IS WHY...
TAK

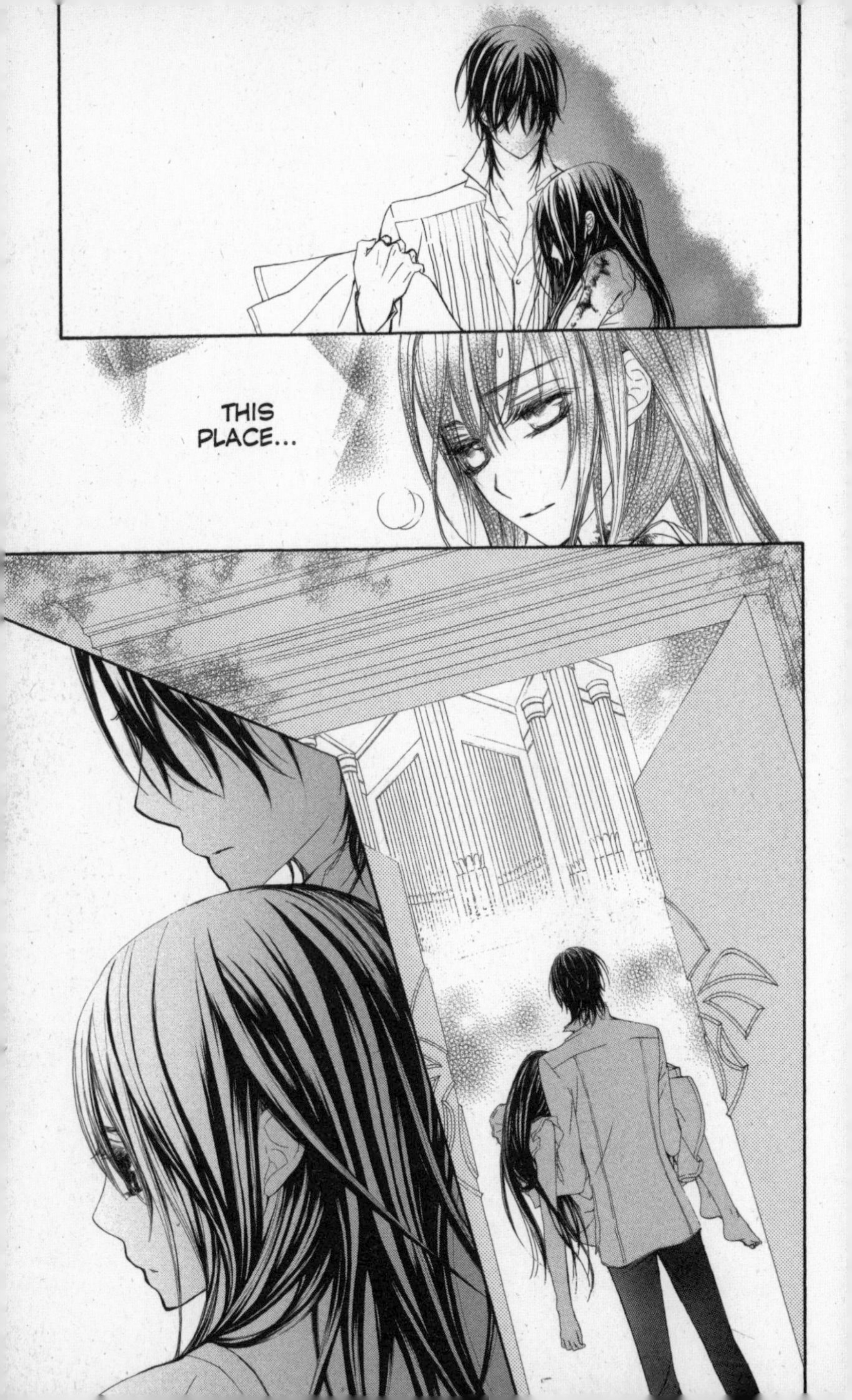
THIS PLACE...

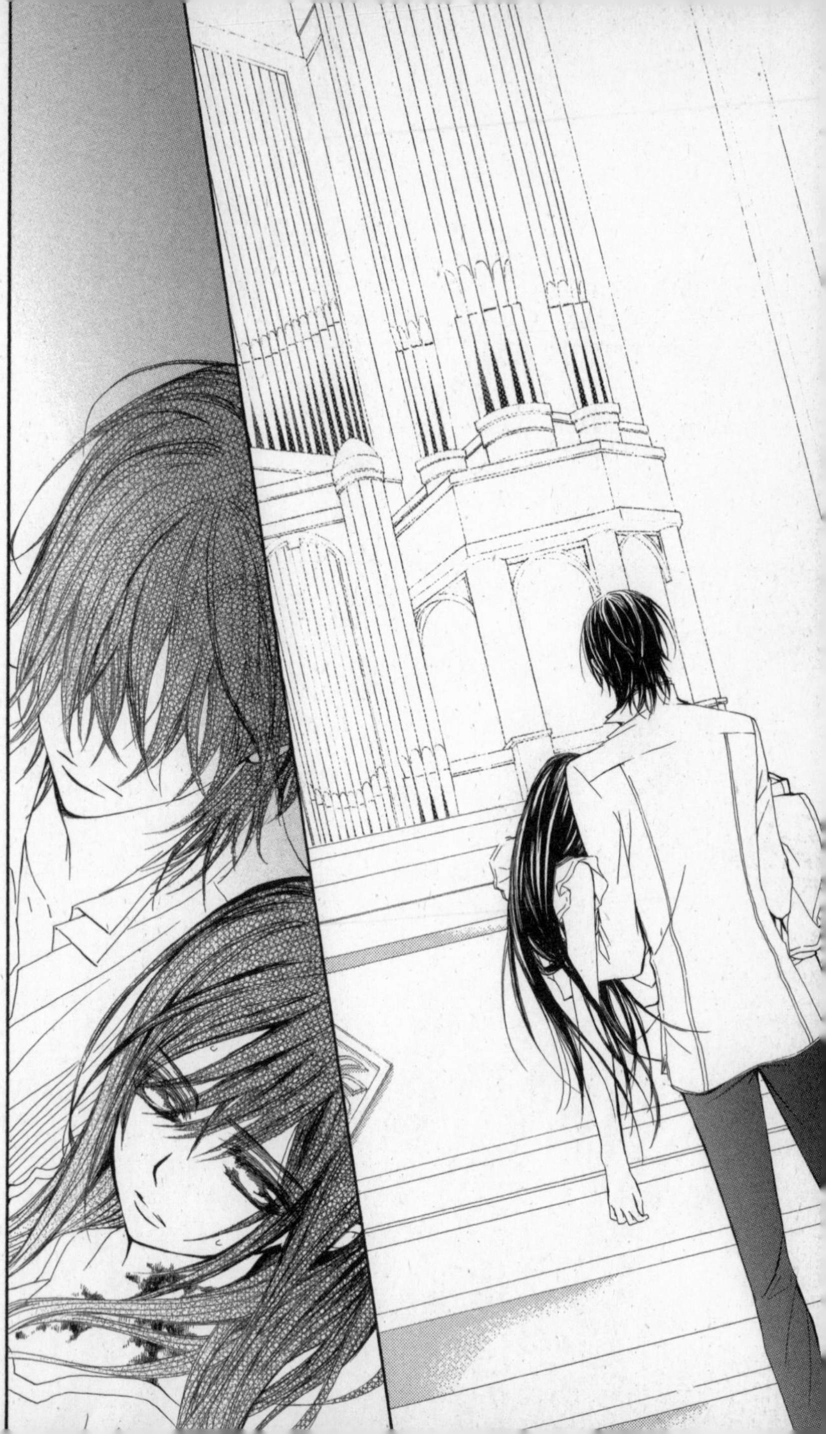

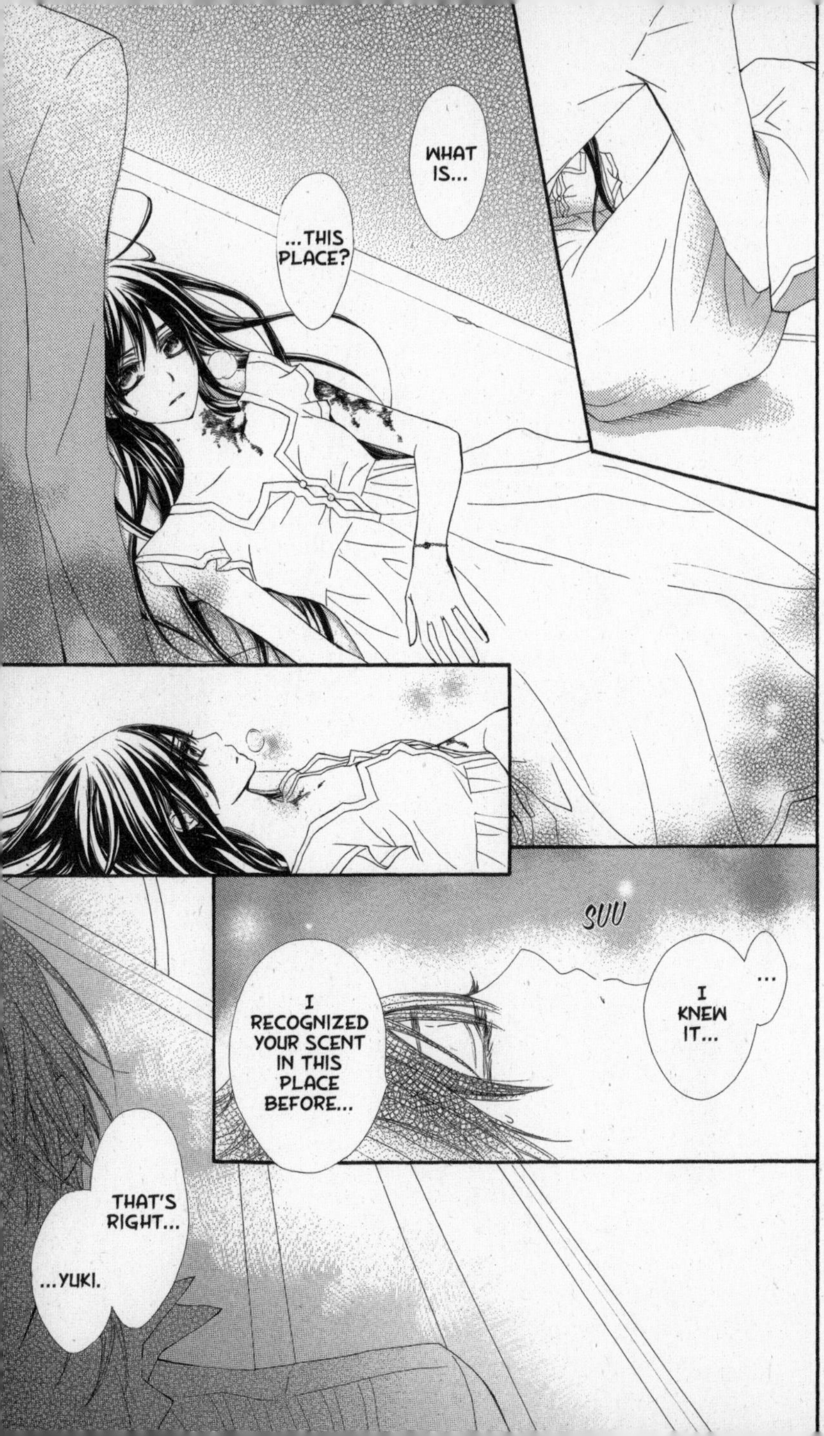
WHAT IS...
...THIS PLACE?
...
I KNEW IT...
SUU
I RECOGNIZED YOUR SCENT IN THIS PLACE BEFORE...
THAT'S RIGHT...
...YUKI.

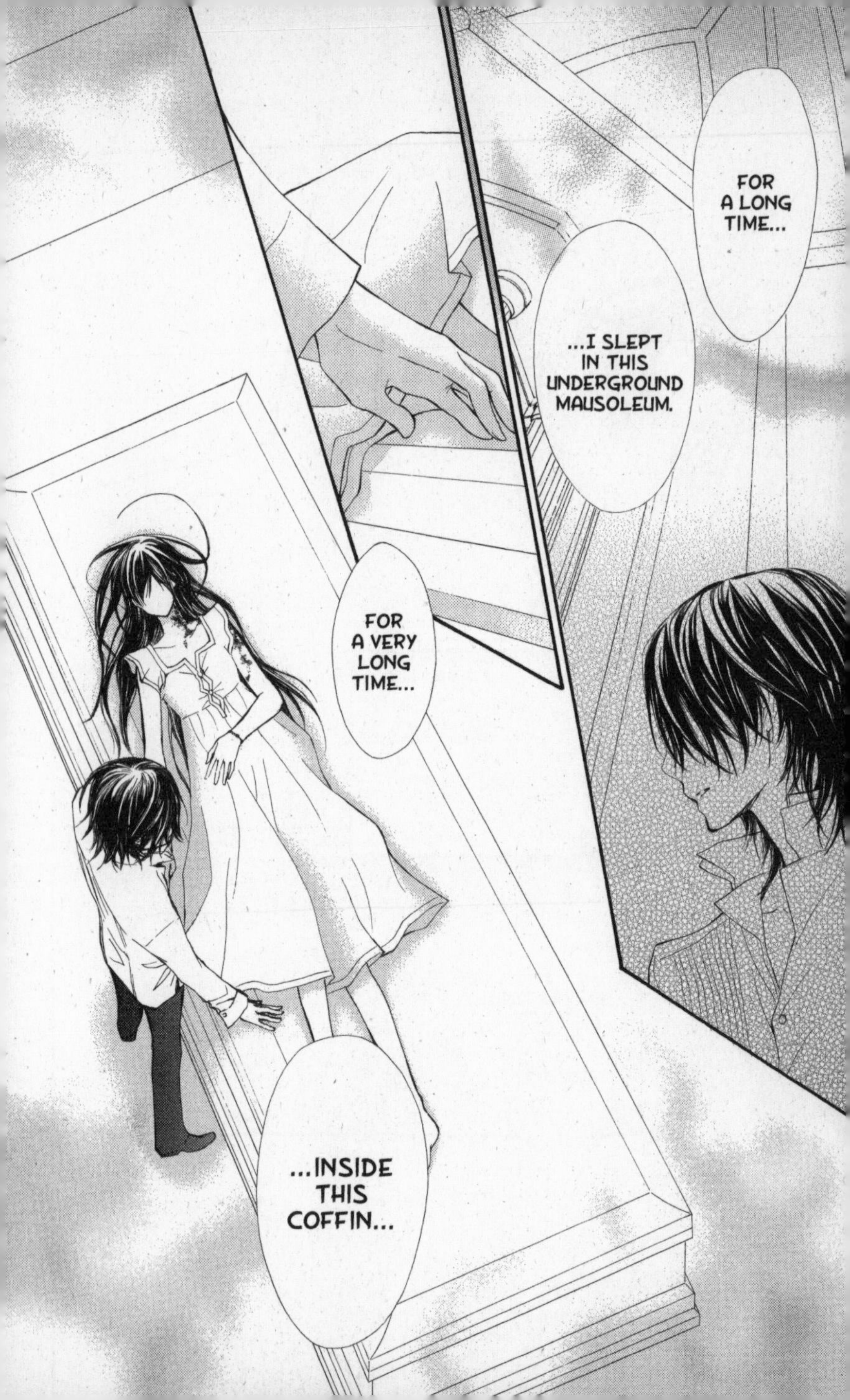
FOR A LONG TIME...
...I SLEPT IN THIS UNDERGROUND MAUSOLEUM.
FOR A VERY LONG TIME...
...INSIDE THIS COFFIN...

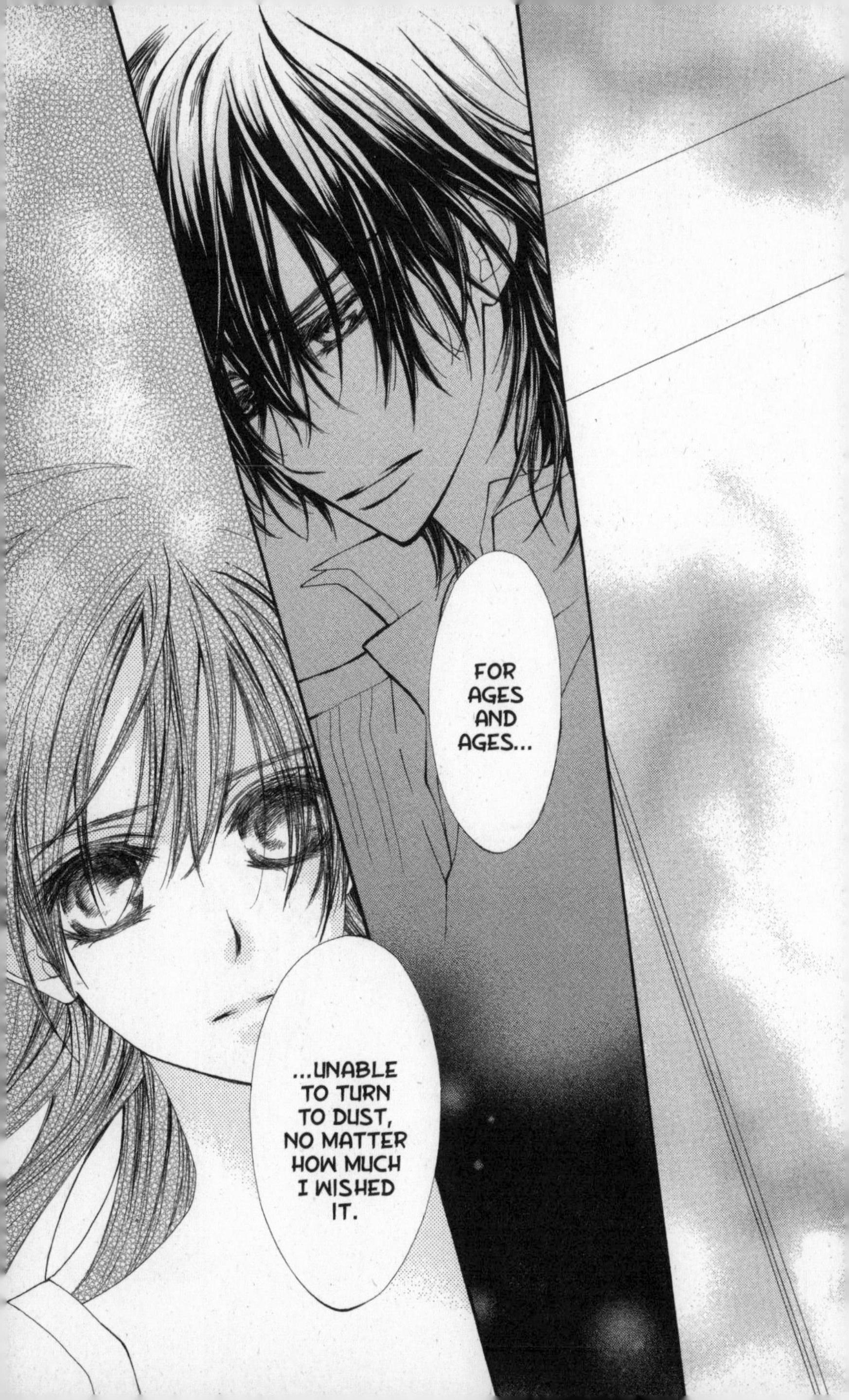
FOR AGES AND AGES...
...UNABLE TO TURN TO DUST, NO MATTER HOW MUCH I WISHED IT.

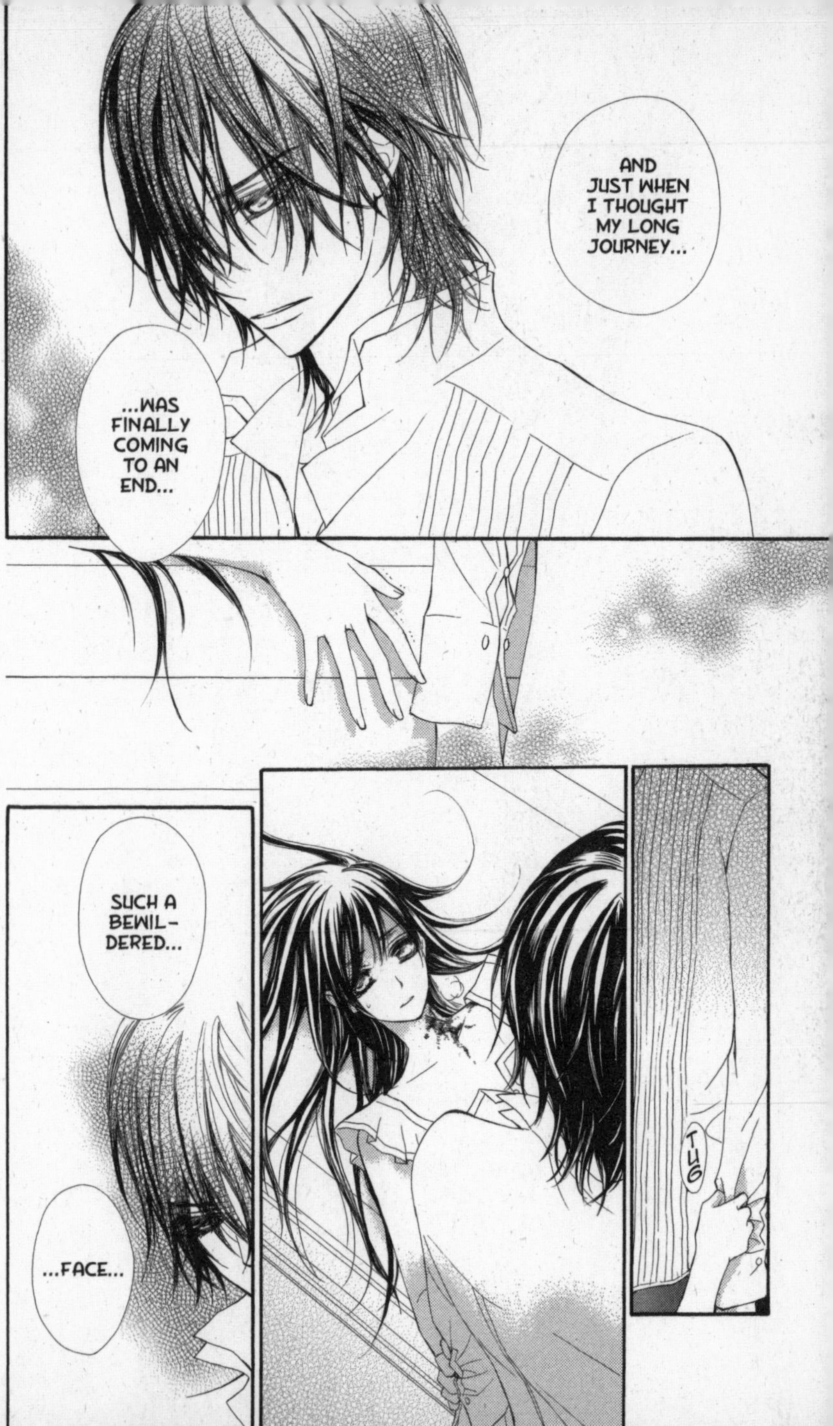
AND JUST WHEN I THOUGHT MY LONG JOURNEY...
...WAS FINALLY COMING TO AN END...
TUG
SUCH A BEWIL-DERED...
...FACE...

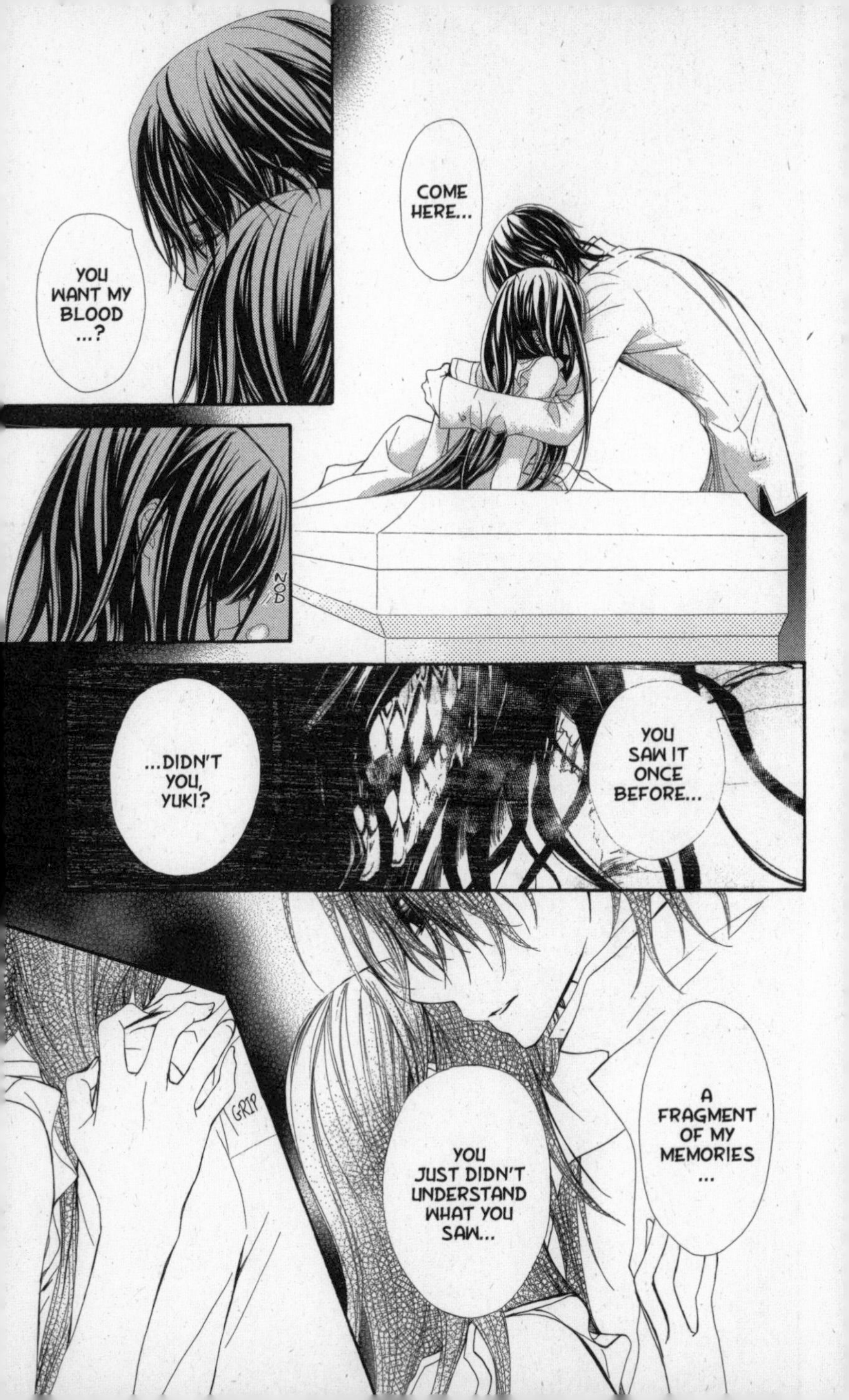
COME HERE...
YOU WANT MY BLOOD ...?
NOD
YOU SAW IT ONCE BEFORE...
...DIDN'T YOU, YUKI?
A FRAGMENT OF MY MEMORIES ...
YOU JUST DIDN'T UNDERSTAND WHAT YOU SAW...
GRIP

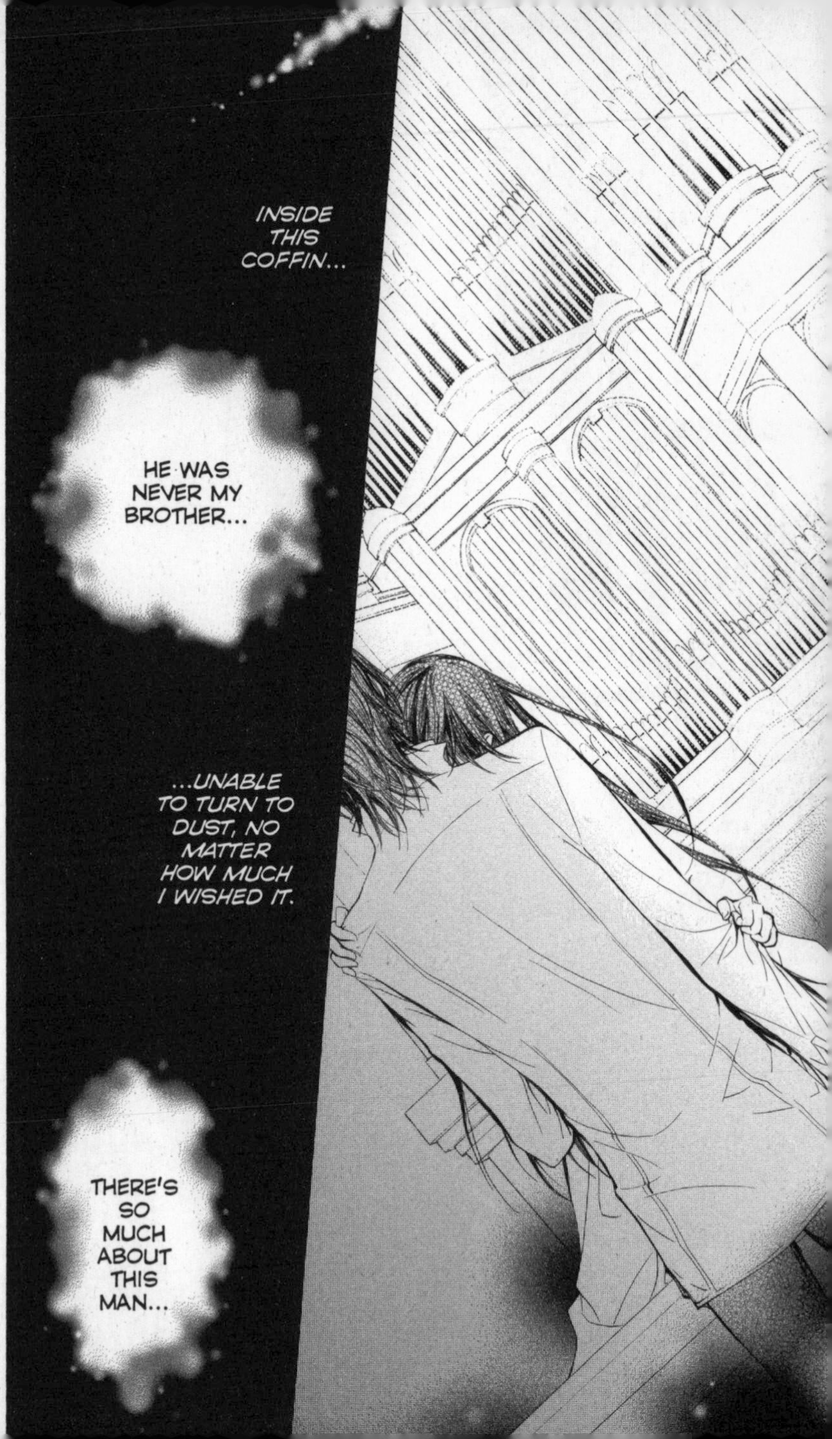
INSIDE THIS COFFIN...
HE WAS NEVER MY BROTHER...
...UNABLE TO TURN TO DUST, NO MATTER HOW MUCH I WISHED IT.
THERE'S SO MUCH ABOUT THIS MAN...

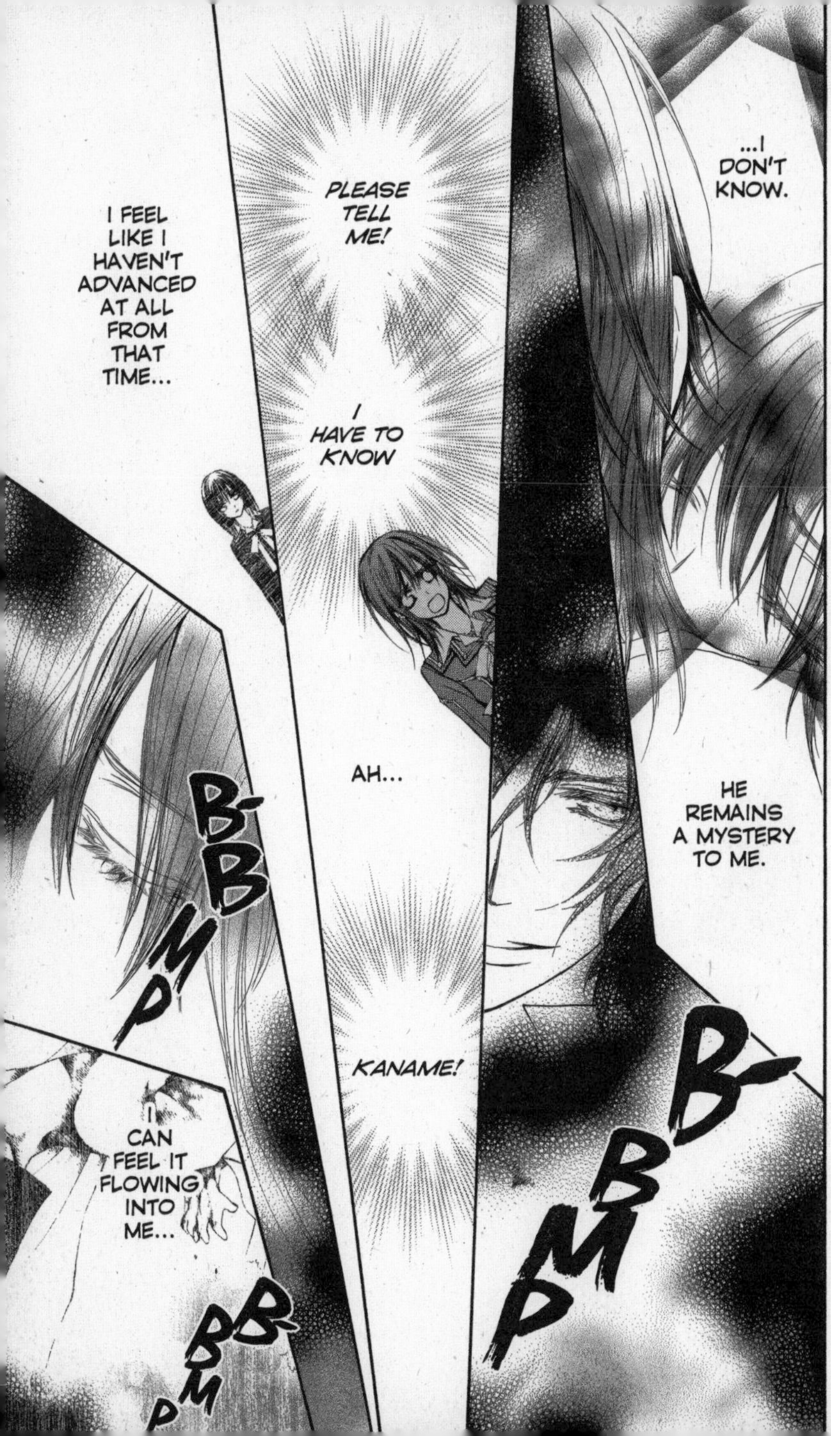

...I DON'T KNOW.
HE REMAINS A MYSTERY TO ME.
B-BMP
PLEASE TELL ME!
I HAVE TO KNOW
AH...
KANAME!
I FEEL LIKE I HAVEN'T ADVANCED AT ALL FROM THAT TIME...
B-BMP
I CAN FEEL IT FLOWING INTO ME...
B-BMP

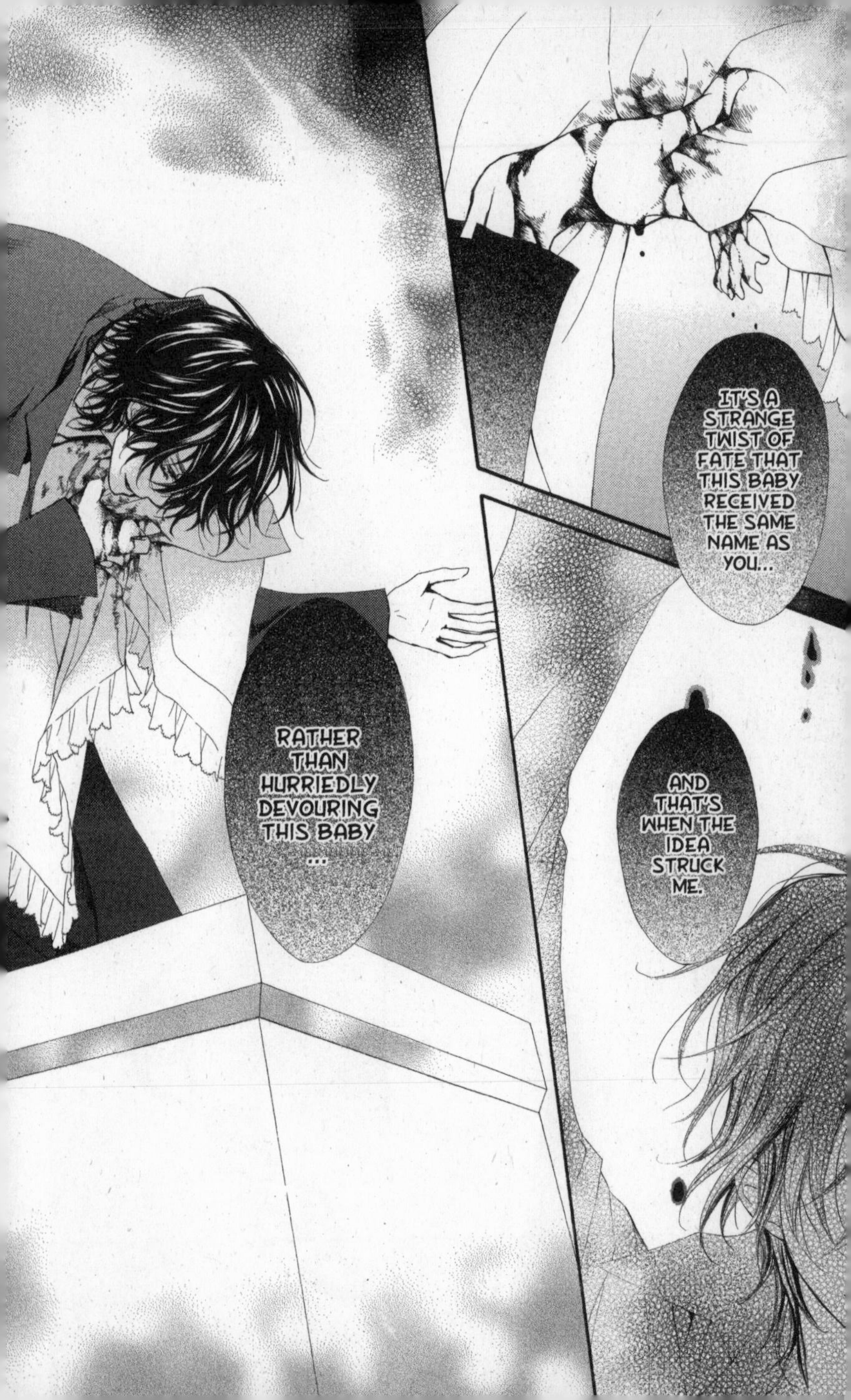
IT'S A STRANGE TWIST OF FATE THAT THIS BABY RECEIVED THE SAME NAME AS YOU...
AND THAT'S WHEN THE IDEA STRUCK ME.
RATHER THAN HURRIEDLY DEVOURING THIS BABY ...

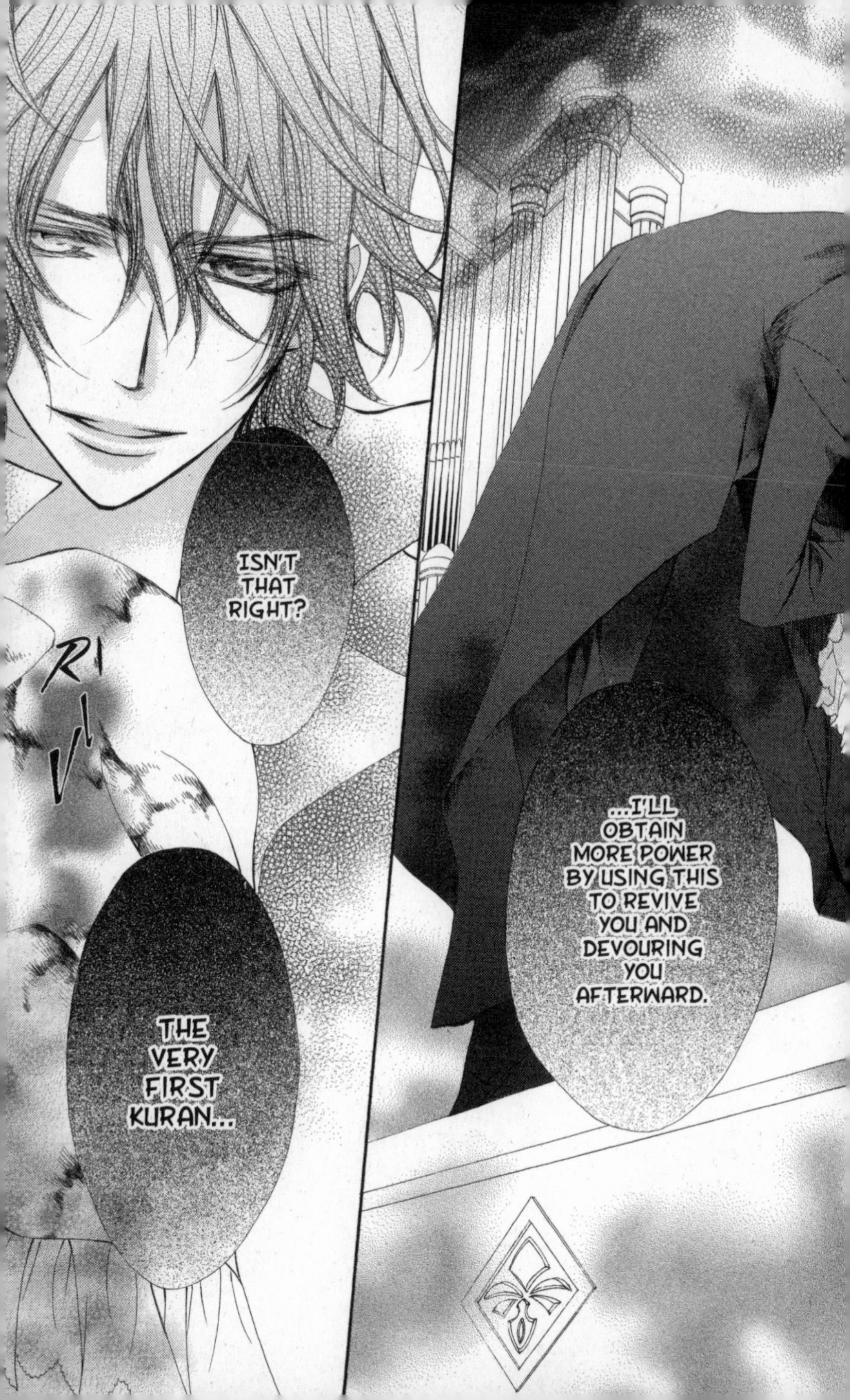
...I'LL OBTAIN MORE POWER BY USING THIS TO REVIVE YOU AND DEVOURING YOU AFTERWARD.
ISN'T THAT RIGHT?
RI VI
THE VERY FIRST KURAN...

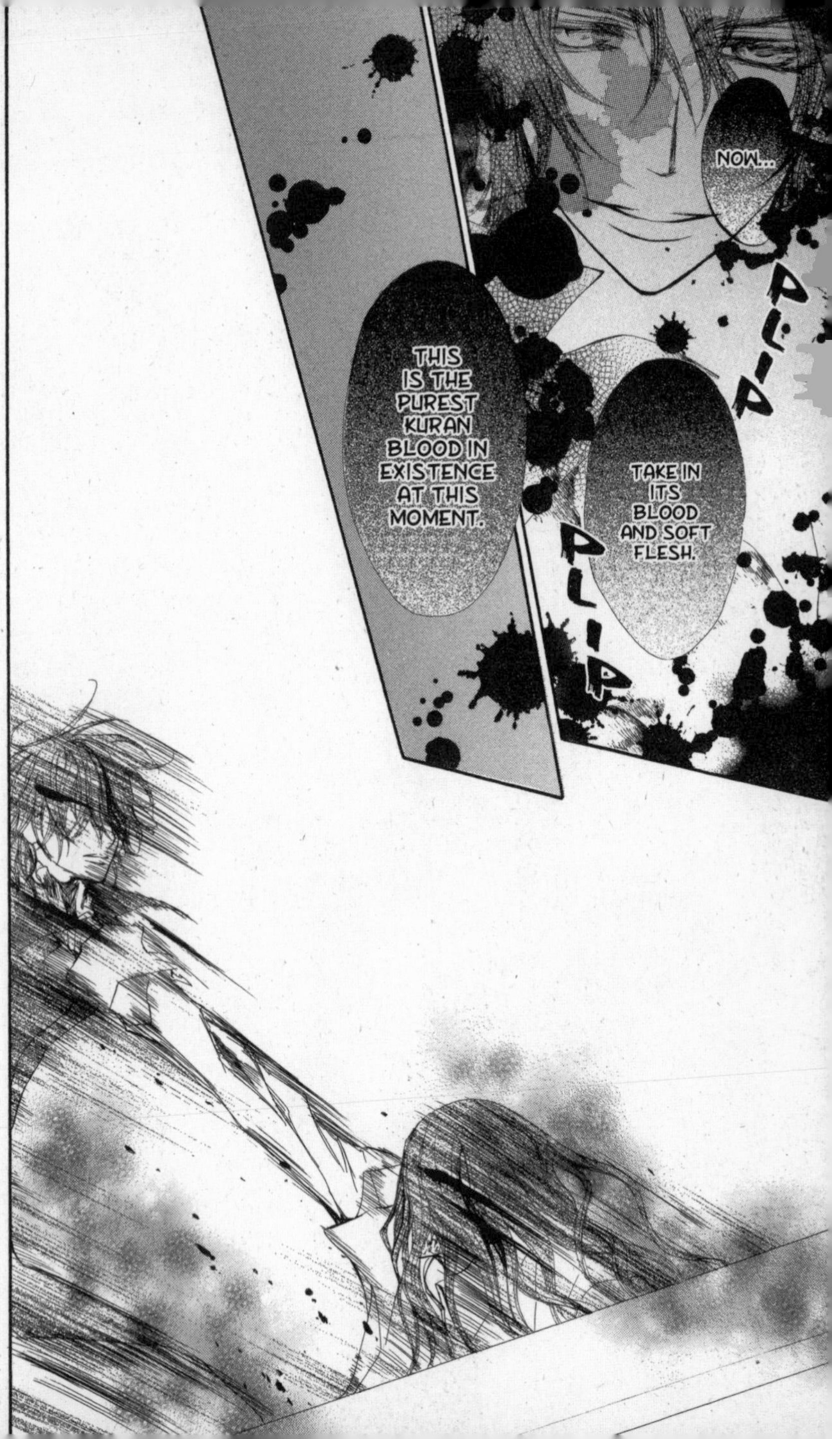
NOW...
PLIP
PLIP
TAKE IN ITS BLOOD AND SOFT FLESH.
THIS IS THE PUREST KURAN BLOOD IN EXISTENCE AT THIS MOMENT.

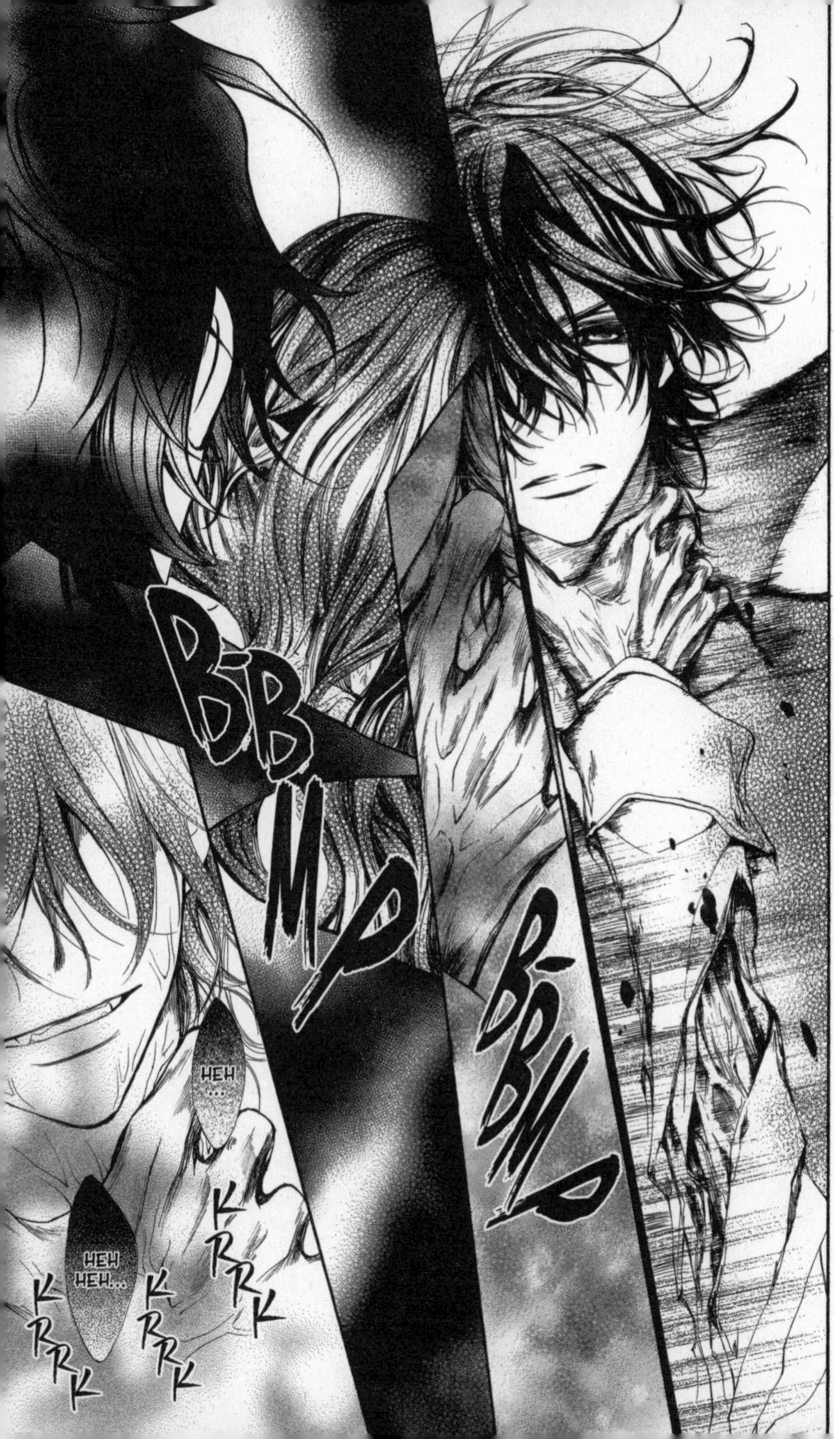
B-BMP
B-BMP
HEH...
KRRRK
HEH HEH...
KRRRK
KRRRK

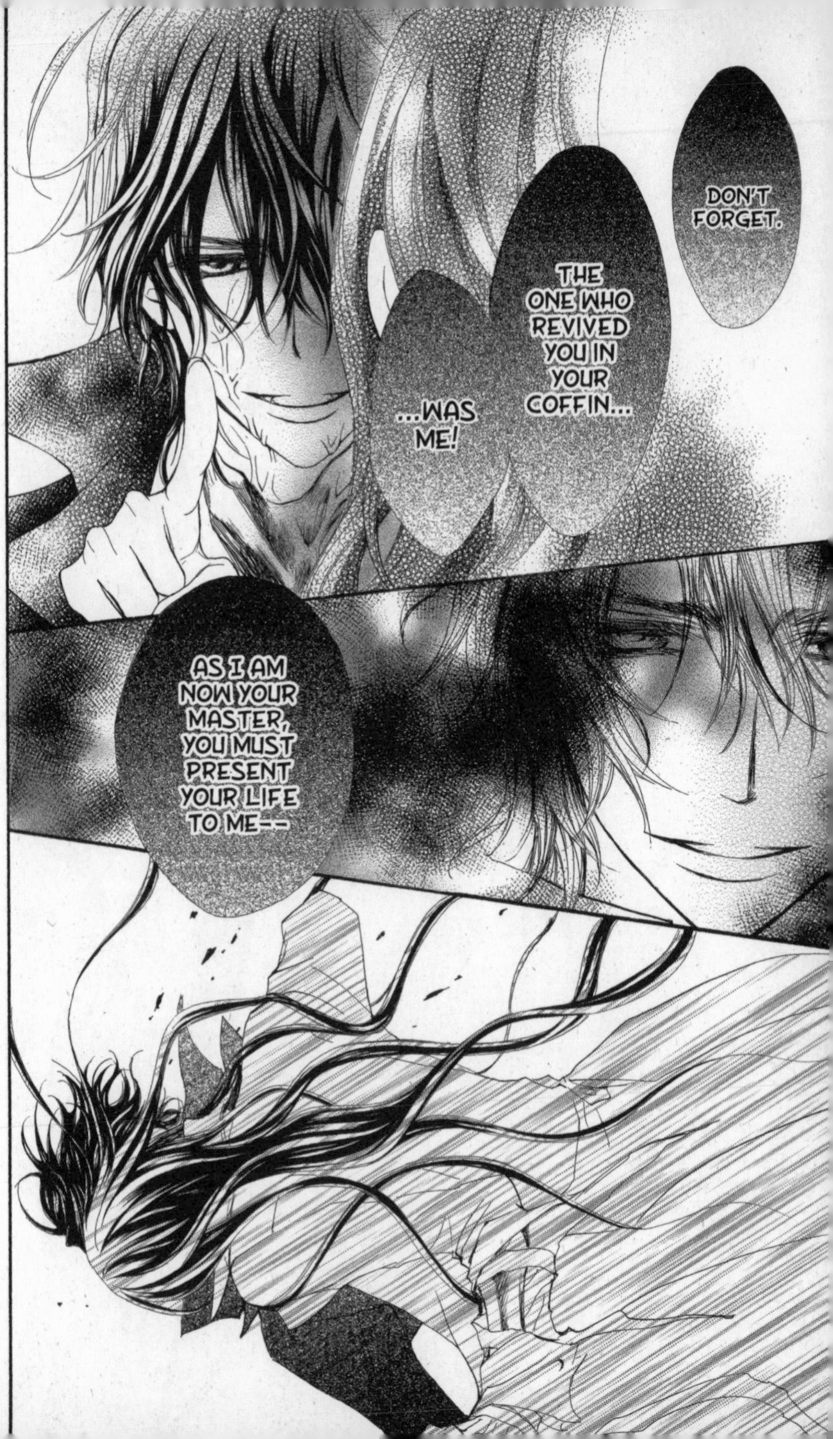
DON'T FORGET.
THE ONE WHO REVIVED YOU IN YOUR COFFIN...
...WAS ME!
AS I AM NOW YOUR MASTER, YOU MUST PRESENT YOUR LIFE TO ME--

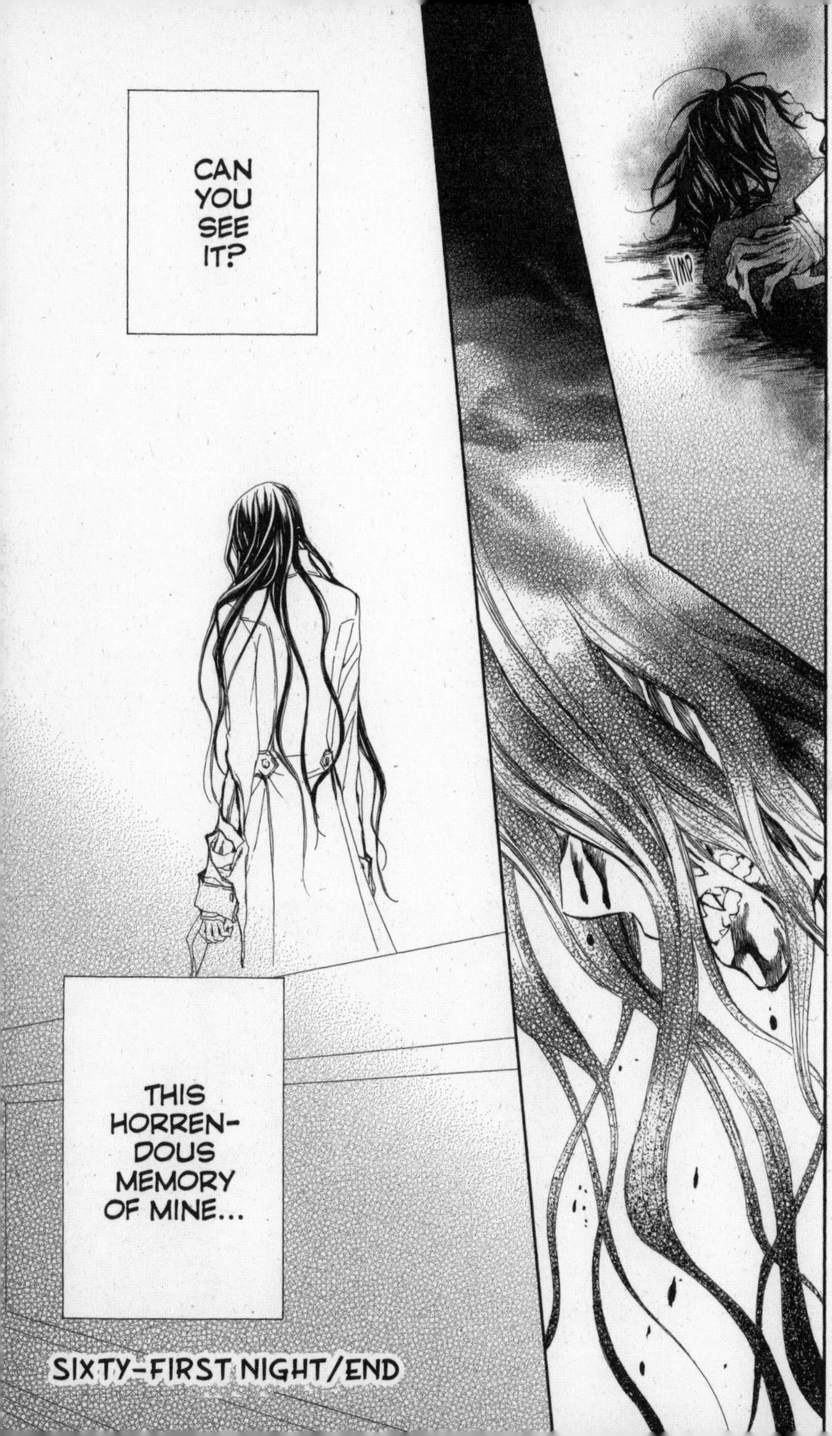
VMP
CAN YOU SEE IT?
THIS HORRENDOUS MEMORY OF MINE...
SIXTY-FIRST NIGHT/END

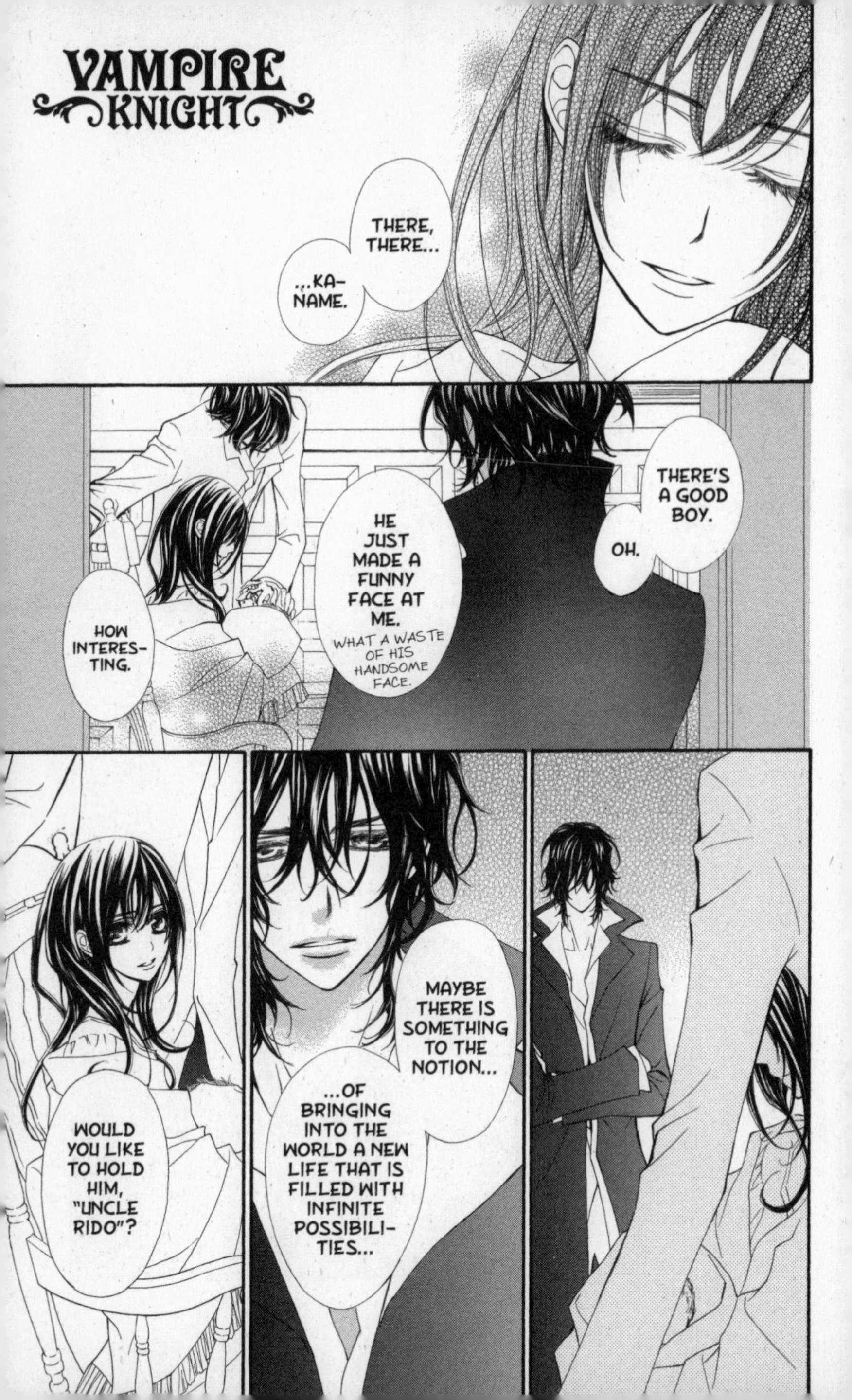
VAMPIRE KNIGHT
THERE, THERE...
...KA-NAME.
THERE'S A GOOD BOY.
OH.
HE JUST MADE A FUNNY FACE AT ME.
WHAT A WASTE OF HIS HANDSOME FACE.
HOW INTERESTING.
MAYBE THERE IS SOMETHING TO THE NOTION...
...OF BRINGING INTO THE WORLD A NEW LIFE THAT IS FILLED WITH INFINITE POSSIBILITIES...
WOULD YOU LIKE TO HOLD HIM, "UNCLE RIDO"?

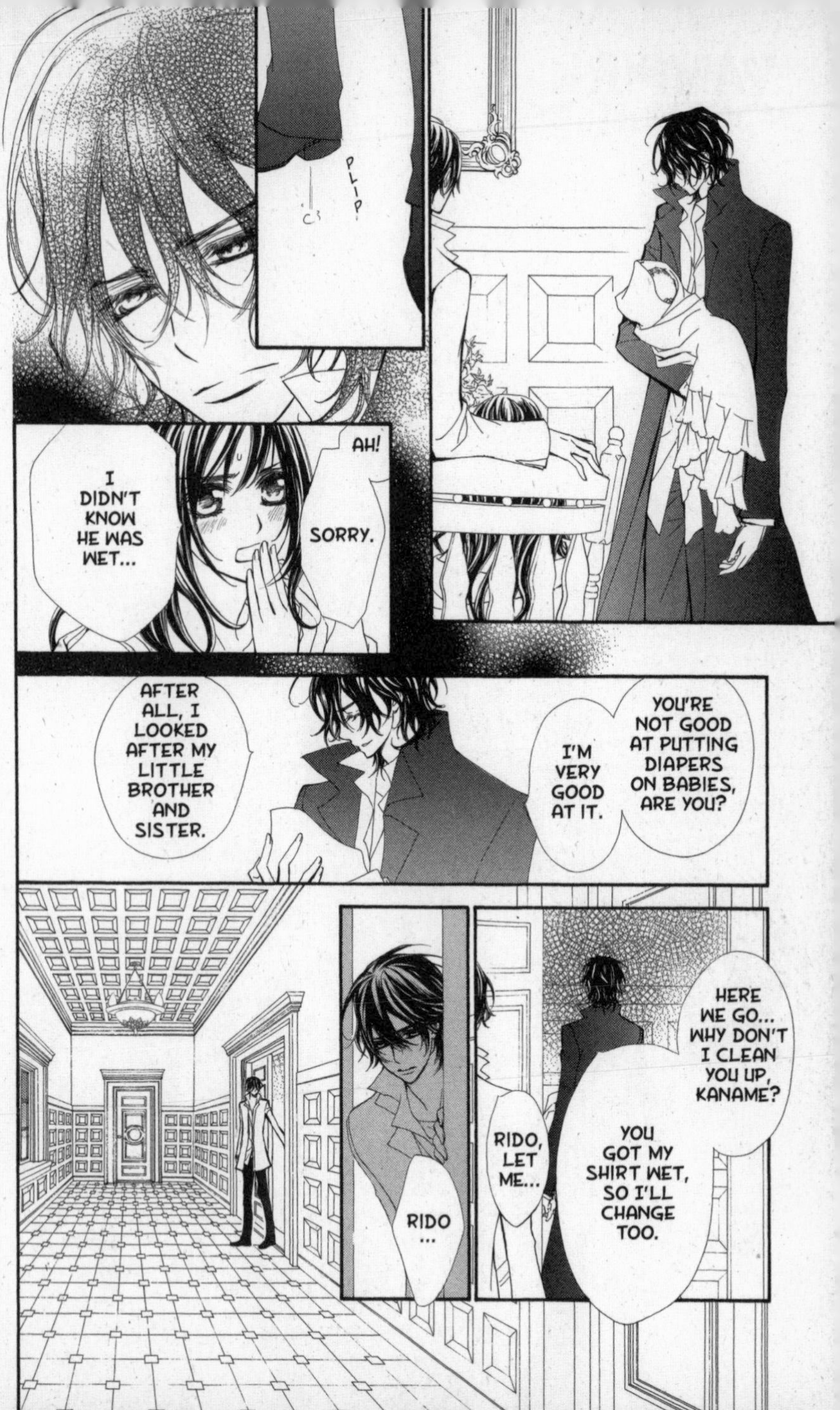
PLIP PLIP
AH!
SORRY.
I DIDN'T KNOW HE WAS WET...
YOU'RE NOT GOOD AT PUTTING DIAPERS ON BABIES, ARE YOU?
I'M VERY GOOD AT IT.
AFTER ALL, I LOOKED AFTER MY LITTLE BROTHER AND SISTER.
HERE WE GO... WHY DON'T I CLEAN YOU UP, KANAME?
YOU GOT MY SHIRT WET, SO I'LL CHANGE TOO.
RIDO, LET ME...
RIDO...

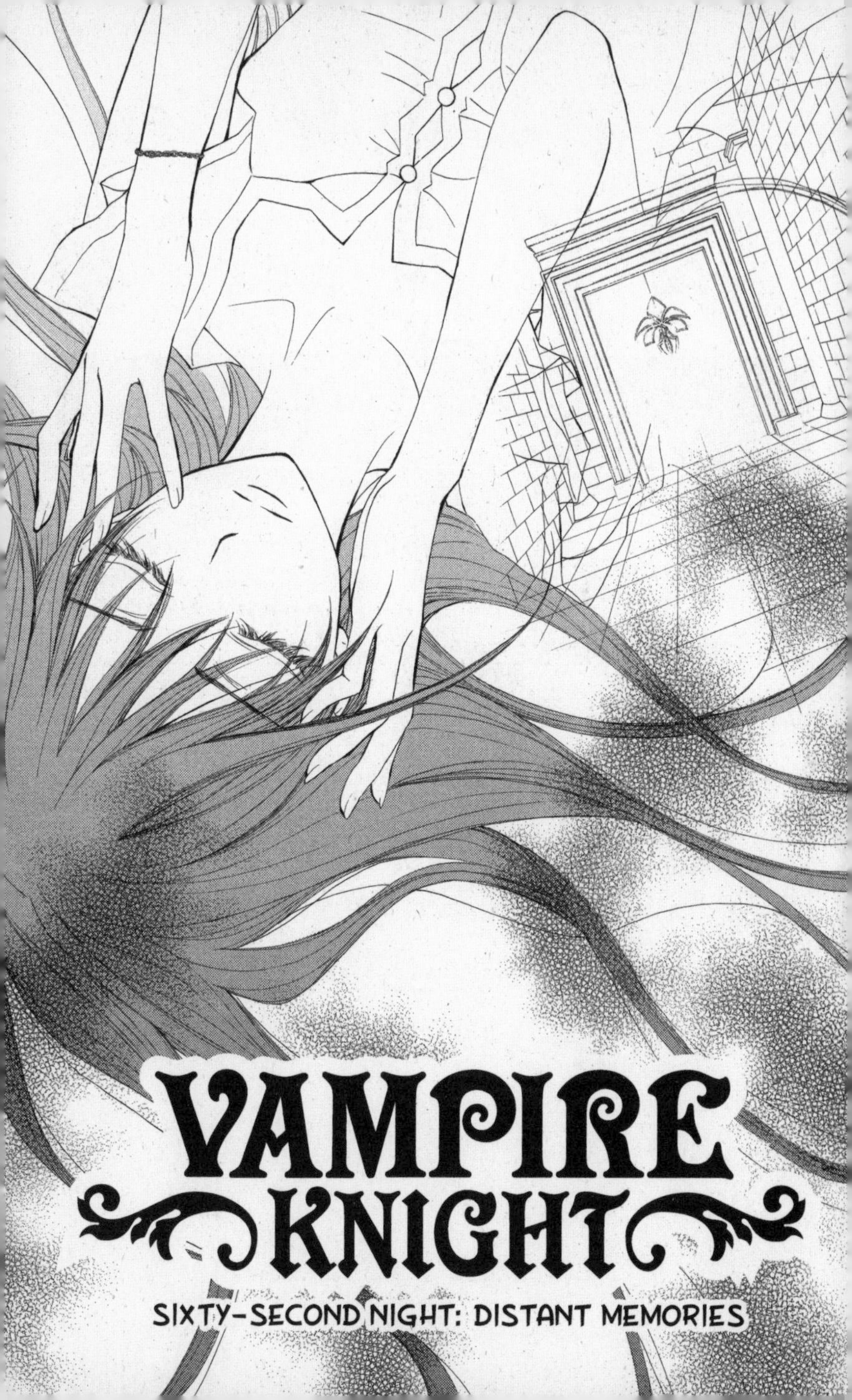
VAMPIRE KNIGHT
SIXTY-SECOND NIGHT: DISTANT MEMORIES

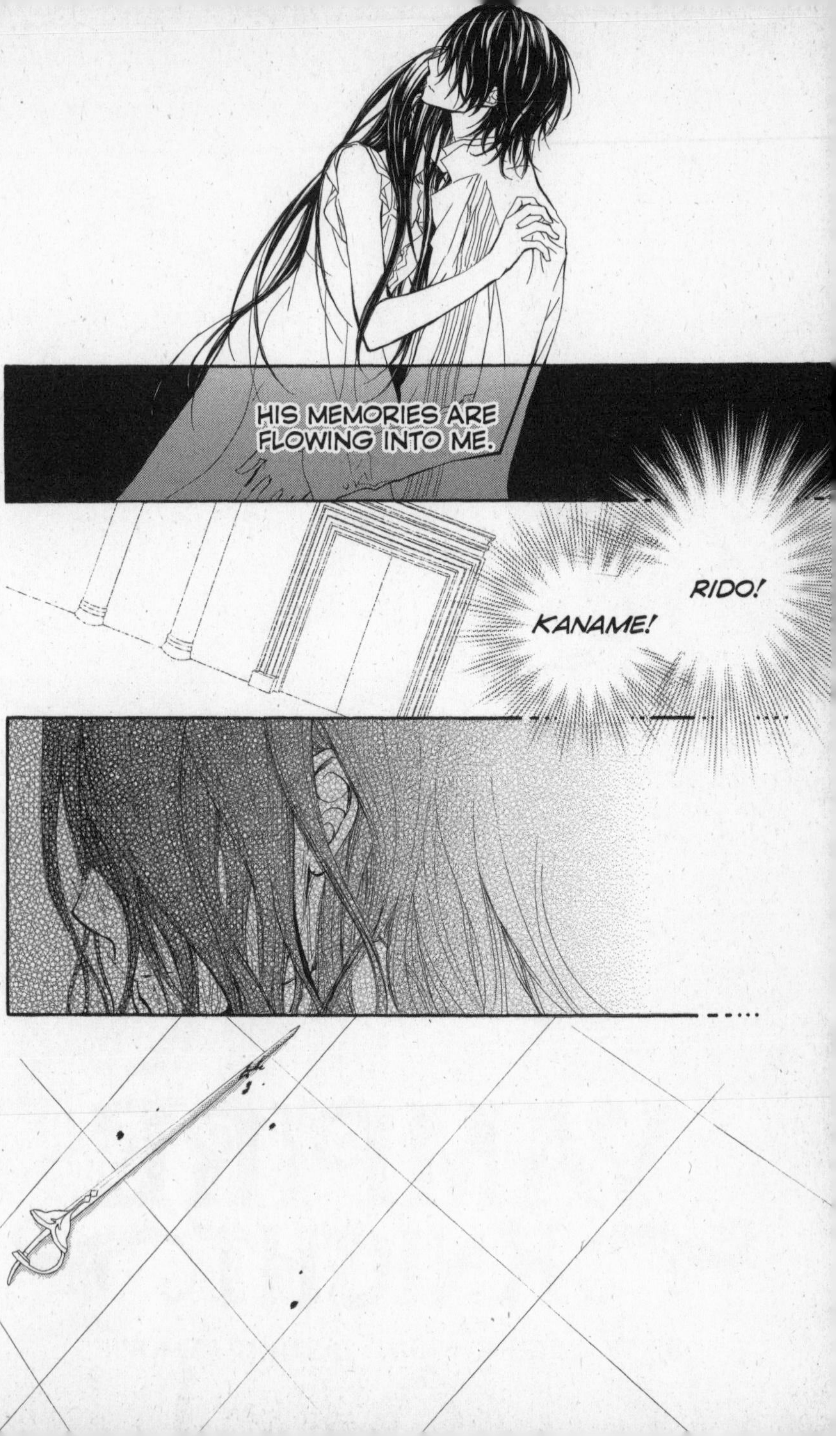
HIS MEMORIES ARE FLOWING INTO ME.
RIDO!
KANAME!

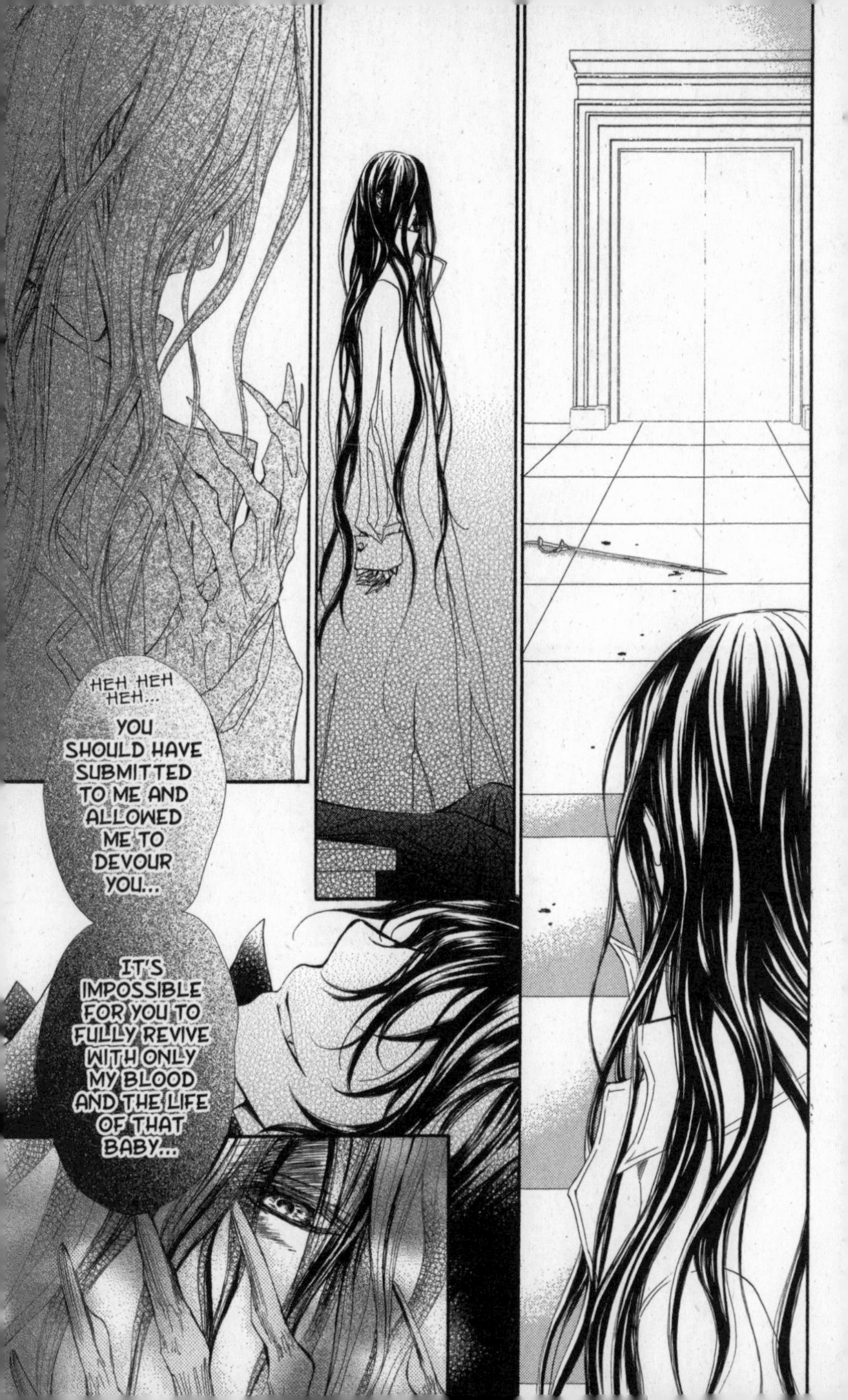
HEH HEH HEH...
YOU SHOULD HAVE SUBMITTED TO ME AND ALLOWED ME TO DEVOUR YOU...
IT'S IMPOSSIBLE FOR YOU TO FULLY REVIVE WITH ONLY MY BLOOD AND THE LIFE OF THAT BABY...

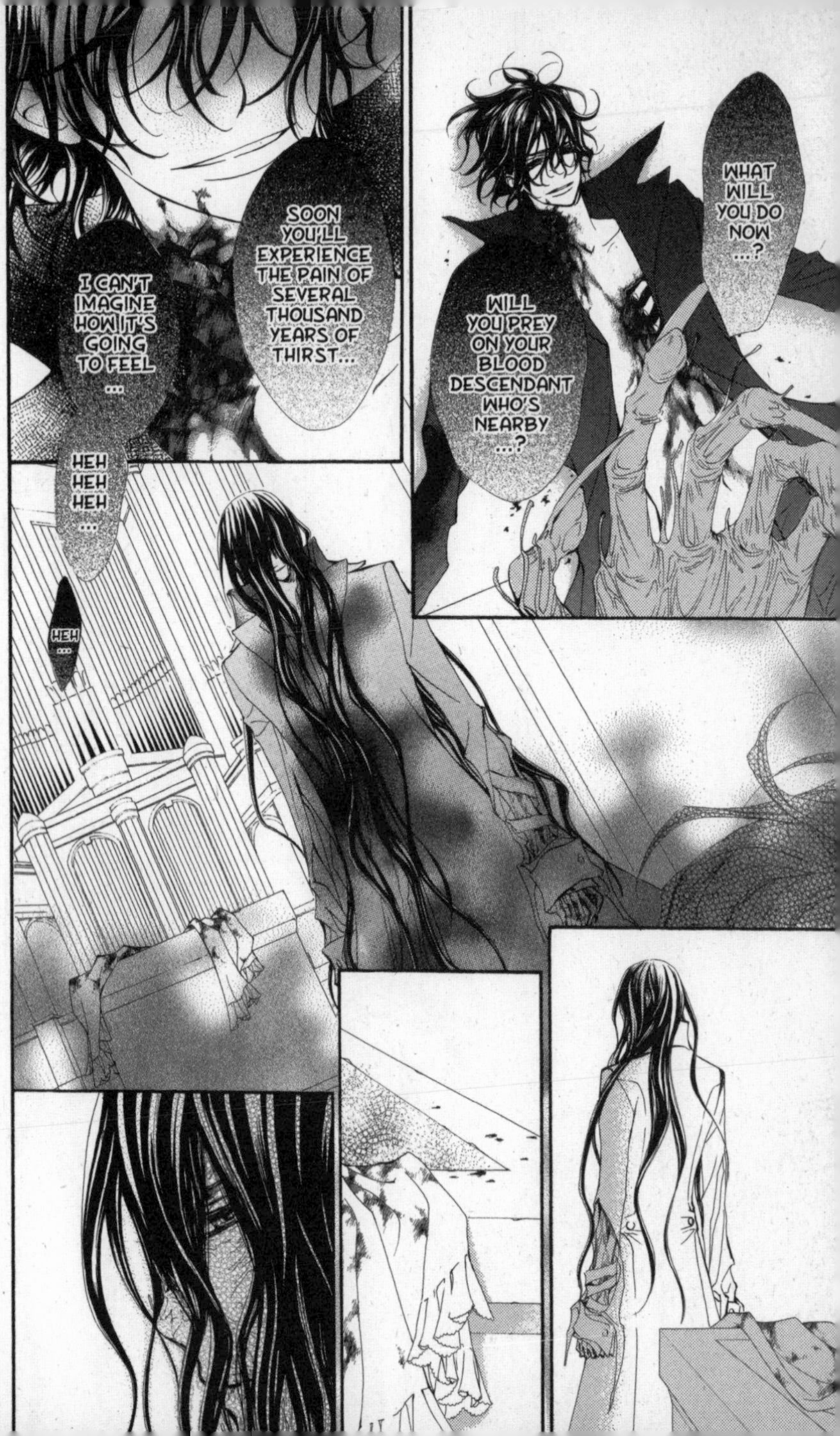
WHAT WILL YOU DO NOW ...?
WILL YOU PREY ON YOUR BLOOD DESCENDANT WHO'S NEARBY ...?
SOON YOU'LL EXPERIENCE THE PAIN OF SEVERAL THOUSAND YEARS OF THIRST...
I CAN'T IMAGINE HOW IT'S GOING TO FEEL ...
HEH HEH HEH ...
HEH ...

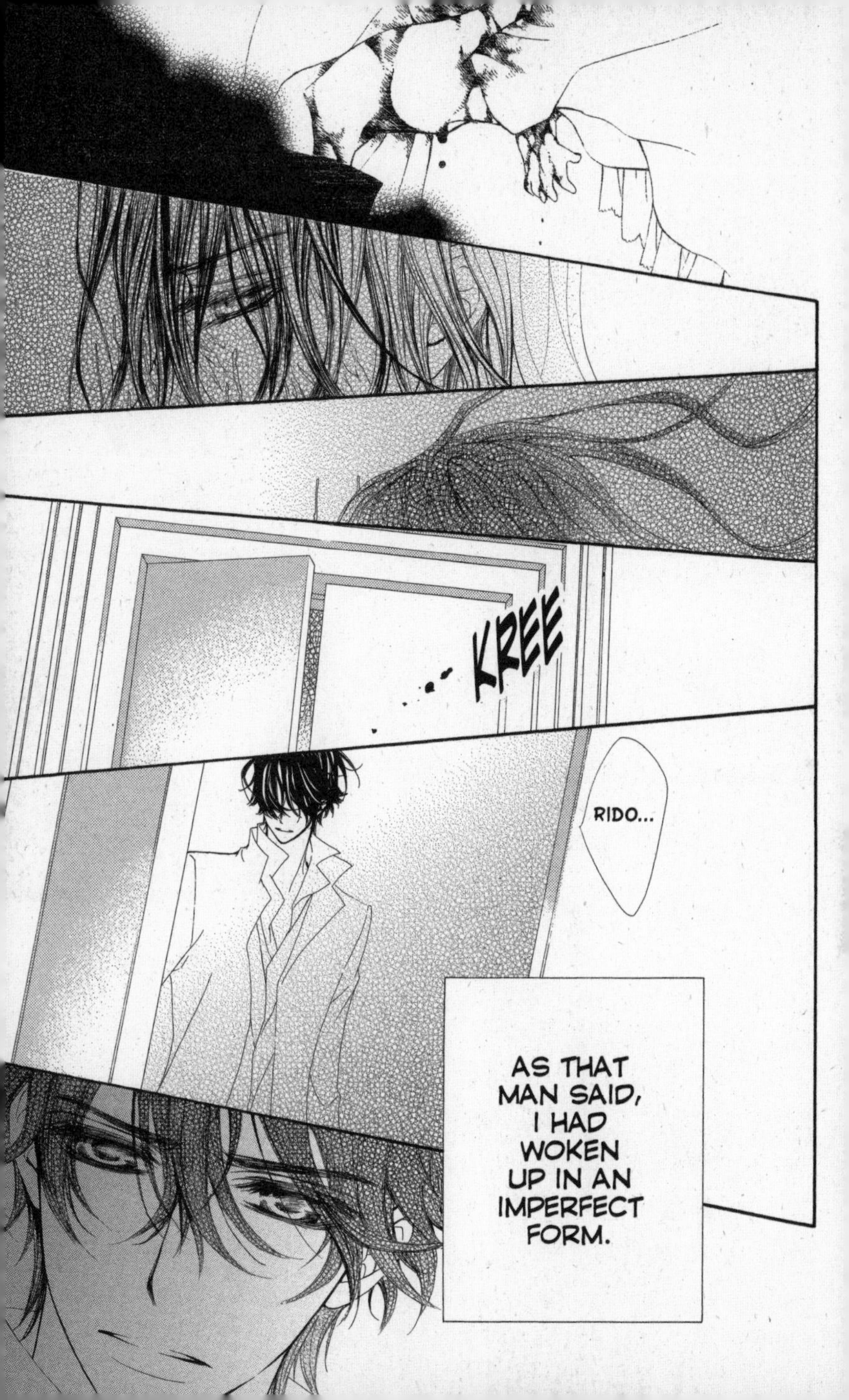
KREE
RIDO...
AS THAT MAN SAID, I HAD WOKEN UP IN AN IMPERFECT FORM.

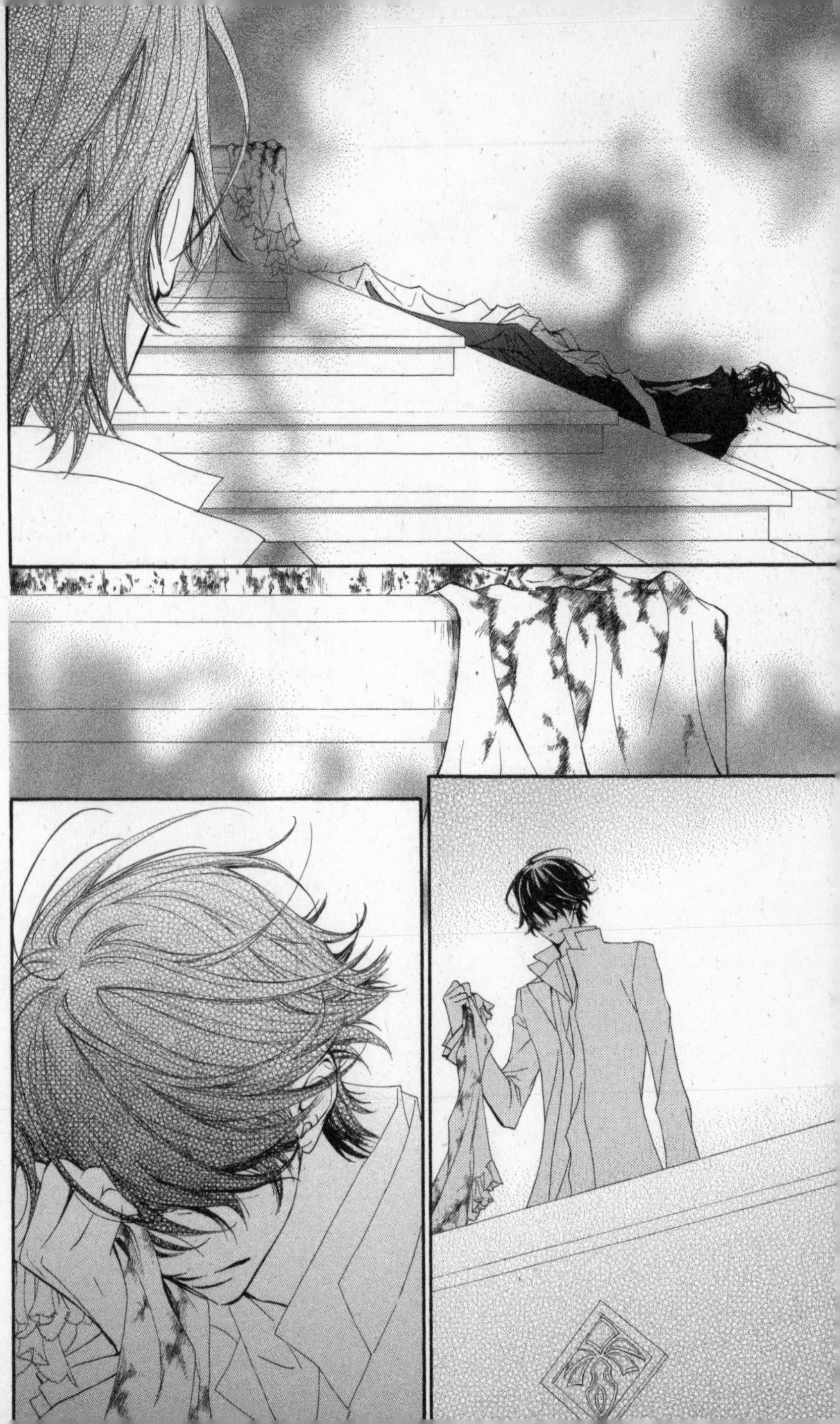

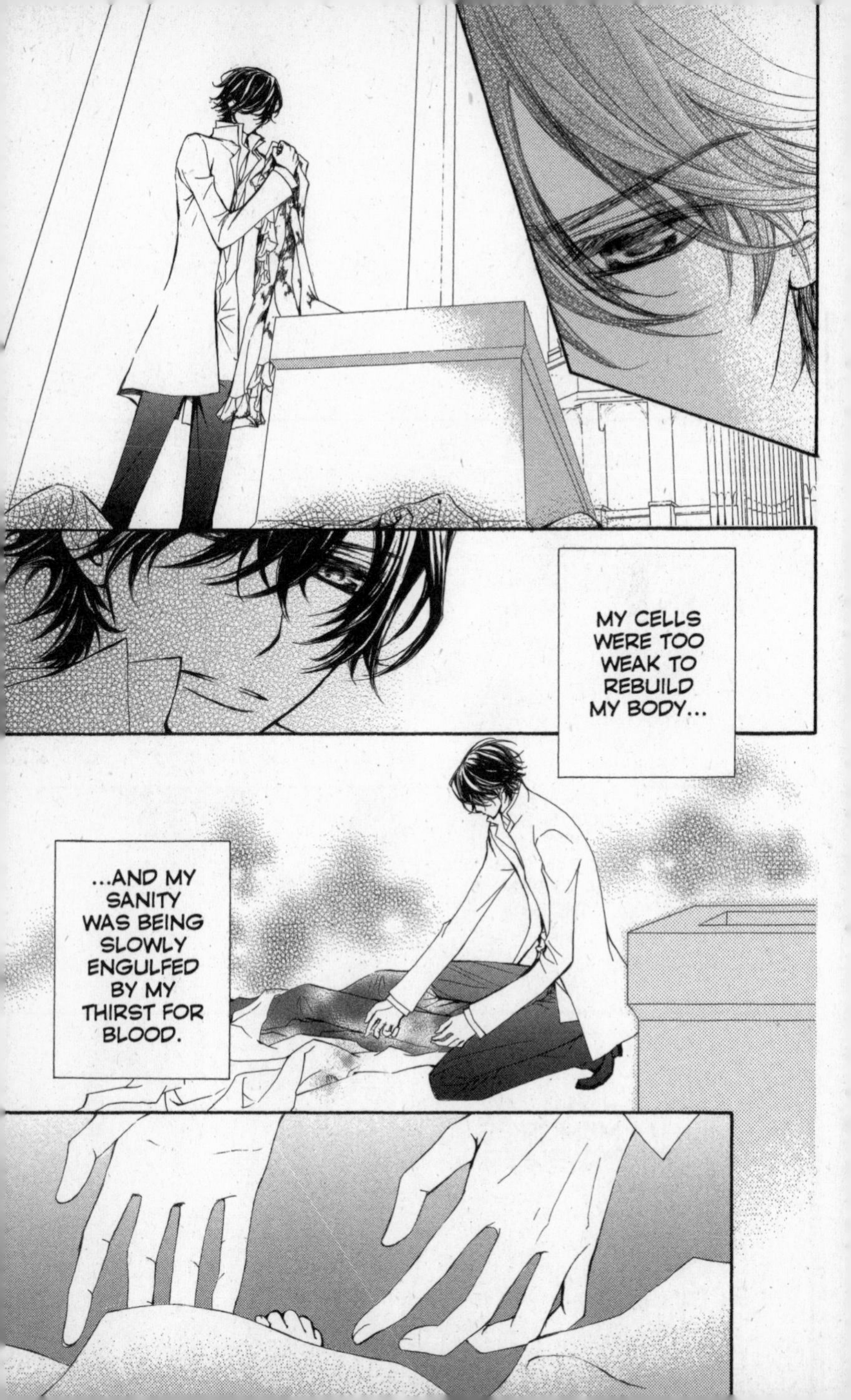
MY CELLS WERE TOO WEAK TO REBUILD MY BODY...
...AND MY SANITY WAS BEING SLOWLY ENGULFED BY MY THIRST FOR BLOOD.

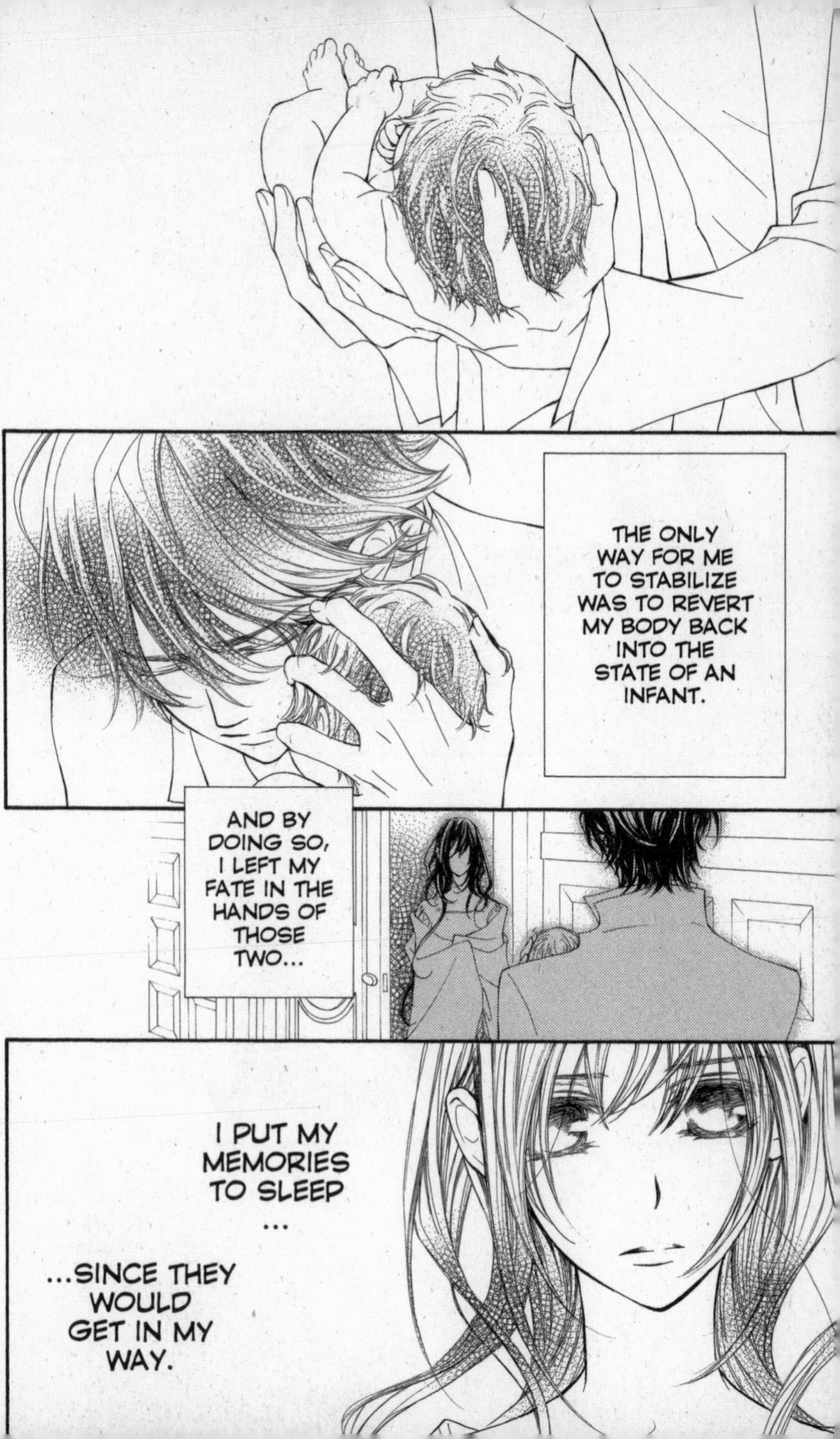
THE ONLY WAY FOR ME TO STABILIZE WAS TO REVERT MY BODY BACK INTO THE STATE OF AN INFANT.
AND BY DOING SO, I LEFT MY FATE IN THE HANDS OF THOSE TWO...
I PUT MY MEMORIES TO SLEEP ...
...SINCE THEY WOULD GET IN MY WAY.

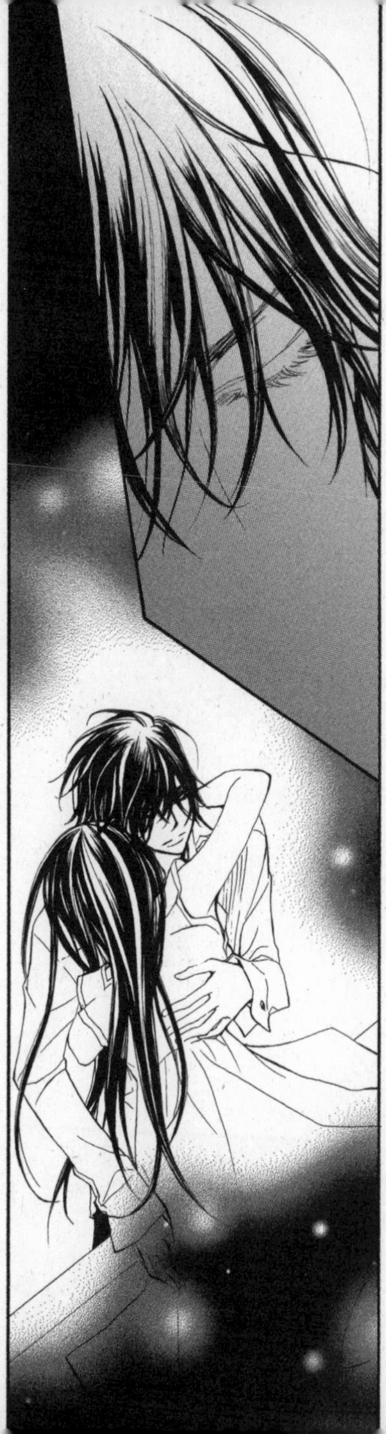

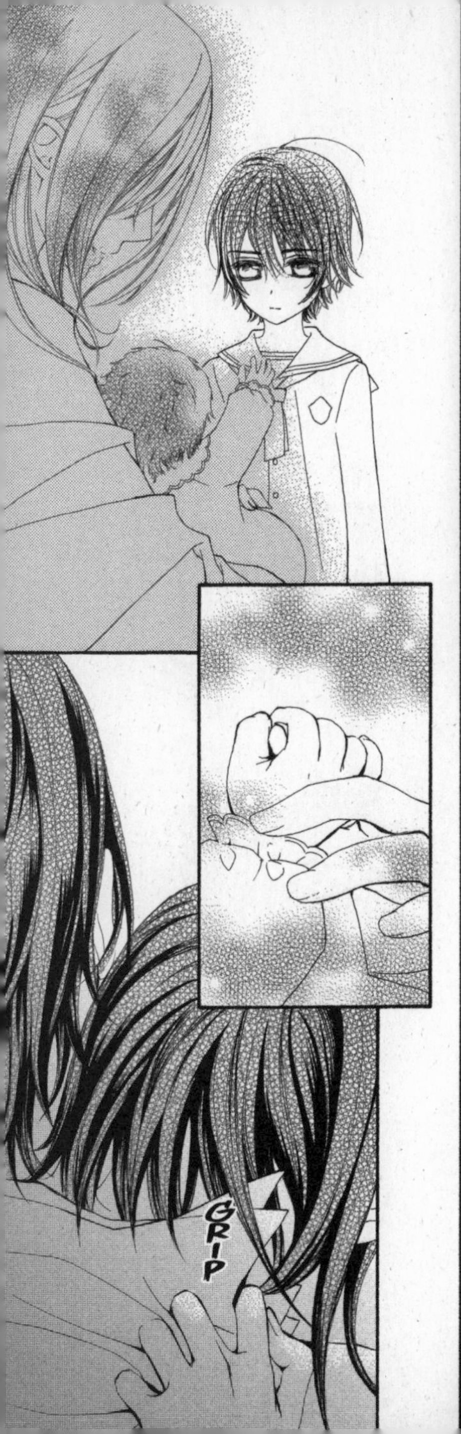
GRIP

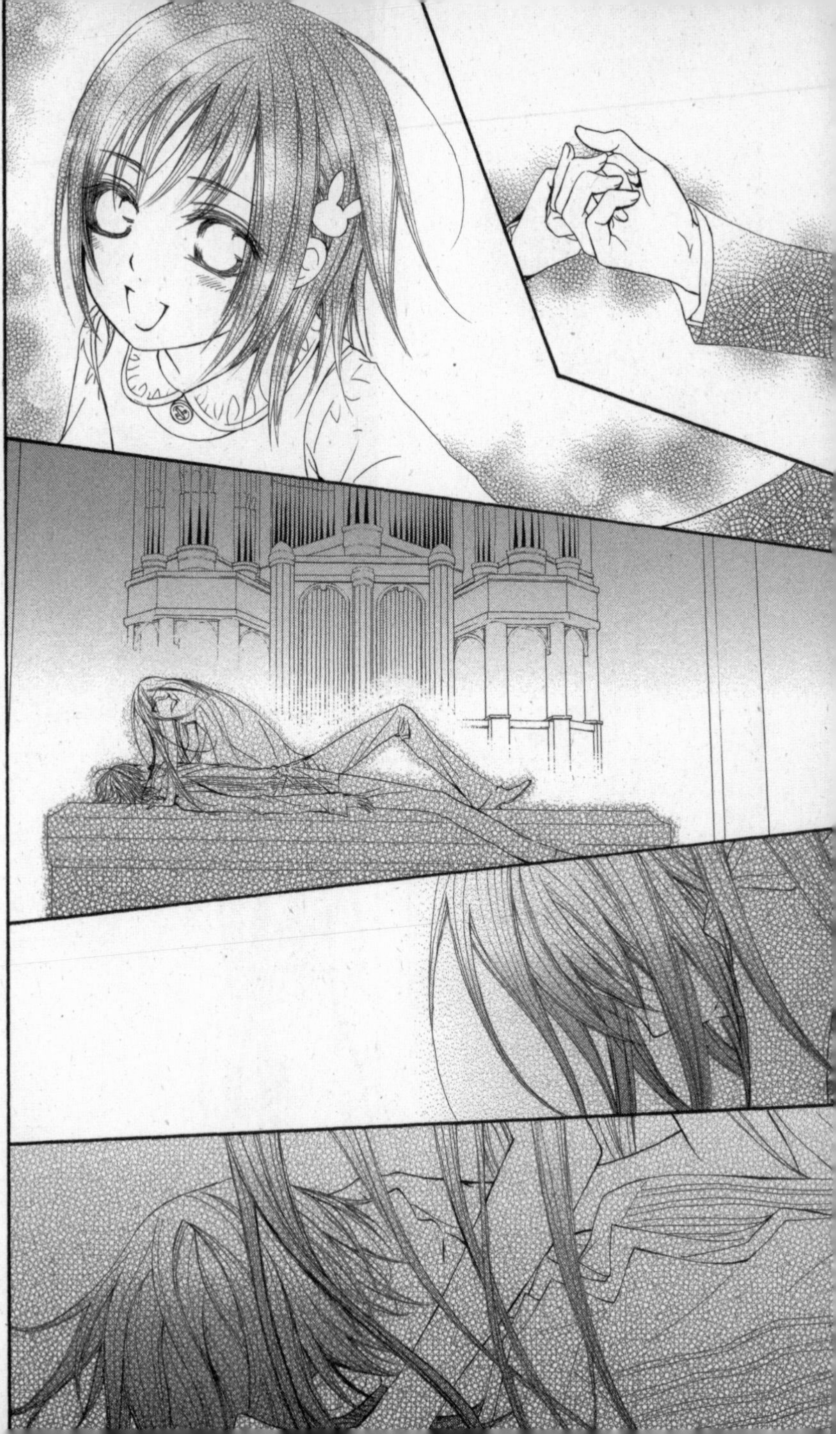

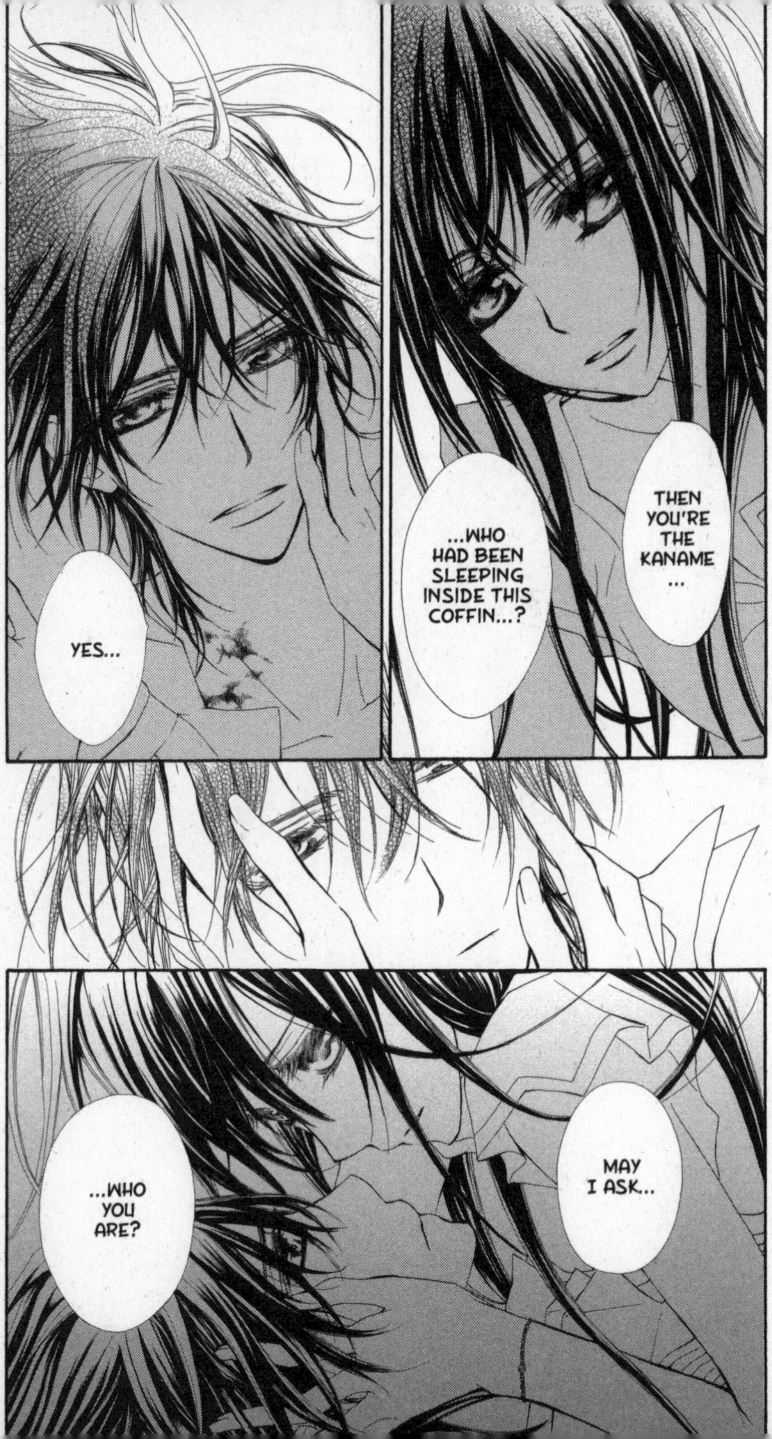
THEN YOU'RE THE KANAME ...
...WHO HAD BEEN SLEEPING INSIDE THIS COFFIN...?
YES...
MAY I ASK...
...WHO YOU ARE?

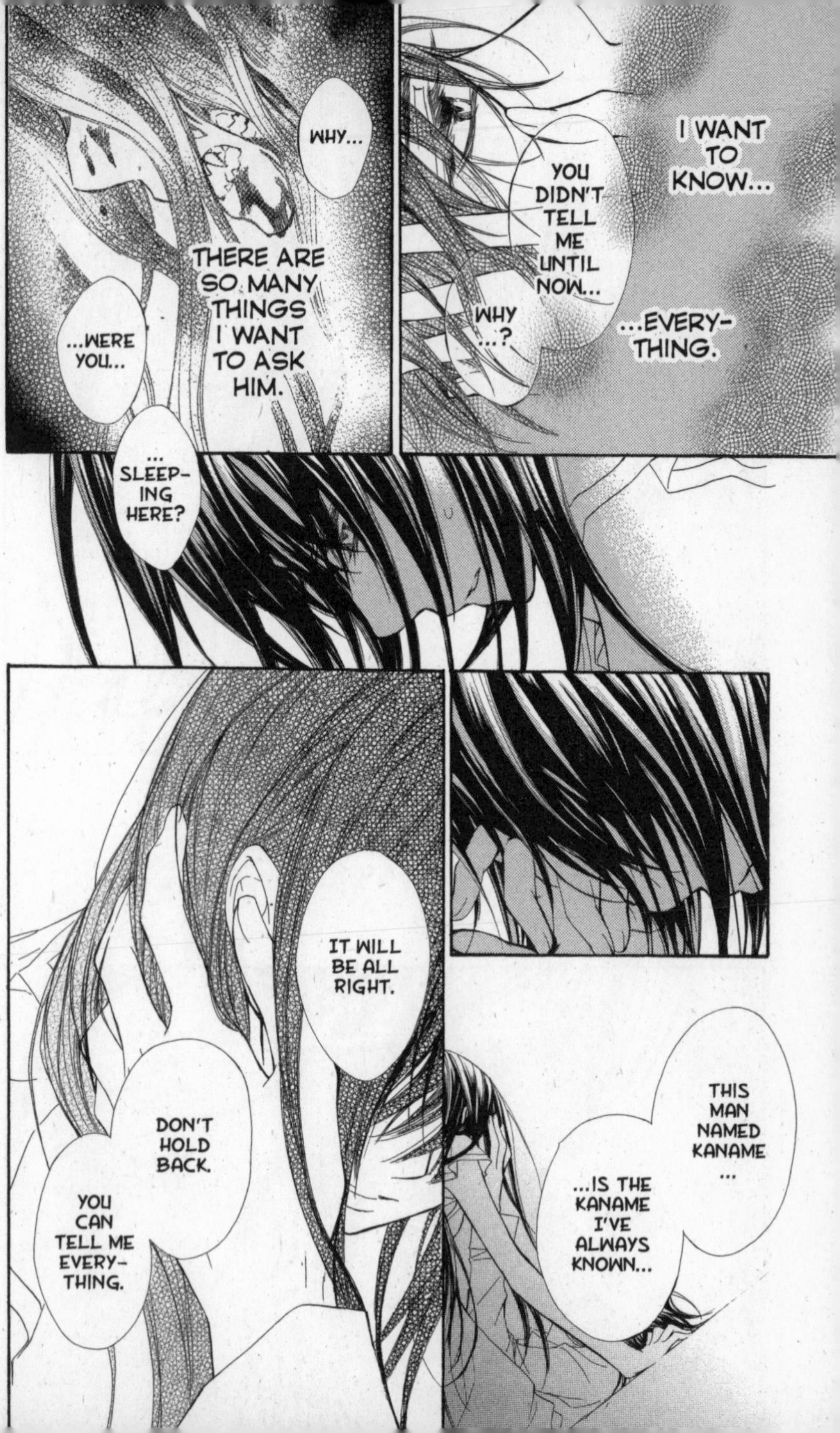
I WANT TO KNOW...
YOU DIDN'T TELL ME UNTIL NOW...
...EVERY-THING.
WHY ...?
WHY...
THERE ARE SO MANY THINGS I WANT TO ASK HIM.
...WERE YOU...
... SLEEP-ING HERE?
THIS MAN NAMED KANAME ...
...IS THE KANAME I'VE ALWAYS KNOWN...
IT WILL BE ALL RIGHT.
DON'T HOLD BACK.
YOU CAN TELL ME EVERY-THING.

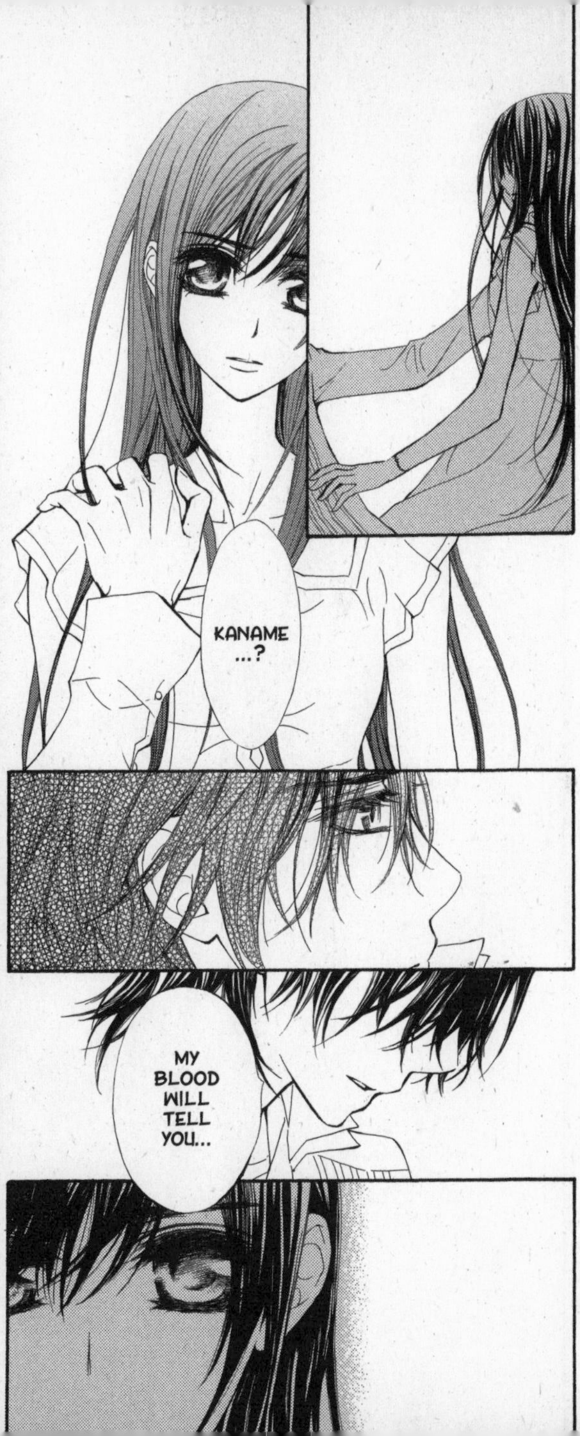
KANAME ...?
MY BLOOD WILL TELL YOU...

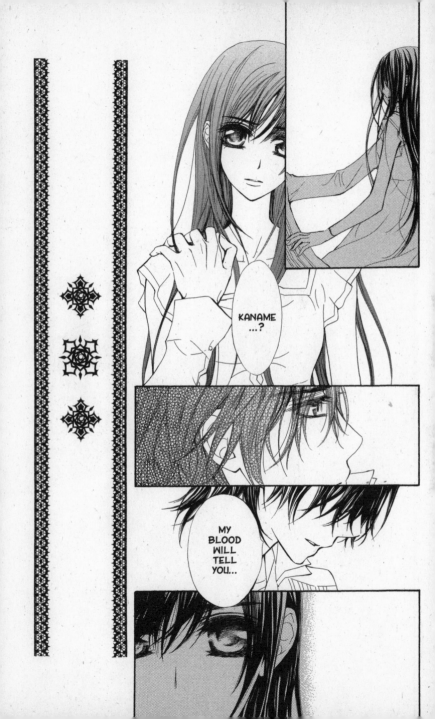

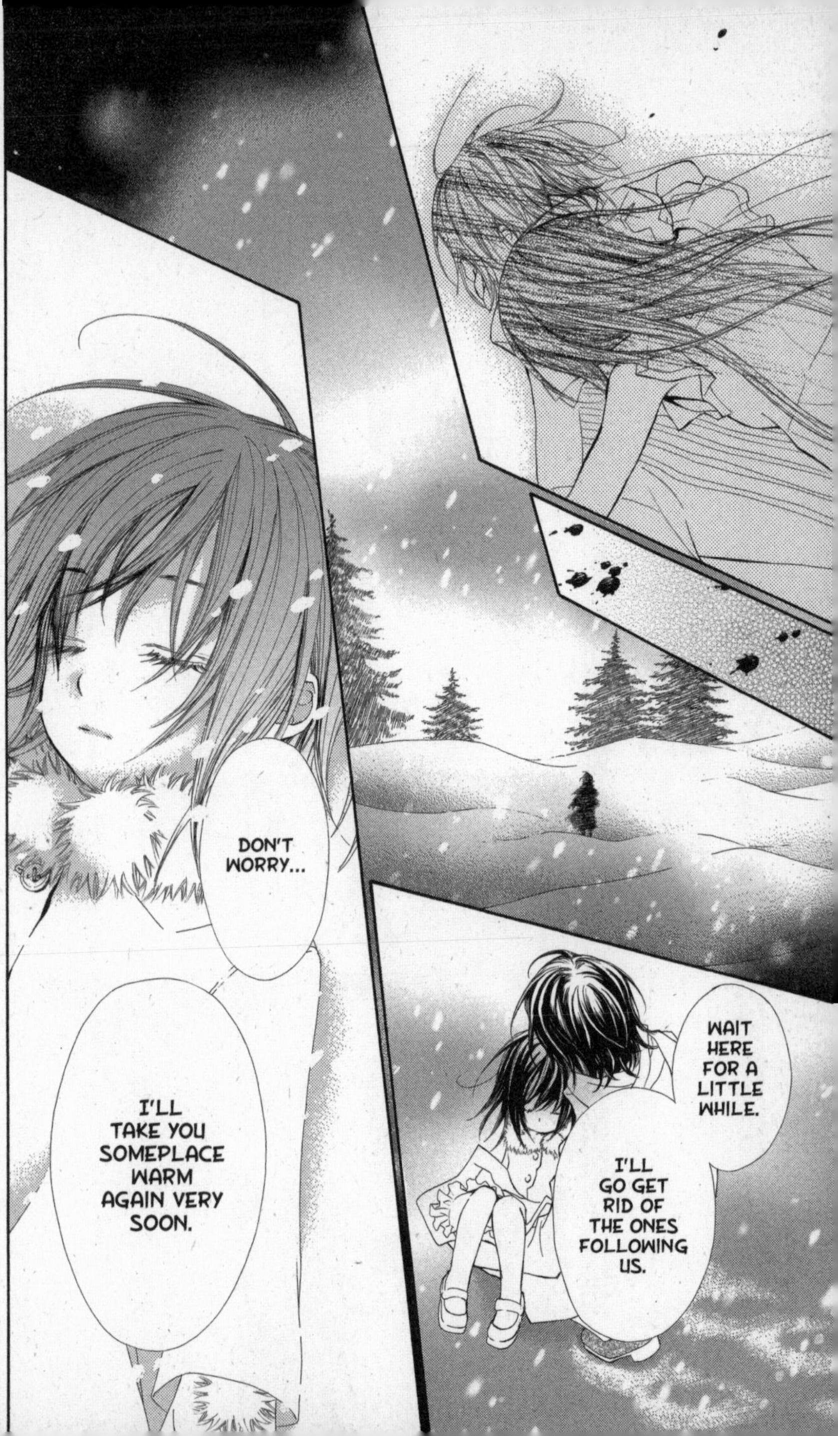
WAIT HERE FOR A LITTLE WHILE.
I'LL GO GET RID OF THE ONES FOLLOWING US.
DON'T WORRY...
I'LL TAKE YOU SOMEPLACE WARM AGAIN VERY SOON.

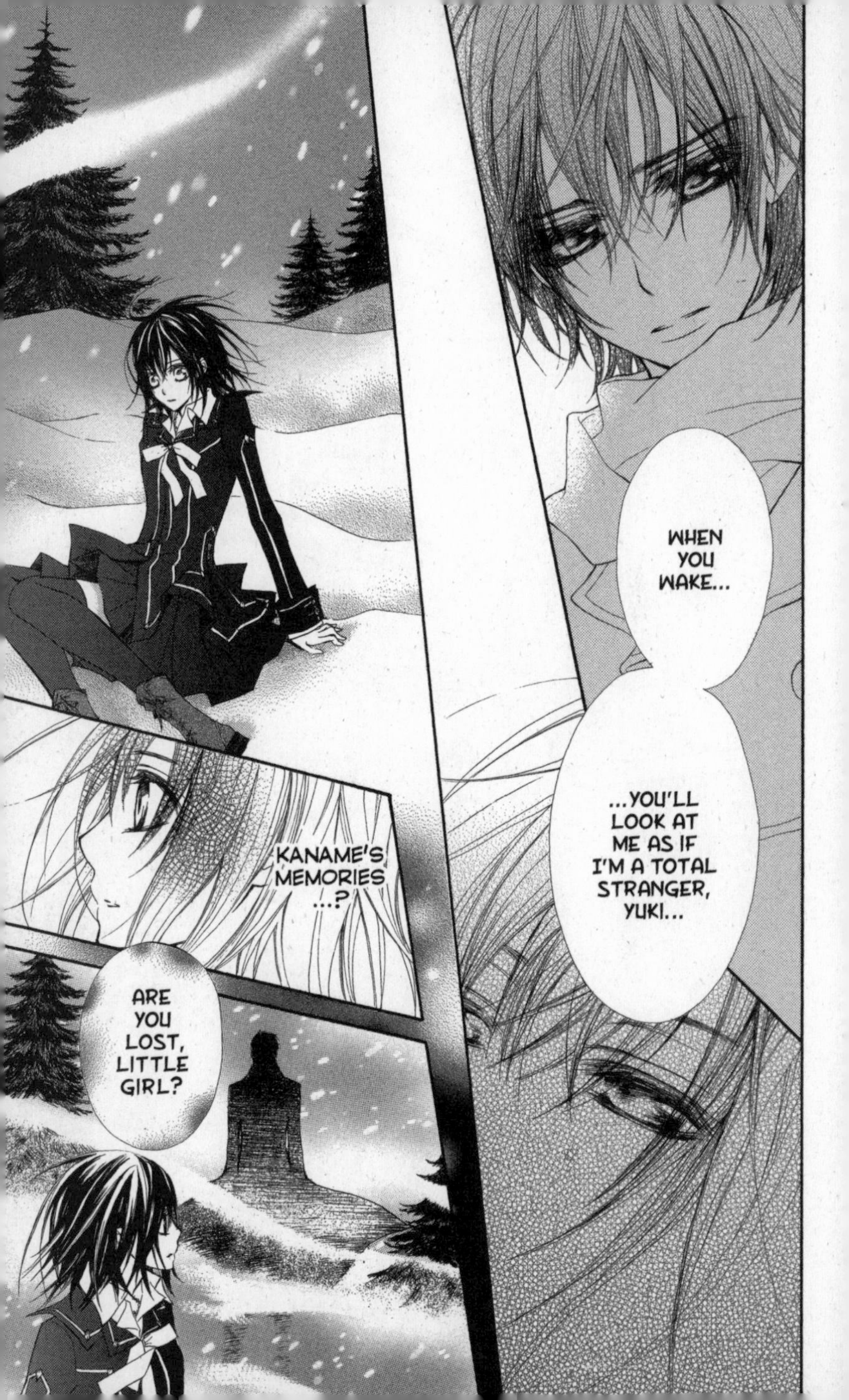
WHEN YOU WAKE...
...YOU'LL LOOK AT ME AS IF I'M A TOTAL STRANGER, YUKI...
KANAME'S MEMORIES ...?
ARE YOU LOST, LITTLE GIRL?

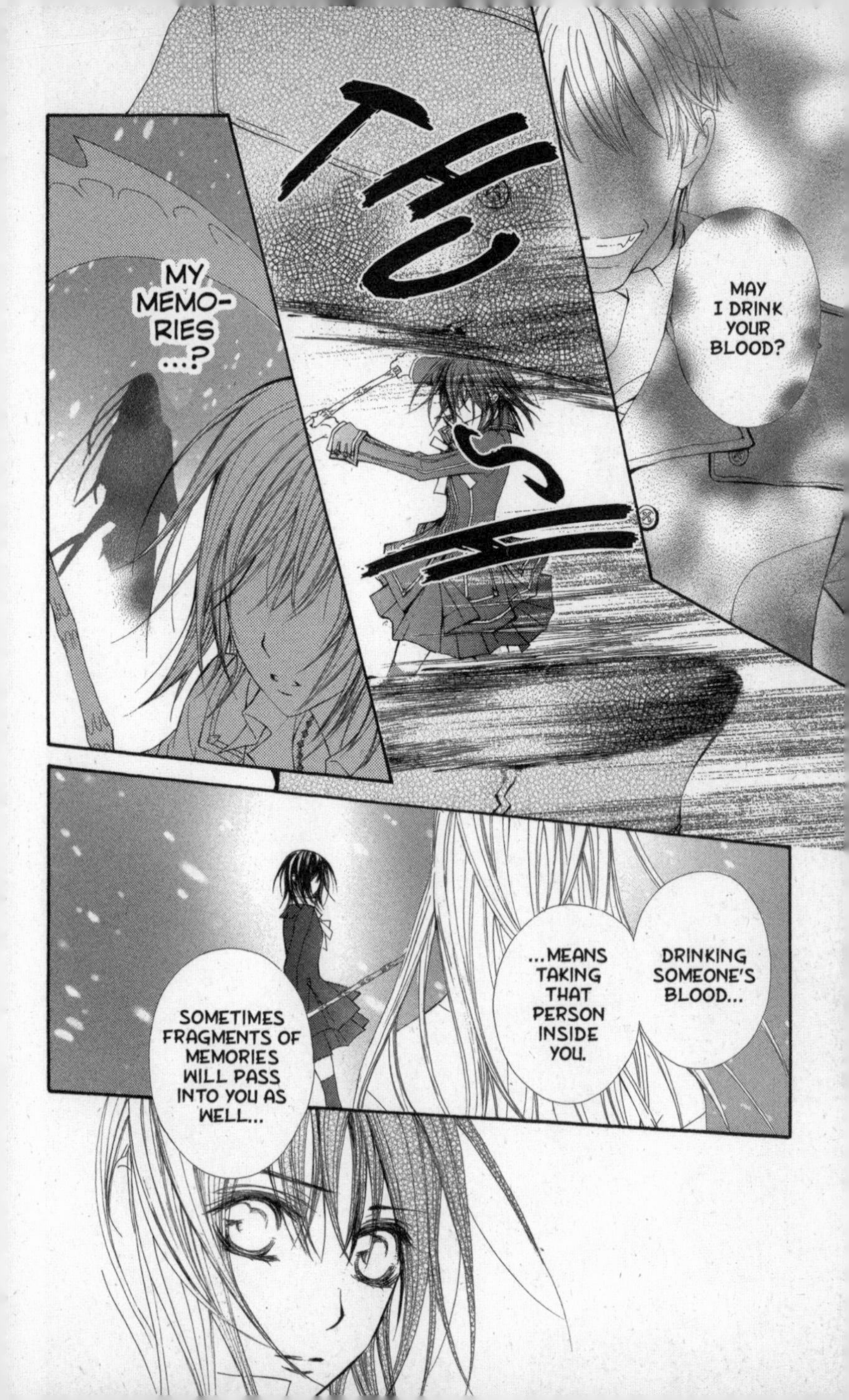
MAY I DRINK YOUR BLOOD?
THUSH
MY MEMO-RIES ...?
DRINKING SOMEONE'S BLOOD...
...MEANS TAKING THAT PERSON INSIDE YOU.
SOMETIMES FRAGMENTS OF MEMORIES WILL PASS INTO YOU AS WELL...

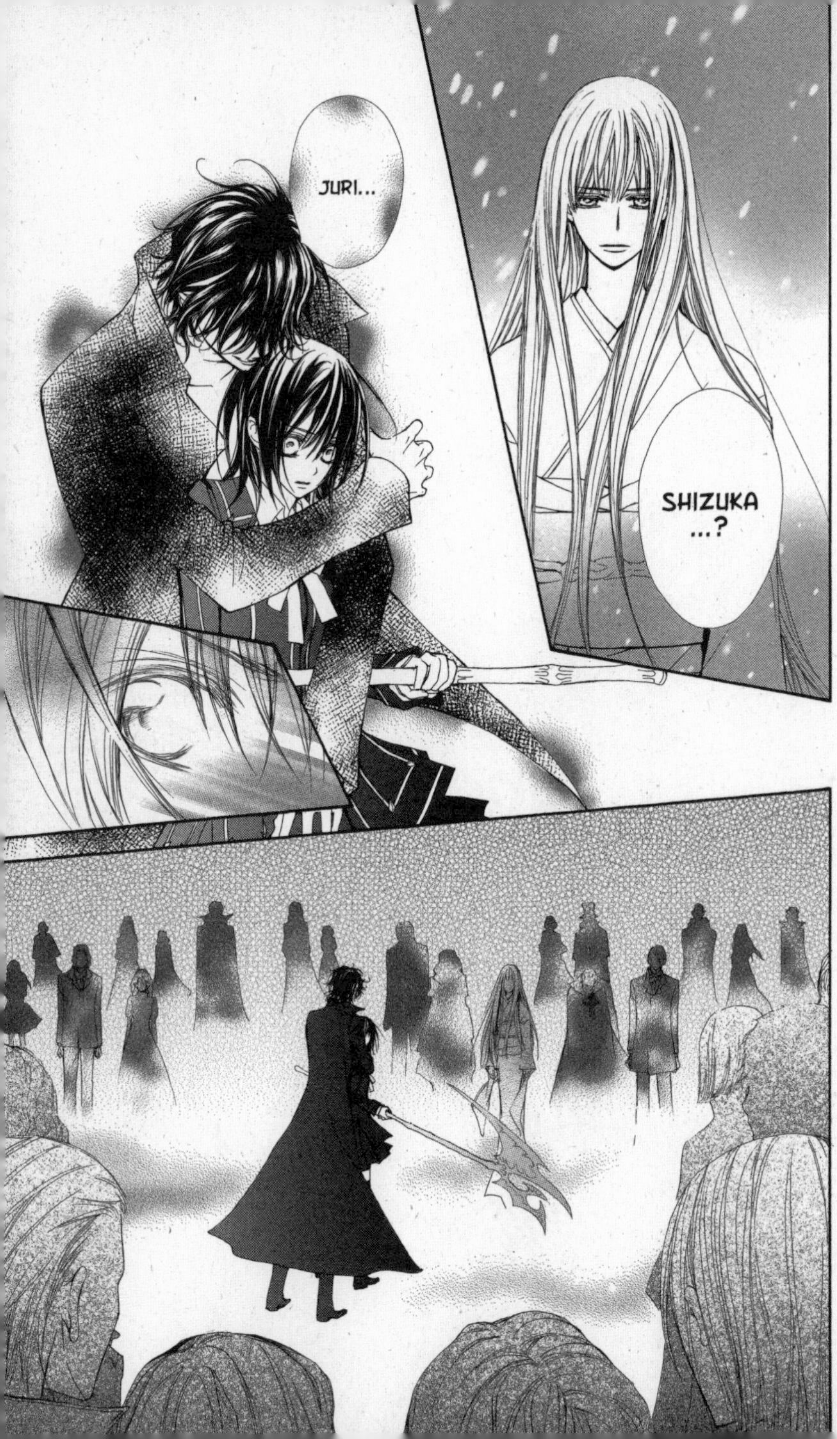
SHIZUKA ...?
JURI...

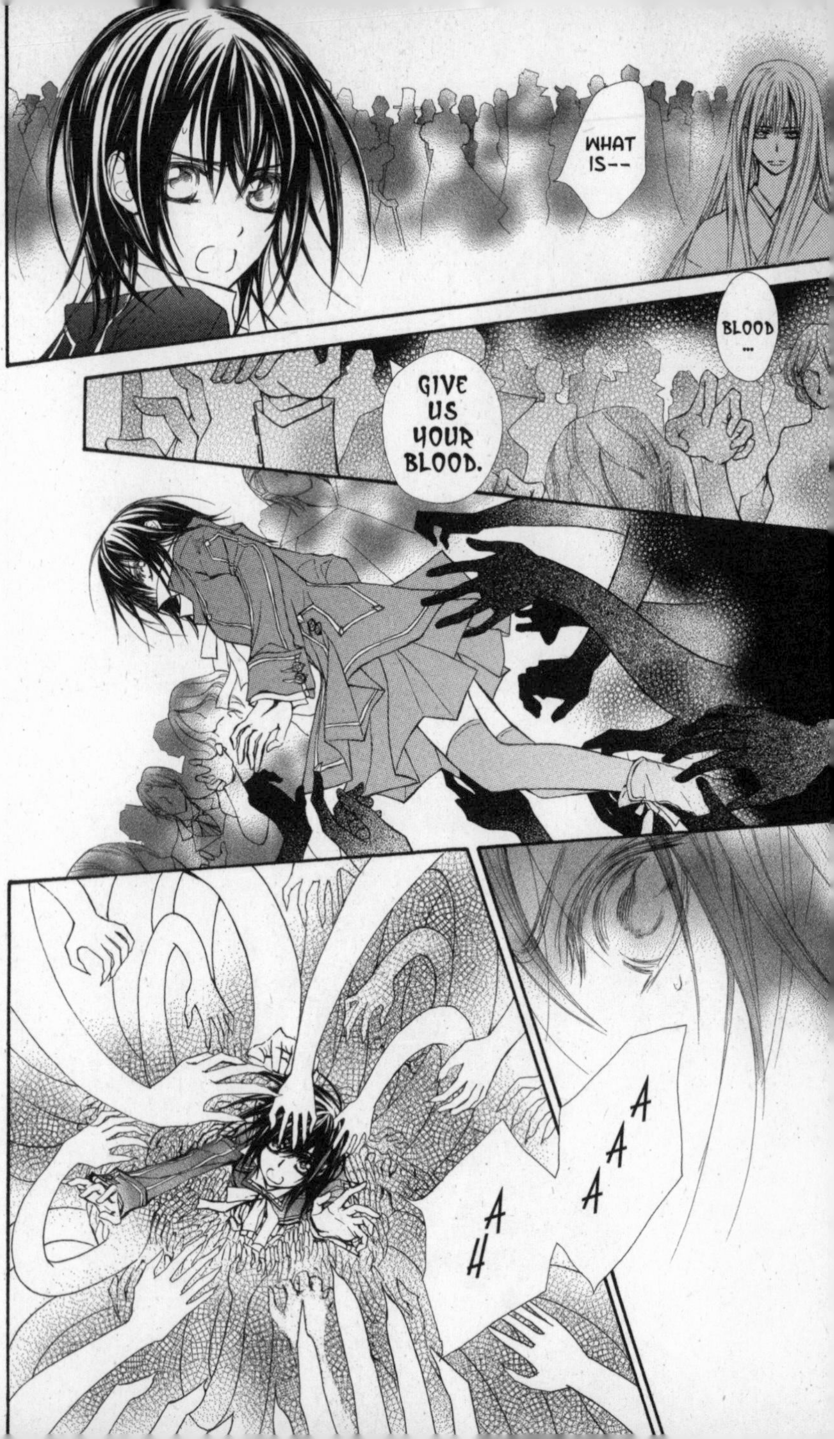
WHAT IS--
BLOOD...
GIVE US YOUR BLOOD.
AAAAH

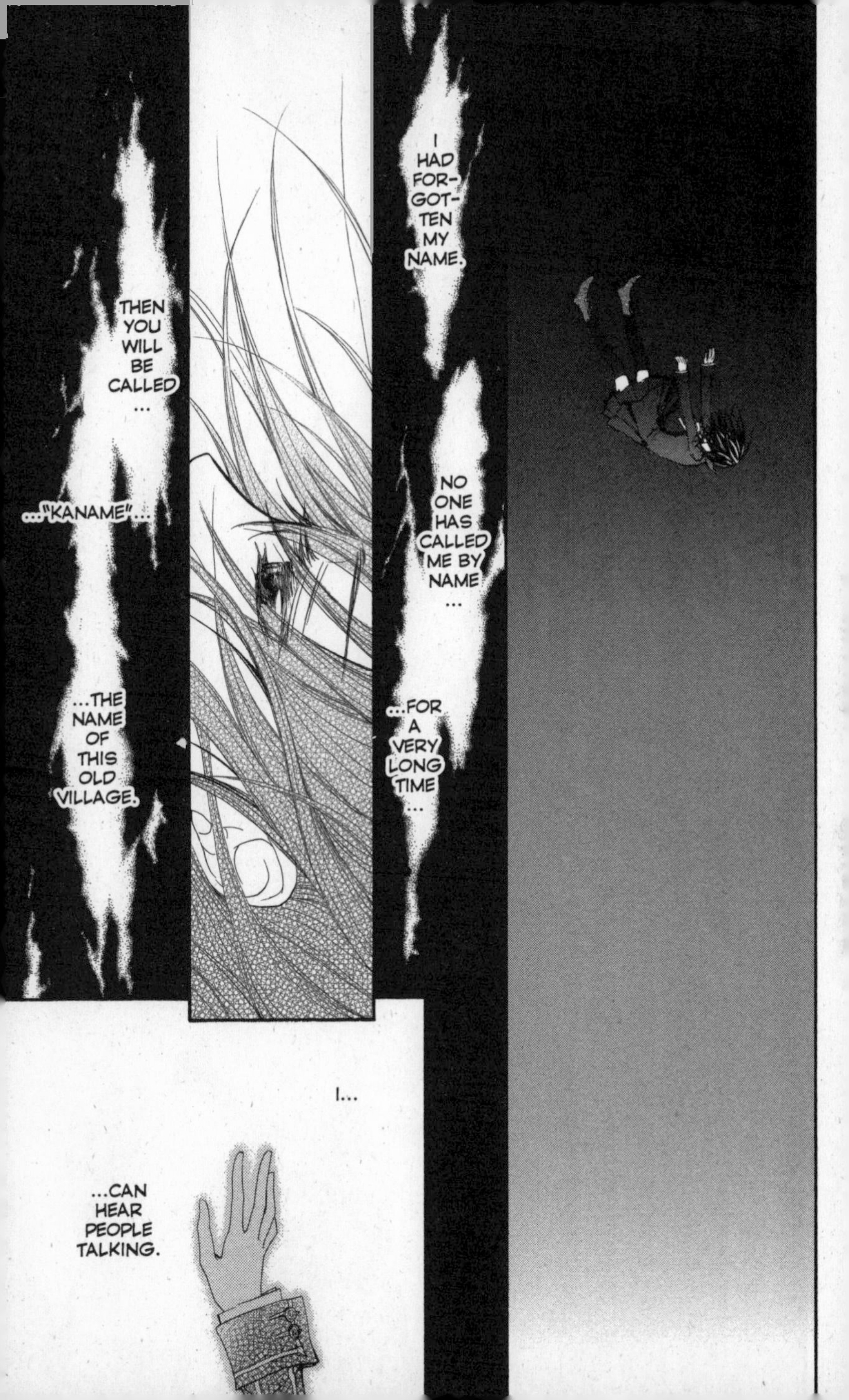
I HAD FOR-GOTTEN MY NAME.
NO ONE HAS CALLED ME BY NAME...
...FOR A VERY LONG TIME...
THEN YOU WILL BE CALLED...
..."KANAME"...
...THE NAME OF THIS OLD VILLAGE.
I...
...CAN HEAR PEOPLE TALKING.

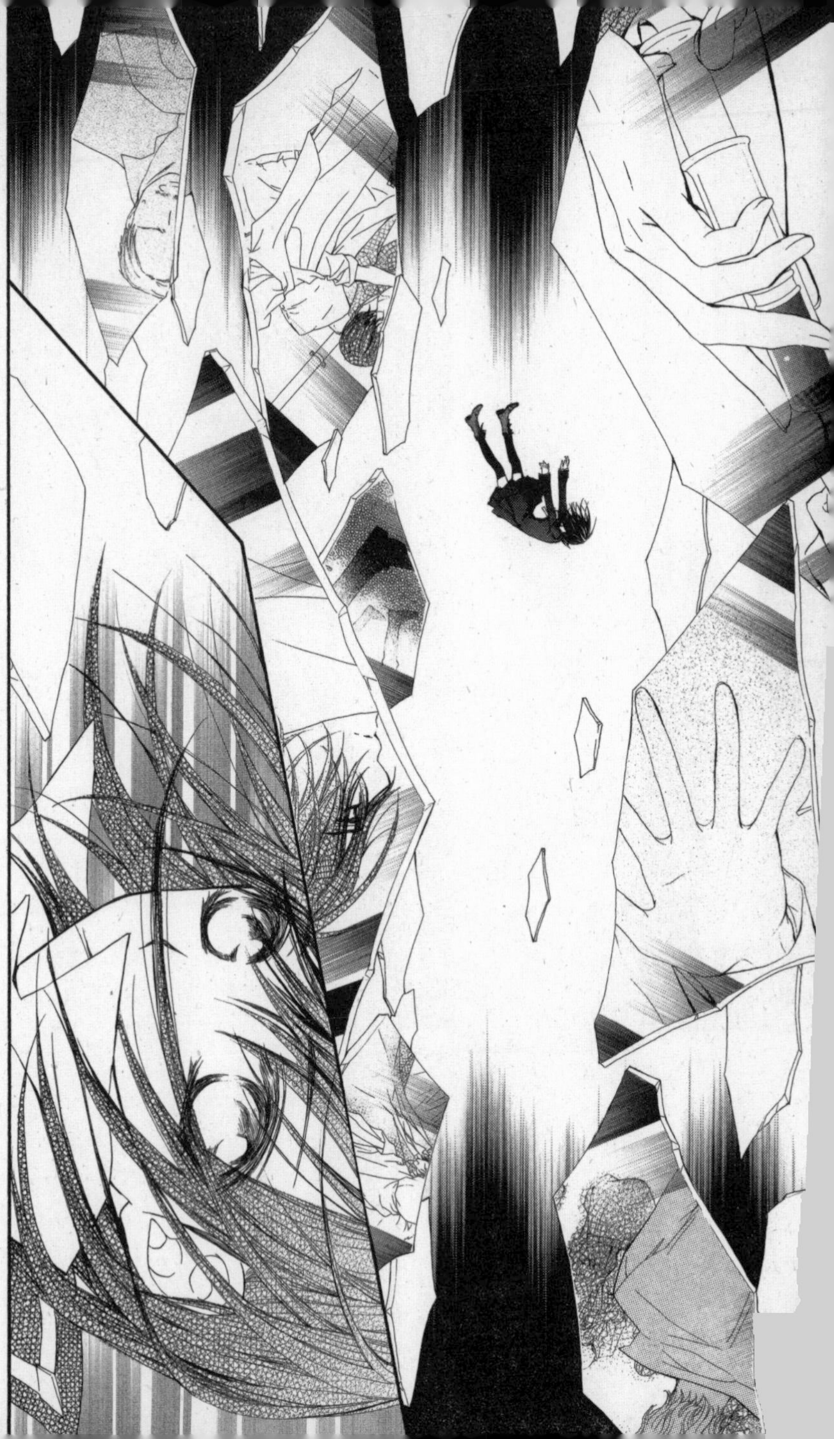

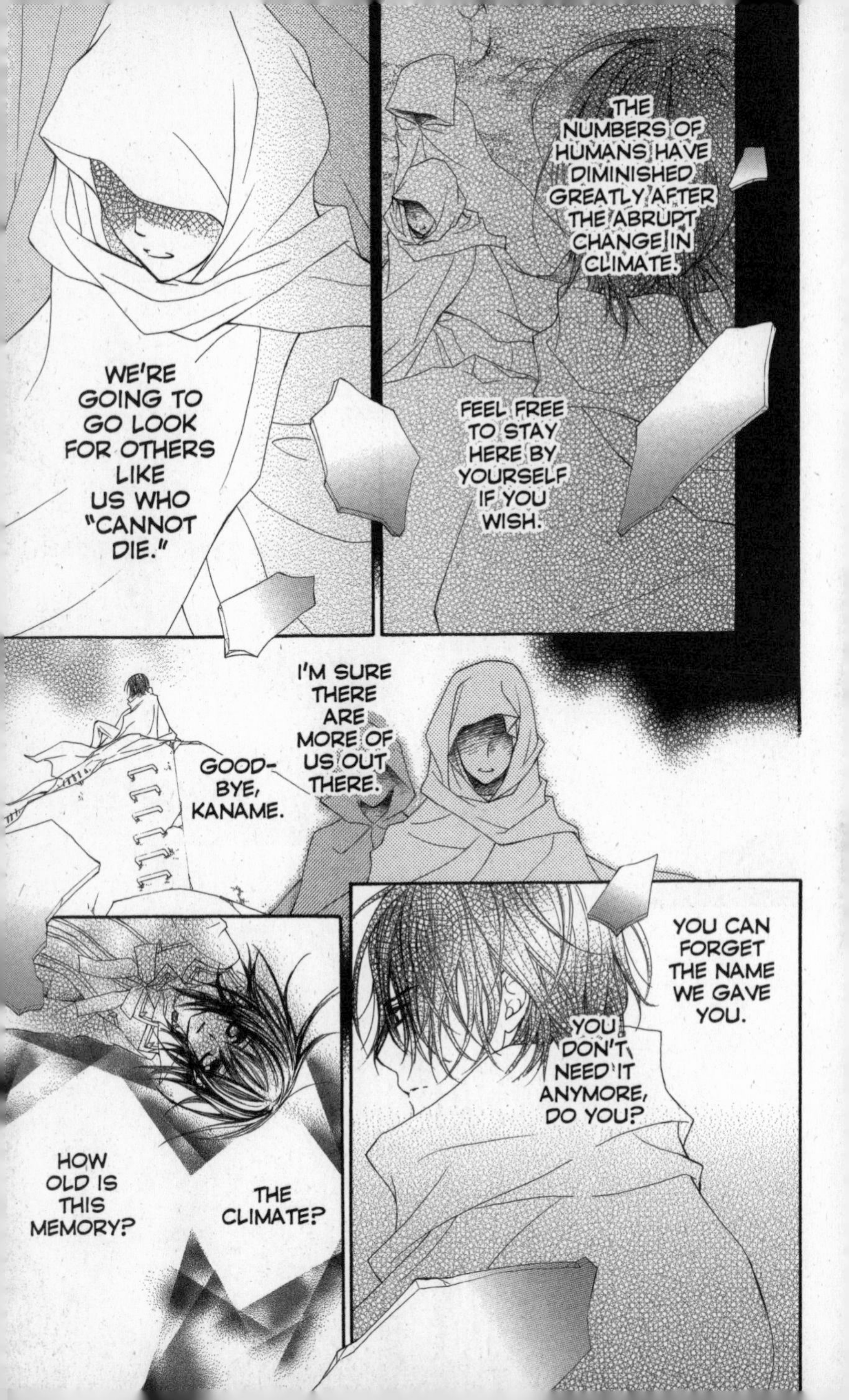
THE NUMBERS OF HUMANS HAVE DIMINISHED GREATLY AFTER THE ABRUPT CHANGE IN CLIMATE.
FEEL FREE TO STAY HERE BY YOURSELF IF YOU WISH.
WE'RE GOING TO GO LOOK FOR OTHERS LIKE US WHO "CANNOT DIE."
I'M SURE THERE ARE MORE OF US OUT THERE.
GOOD-BYE, KANAME.
YOU CAN FORGET THE NAME WE GAVE YOU.
YOU DON'T NEED IT ANYMORE, DO YOU?
HOW OLD IS THIS MEMORY?
THE CLIMATE?

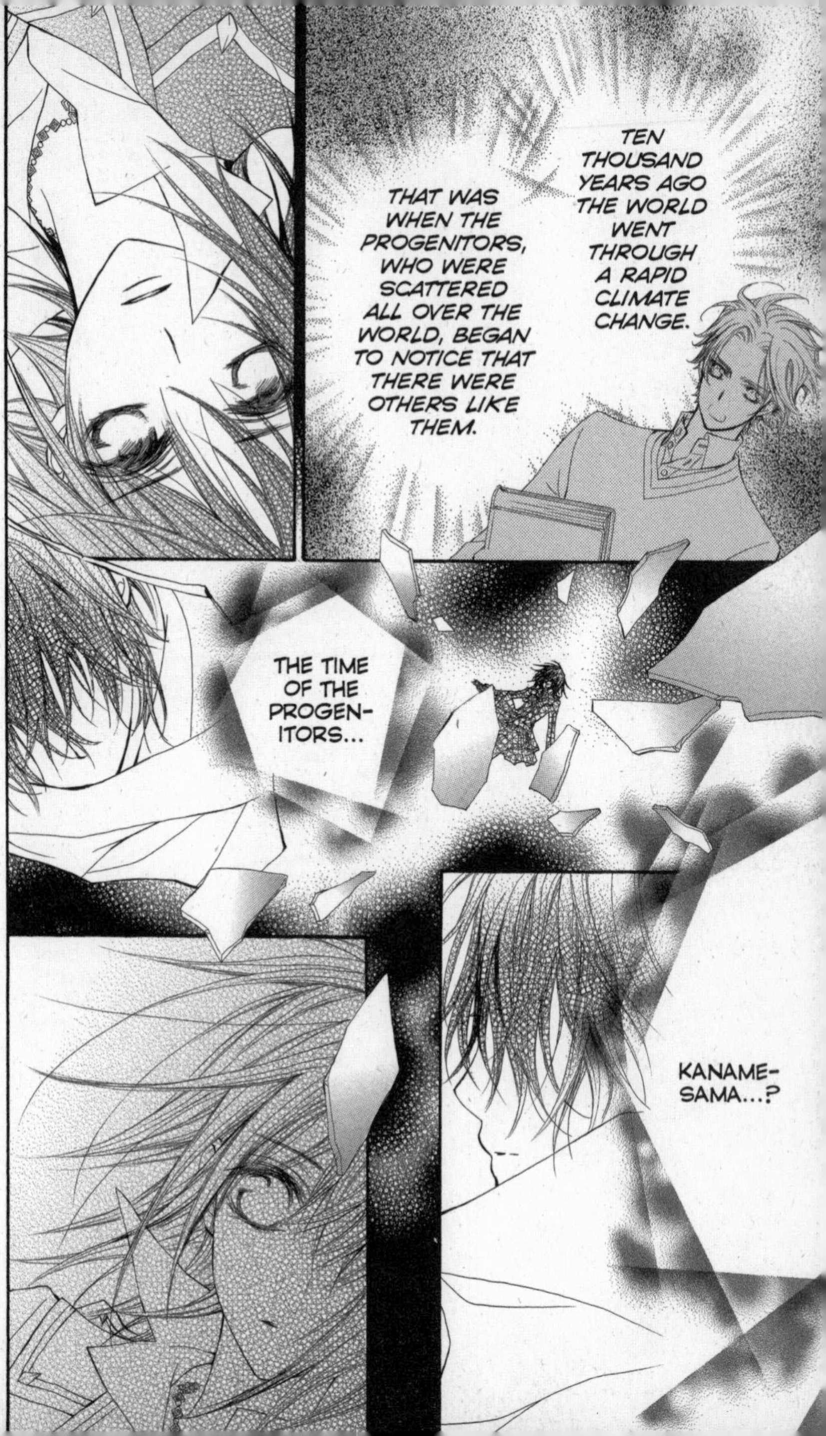
TEN THOUSAND YEARS AGO THE WORLD WENT THROUGH A RAPID CLIMATE CHANGE.
THAT WAS WHEN THE PROGENITORS, WHO WERE SCATTERED ALL OVER THE WORLD, BEGAN TO NOTICE THAT THERE WERE OTHERS LIKE THEM.
THE TIME OF THE PROGEN-ITORS...
KANAME-SAMA...?

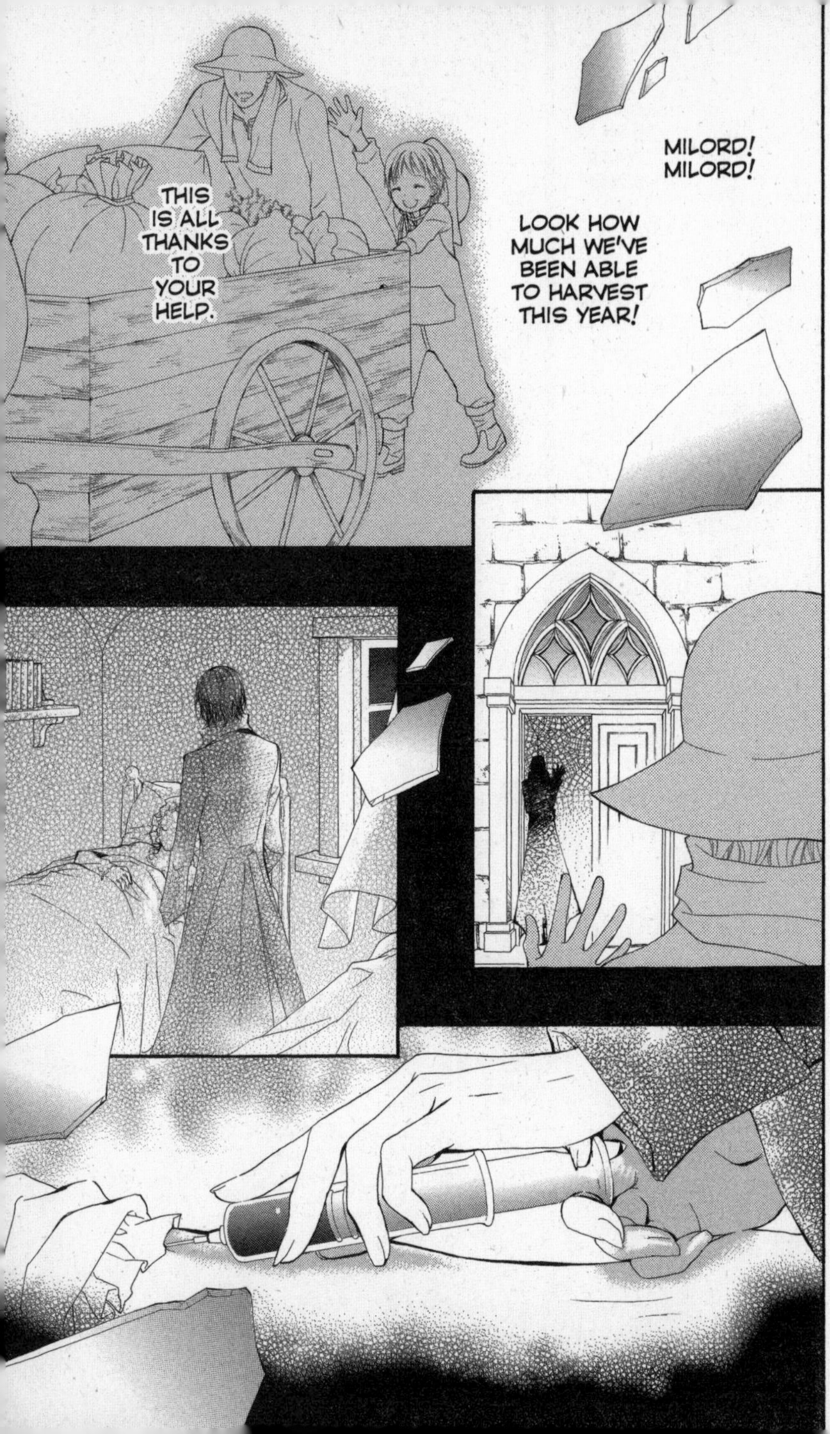
MILORD! MILORD!
LOOK HOW MUCH WE'VE BEEN ABLE TO HARVEST THIS YEAR!
THIS IS ALL THANKS TO YOUR HELP.

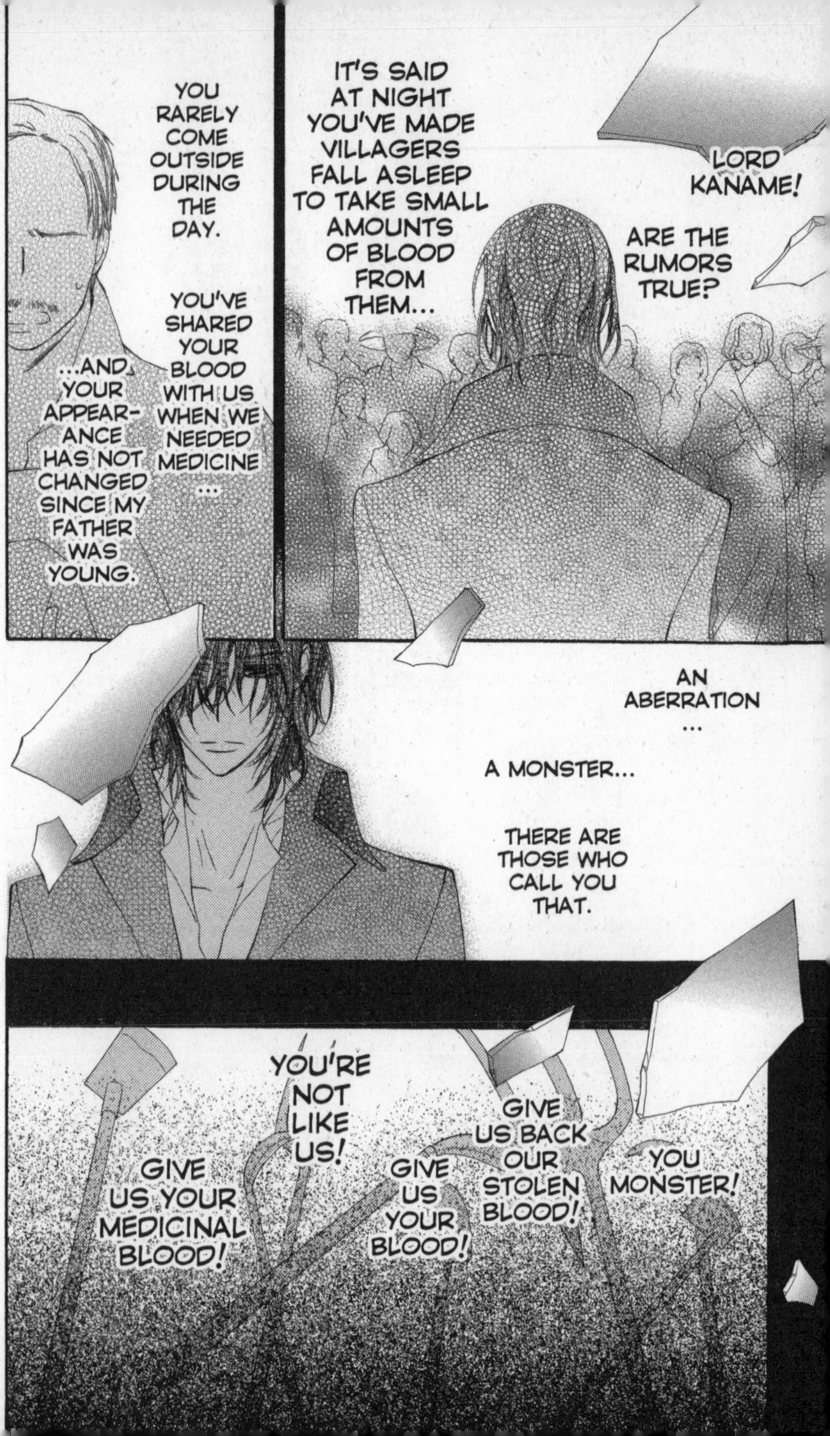
LORD KANAME!
ARE THE RUMORS TRUE?
IT'S SAID AT NIGHT YOU'VE MADE VILLAGERS FALL ASLEEP TO TAKE SMALL AMOUNTS OF BLOOD FROM THEM...
YOU RARELY COME OUTSIDE DURING THE DAY.
YOU'VE SHARED YOUR BLOOD WITH US WHEN WE NEEDED MEDICINE...
...AND YOUR APPEAR-ANCE HAS NOT CHANGED SINCE MY FATHER WAS YOUNG.
AN ABERRATION...
A MONSTER...
THERE ARE THOSE WHO CALL YOU THAT.
YOU MONSTER!
GIVE US BACK OUR STOLEN BLOOD!
GIVE US YOUR BLOOD!
YOU'RE NOT LIKE US!
GIVE US YOUR MEDICINAL BLOOD!

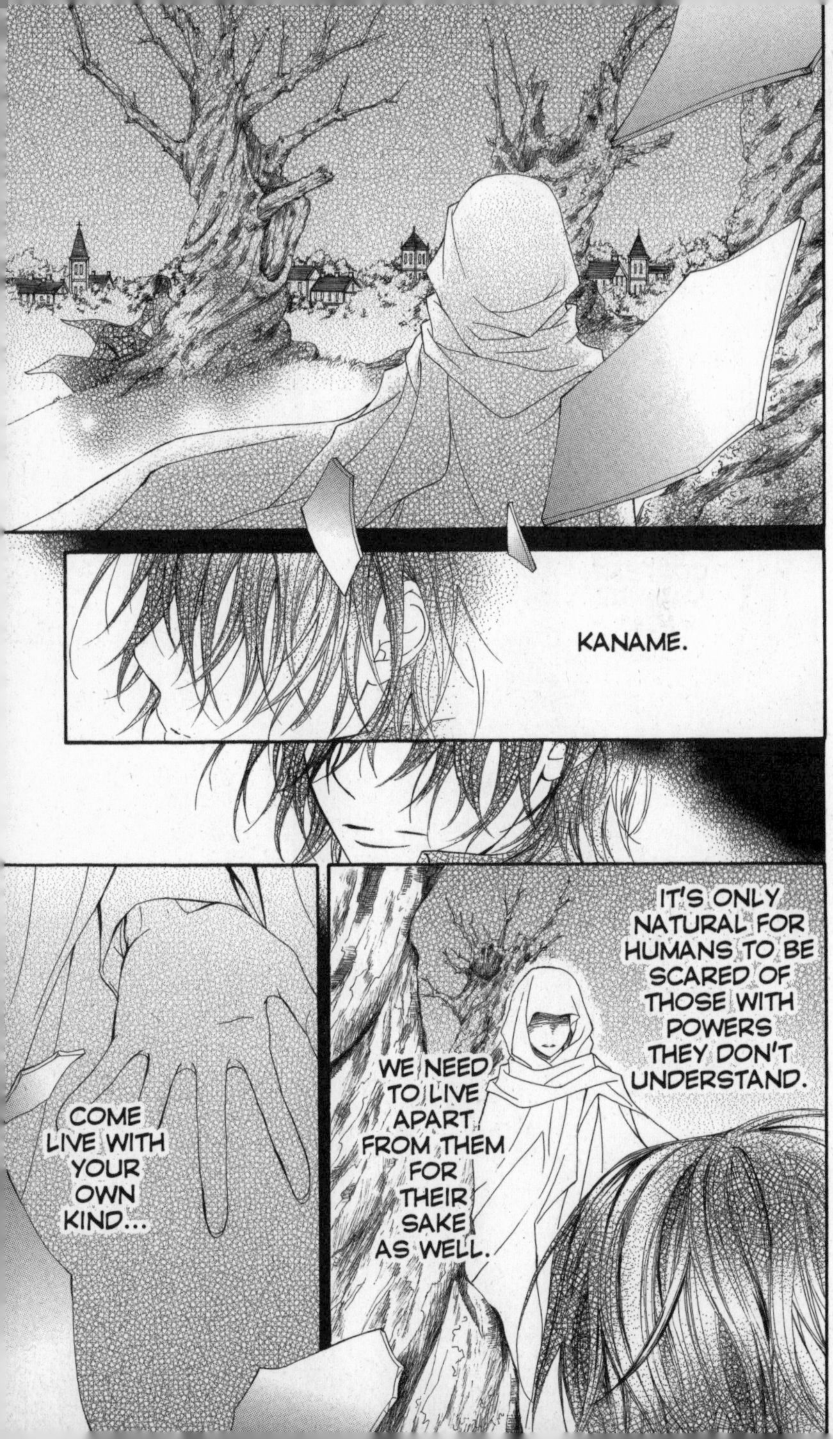
KANAME.
IT'S ONLY NATURAL FOR HUMANS TO BE SCARED OF THOSE WITH POWERS THEY DON'T UNDERSTAND.
WE NEED TO LIVE APART FROM THEM FOR THEIR SAKE AS WELL.
COME LIVE WITH YOUR OWN KIND...

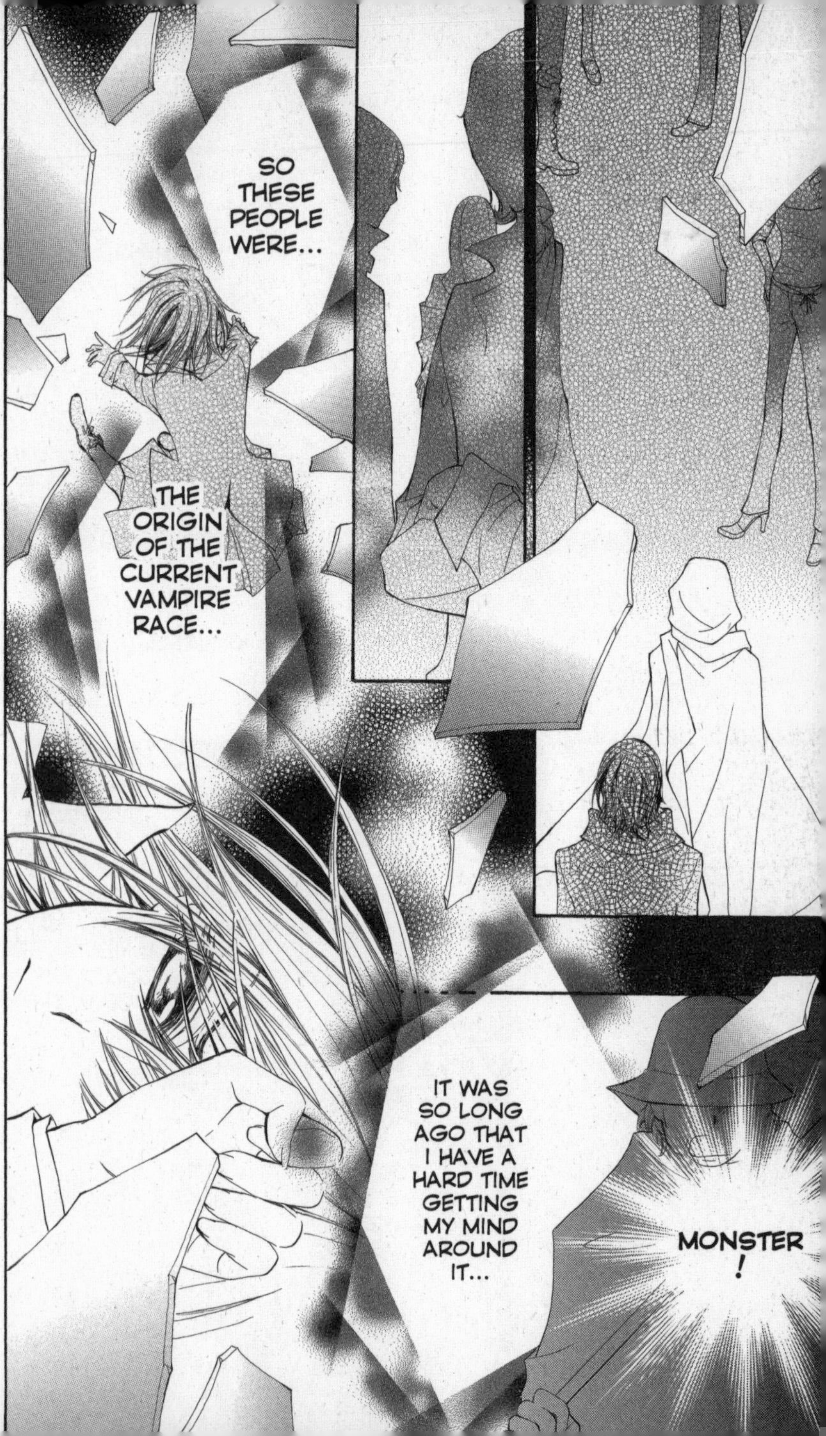
SO THESE PEOPLE WERE...
THE ORIGIN OF THE CURRENT VAMPIRE RACE...
IT WAS SO LONG AGO THAT I HAVE A HARD TIME GETTING MY MIND AROUND IT...
MONSTER!

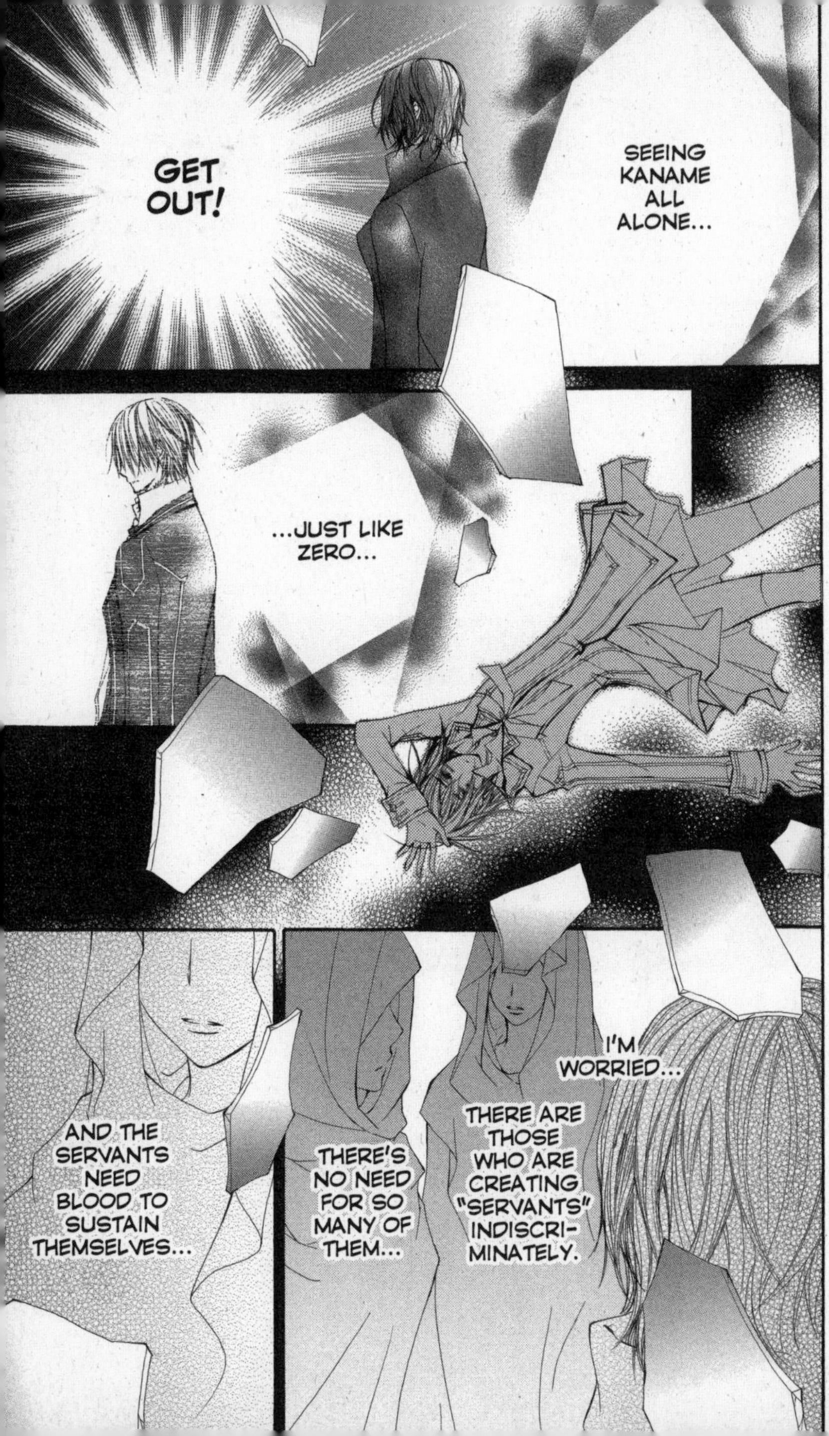
SEEING KANAME ALL ALONE...
GET OUT!
...JUST LIKE ZERO...
I'M WORRIED...
THERE ARE THOSE WHO ARE CREATING "SERVANTS" INDISCRIMINATELY.
THERE'S NO NEED FOR SO MANY OF THEM...
AND THE SERVANTS NEED BLOOD TO SUSTAIN THEMSELVES...

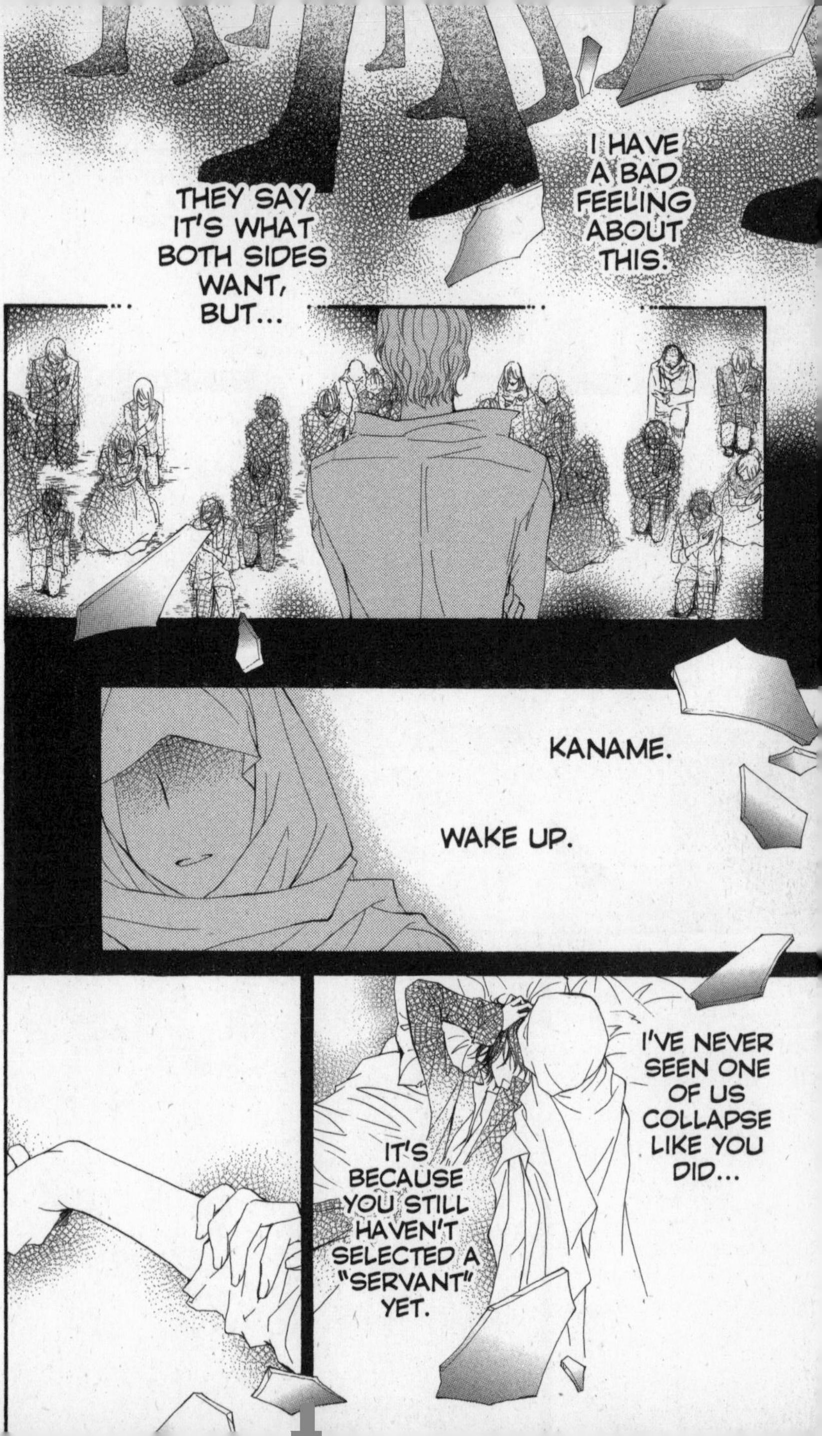
I HAVE A BAD FEELING ABOUT THIS.
THEY SAY IT'S WHAT BOTH SIDES WANT, BUT...
KANAME.
WAKE UP.
I'VE NEVER SEEN ONE OF US COLLAPSE LIKE YOU DID...
IT'S BECAUSE YOU STILL HAVEN'T SELECTED A "SERVANT" YET.

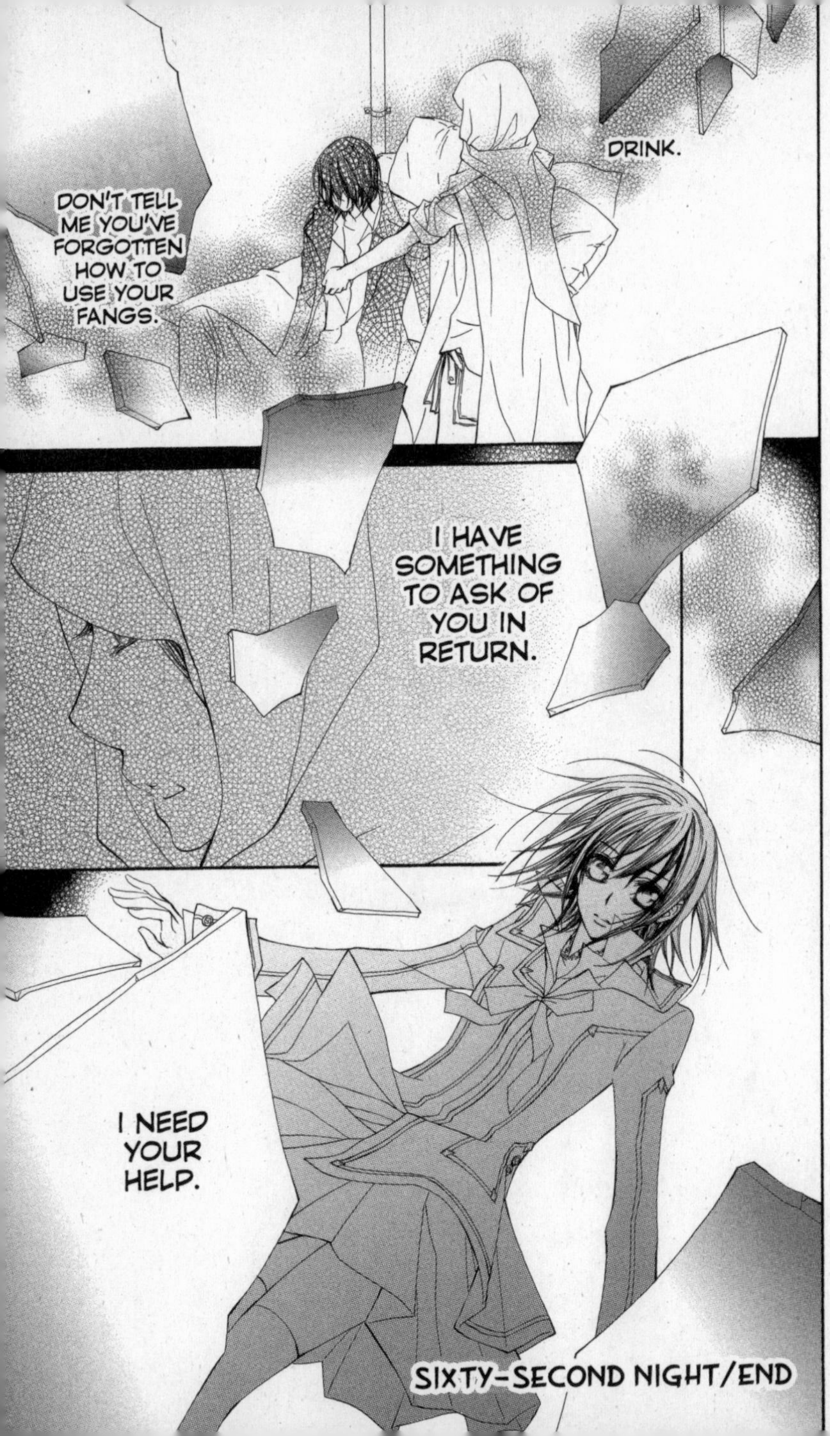
DRINK.
DON'T TELL ME YOU'VE FORGOTTEN HOW TO USE YOUR FANGS.
I HAVE SOMETHING TO ASK OF YOU IN RETURN.
I NEED YOUR HELP.
SIXTY-SECOND NIGHT/END

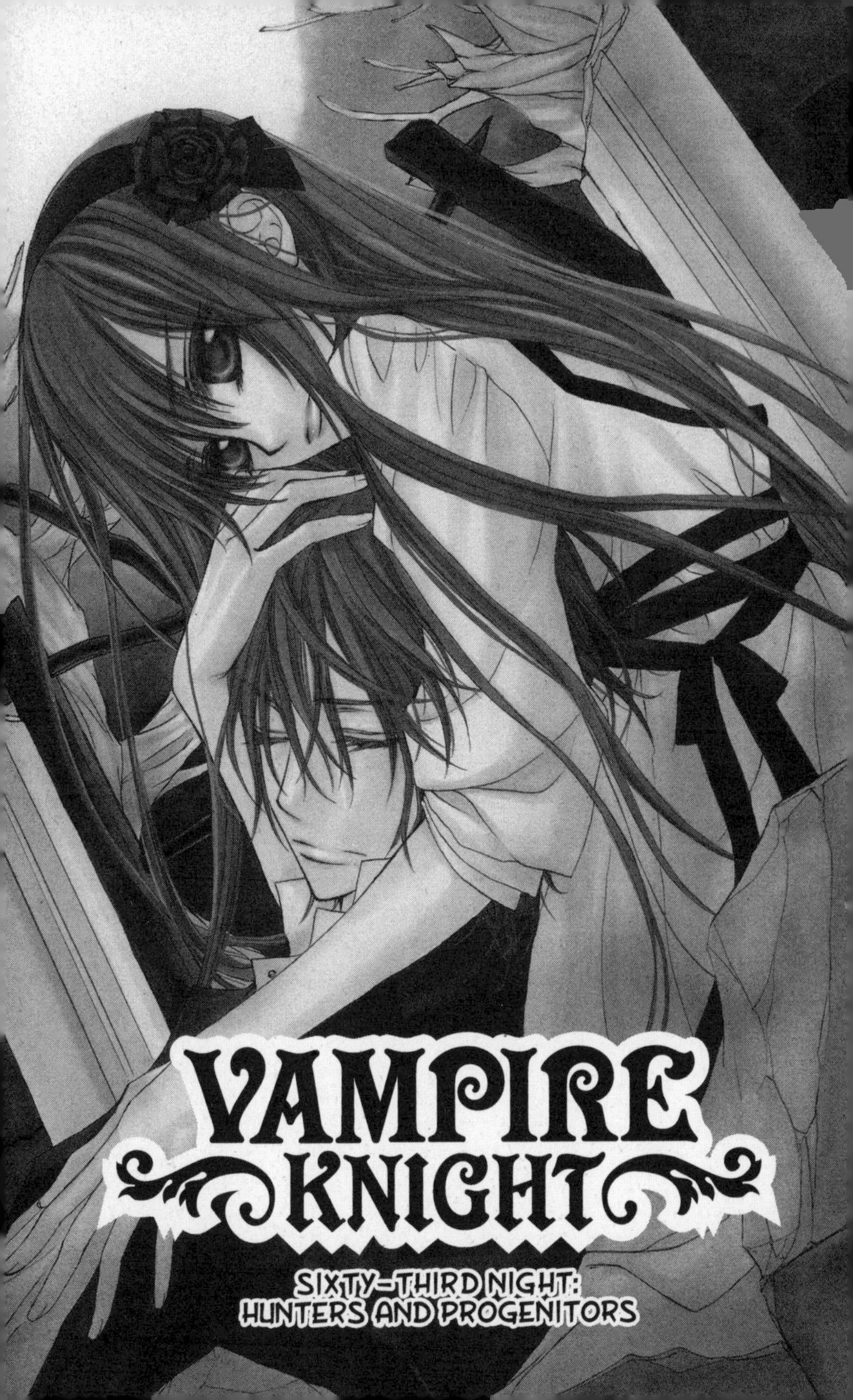
VAMPIRE KNIGHT
SIXTY-THIRD NIGHT:
HUNTERS AND PROGENITORS

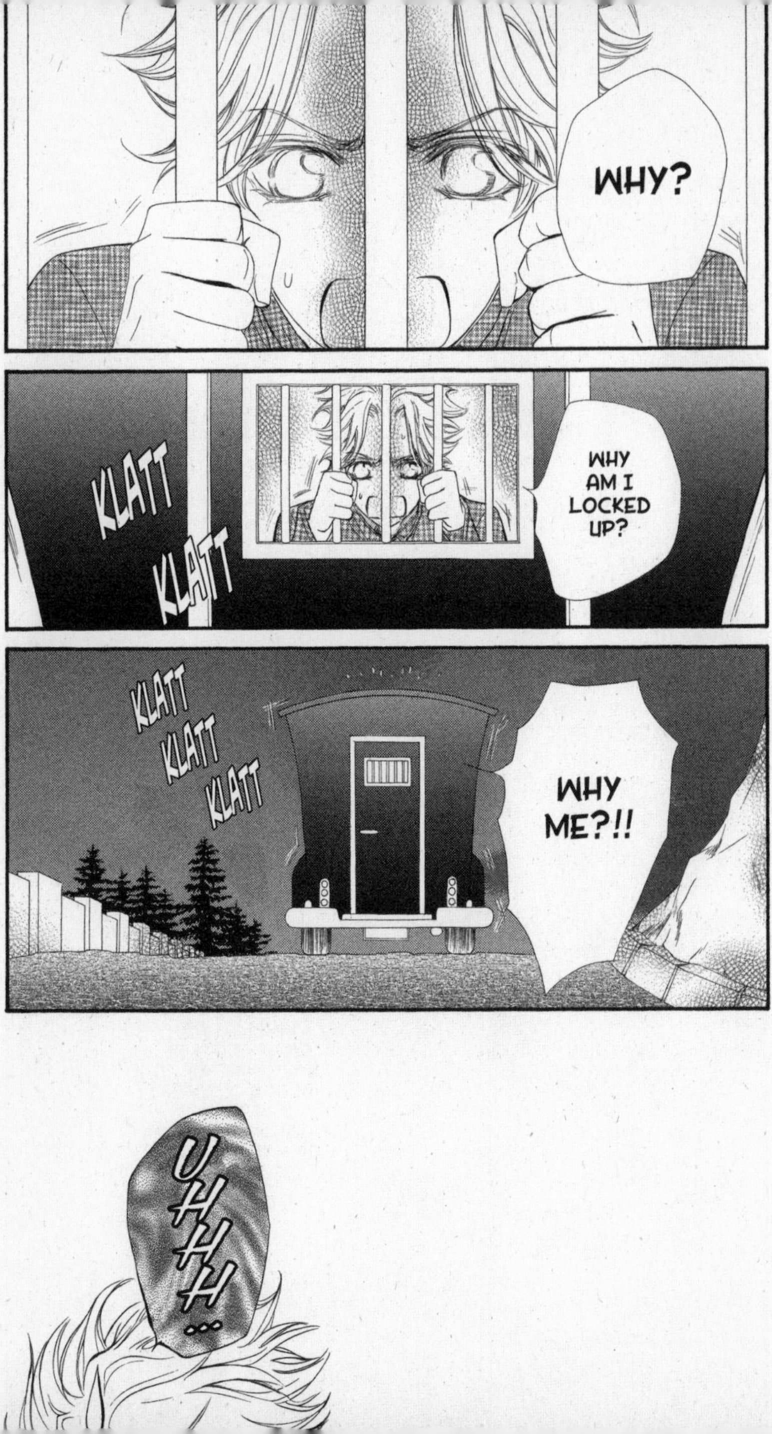
WHY?
WHY AM I LOCKED UP?
KLATT KLATT
WHY ME?!!
KLATT KLATT KLATT
UHHH..

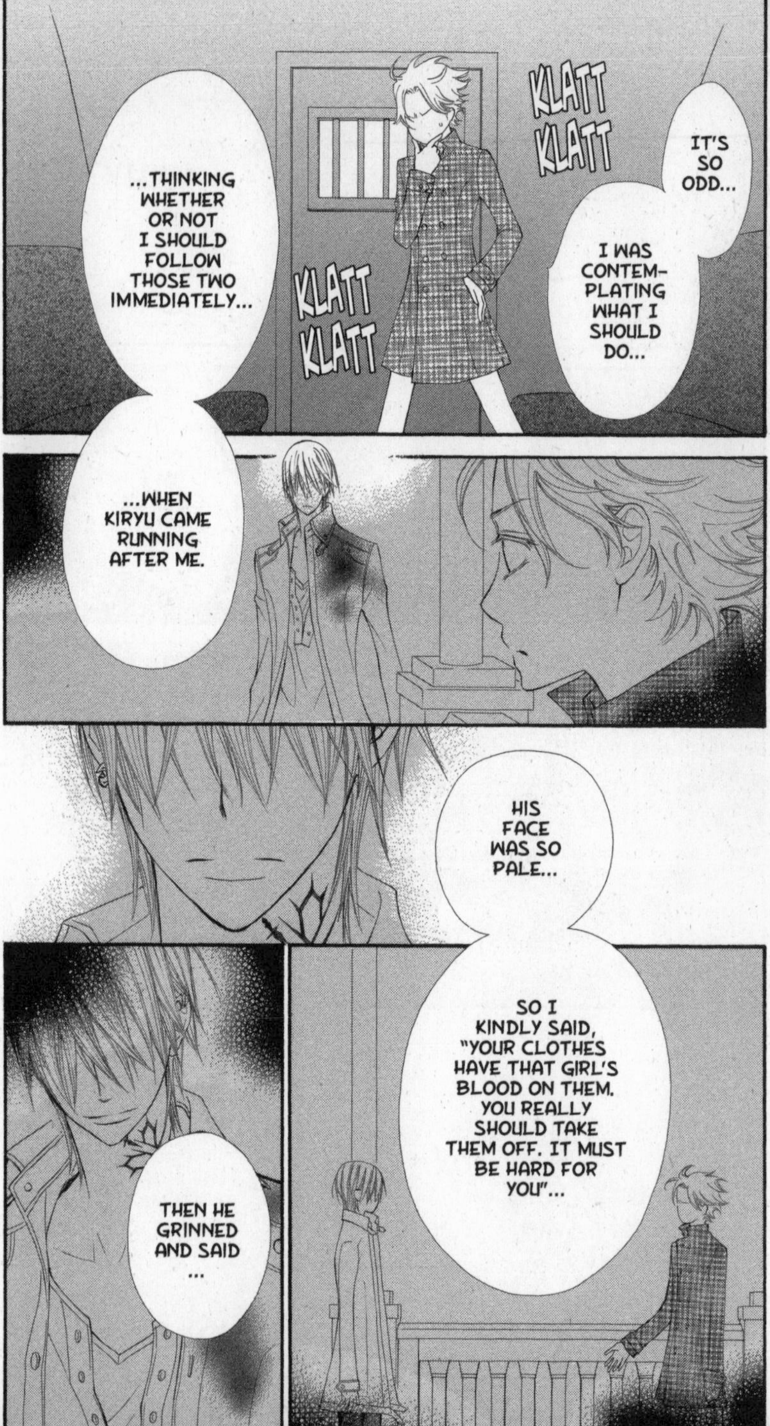
IT'S SO ODD...
I WAS CONTEMPLATING WHAT I SHOULD DO...
KLATT KLATT
...THINKING WHETHER OR NOT I SHOULD FOLLOW THOSE TWO IMMEDIATELY...
KLATT KLATT
...WHEN KIRYU CAME RUNNING AFTER ME.
HIS FACE WAS SO PALE...
SO I KINDLY SAID, "YOUR CLOTHES HAVE THAT GIRL'S BLOOD ON THEM. YOU REALLY SHOULD TAKE THEM OFF. IT MUST BE HARD FOR YOU"...
THEN HE GRINNED AND SAID ...

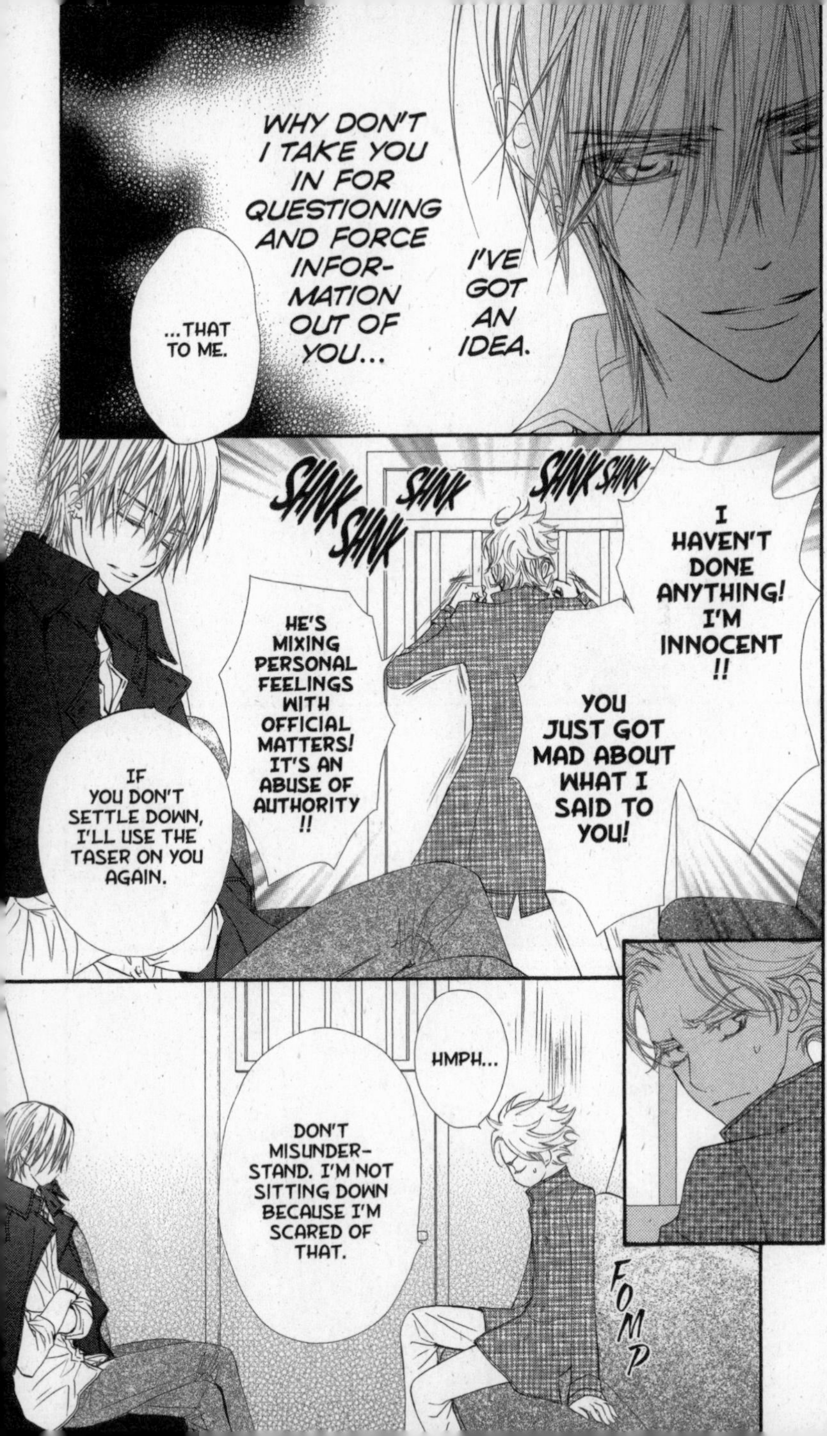
I'VE GOT AN IDEA.
WHY DON'T I TAKE YOU IN FOR QUESTIONING AND FORCE INFOR-MATION OUT OF YOU...
...THAT TO ME.
SHINK SHINK
SHINK
SHINK SHINK
I HAVEN'T DONE ANYTHING! I'M INNOCENT !!
YOU JUST GOT MAD ABOUT WHAT I SAID TO YOU!
HE'S MIXING PERSONAL FEELINGS WITH OFFICIAL MATTERS! IT'S AN ABUSE OF AUTHORITY !!
IF YOU DON'T SETTLE DOWN, I'LL USE THE TASER ON YOU AGAIN.
FOMP
HMPH...
DON'T MISUNDER-STAND. I'M NOT SITTING DOWN BECAUSE I'M SCARED OF THAT.

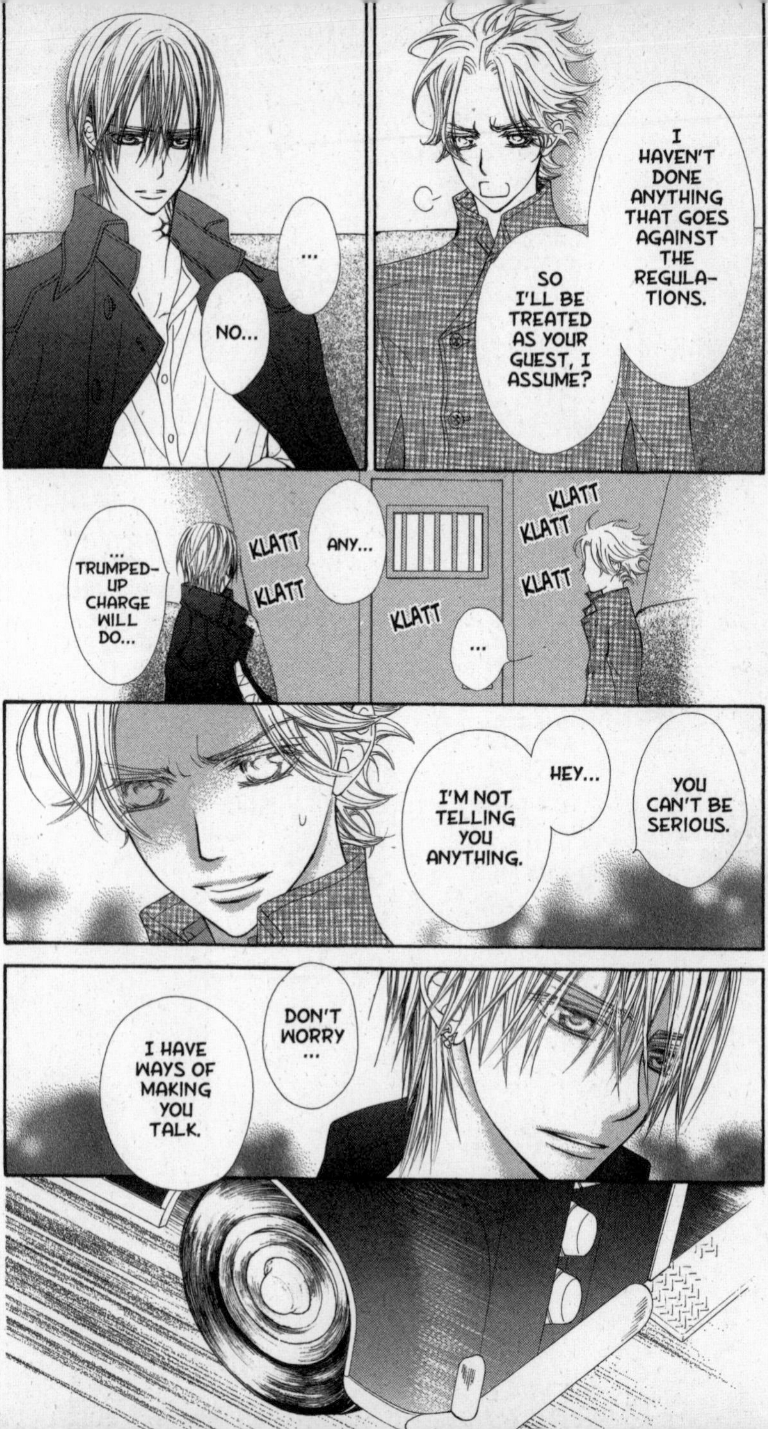
I HAVEN'T DONE ANYTHING THAT GOES AGAINST THE REGULATIONS.
SO I'LL BE TREATED AS YOUR GUEST, I ASSUME?
...
NO...
KLATT
KLATT
KLATT
...
KLATT
ANY...
KLATT
KLATT
... TRUMPED-UP CHARGE WILL DO...
YOU CAN'T BE SERIOUS.
HEY...
I'M NOT TELLING YOU ANYTHING.
DON'T WORRY...
I HAVE WAYS OF MAKING YOU TALK.

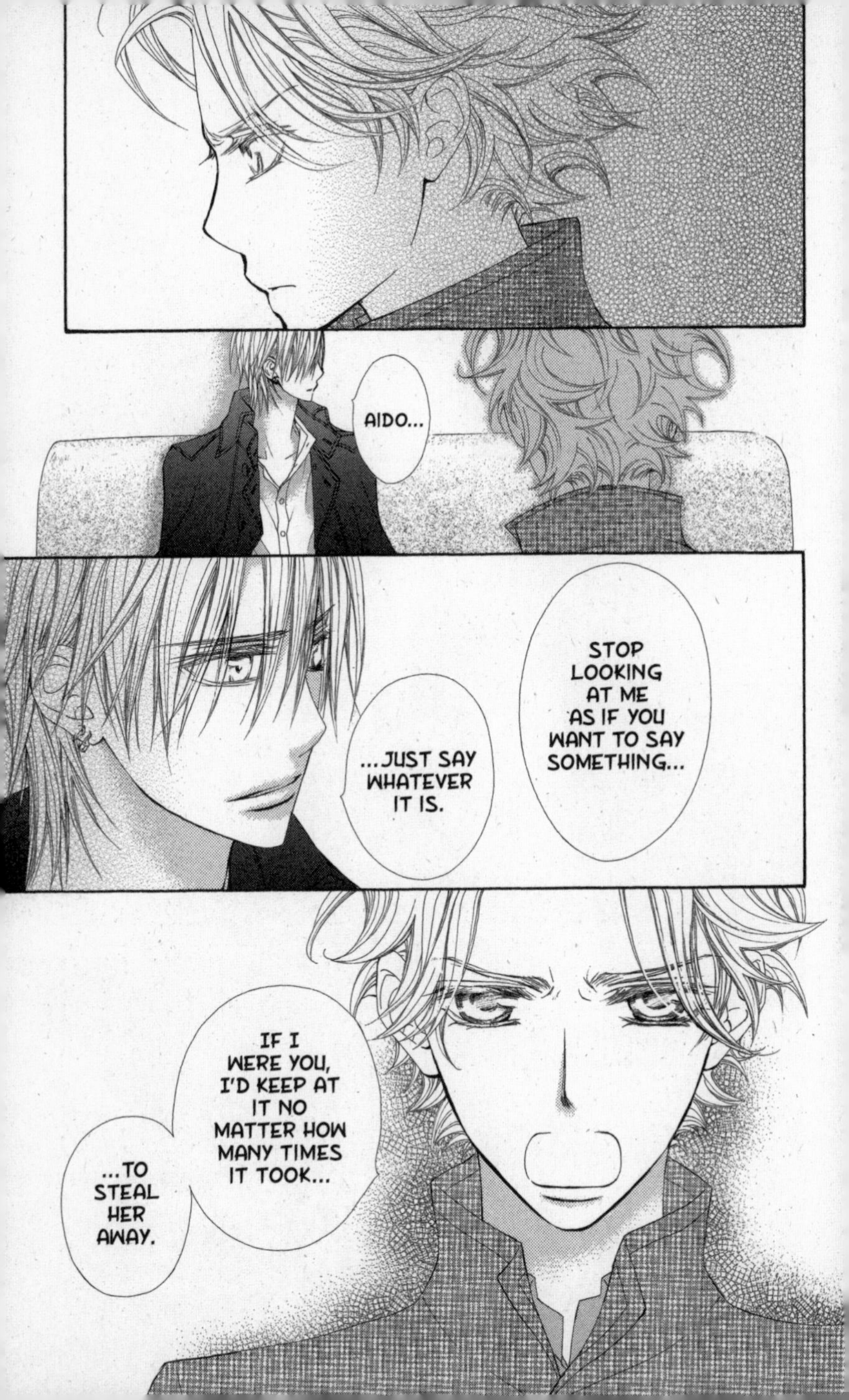
AIDO...
STOP LOOKING AT ME AS IF YOU WANT TO SAY SOMETHING...
...JUST SAY WHATEVER IT IS.
IF I WERE YOU, I'D KEEP AT IT NO MATTER HOW MANY TIMES IT TOOK...
...TO STEAL HER AWAY.

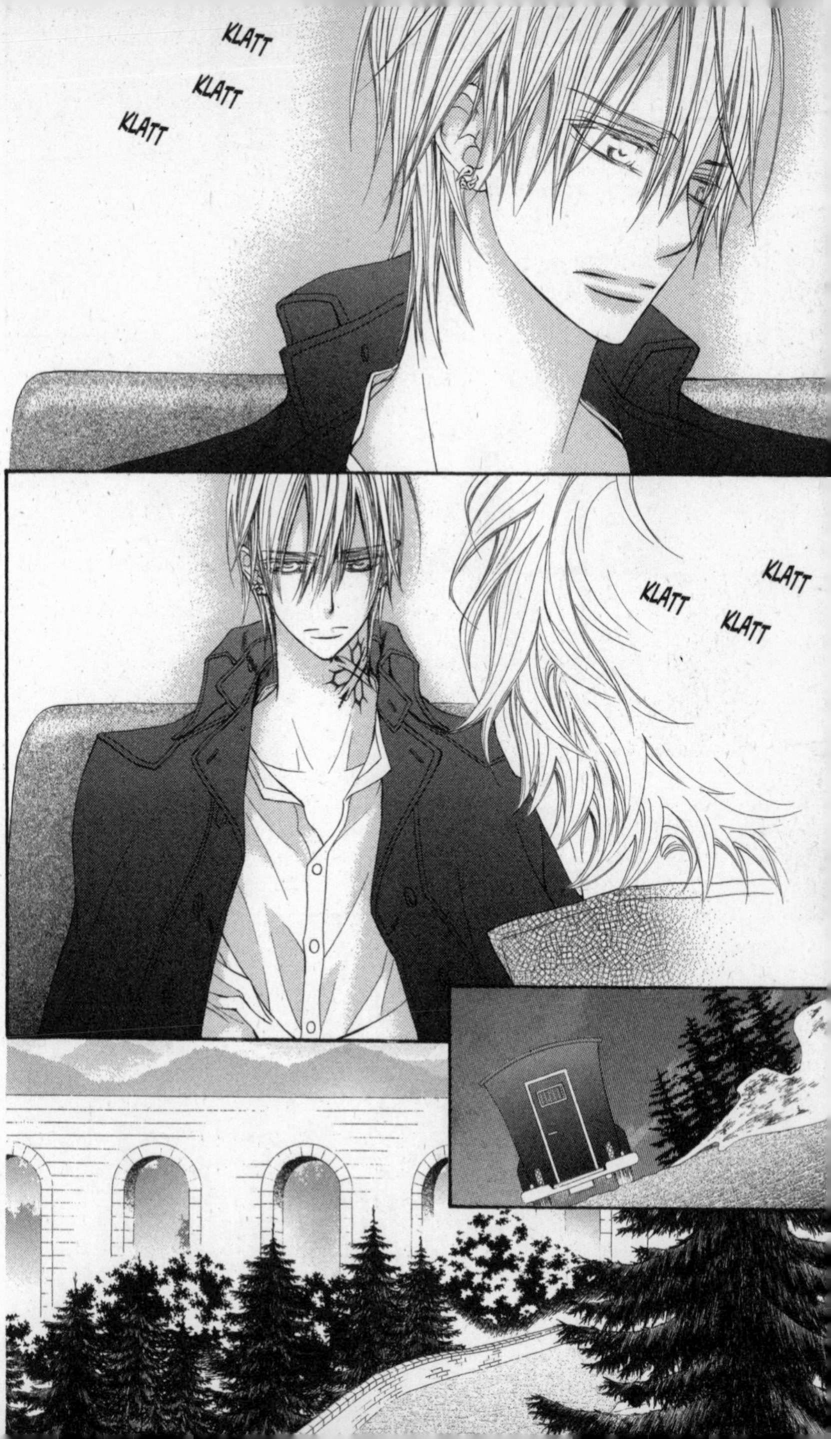
KLATT
KLATT
KLATT
KLATT
KLATT
KLATT

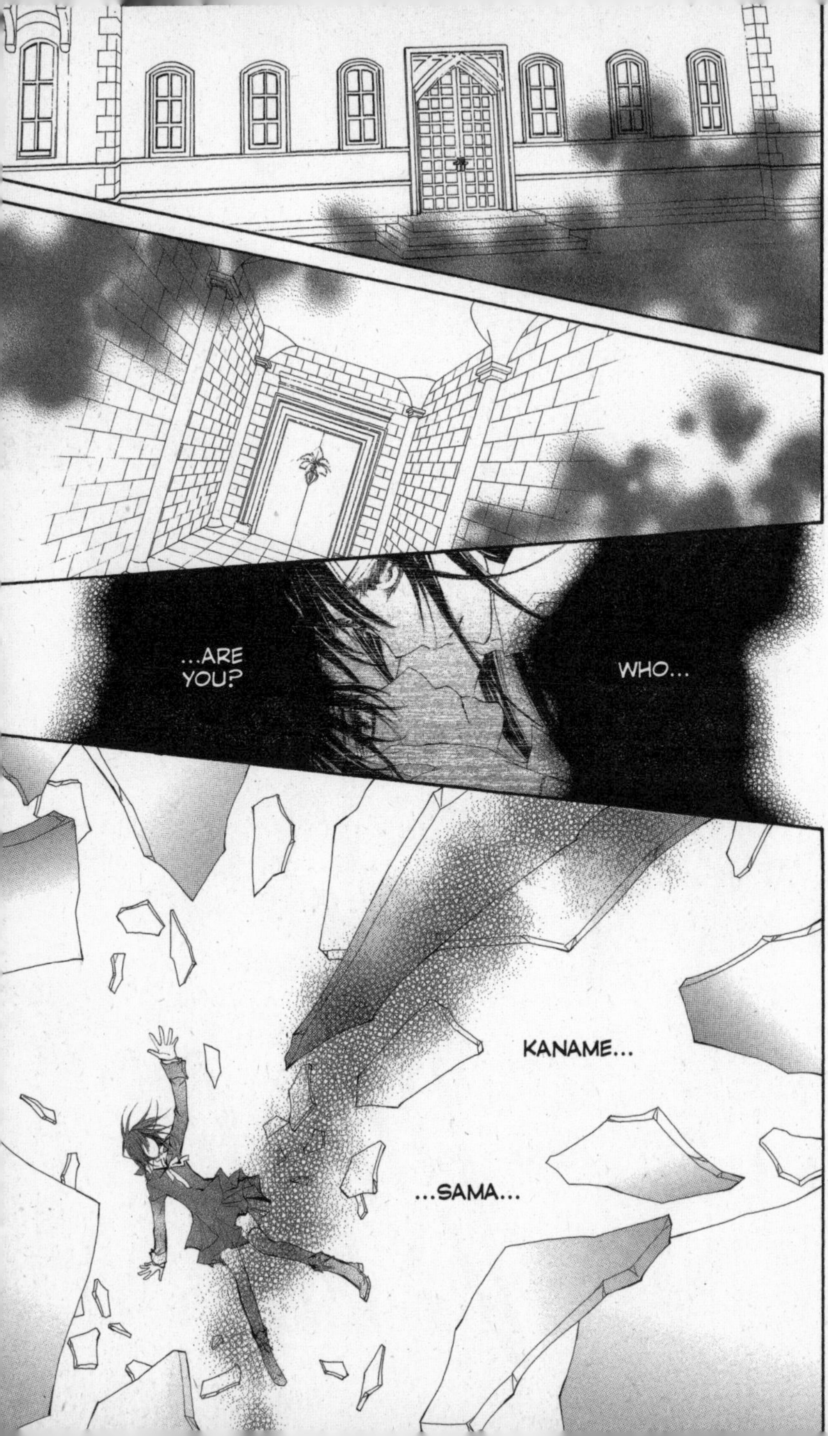
WHO...
...ARE YOU?
KANAME...
...SAMA...

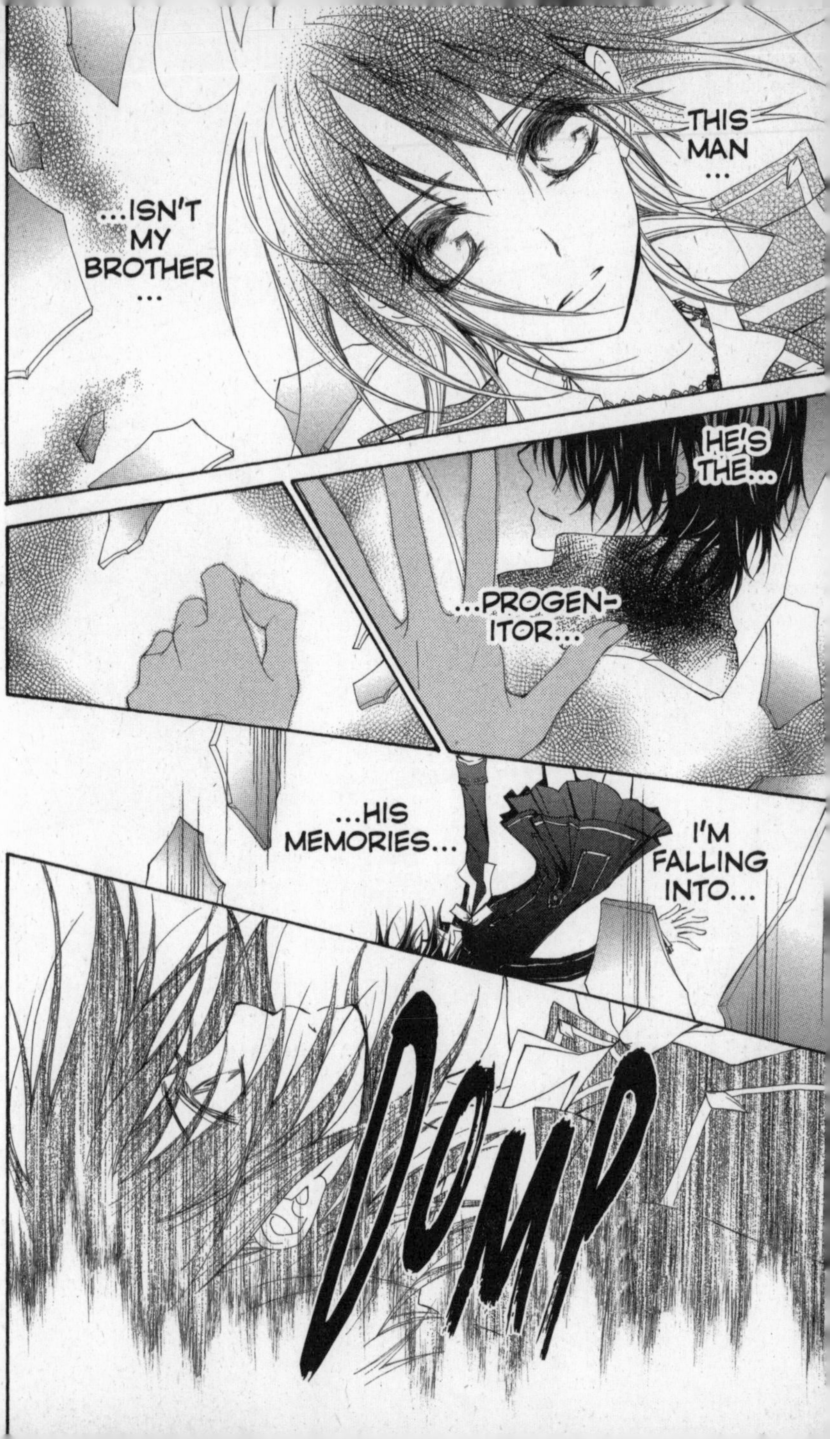
THIS MAN ...
...ISN'T MY BROTHER ...
HE'S THE...
...PROGEN-ITOR...
I'M FALLING INTO...
...HIS MEMORIES...
DOMP

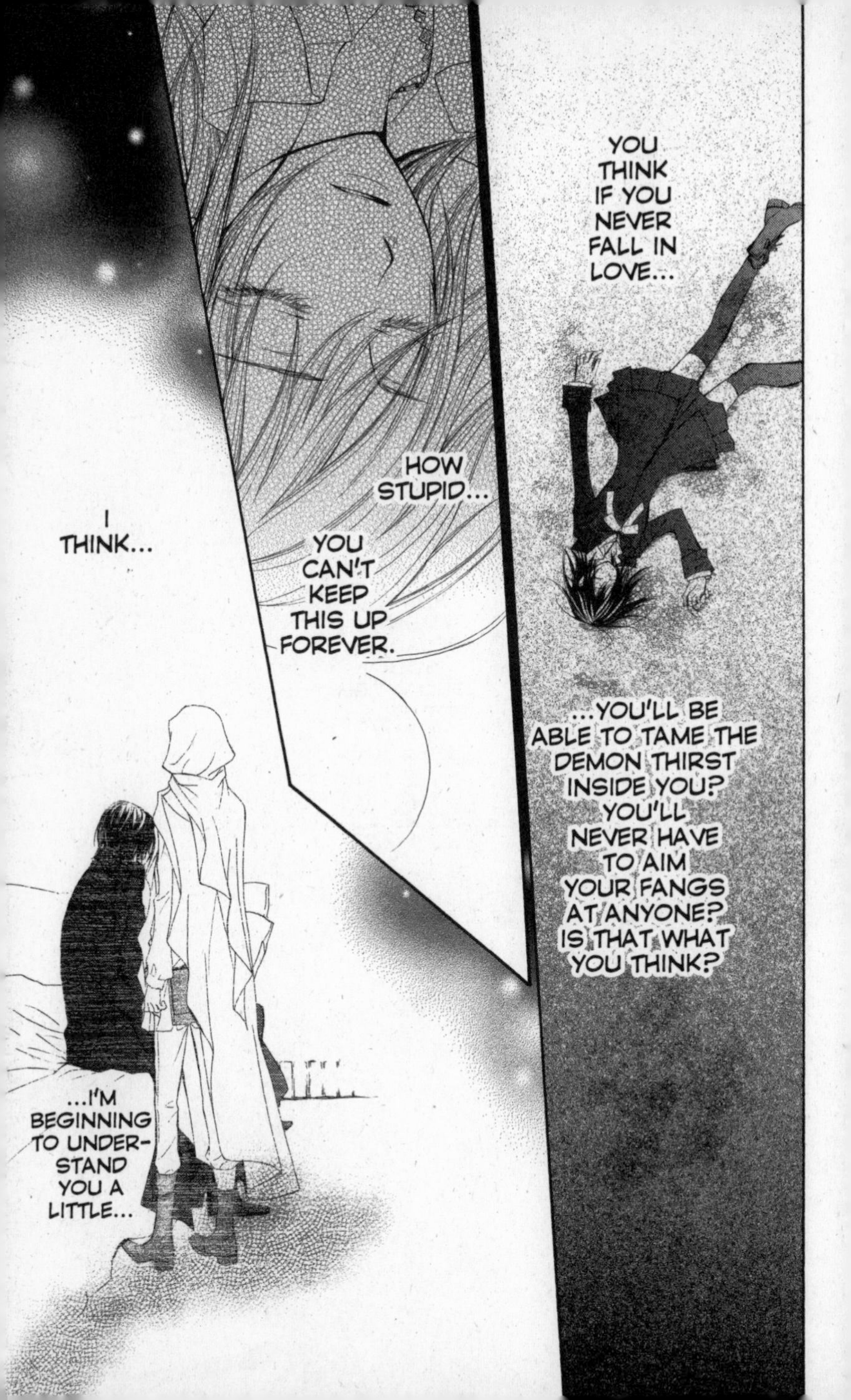
YOU THINK IF YOU NEVER FALL IN LOVE...
...YOU'LL BE ABLE TO TAME THE DEMON THIRST INSIDE YOU? YOU'LL NEVER HAVE TO AIM YOUR FANGS AT ANYONE? IS THAT WHAT YOU THINK?
HOW STUPID...
YOU CAN'T KEEP THIS UP FOREVER.
I THINK...
...I'M BEGINNING TO UNDER-STAND YOU A LITTLE...

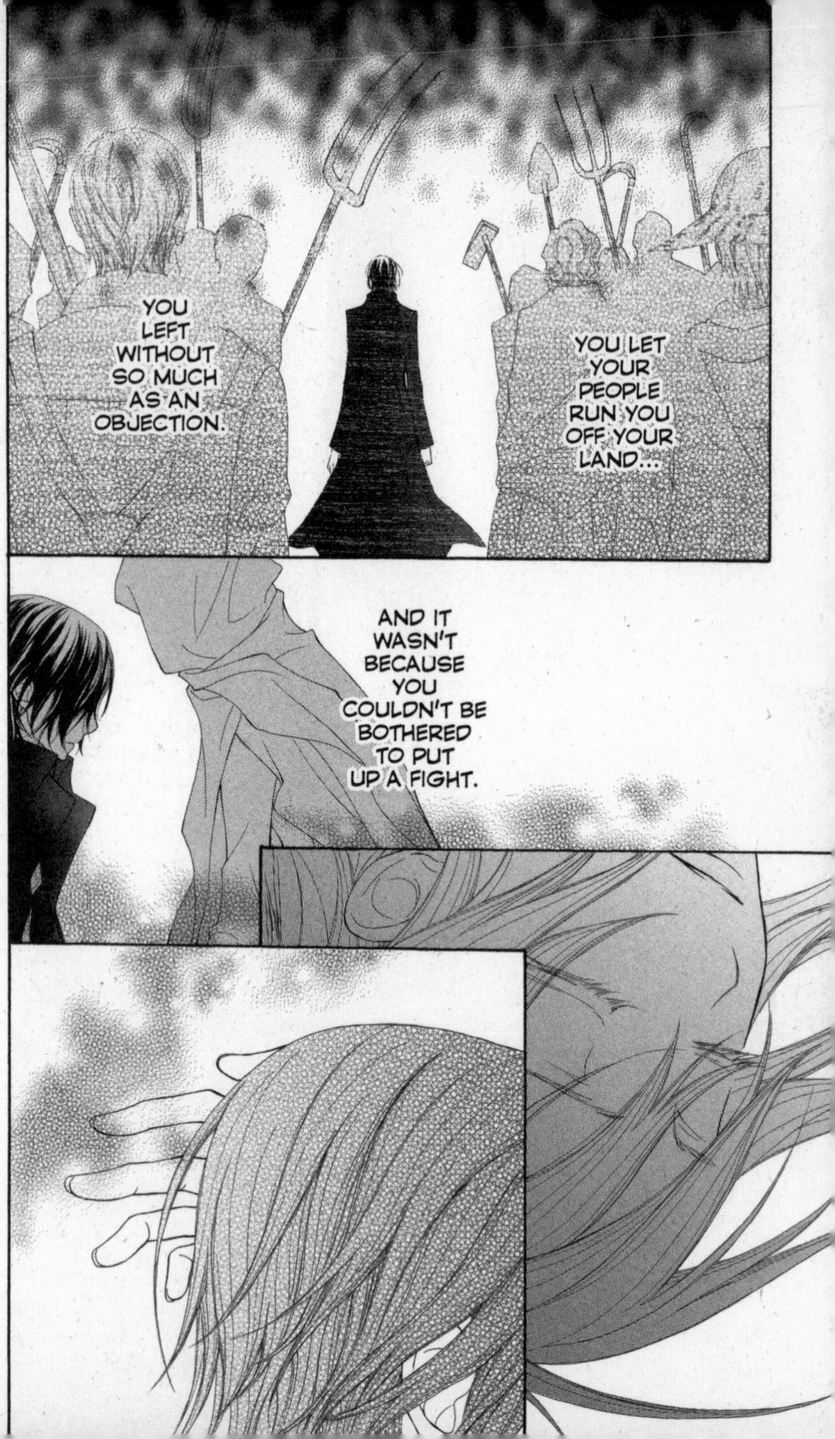
YOU LET YOUR PEOPLE RUN YOU OFF YOUR LAND...
YOU LEFT WITHOUT SO MUCH AS AN OBJECTION.
AND IT WASN'T BECAUSE YOU COULDN'T BE BOTHERED TO PUT UP A FIGHT.

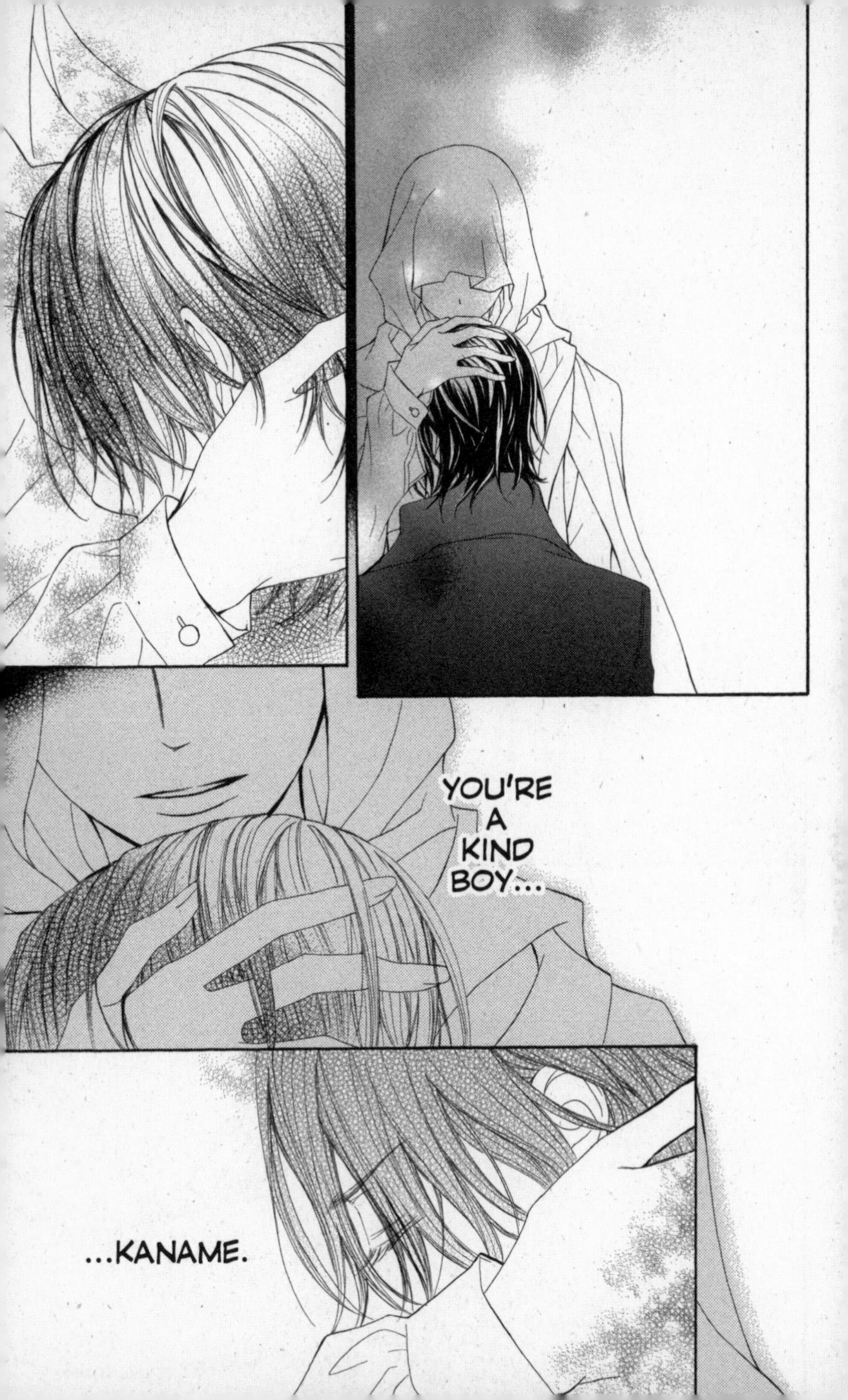
YOU'RE A KIND BOY...
...KANAME.

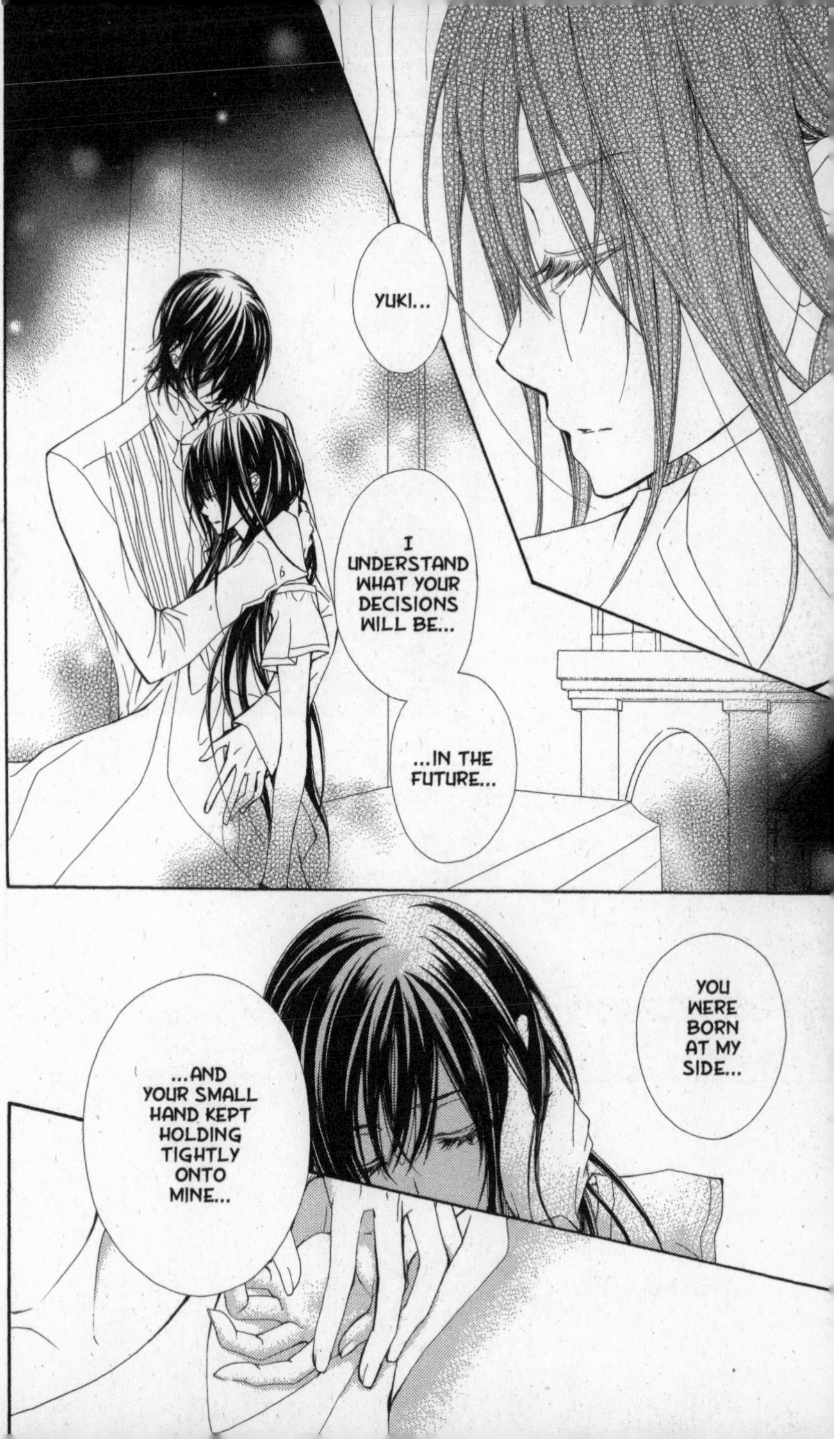
YUKI...
I UNDERSTAND WHAT YOUR DECISIONS WILL BE...
...IN THE FUTURE...
YOU WERE BORN AT MY SIDE...
...AND YOUR SMALL HAND KEPT HOLDING TIGHTLY ONTO MINE...

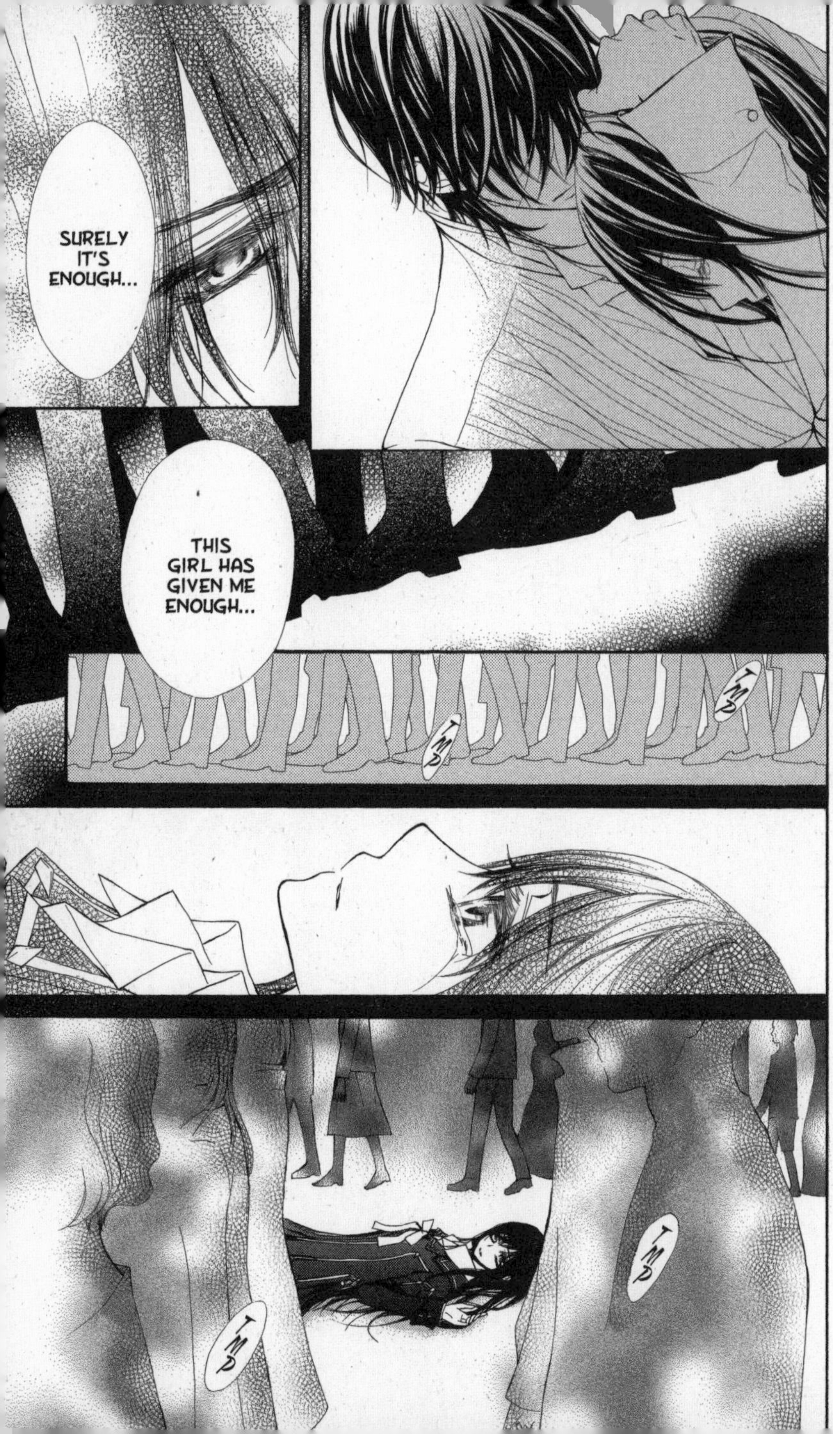
SURELY IT'S ENOUGH...
THIS GIRL HAS GIVEN ME ENOUGH...
TMP
TMP
TMP
TMP

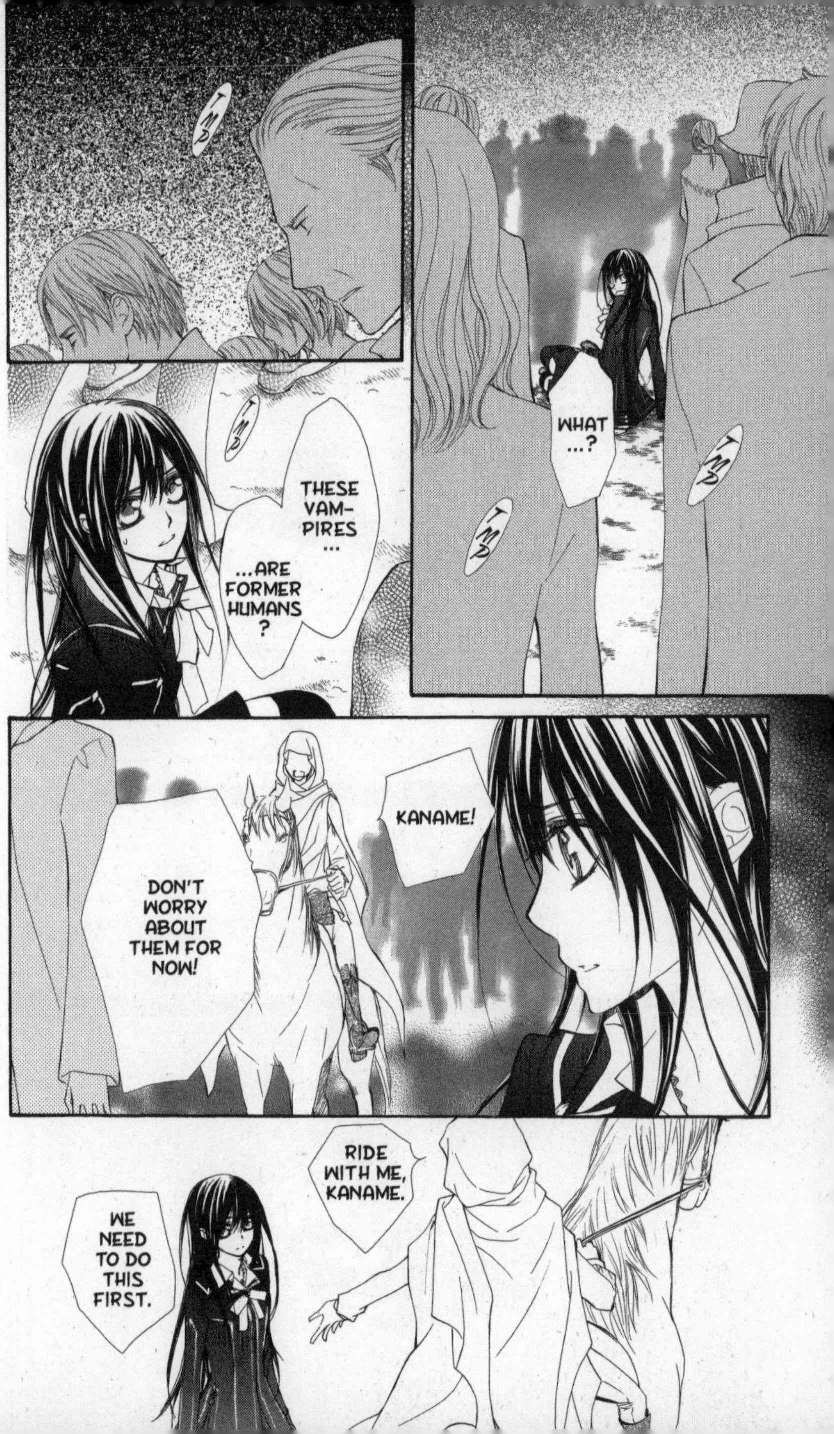

TMP
TMP
WHAT ...?
TMP
TMP
TMP
THESE VAMPIRES ...
...ARE FORMER HUMANS?
KANAME!
DON'T WORRY ABOUT THEM FOR NOW!
RIDE WITH ME, KANAME.
WE NEED TO DO THIS FIRST.

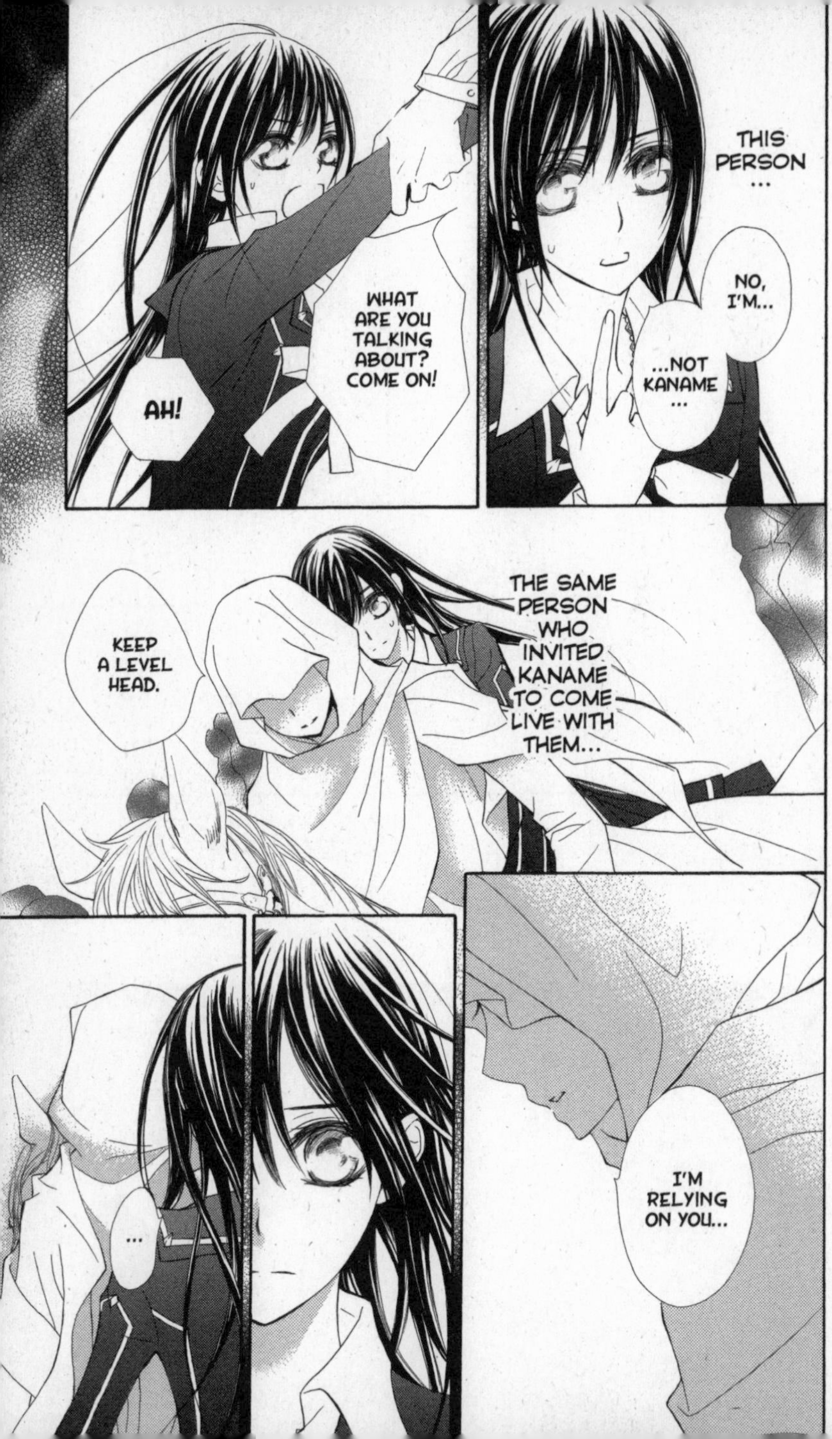
THIS PERSON ...
NO, I'M...
...NOT KANAME ...
WHAT ARE YOU TALKING ABOUT? COME ON!
AH!
THE SAME PERSON WHO INVITED KANAME TO COME LIVE WITH THEM...
KEEP A LEVEL HEAD.
I'M RELYING ON YOU...
...

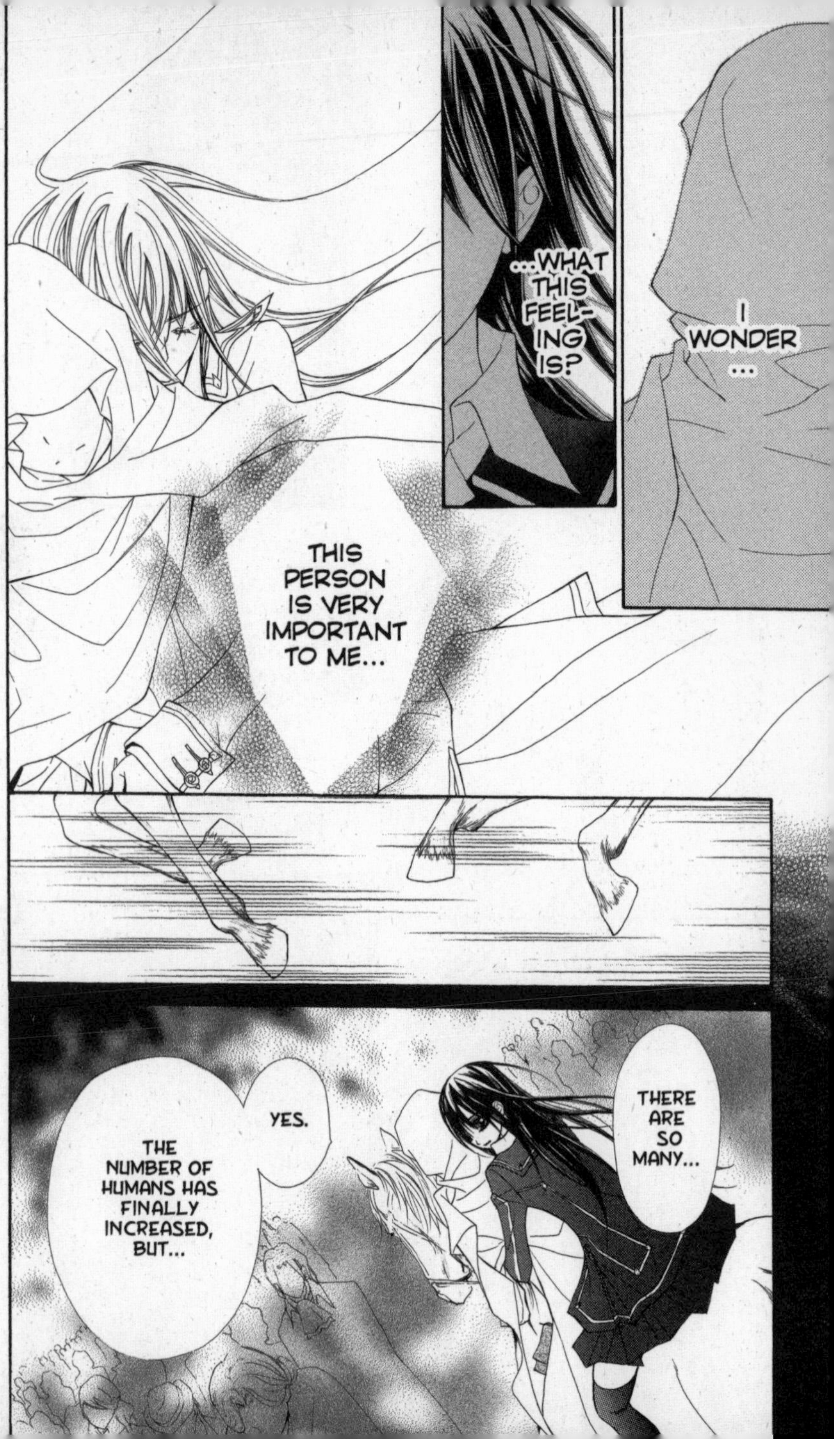
I WONDER...
...WHAT THIS FEEL-ING IS?
THIS PERSON IS VERY IMPORTANT TO ME...
THERE ARE SO MANY...
YES.
THE NUMBER OF HUMANS HAS FINALLY INCREASED, BUT...

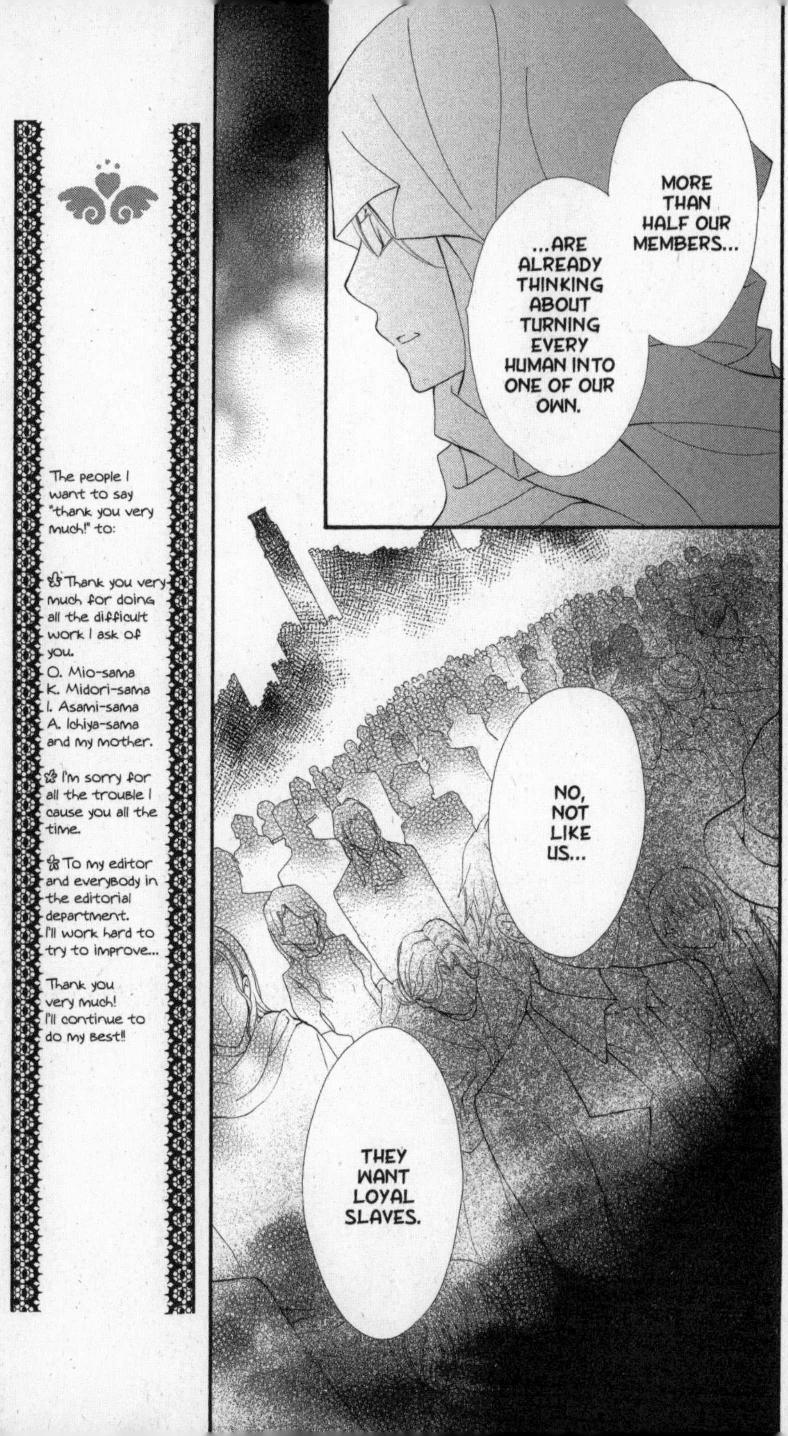
MORE THAN HALF OUR MEMBERS...
...ARE ALREADY THINKING ABOUT TURNING EVERY HUMAN INTO ONE OF OUR OWN.
NO, NOT LIKE US...
THEY WANT LOYAL SLAVES.

The people I want to say "thank you very much!" to:

✿ Thank you very much for doing all the difficult work I ask of you.
O. Mio-sama
K. Midori-sama
I. Asami-sama
A. Ichiya-sama
and my mother.

✿ I'm sorry for all the trouble I cause you all the time.

✿ To my editor and everybody in the editorial department.
I'll work hard to try to improve...

Thank you very much!
I'll continue to do my best!!

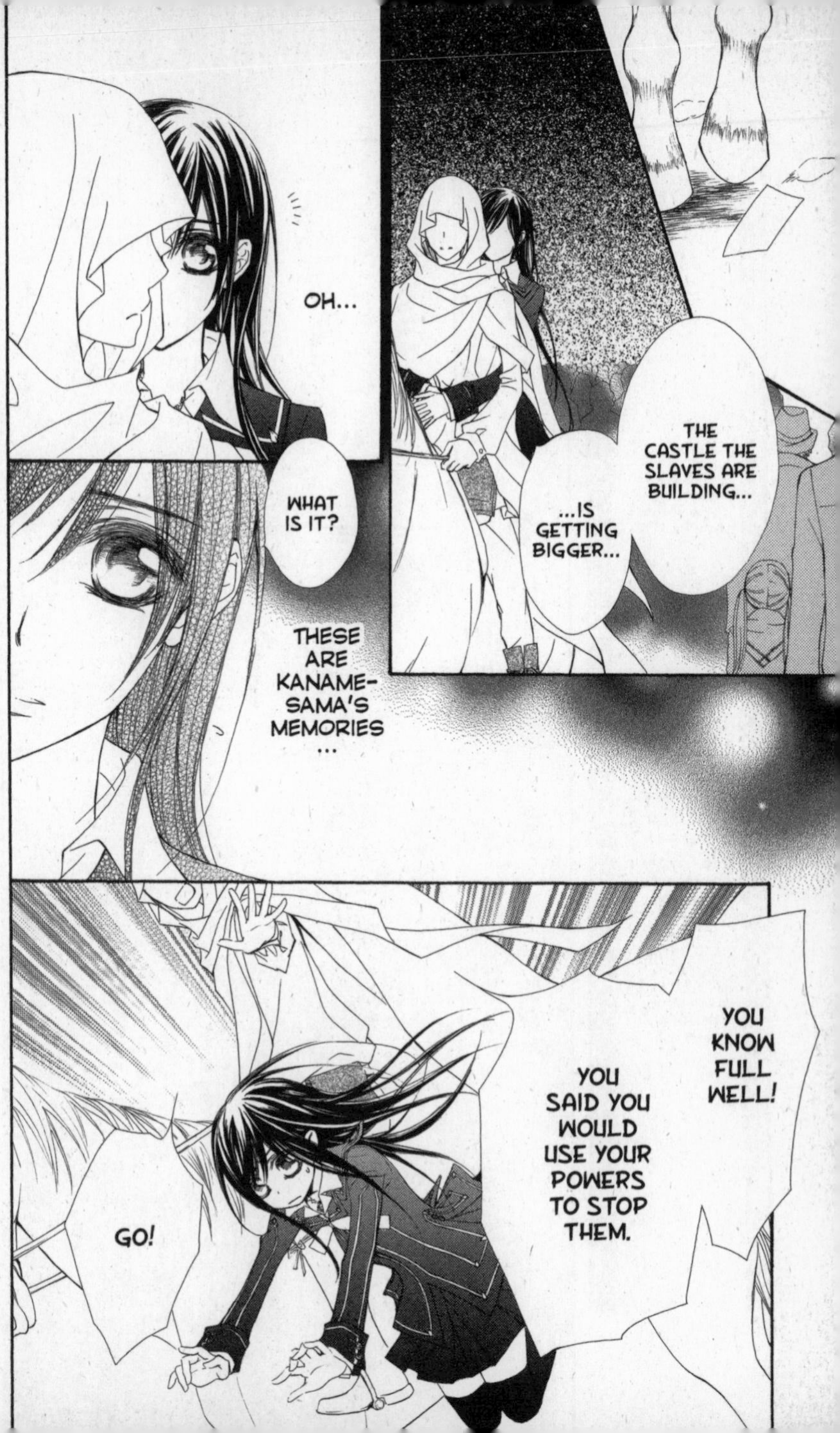
THE CASTLE THE SLAVES ARE BUILDING...
...IS GETTING BIGGER...
OH...
WHAT IS IT?
THESE ARE KANAME-SAMA'S MEMORIES...
YOU KNOW FULL WELL!
YOU SAID YOU WOULD USE YOUR POWERS TO STOP THEM.
GO!

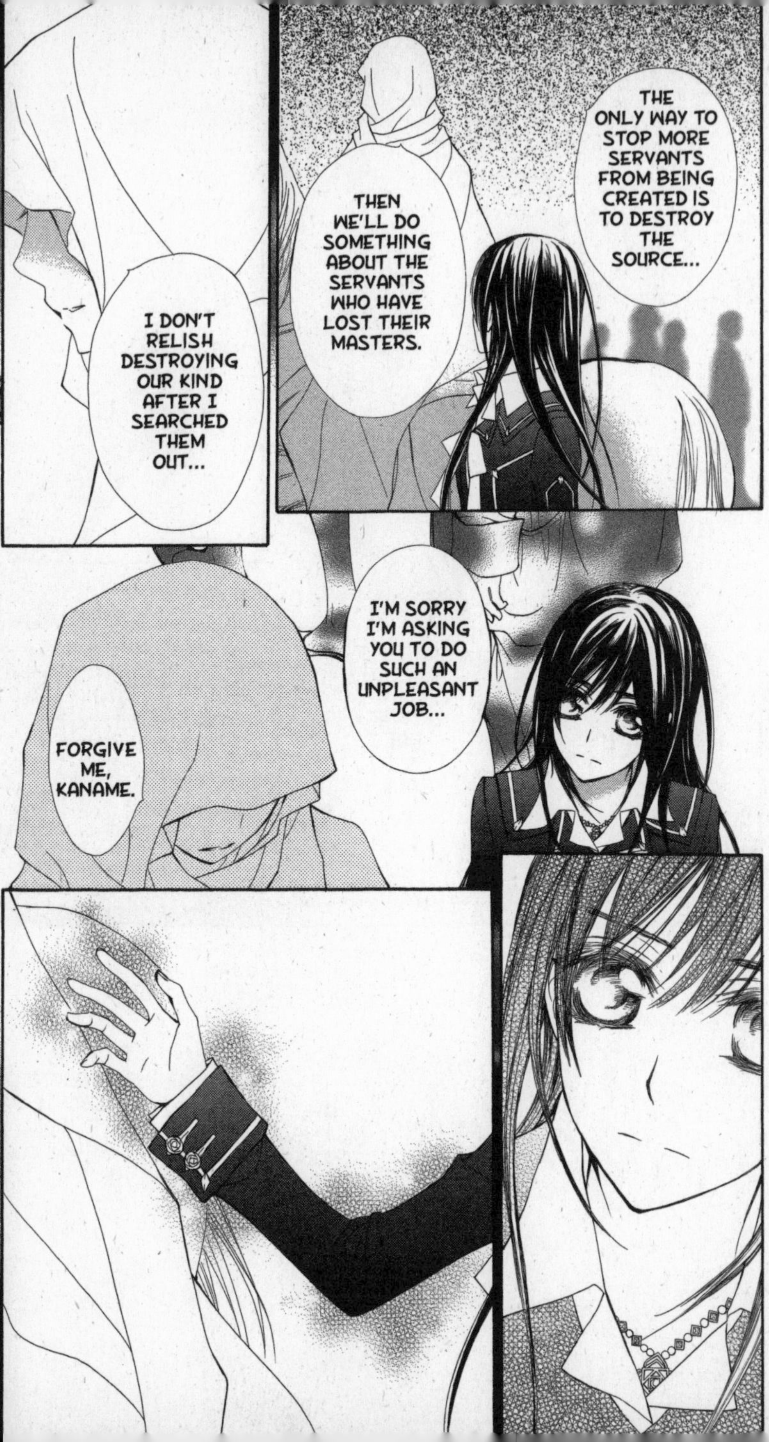
THE ONLY WAY TO STOP MORE SERVANTS FROM BEING CREATED IS TO DESTROY THE SOURCE...
THEN WE'LL DO SOMETHING ABOUT THE SERVANTS WHO HAVE LOST THEIR MASTERS.
I DON'T RELISH DESTROYING OUR KIND AFTER I SEARCHED THEM OUT...
I'M SORRY I'M ASKING YOU TO DO SUCH AN UNPLEASANT JOB...
FORGIVE ME, KANAME.

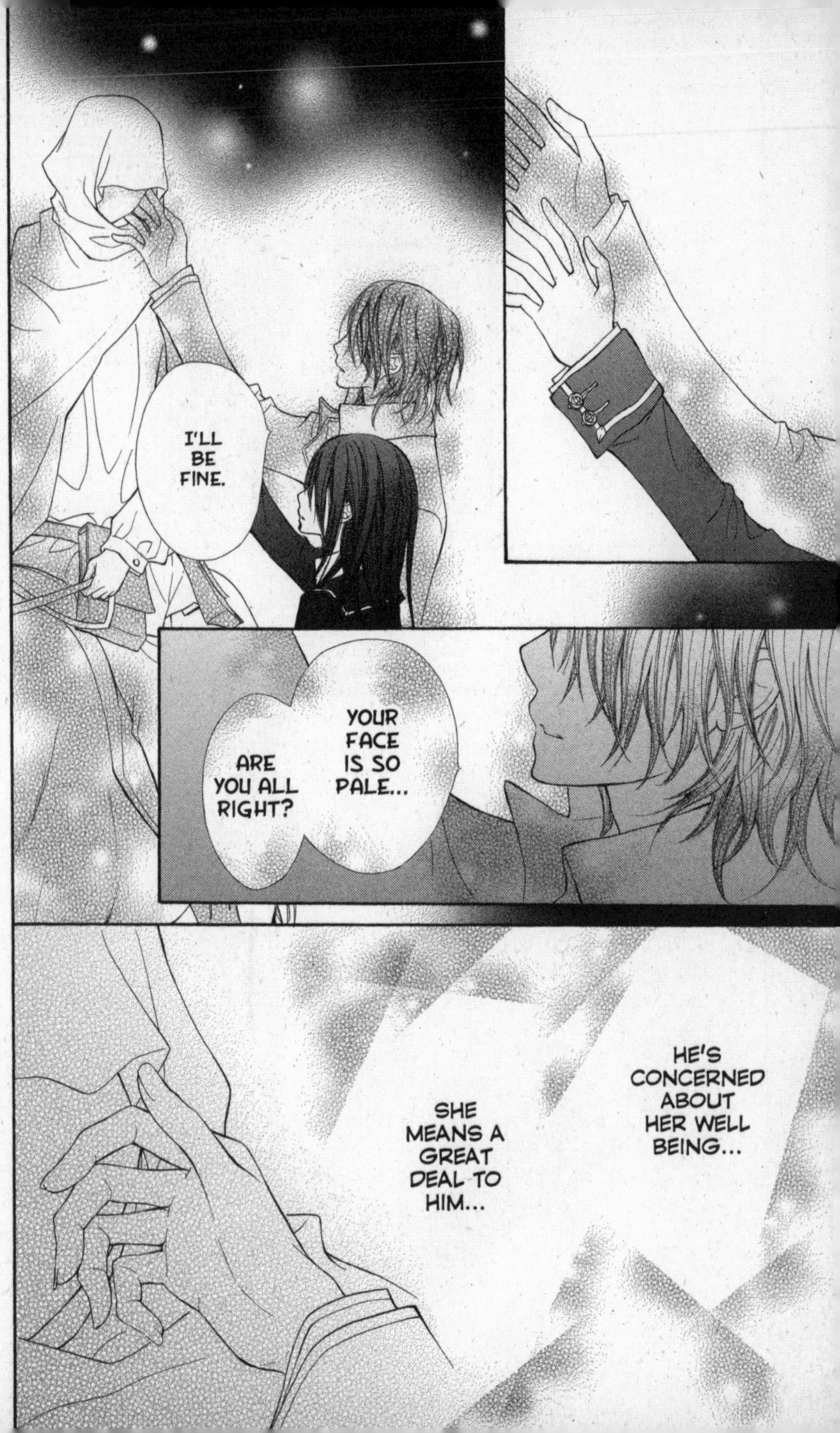
I'LL BE FINE.
YOUR FACE IS SO PALE...
ARE YOU ALL RIGHT?
HE'S CONCERNED ABOUT HER WELL BEING...
SHE MEANS A GREAT DEAL TO HIM...

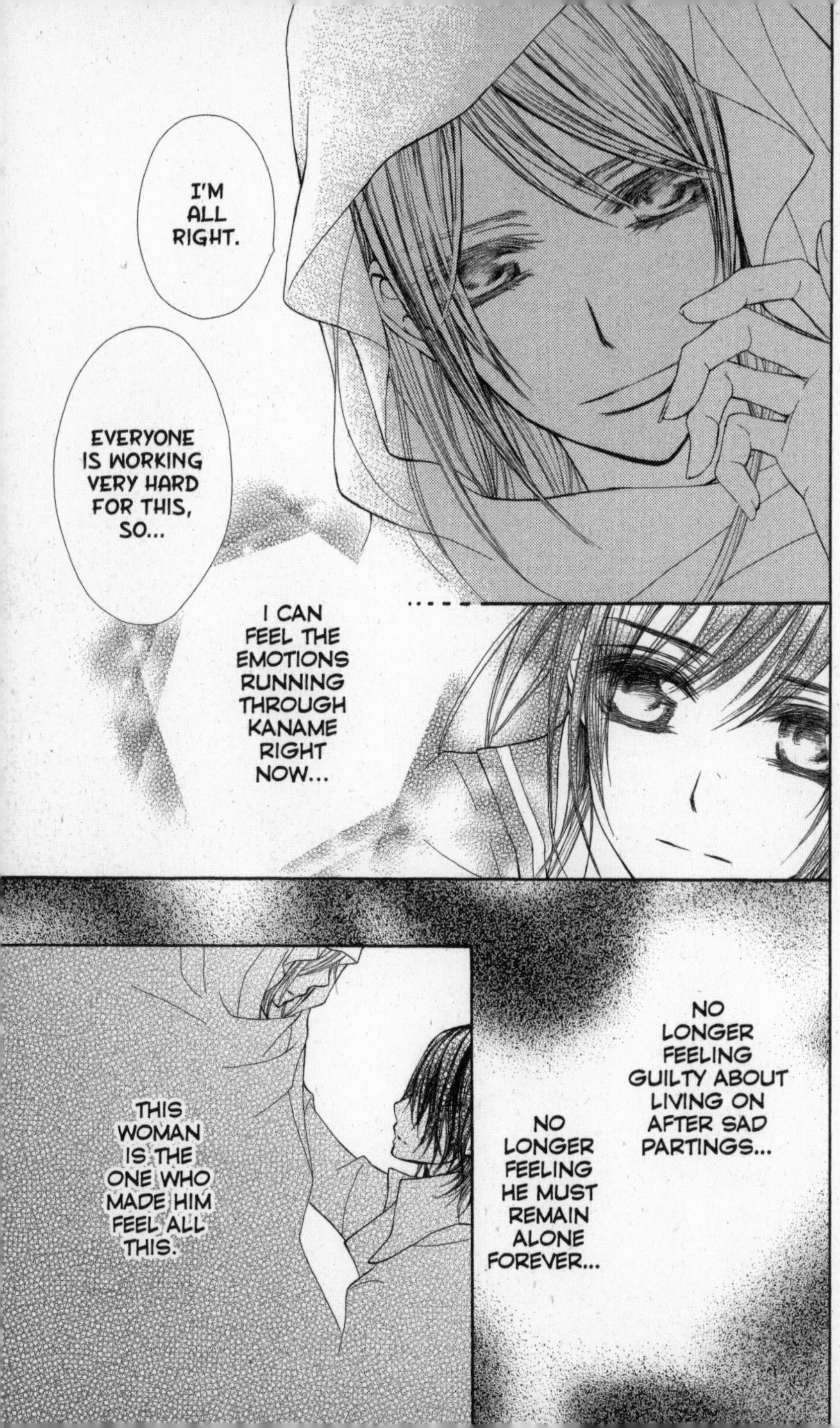
I'M ALL RIGHT.
EVERYONE IS WORKING VERY HARD FOR THIS, SO...
I CAN FEEL THE EMOTIONS RUNNING THROUGH KANAME RIGHT NOW...
NO LONGER FEELING GUILTY ABOUT LIVING ON AFTER SAD PARTINGS...
NO LONGER FEELING HE MUST REMAIN ALONE FOREVER...
THIS WOMAN IS THE ONE WHO MADE HIM FEEL ALL THIS.

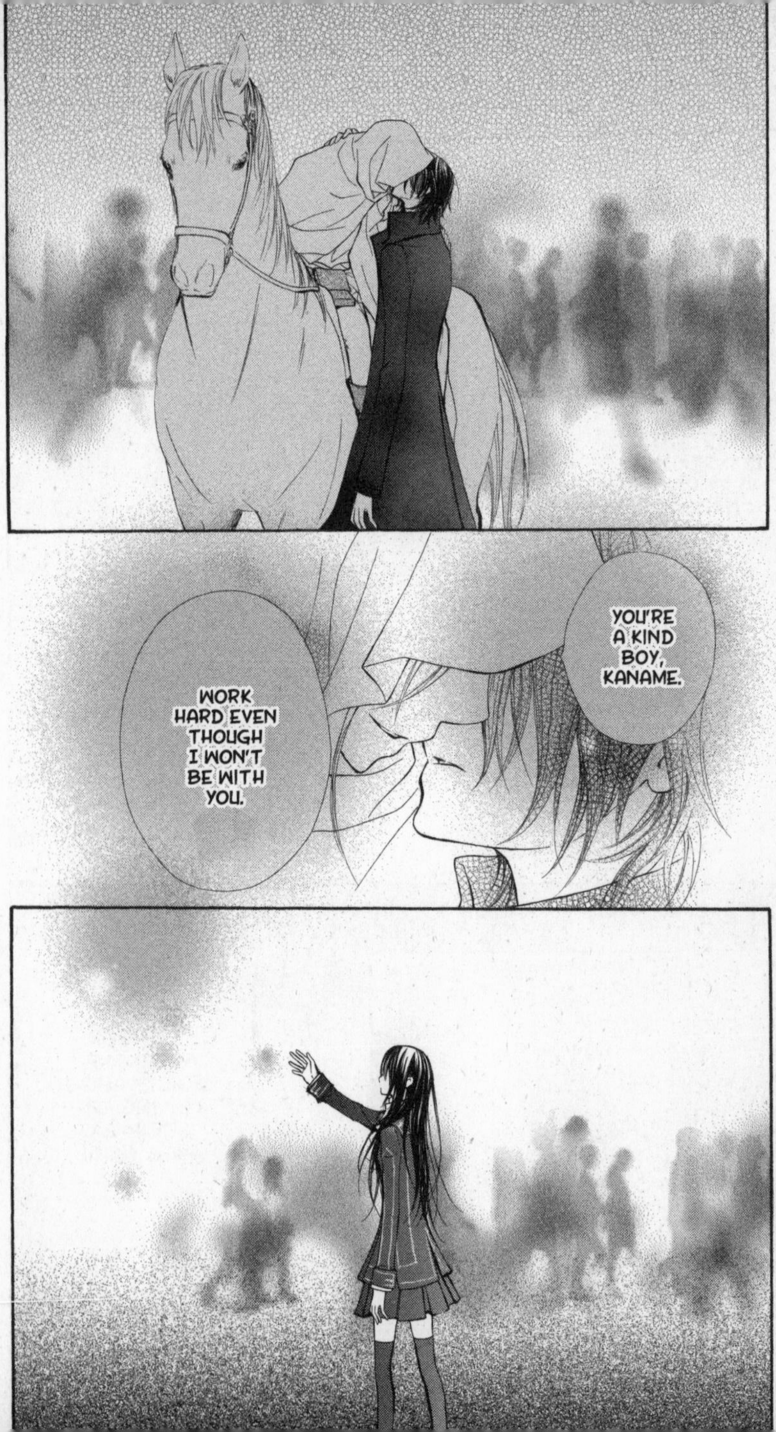
YOU'RE A KIND BOY, KANAME.
WORK HARD EVEN THOUGH I WON'T BE WITH YOU.

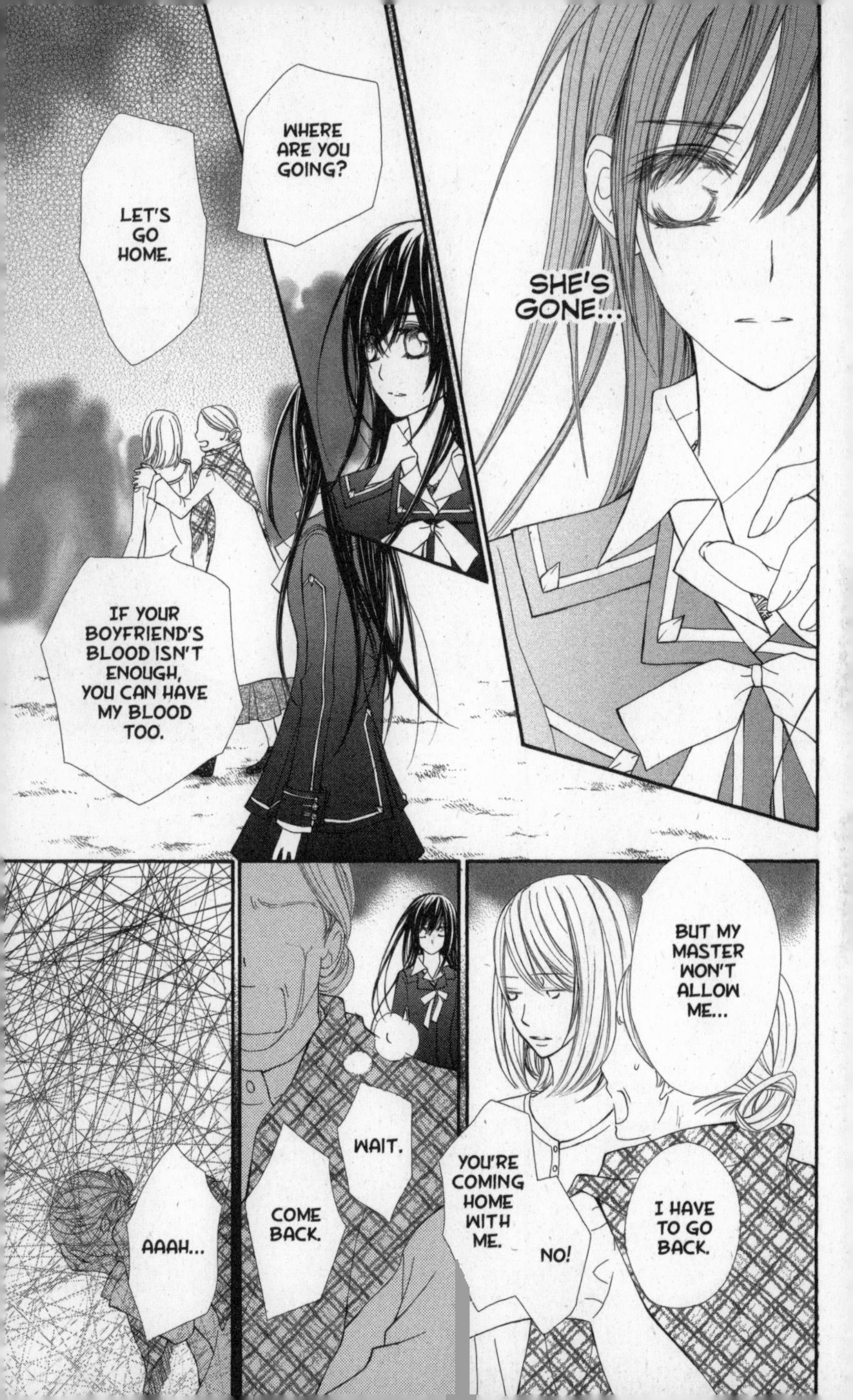
SHE'S GONE...
WHERE ARE YOU GOING?
LET'S GO HOME.
IF YOUR BOYFRIEND'S BLOOD ISN'T ENOUGH, YOU CAN HAVE MY BLOOD TOO.
BUT MY MASTER WON'T ALLOW ME...
I HAVE TO GO BACK.
NO!
YOU'RE COMING HOME WITH ME.
WAIT.
COME BACK.
AAAH...

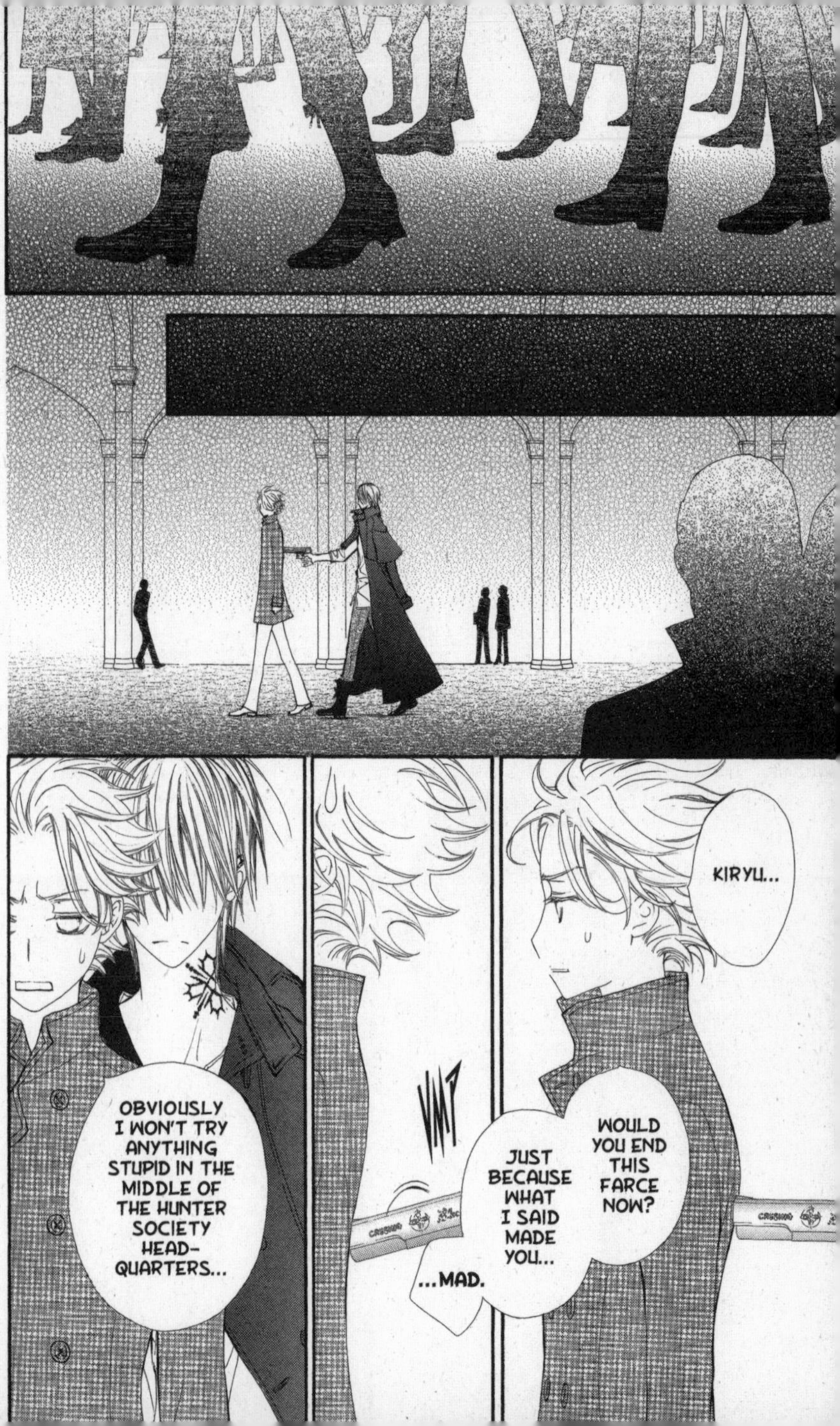
KIRYU...
WOULD YOU END THIS FARCE NOW?
JUST BECAUSE WHAT I SAID MADE YOU...
...MAD.
OBVIOUSLY I WON'T TRY ANYTHING STUPID IN THE MIDDLE OF THE HUNTER SOCIETY HEAD-QUARTERS...

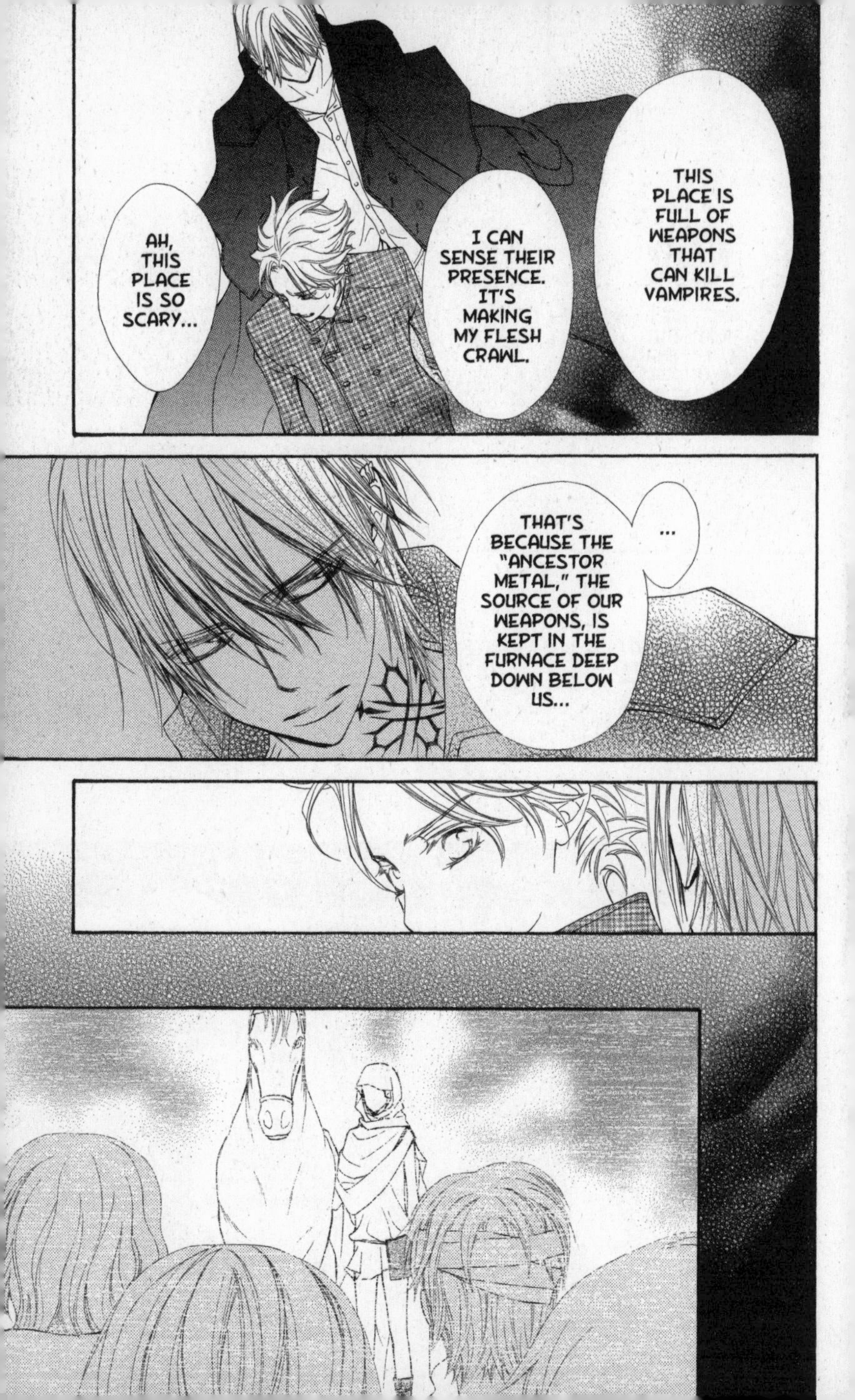
THIS PLACE IS FULL OF WEAPONS THAT CAN KILL VAMPIRES.
I CAN SENSE THEIR PRESENCE. IT'S MAKING MY FLESH CRAWL.
AH, THIS PLACE IS SO SCARY...
...
THAT'S BECAUSE THE "ANCESTOR METAL," THE SOURCE OF OUR WEAPONS, IS KEPT IN THE FURNACE DEEP DOWN BELOW US...

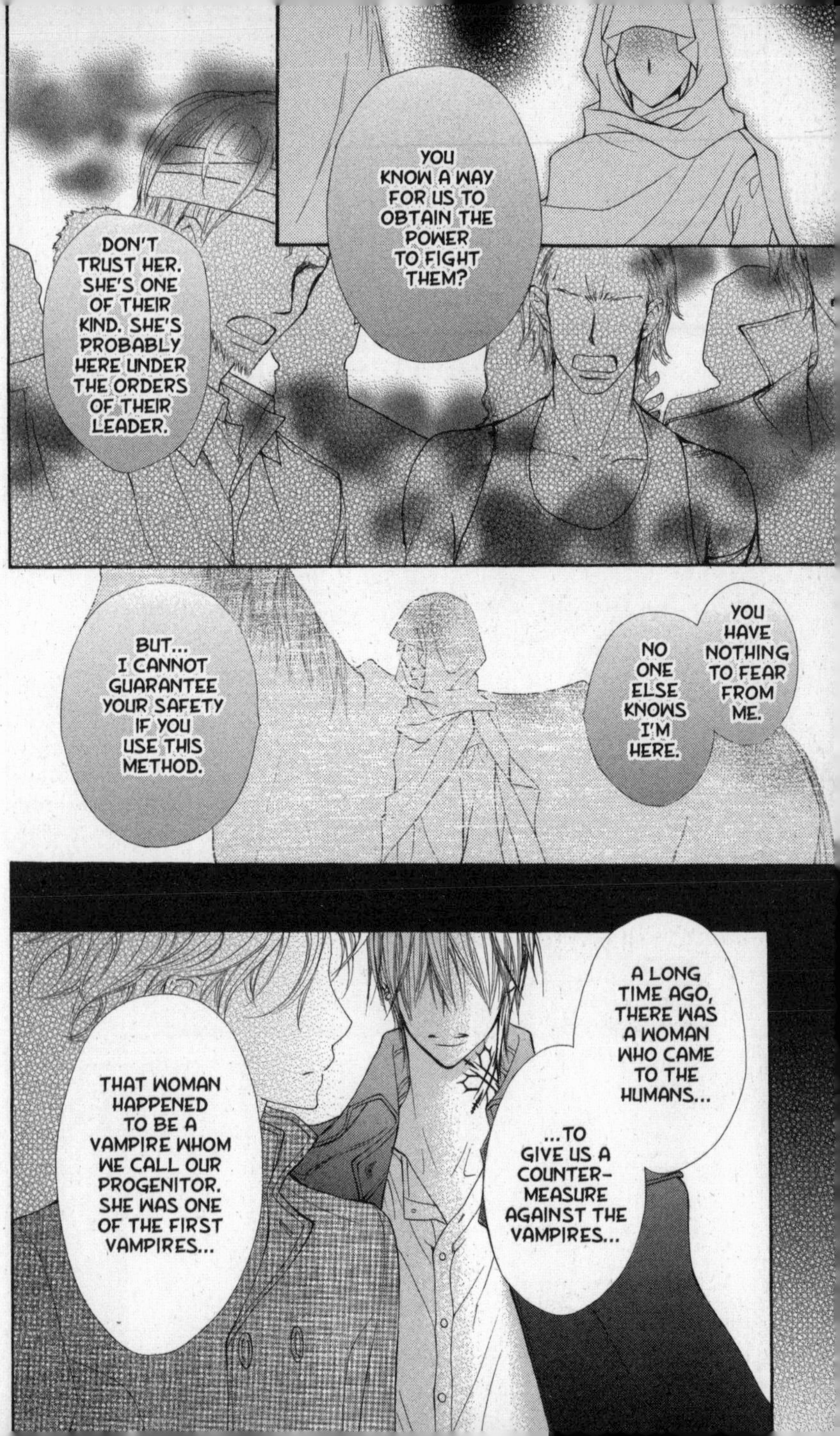
YOU KNOW A WAY FOR US TO OBTAIN THE POWER TO FIGHT THEM?
DON'T TRUST HER. SHE'S ONE OF THEIR KIND. SHE'S PROBABLY HERE UNDER THE ORDERS OF THEIR LEADER.
YOU HAVE NOTHING TO FEAR FROM ME.
NO ONE ELSE KNOWS I'M HERE.
BUT... I CANNOT GUARANTEE YOUR SAFETY IF YOU USE THIS METHOD.
A LONG TIME AGO, THERE WAS A WOMAN WHO CAME TO THE HUMANS...
...TO GIVE US A COUNTER-MEASURE AGAINST THE VAMPIRES...
THAT WOMAN HAPPENED TO BE A VAMPIRE WHOM WE CALL OUR PROGENITOR. SHE WAS ONE OF THE FIRST VAMPIRES...

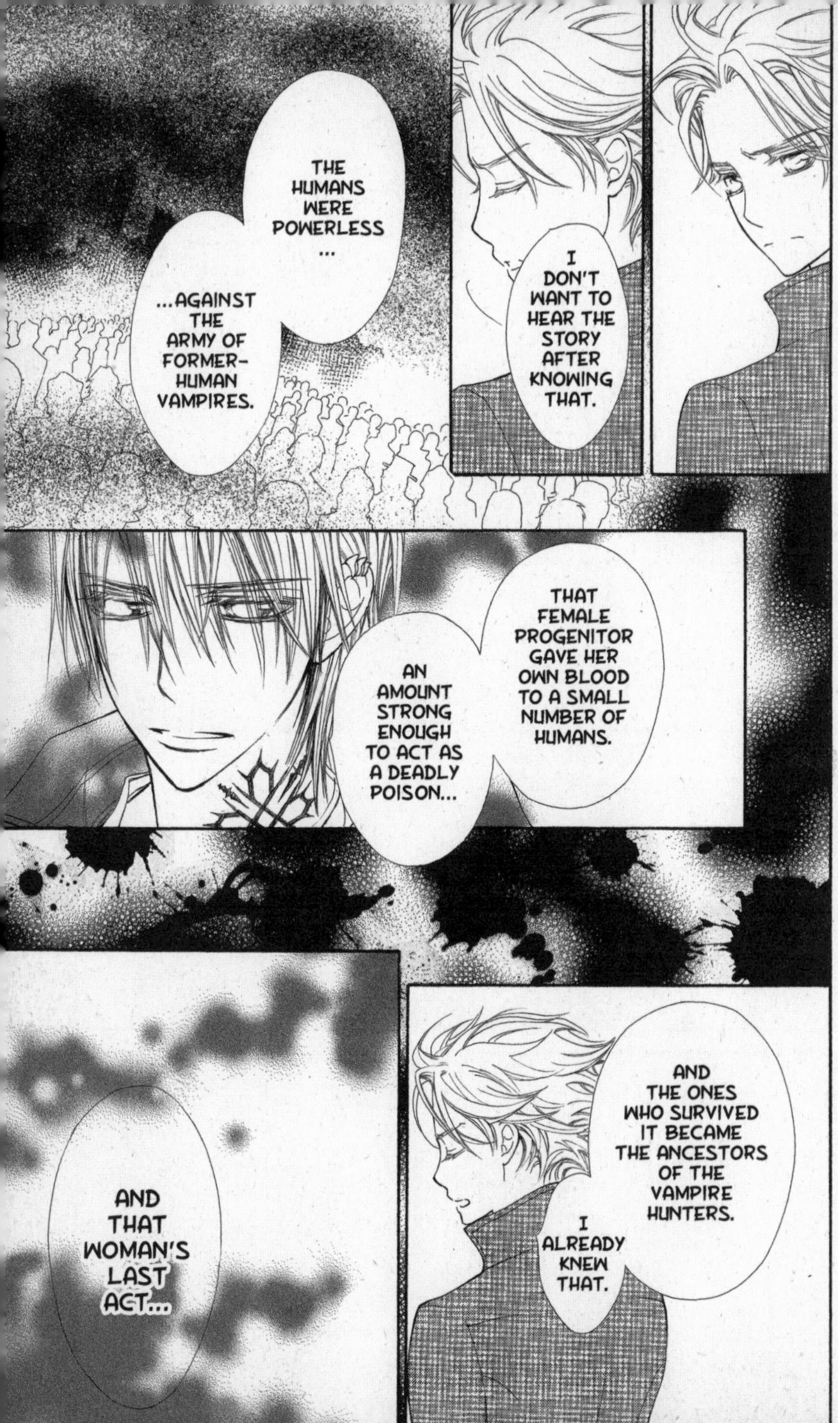
I DON'T WANT TO HEAR THE STORY AFTER KNOWING THAT.
THE HUMANS WERE POWERLESS...
...AGAINST THE ARMY OF FORMER-HUMAN VAMPIRES.
THAT FEMALE PROGENITOR GAVE HER OWN BLOOD TO A SMALL NUMBER OF HUMANS.
AN AMOUNT STRONG ENOUGH TO ACT AS A DEADLY POISON...
AND THE ONES WHO SURVIVED IT BECAME THE ANCESTORS OF THE VAMPIRE HUNTERS.
I ALREADY KNEW THAT.
AND THAT WOMAN'S LAST ACT...

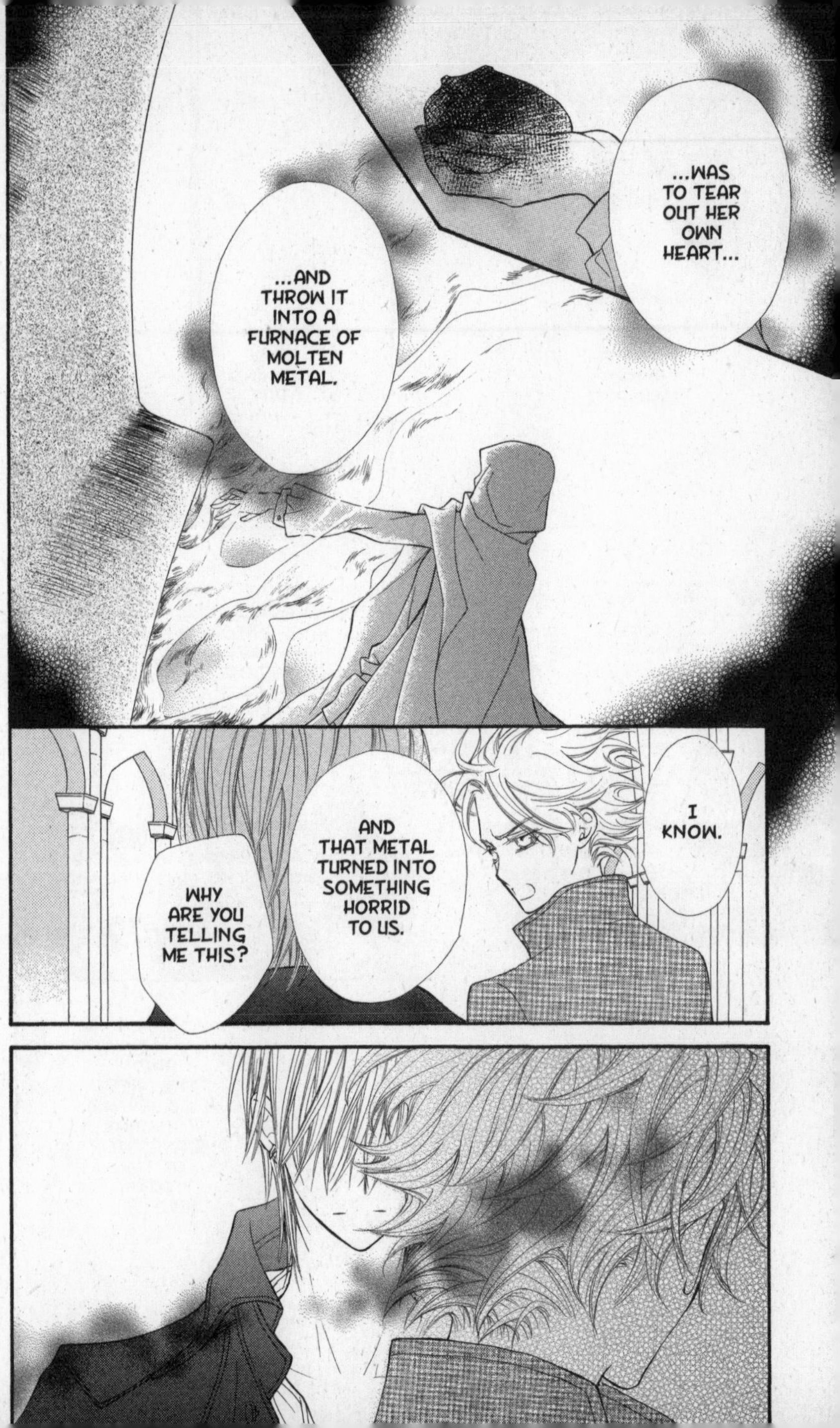
...WAS TO TEAR OUT HER OWN HEART...
...AND THROW IT INTO A FURNACE OF MOLTEN METAL.
I KNOW.
AND THAT METAL TURNED INTO SOMETHING HORRID TO US.
WHY ARE YOU TELLING ME THIS?

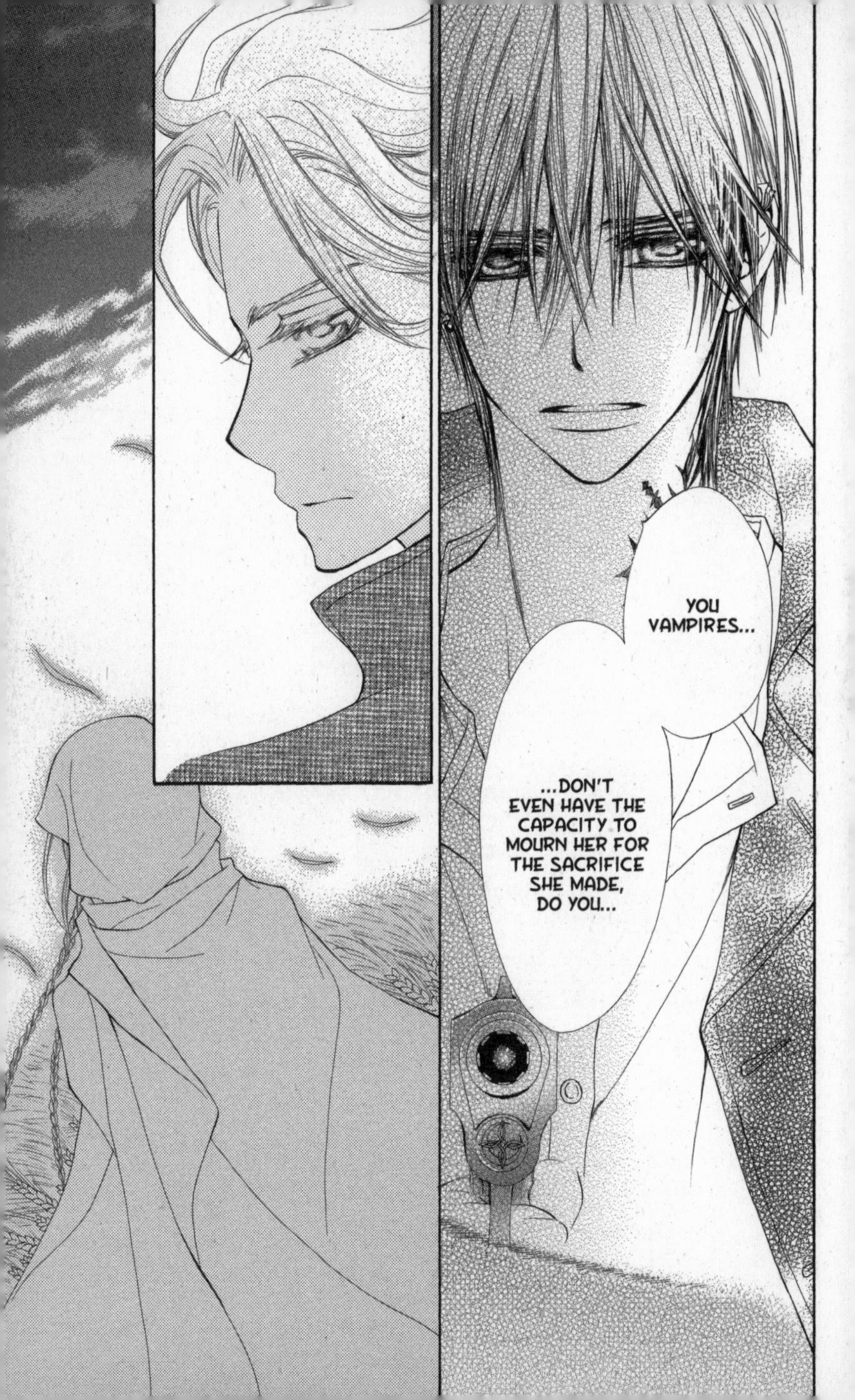
YOU VAMPIRES...
...DON'T EVEN HAVE THE CAPACITY TO MOURN HER FOR THE SACRIFICE SHE MADE, DO YOU...

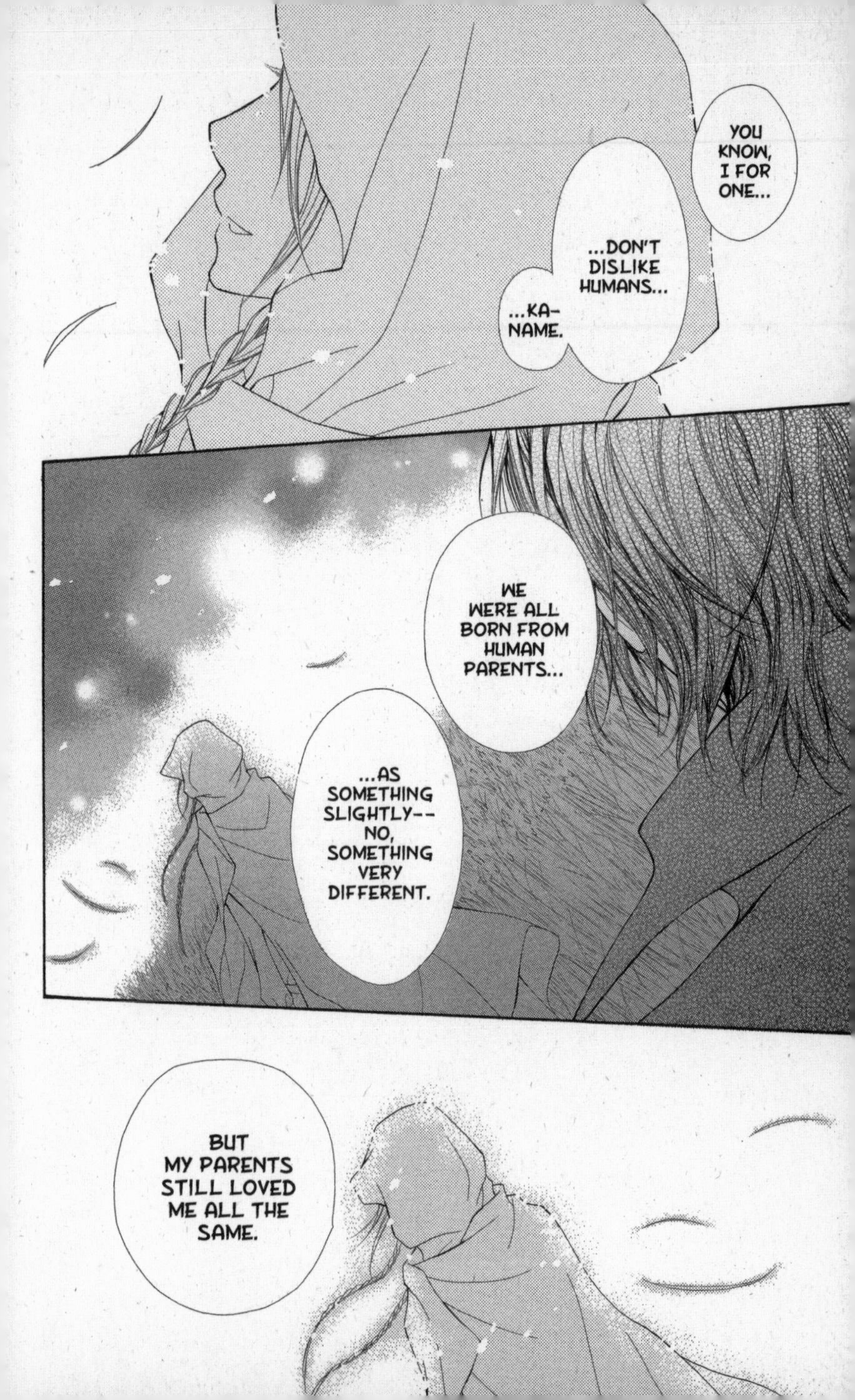
YOU KNOW, I FOR ONE...
...DON'T DISLIKE HUMANS...
...KA-NAME.
WE WERE ALL BORN FROM HUMAN PARENTS...
...AS SOMETHING SLIGHTLY-- NO, SOMETHING VERY DIFFERENT.
BUT MY PARENTS STILL LOVED ME ALL THE SAME.

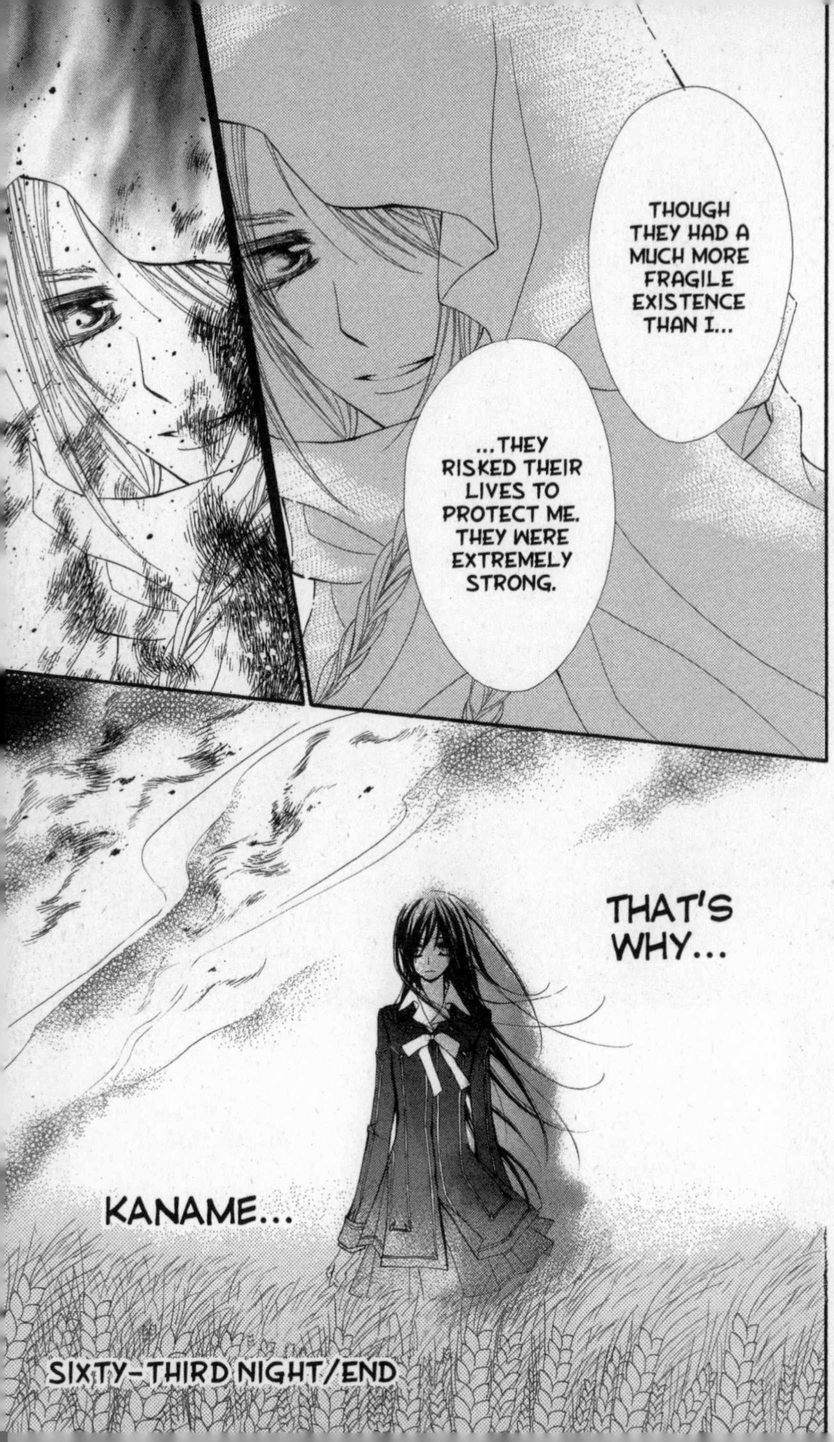
THOUGH THEY HAD A MUCH MORE FRAGILE EXISTENCE THAN I...
...THEY RISKED THEIR LIVES TO PROTECT ME. THEY WERE EXTREMELY STRONG.
THAT'S WHY...
KANAME...
SIXTY-THIRD NIGHT/END

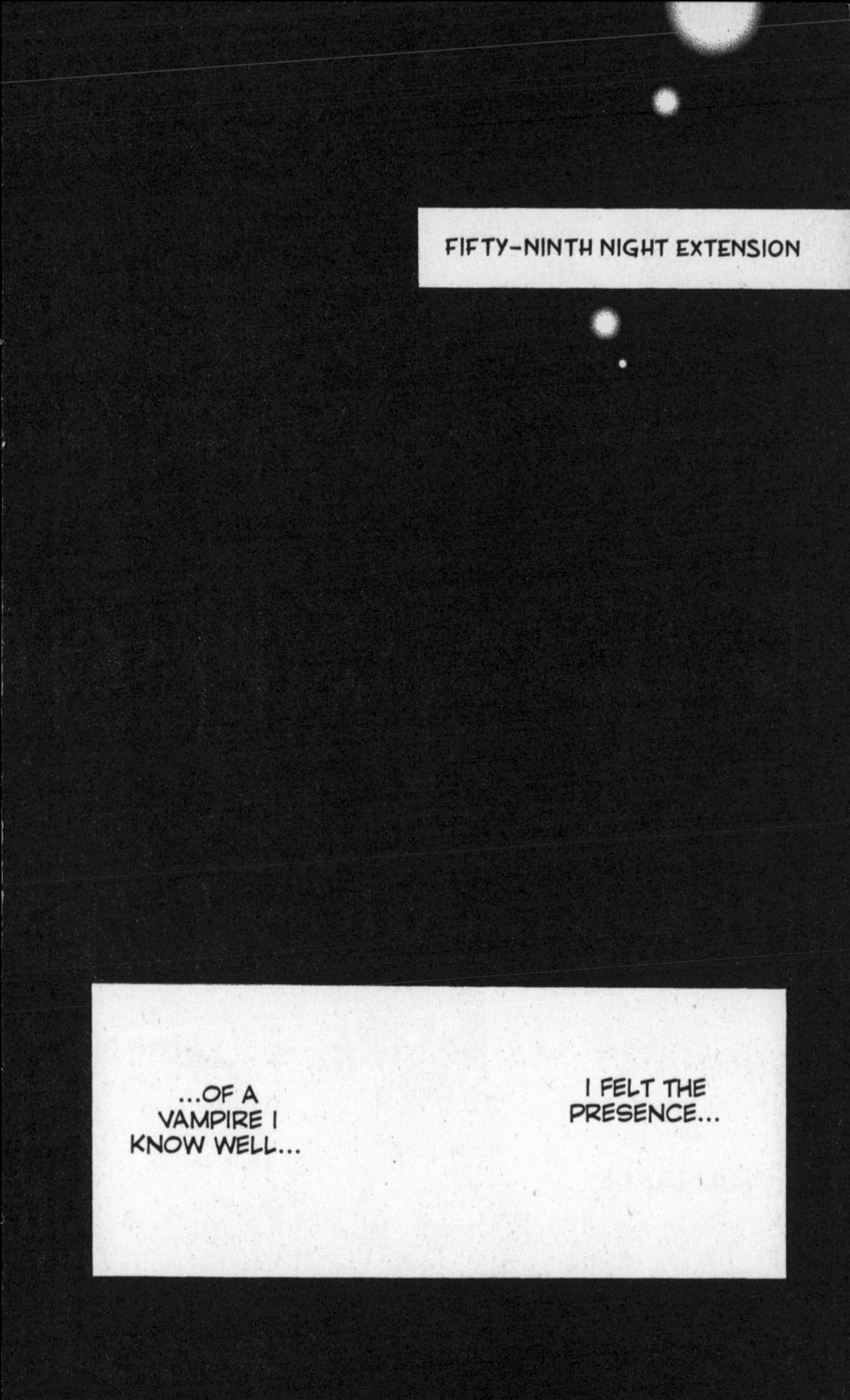
FIFTY-NINTH NIGHT EXTENSION
I FELT THE PRESENCE...
...OF A VAMPIRE I KNOW WELL...

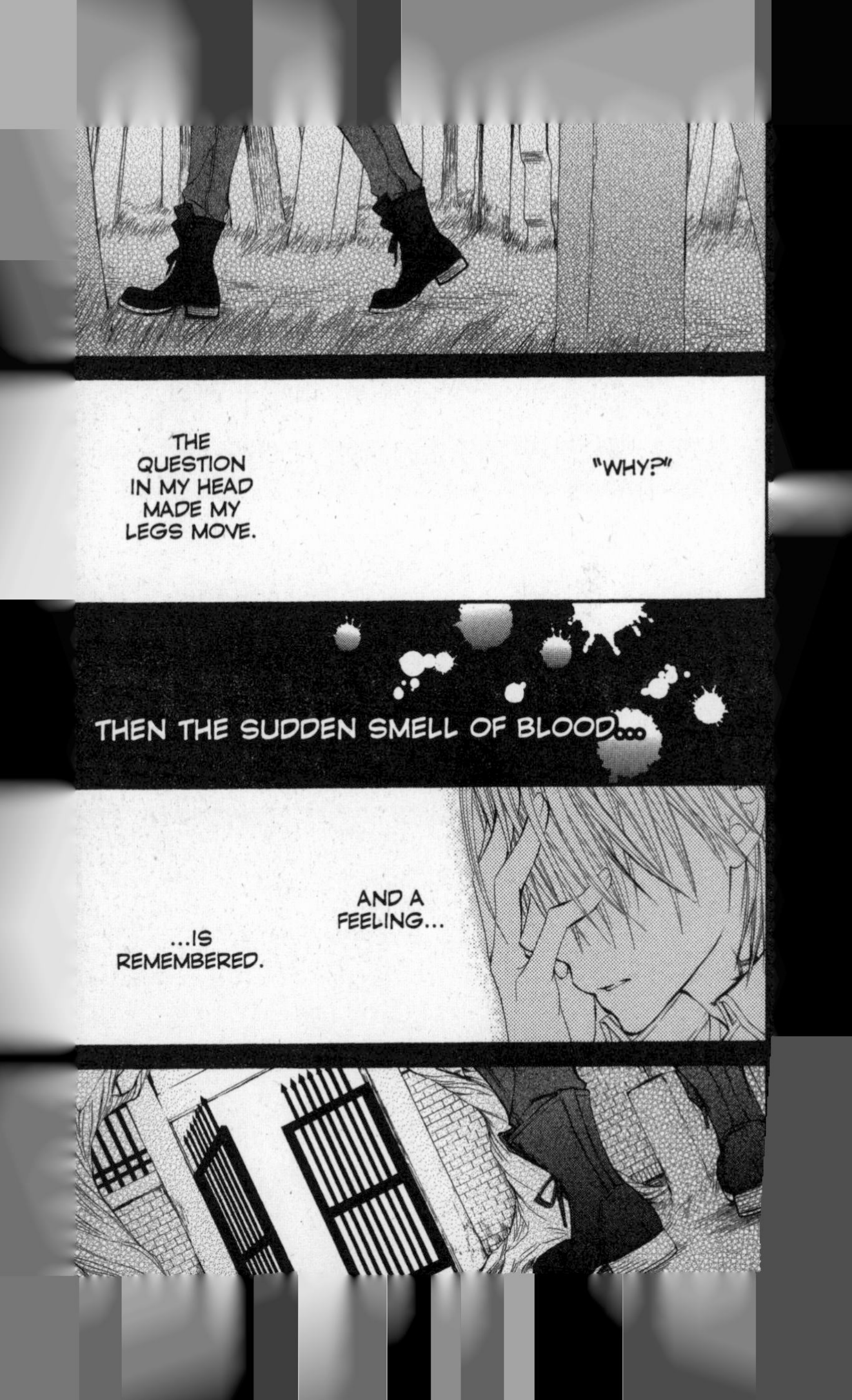
"WHY?"
THE QUESTION IN MY HEAD MADE MY LEGS MOVE.
THEN THE SUDDEN SMELL OF BLOOD...
AND A FEELING...
...IS REMEMBERED.

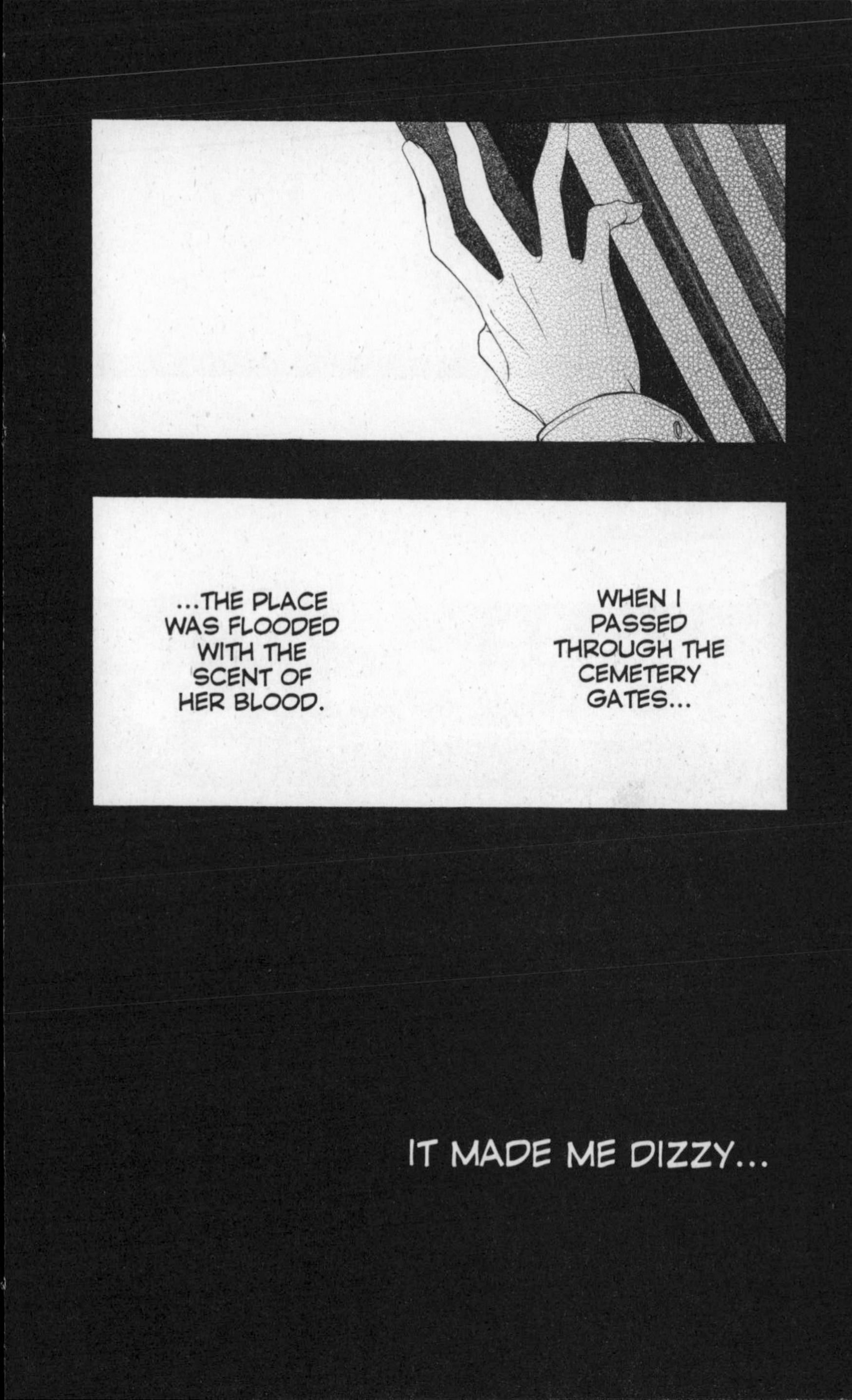
WHEN I PASSED THROUGH THE CEMETERY GATES...
...THE PLACE WAS FLOODED WITH THE SCENT OF HER BLOOD.
IT MADE ME DIZZY...

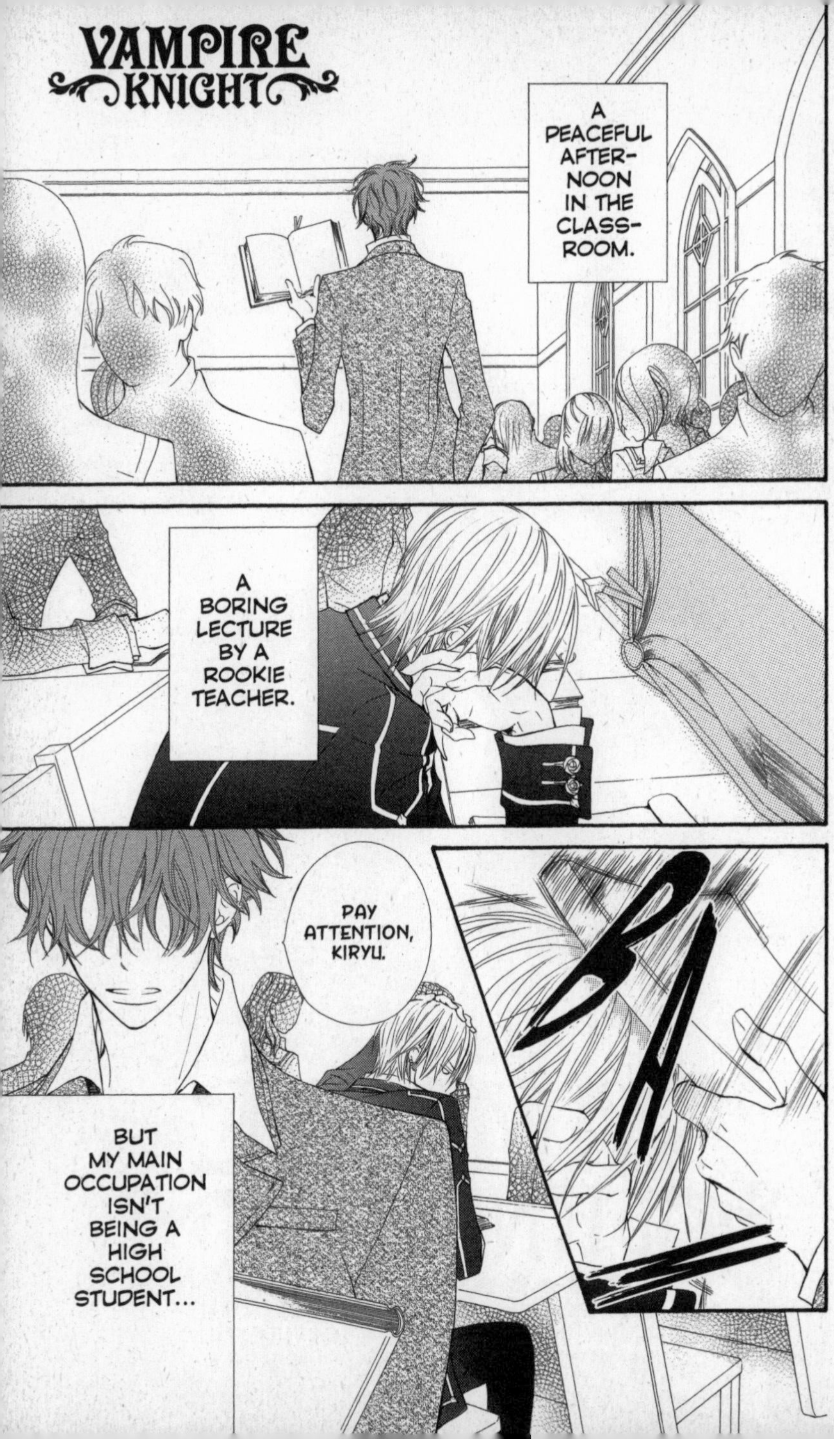
VAMPIRE KNIGHT
A PEACEFUL AFTERNOON IN THE CLASSROOM.
A BORING LECTURE BY A ROOKIE TEACHER.
PAY ATTENTION, KIRYU.
BUT MY MAIN OCCUPATION ISN'T BEING A HIGH SCHOOL STUDENT...

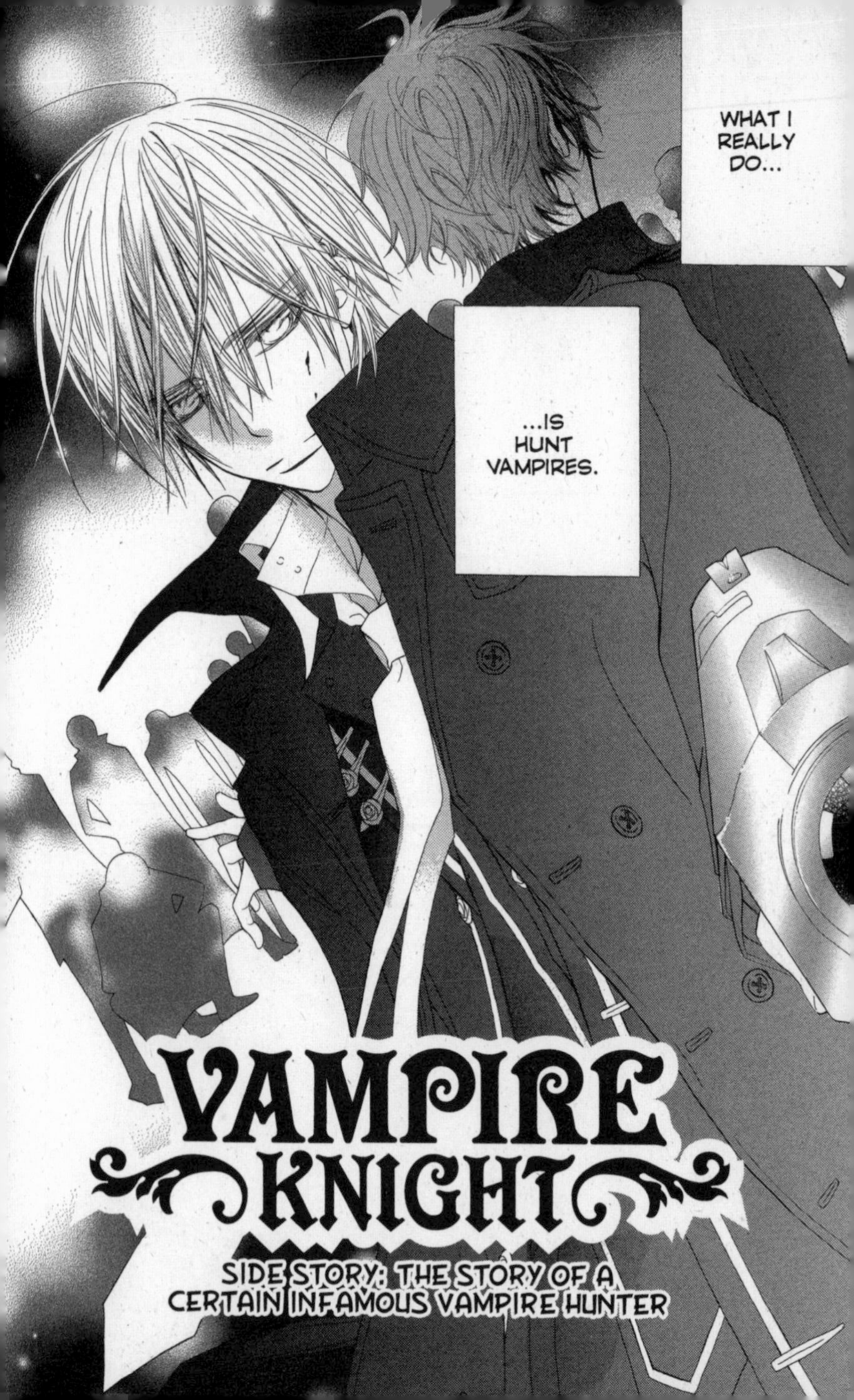
WHAT I REALLY DO...
...IS HUNT VAMPIRES.
VAMPIRE KNIGHT
SIDE STORY: THE STORY OF A CERTAIN INFAMOUS VAMPIRE HUNTER

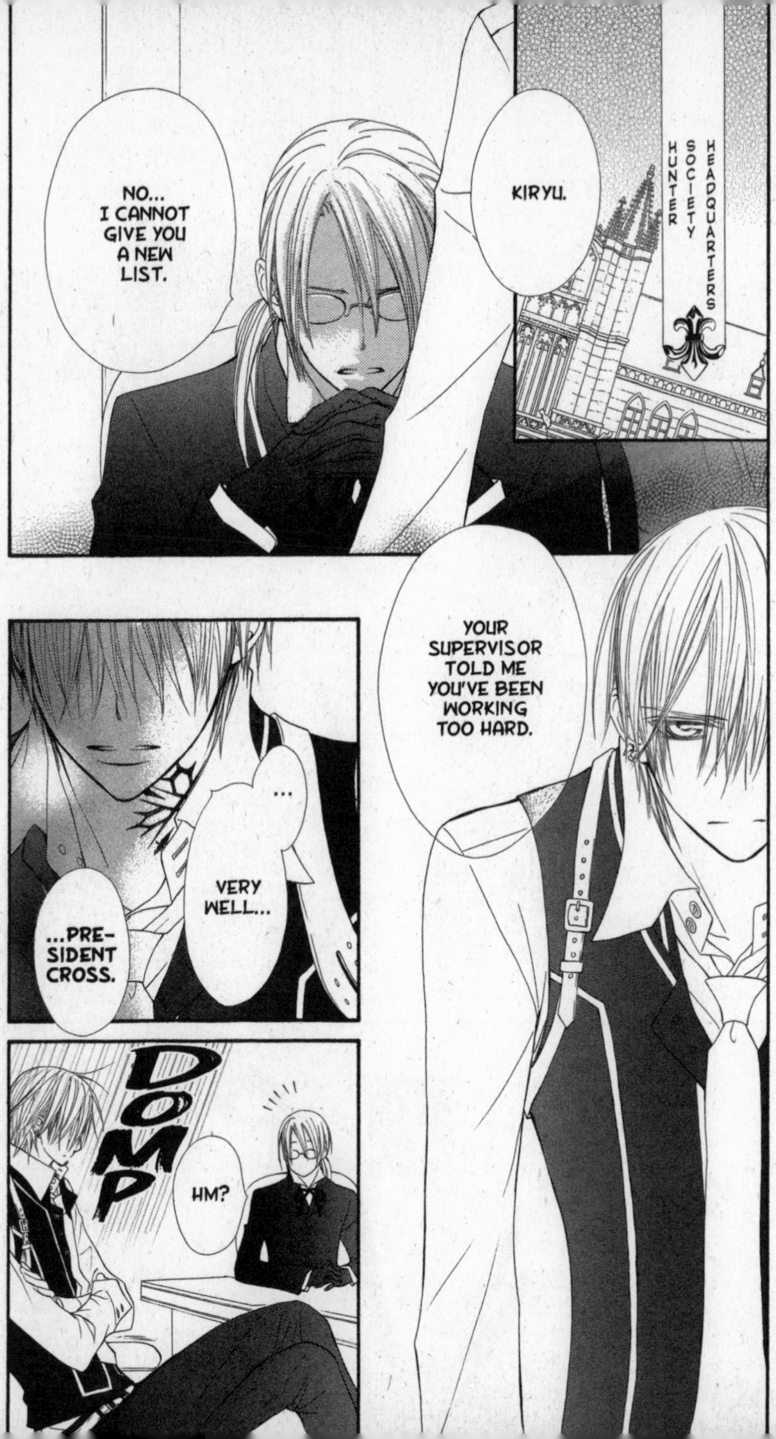
HUNTER SOCIETY HEADQUARTERS
KIRYU.
NO... I CANNOT GIVE YOU A NEW LIST.
YOUR SUPERVISOR TOLD ME YOU'VE BEEN WORKING TOO HARD.
...
VERY WELL...
...PRE-SIDENT CROSS.
DOMP
HM?

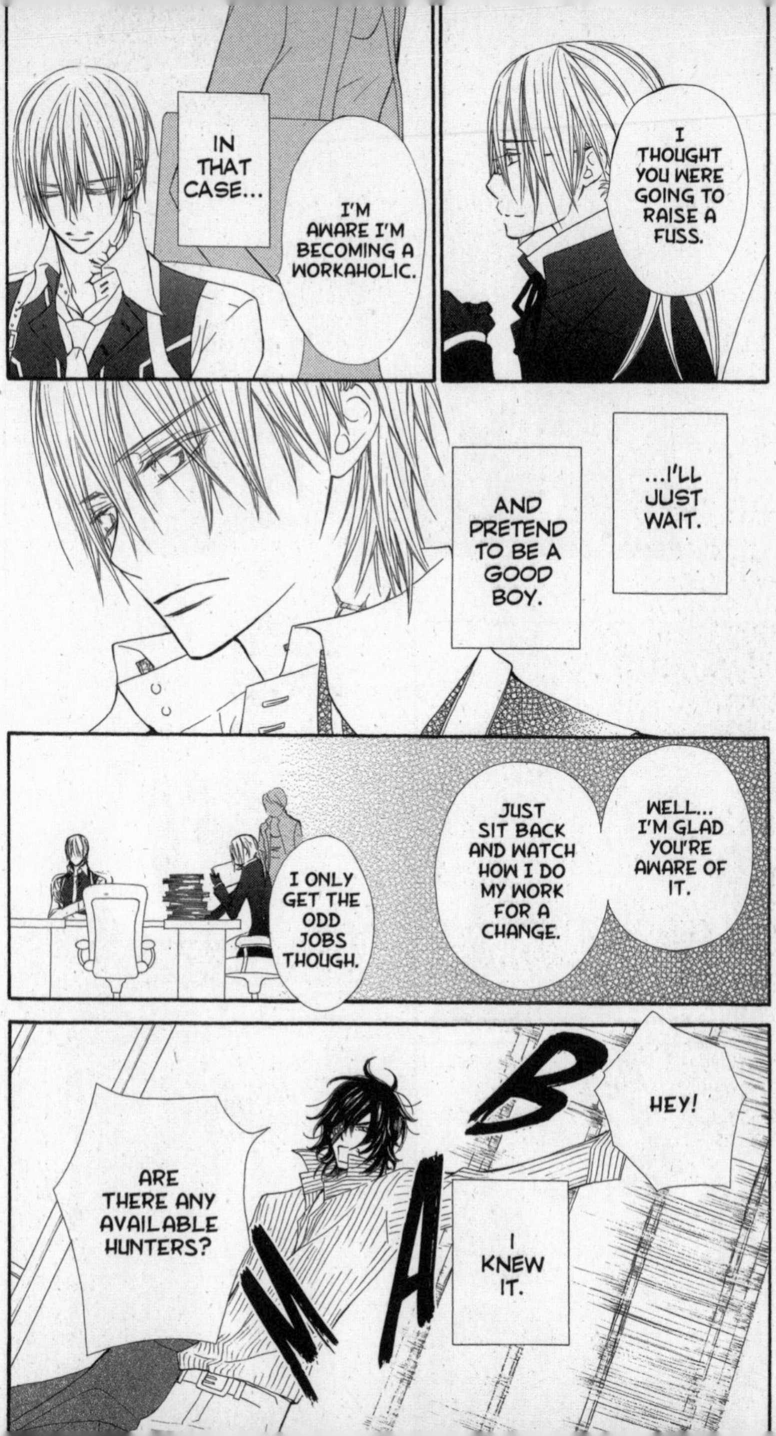
I THOUGHT YOU WERE GOING TO RAISE A FUSS.
I'M AWARE I'M BECOMING A WORKAHOLIC.
IN THAT CASE...
...I'LL JUST WAIT.
AND PRETEND TO BE A GOOD BOY.
WELL... I'M GLAD YOU'RE AWARE OF IT.
JUST SIT BACK AND WATCH HOW I DO MY WORK FOR A CHANGE.
I ONLY GET THE ODD JOBS THOUGH.
HEY!
BAM
I KNEW IT.
ARE THERE ANY AVAILABLE HUNTERS?

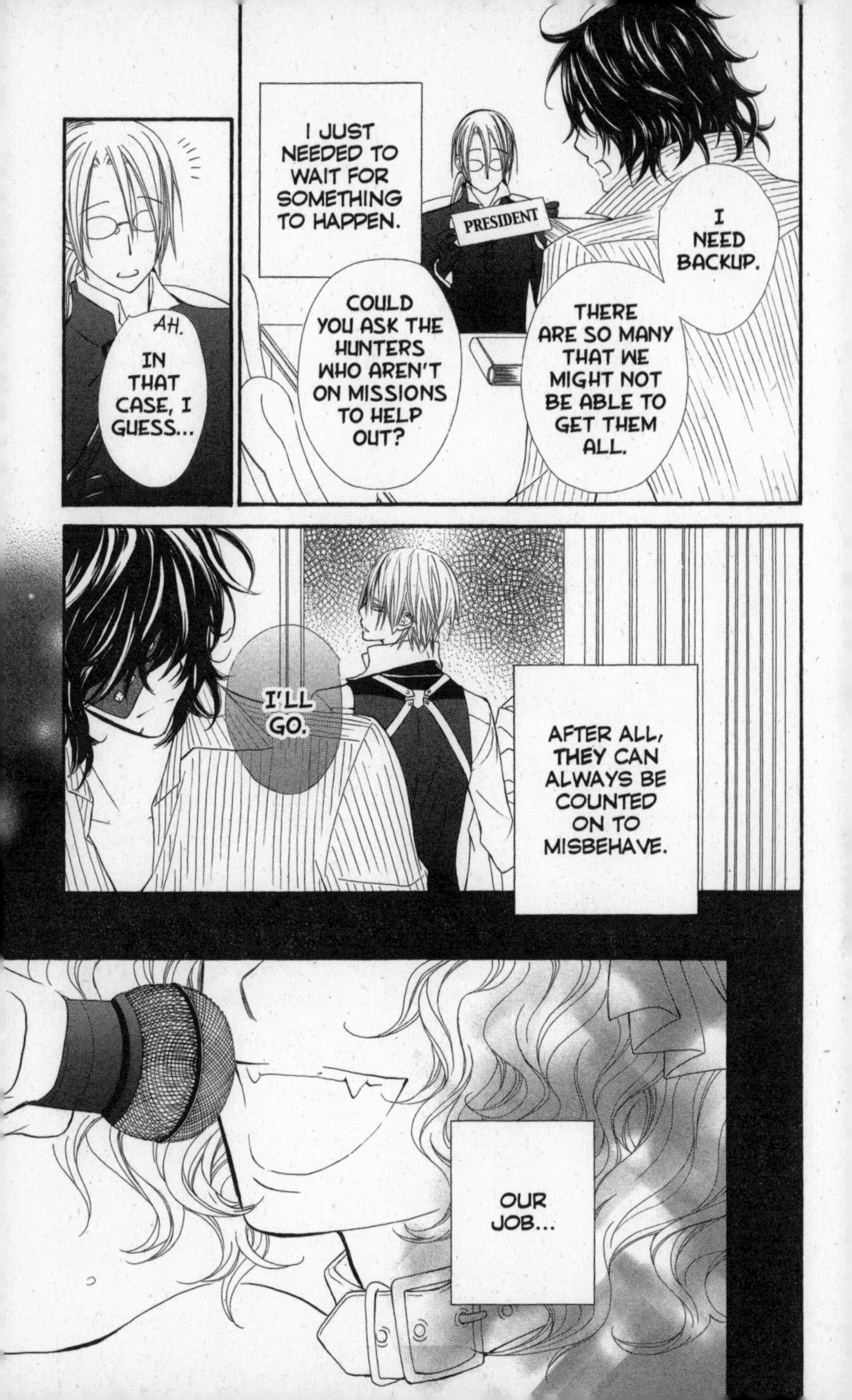
I JUST NEEDED TO WAIT FOR SOMETHING TO HAPPEN.
PRESIDENT
I NEED BACKUP.
THERE ARE SO MANY THAT WE MIGHT NOT BE ABLE TO GET THEM ALL.
COULD YOU ASK THE HUNTERS WHO AREN'T ON MISSIONS TO HELP OUT?
AH.
IN THAT CASE, I GUESS...
AFTER ALL, THEY CAN ALWAYS BE COUNTED ON TO MISBEHAVE.
I'LL GO.
OUR JOB...

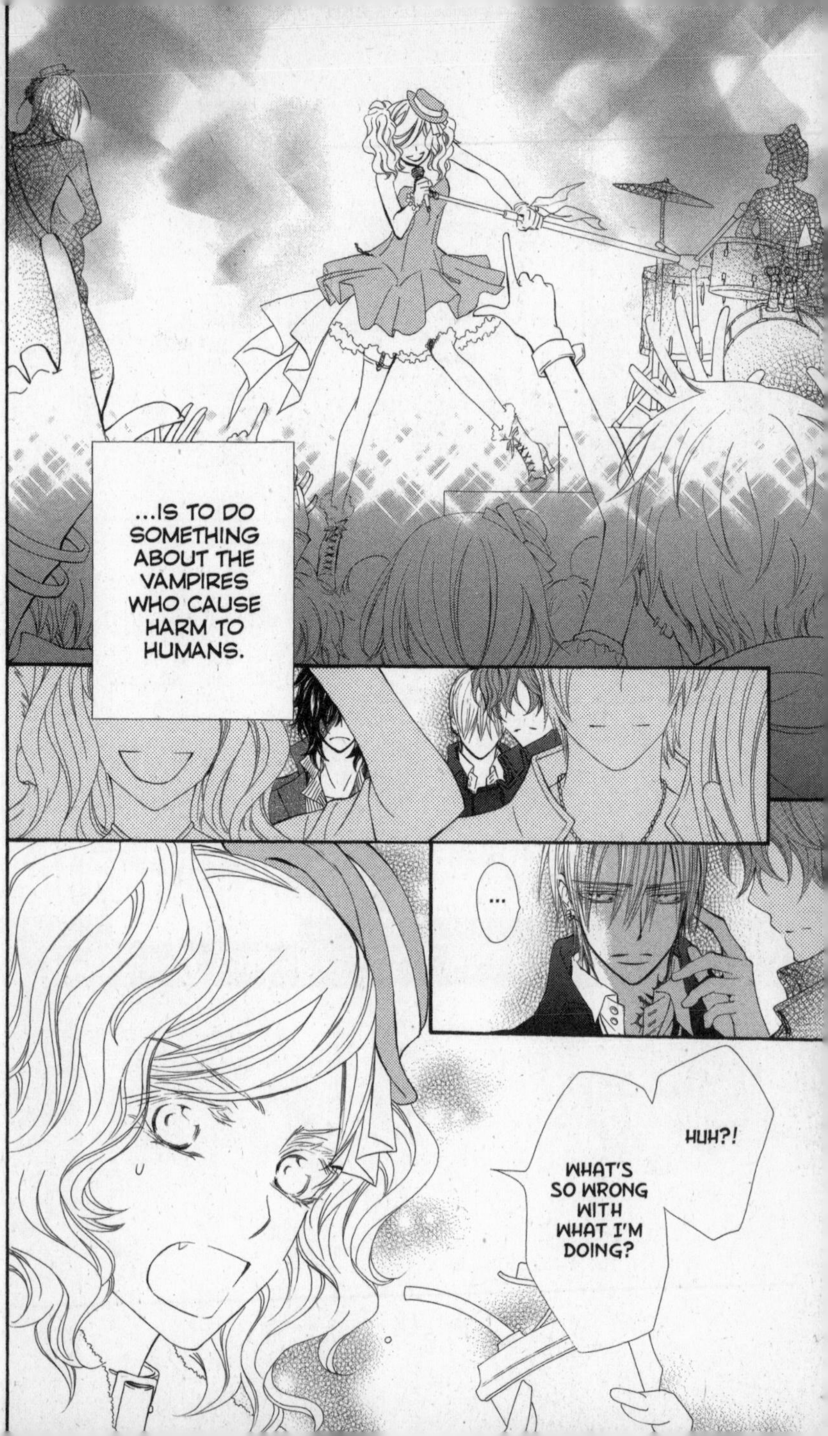
...IS TO DO SOMETHING ABOUT THE VAMPIRES WHO CAUSE HARM TO HUMANS.
...
HUH?!
WHAT'S SO WRONG WITH WHAT I'M DOING?

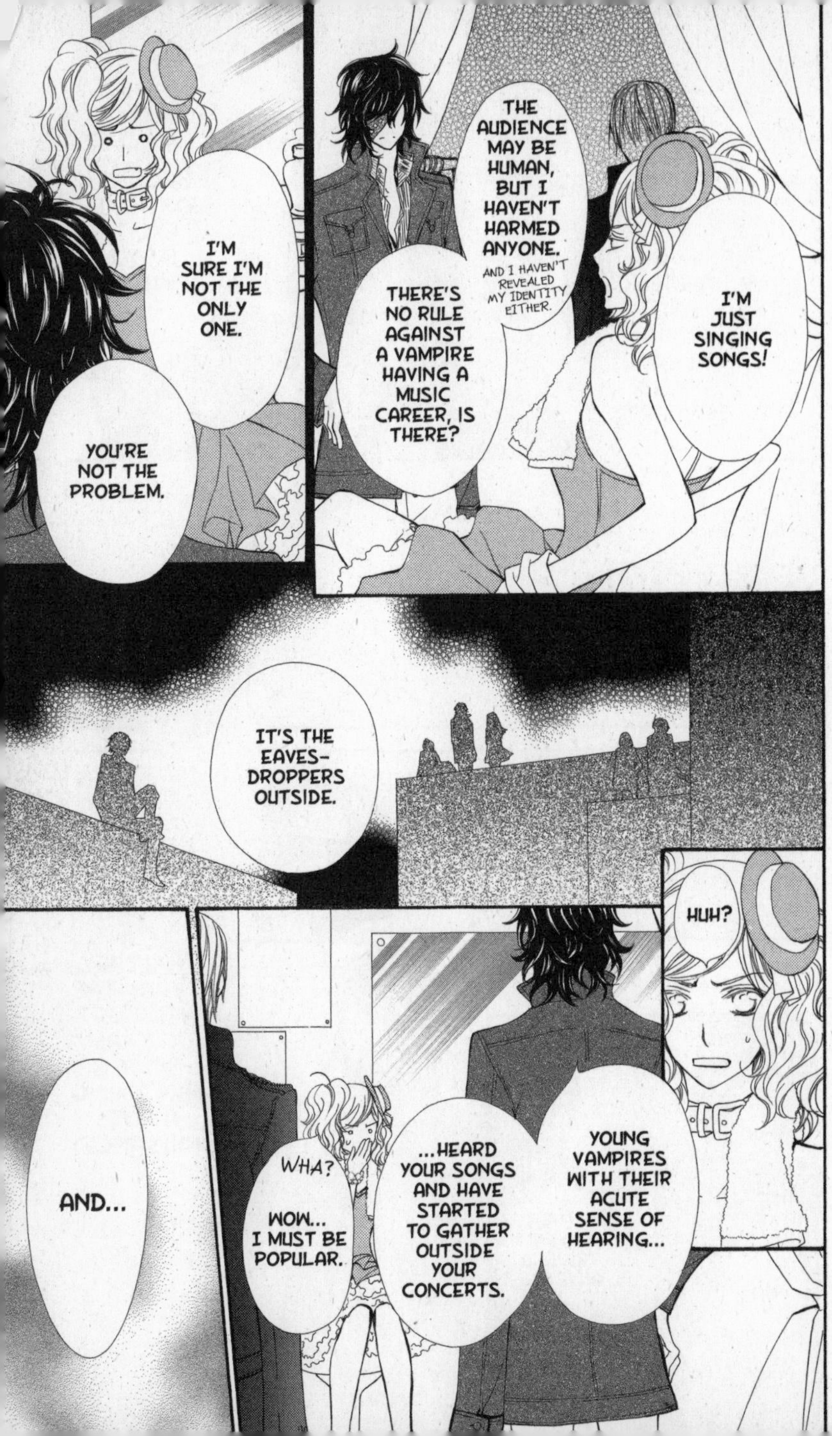
I'M JUST SINGING SONGS!
THE AUDIENCE MAY BE HUMAN, BUT I HAVEN'T HARMED ANYONE.
AND I HAVEN'T REVEALED MY IDENTITY EITHER.
THERE'S NO RULE AGAINST A VAMPIRE HAVING A MUSIC CAREER, IS THERE?
I'M SURE I'M NOT THE ONLY ONE.
YOU'RE NOT THE PROBLEM.
IT'S THE EAVES-DROPPERS OUTSIDE.
HUH?
YOUNG VAMPIRES WITH THEIR ACUTE SENSE OF HEARING...
...HEARD YOUR SONGS AND HAVE STARTED TO GATHER OUTSIDE YOUR CONCERTS.
WHA?
WOW... I MUST BE POPULAR.
AND...

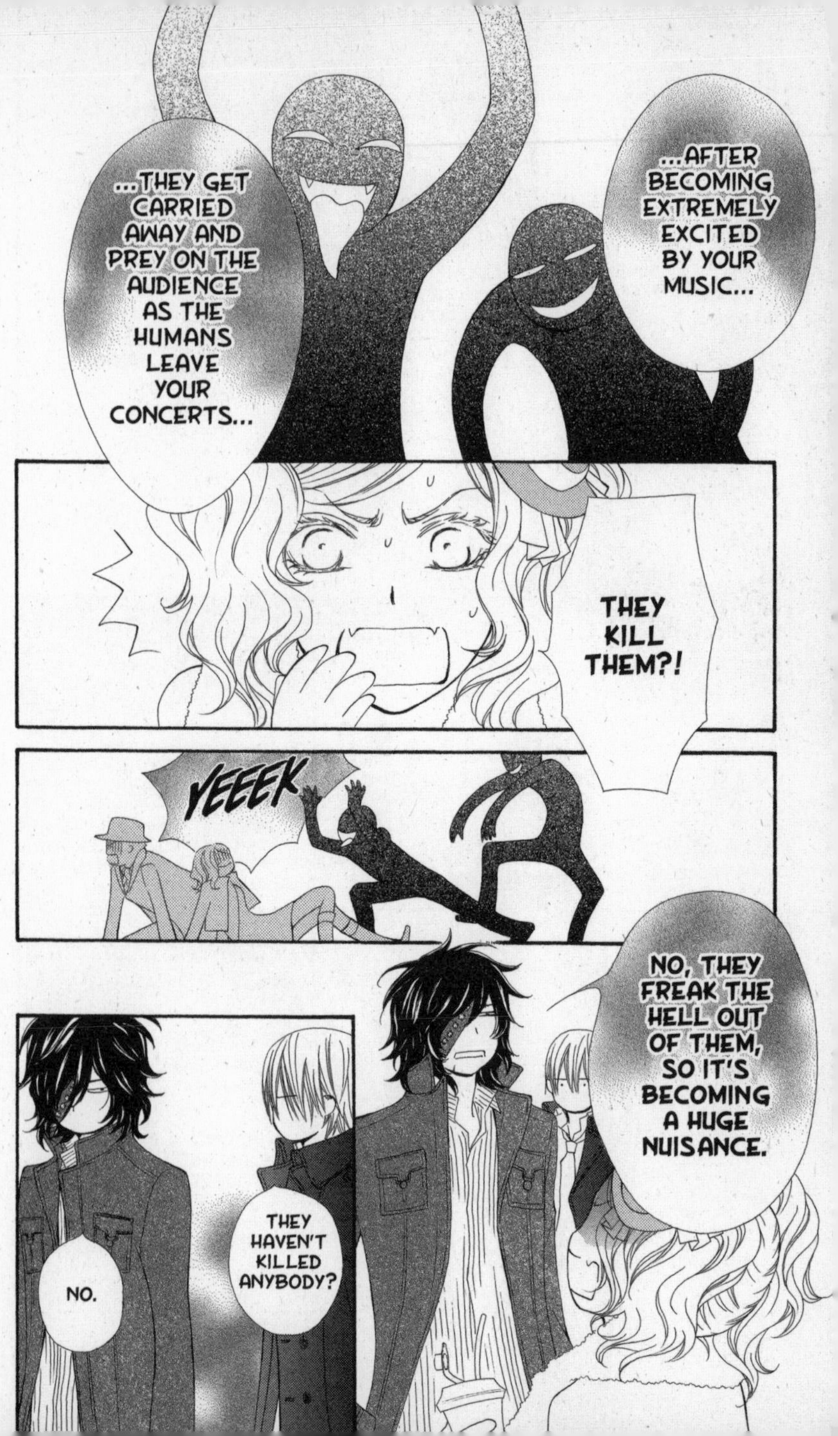
...AFTER BECOMING EXTREMELY EXCITED BY YOUR MUSIC...
...THEY GET CARRIED AWAY AND PREY ON THE AUDIENCE AS THE HUMANS LEAVE YOUR CONCERTS...
THEY KILL THEM?!
YEEEK
NO, THEY FREAK THE HELL OUT OF THEM, SO IT'S BECOMING A HUGE NUISANCE.
THEY HAVEN'T KILLED ANYBODY?
NO.

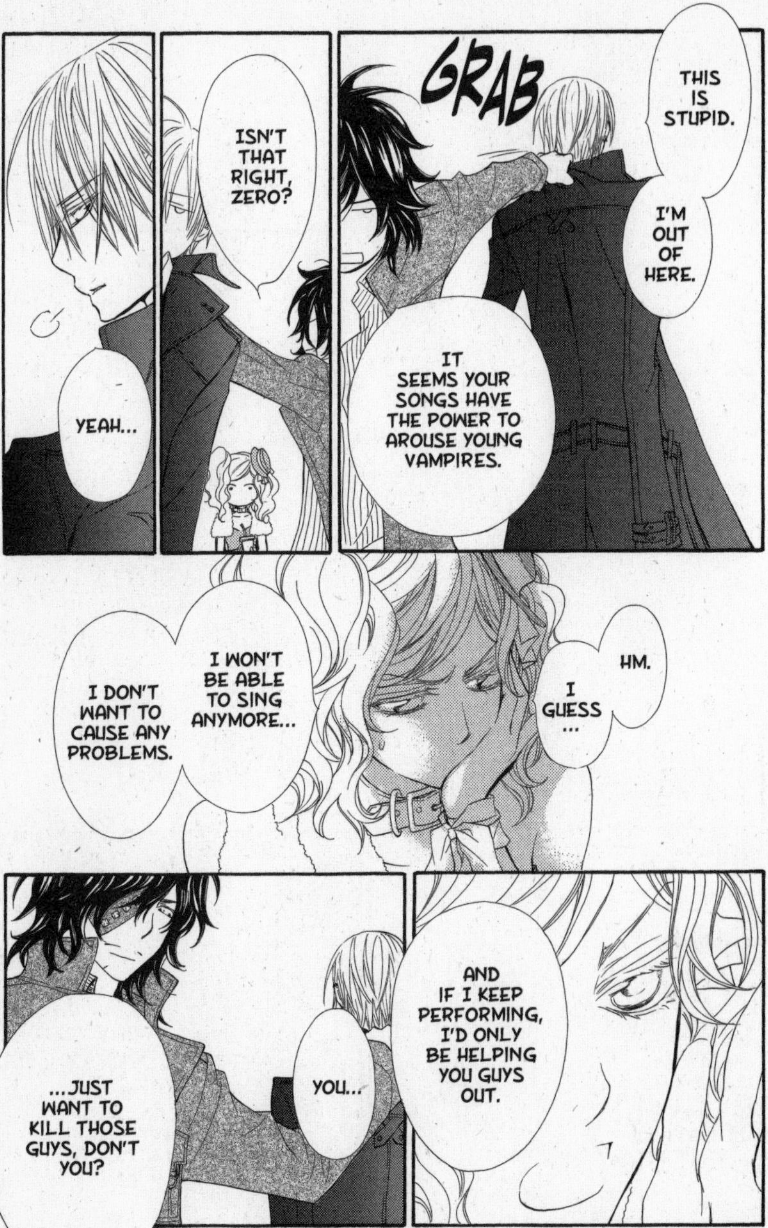
THIS IS STUPID.
GRAB
I'M OUT OF HERE.
IT SEEMS YOUR SONGS HAVE THE POWER TO AROUSE YOUNG VAMPIRES.
ISN'T THAT RIGHT, ZERO?
YEAH...
HM. I GUESS...
I WON'T BE ABLE TO SING ANYMORE...
I DON'T WANT TO CAUSE ANY PROBLEMS.
AND IF I KEEP PERFORMING, I'D ONLY BE HELPING YOU GUYS OUT.
YOU...
...JUST WANT TO KILL THOSE GUYS, DON'T YOU?

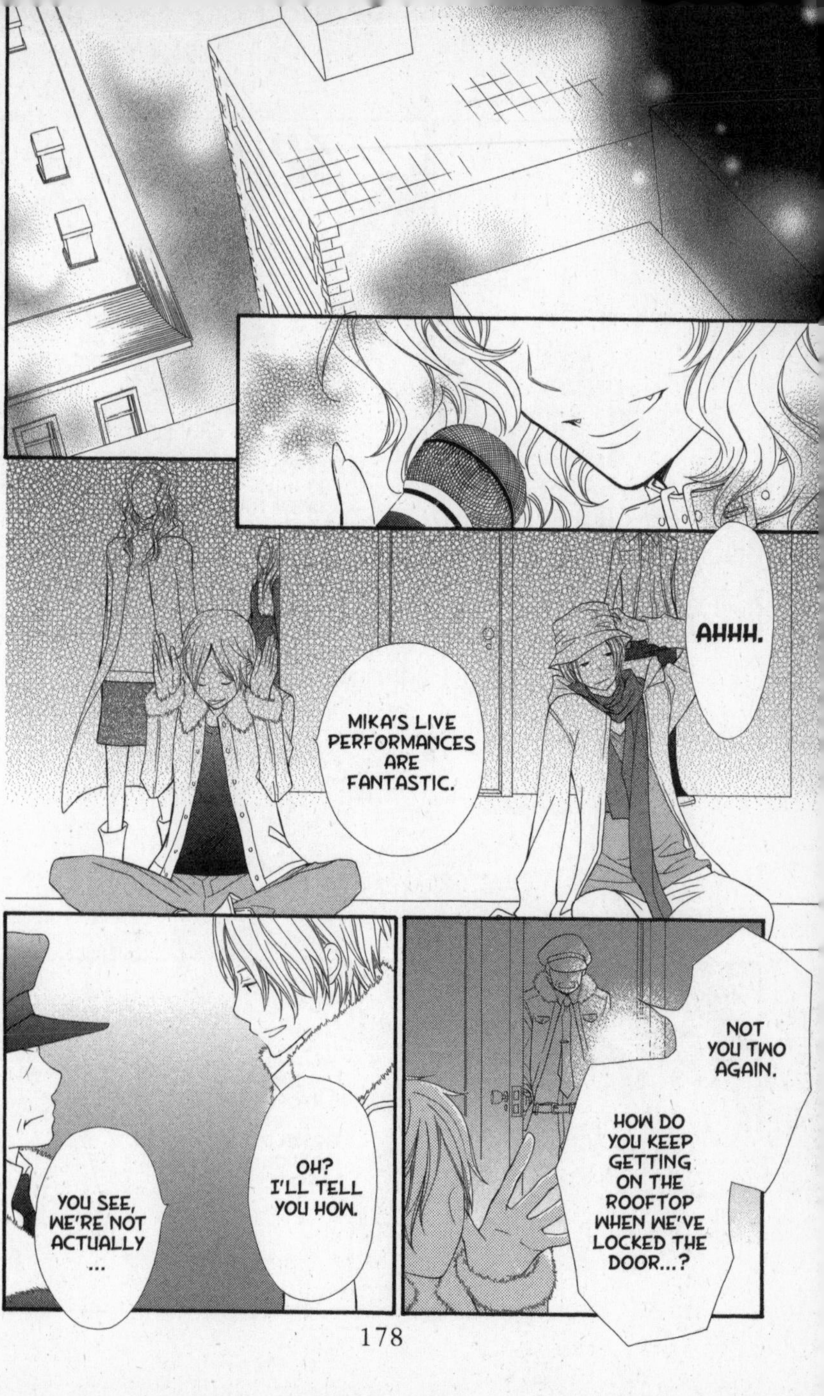
AHHH.
MIKA'S LIVE PERFORMANCES ARE FANTASTIC.
NOT YOU TWO AGAIN.
HOW DO YOU KEEP GETTING ON THE ROOFTOP WHEN WE'VE LOCKED THE DOOR...?
OH? I'LL TELL YOU HOW.
YOU SEE, WE'RE NOT ACTUALLY ...

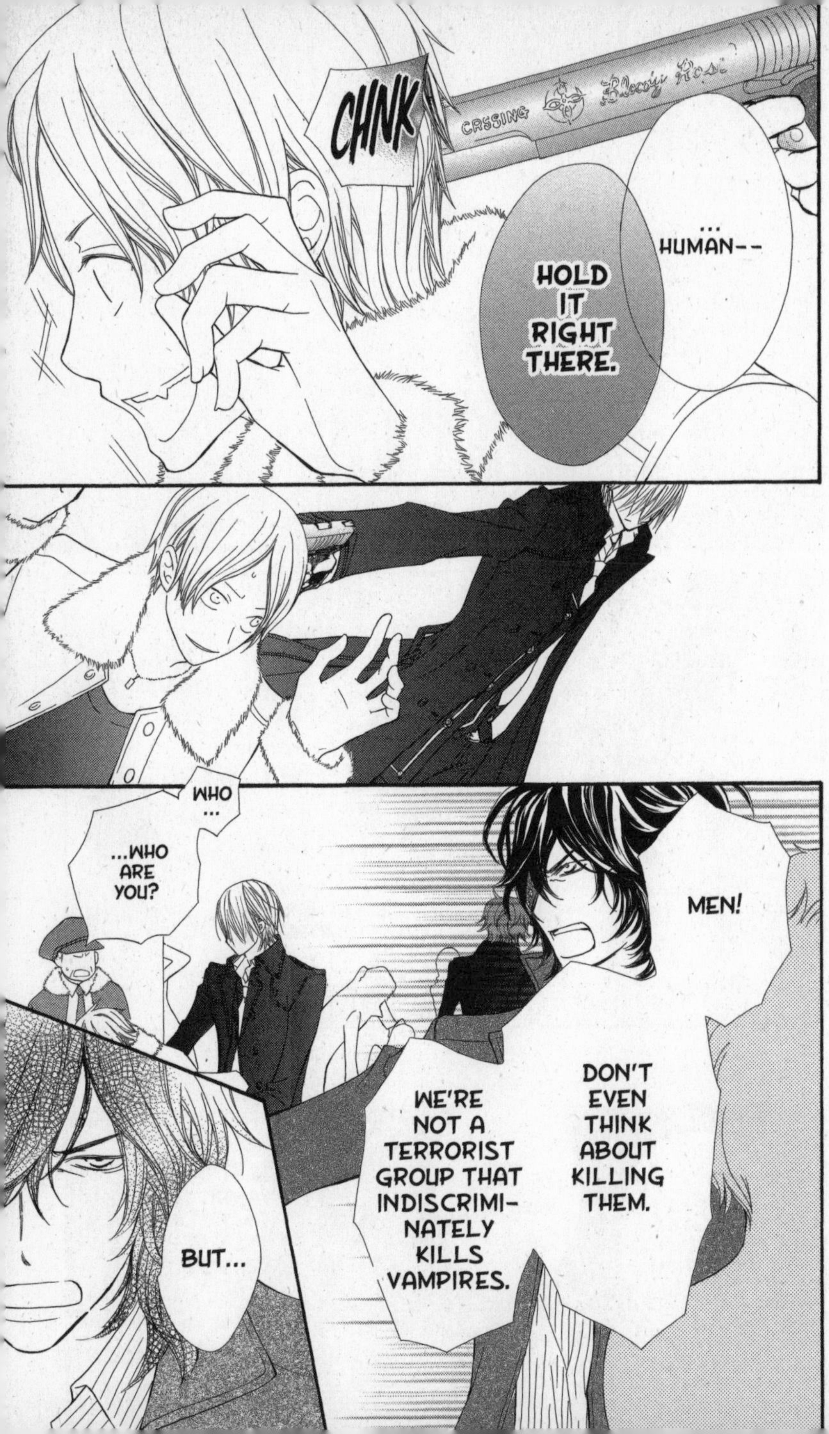
...HUMAN--
HOLD IT RIGHT THERE.
CHNK
MEN!
WHO ...
...WHO ARE YOU?
DON'T EVEN THINK ABOUT KILLING THEM.
WE'RE NOT A TERRORIST GROUP THAT INDISCRIMI-NATELY KILLS VAMPIRES.
BUT...

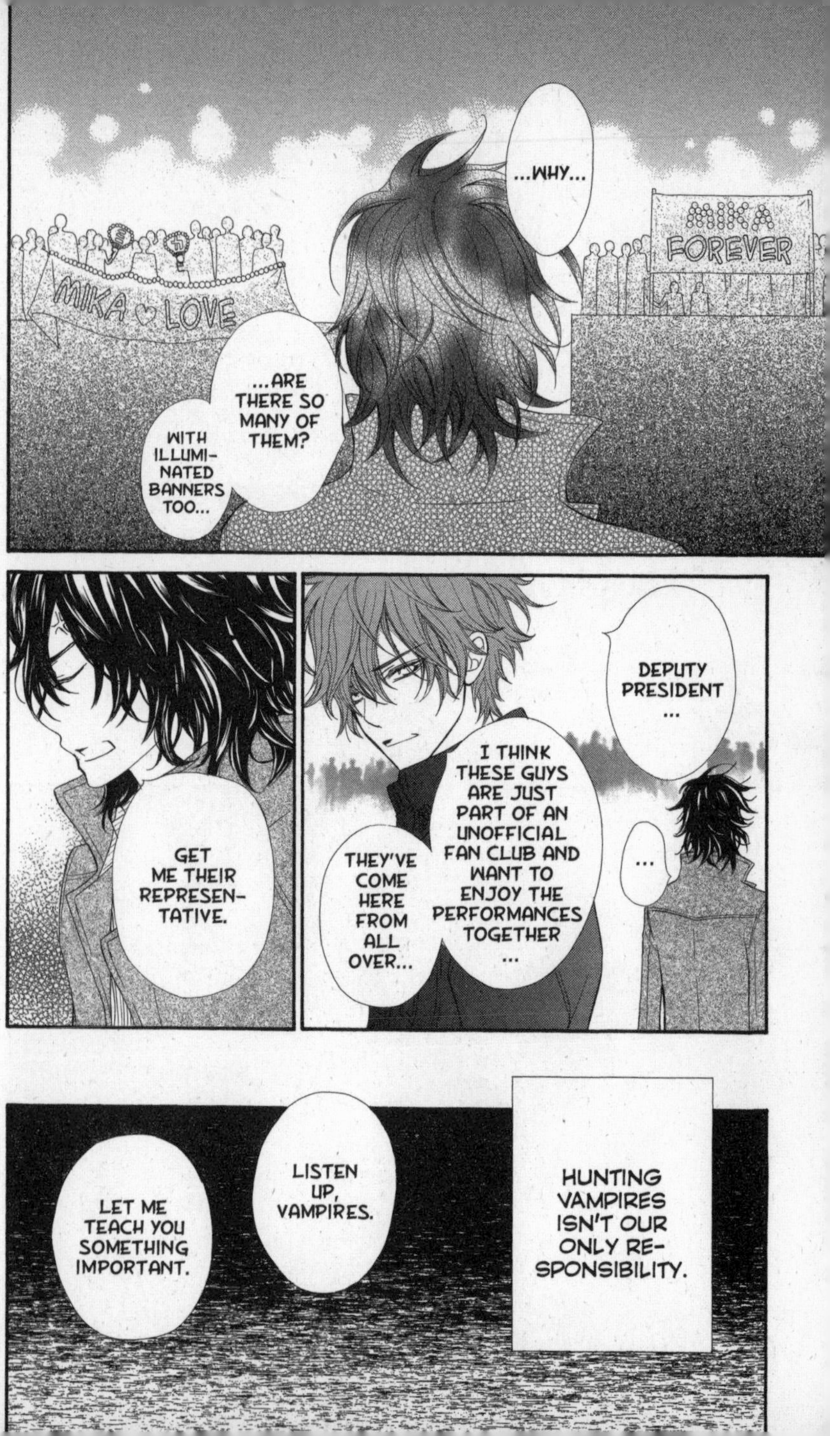
...WHY...
MIKA FOREVER
MIKA ♡ LOVE
...ARE THERE SO MANY OF THEM?
WITH ILLUMINATED BANNERS TOO...
DEPUTY PRESIDENT ...
...
I THINK THESE GUYS ARE JUST PART OF AN UNOFFICIAL FAN CLUB AND WANT TO ENJOY THE PERFORMANCES TOGETHER ...
THEY'VE COME HERE FROM ALL OVER...
GET ME THEIR REPRESENTATIVE.
HUNTING VAMPIRES ISN'T OUR ONLY RESPONSIBILITY.
LISTEN UP, VAMPIRES.
LET ME TEACH YOU SOMETHING IMPORTANT.

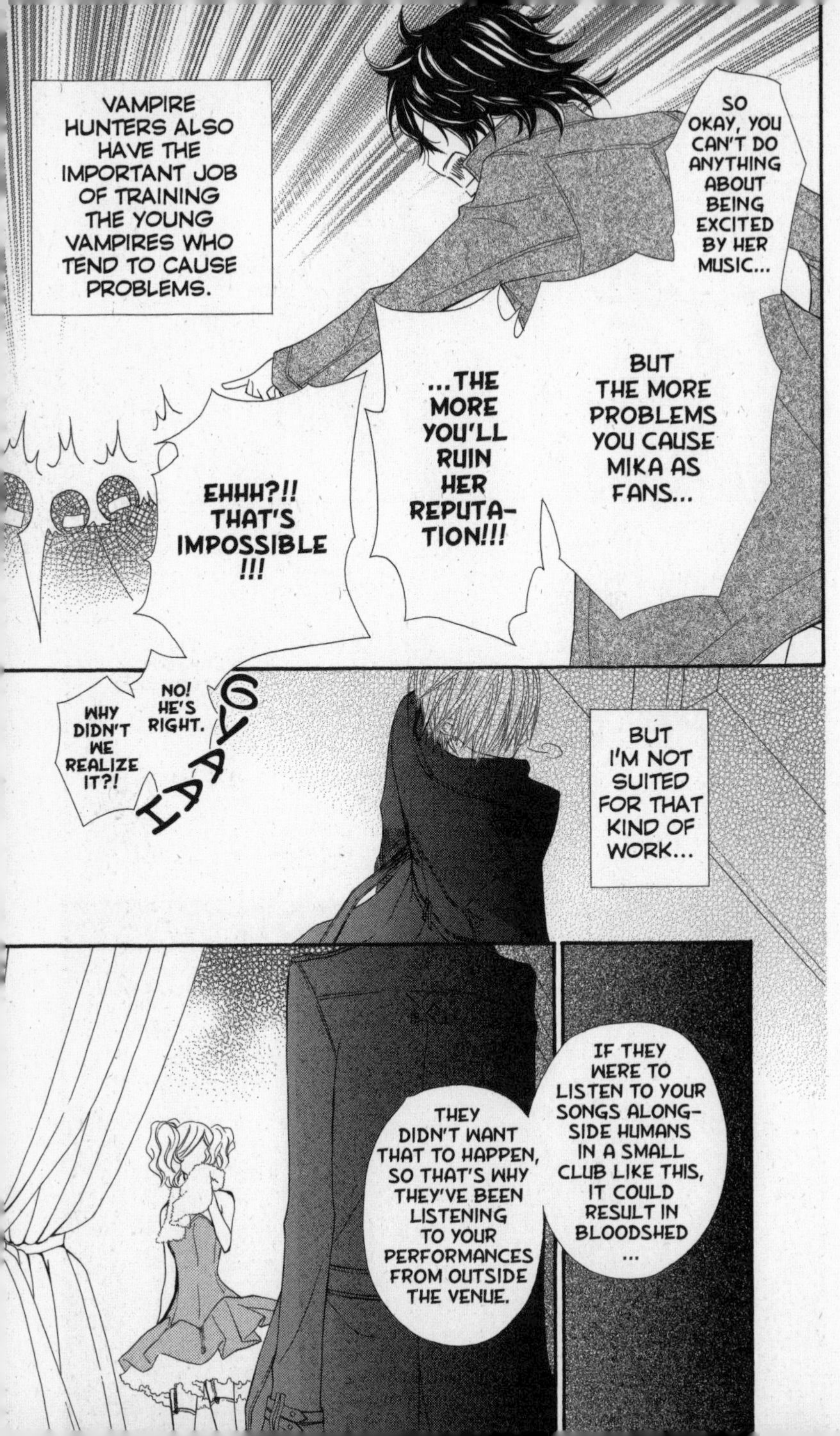
SO OKAY, YOU CAN'T DO ANYTHING ABOUT BEING EXCITED BY HER MUSIC...
VAMPIRE HUNTERS ALSO HAVE THE IMPORTANT JOB OF TRAINING THE YOUNG VAMPIRES WHO TEND TO CAUSE PROBLEMS.
BUT THE MORE PROBLEMS YOU CAUSE MIKA AS FANS...
...THE MORE YOU'LL RUIN HER REPUTA-TION!!!
EHHH?!! THAT'S IMPOSSIBLE !!!
BUT I'M NOT SUITED FOR THAT KIND OF WORK...
GYAAH
NO! HE'S RIGHT.
WHY DIDN'T WE REALIZE IT?!
IF THEY WERE TO LISTEN TO YOUR SONGS ALONG-SIDE HUMANS IN A SMALL CLUB LIKE THIS, IT COULD RESULT IN BLOODSHED ...
THEY DIDN'T WANT THAT TO HAPPEN, SO THAT'S WHY THEY'VE BEEN LISTENING TO YOUR PERFORMANCES FROM OUTSIDE THE VENUE.

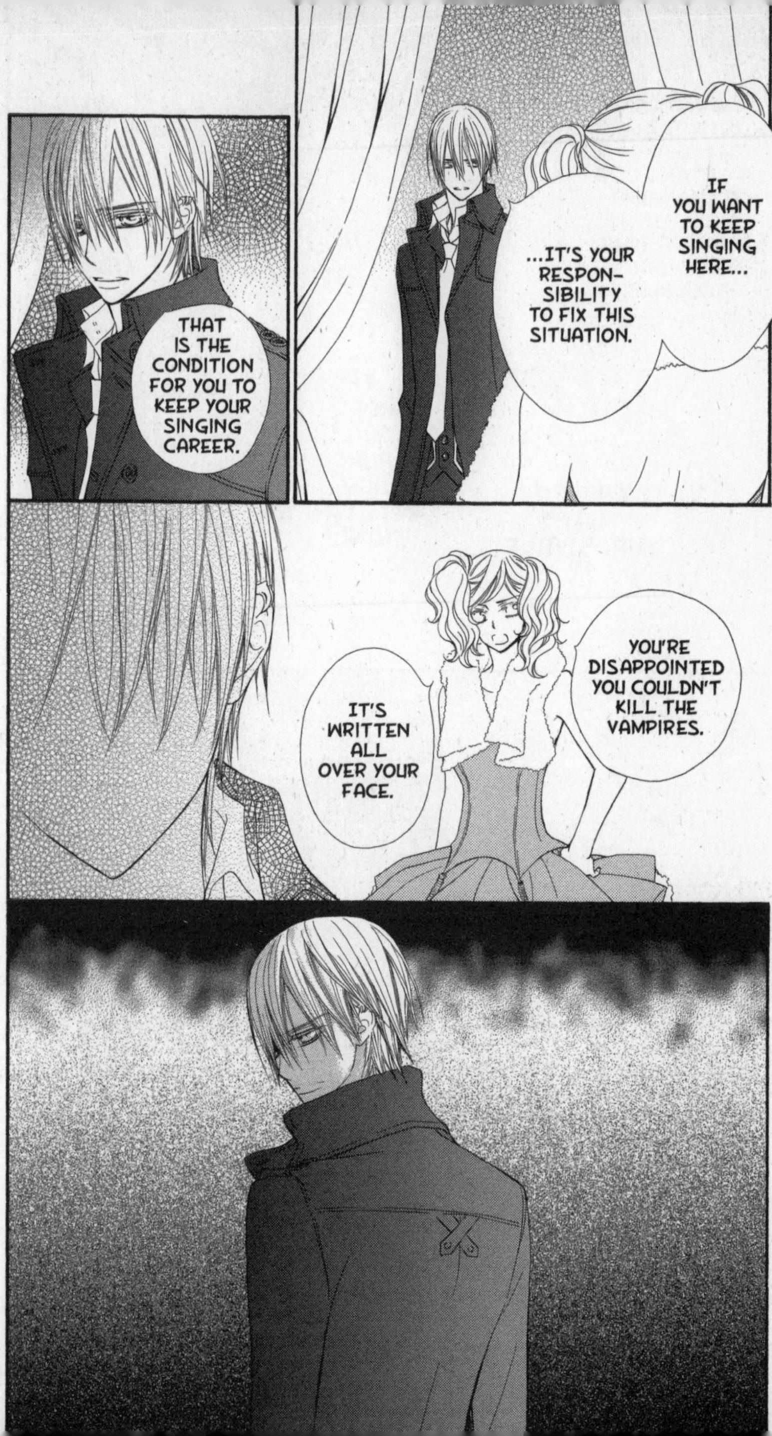
IF YOU WANT TO KEEP SINGING HERE...
...IT'S YOUR RESPON-SIBILITY TO FIX THIS SITUATION.
THAT IS THE CONDITION FOR YOU TO KEEP YOUR SINGING CAREER.
YOU'RE DISAPPOINTED YOU COULDN'T KILL THE VAMPIRES.
IT'S WRITTEN ALL OVER YOUR FACE.

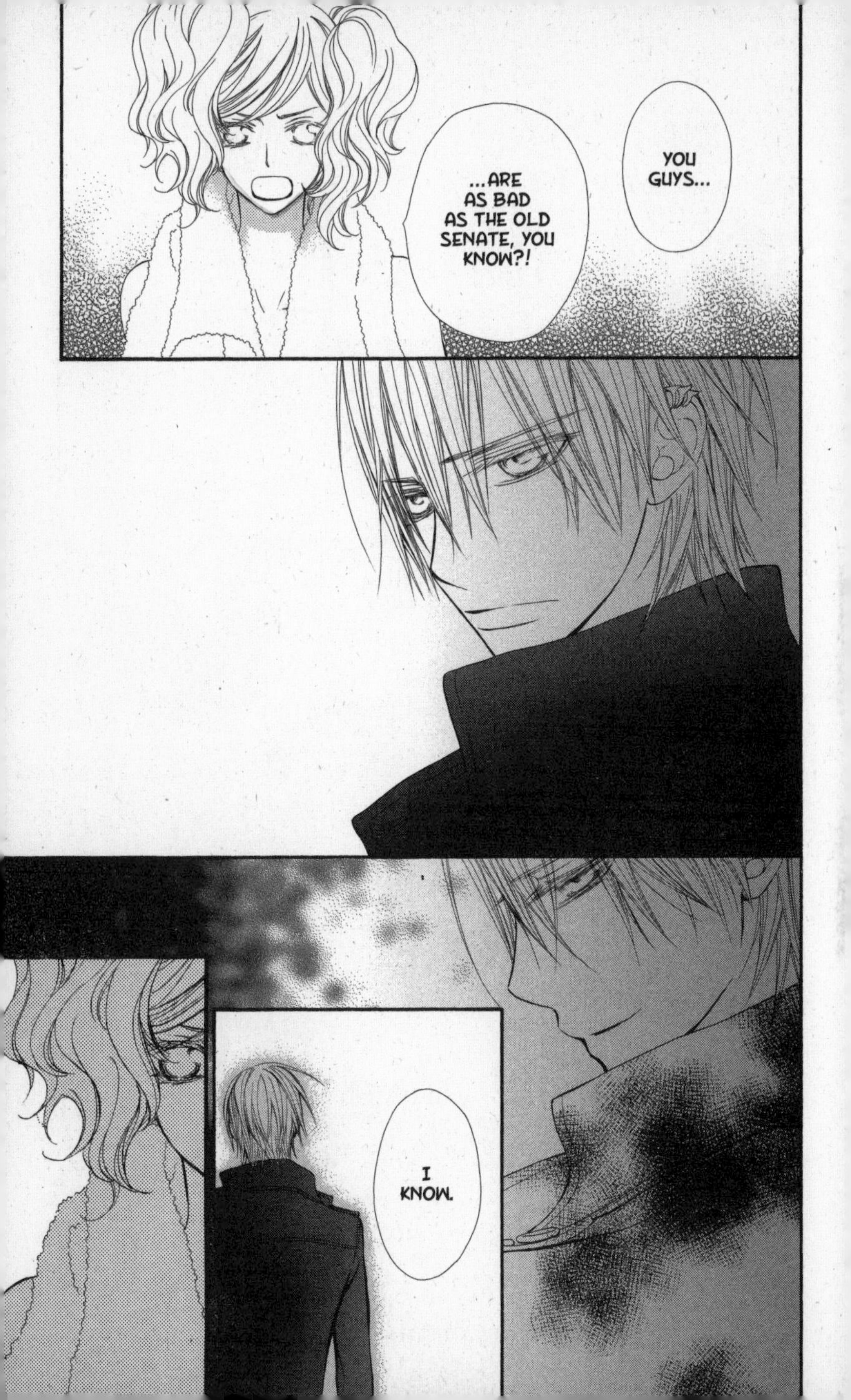
YOU GUYS...
...ARE AS BAD AS THE OLD SENATE, YOU KNOW?!
I KNOW.

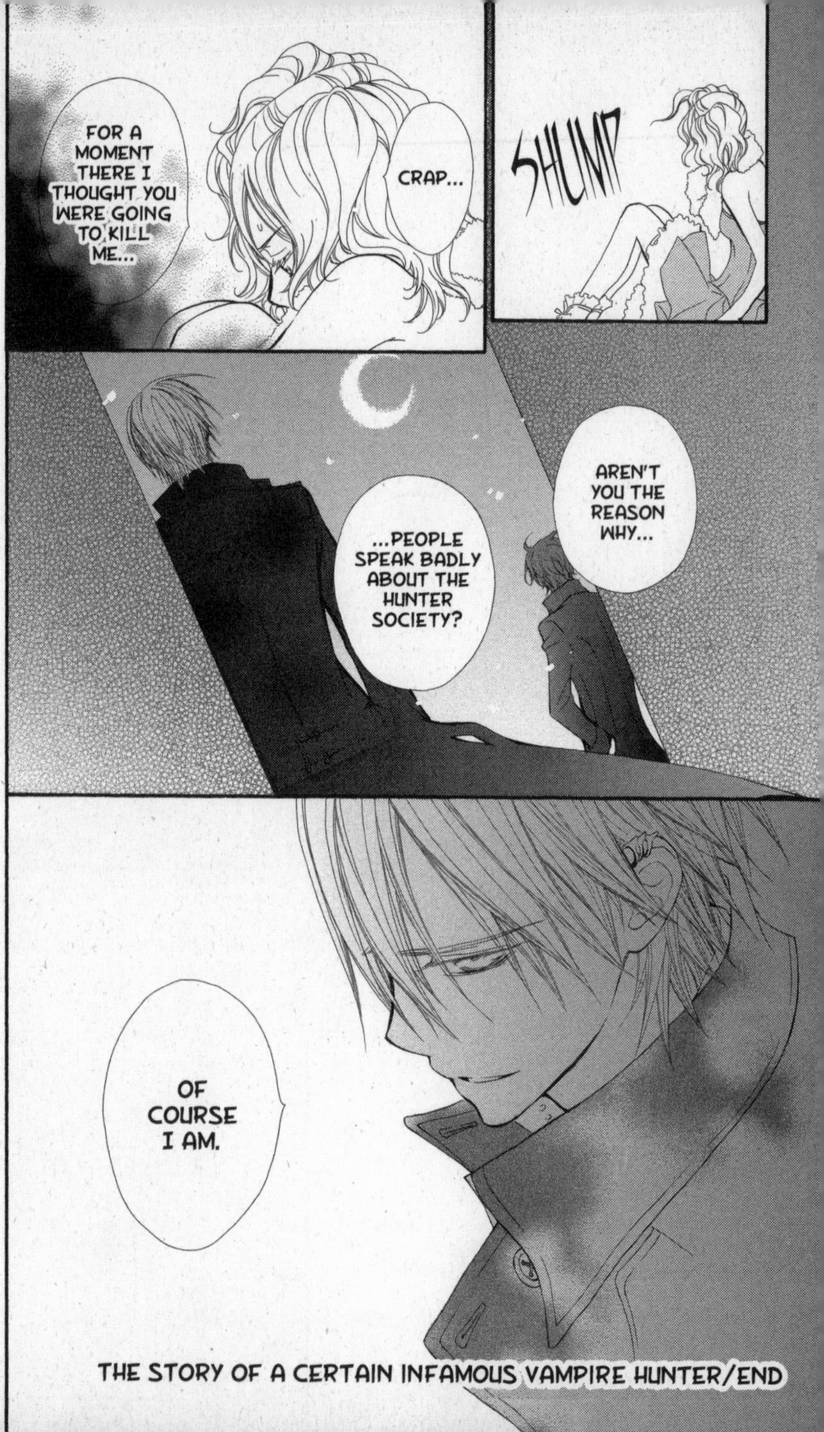
SHUMP
CRAP...
FOR A MOMENT THERE I THOUGHT YOU WERE GOING TO KILL ME...
AREN'T YOU THE REASON WHY...
...PEOPLE SPEAK BADLY ABOUT THE HUNTER SOCIETY?
OF COURSE I AM.
THE STORY OF A CERTAIN INFAMOUS VAMPIRE HUNTER/END

KANAME AND THE COLLAR

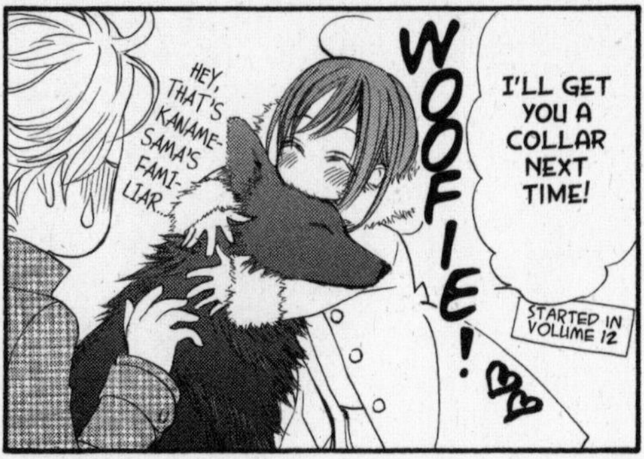
I'LL GET YOU A COLLAR NEXT TIME!
WOOFIE!
STARTED IN VOLUME 12
HEY, THAT'S KANAME-SAMA'S FAMILIAR...

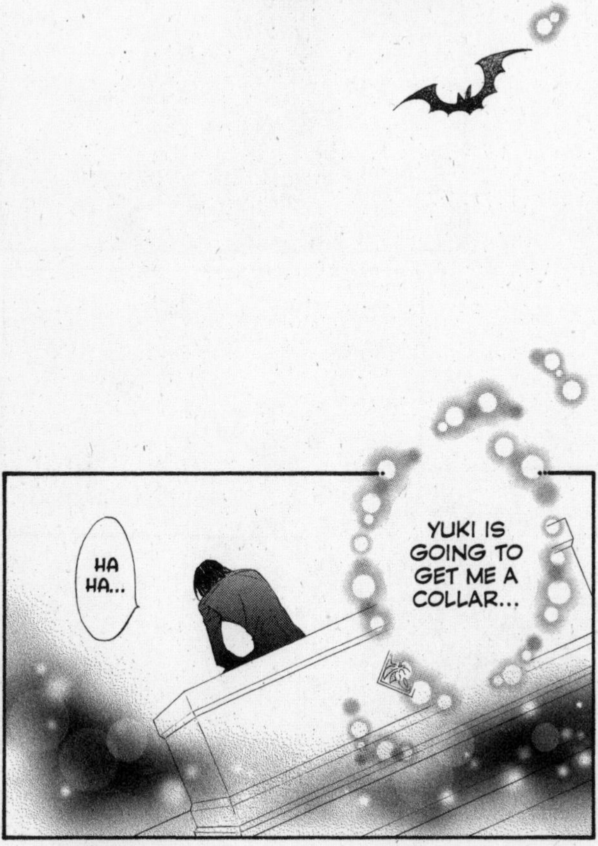
YUKI IS GOING TO GET ME A COLLAR...
HA HA...

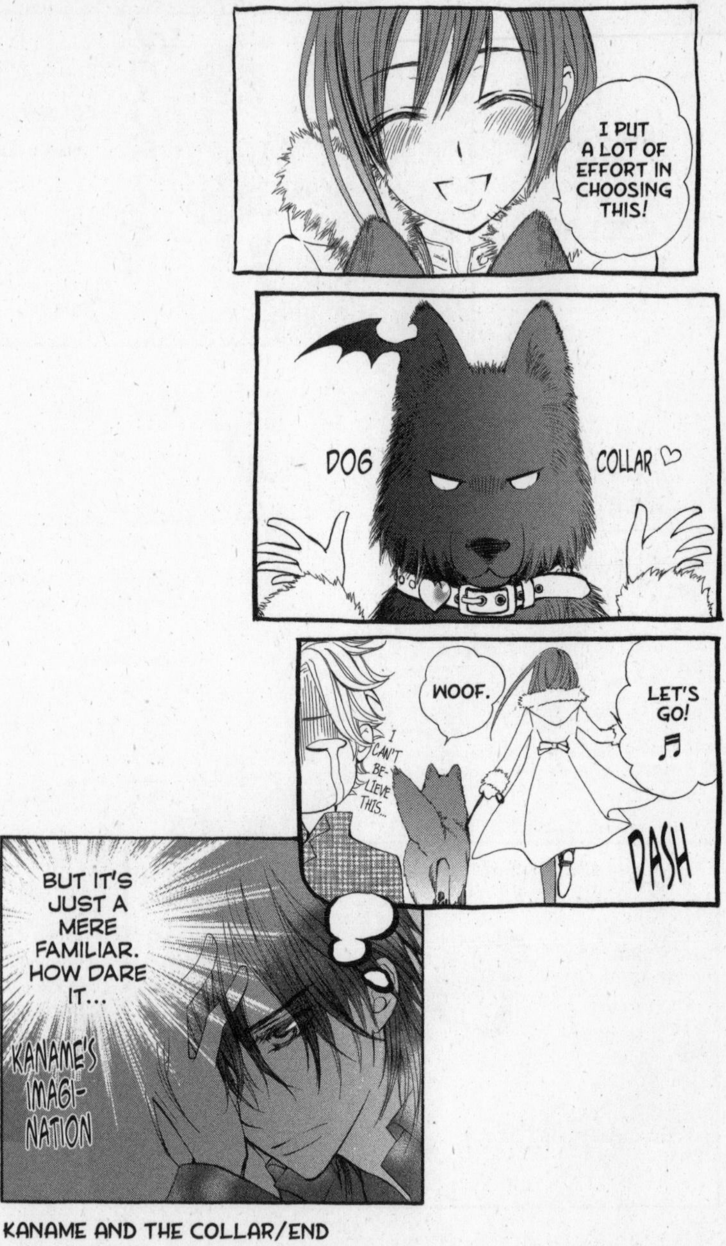
I PUT A LOT OF EFFORT IN CHOOSING THIS!
DOG
COLLAR ♡
LET'S GO! ♬
WOOF.
I CAN'T BE-LIEVE THIS...
DASH
BUT IT'S JUST A MERE FAMILIAR. HOW DARE IT...
KANAME'S IMAGI-NATION

KANAME AND THE COLLAR/END

EDITOR'S NOTES

Characters

Matsuri Hino puts careful thought into the names of her characters in *Vampire Knight*. Below is the collection of characters through volume 13. Each character's name is presented family name first, per the kanji reading.

黒主優姫

Cross Yuki

Yuki's last name, *Kurosu*, is the Japanese pronunciation of the English word "cross." However, the kanji has a different meaning—*kuro* means "black" and *su* means "master." Her first name is a combination of *yuu*, meaning "tender" or "kind," and *ki*, meaning "princess."

錐生零

Kiryu Zero

Zero's first name is the kanji for *rei*, meaning "zero." In his last name, *Kiryu*, the *ki* means "auger" or "drill," and the *ryu* means "life."

玖蘭枢

Kuran Kaname

Kaname means "hinge" or "door." The kanji for his last name is a combination of the old-fashioned way of writing *ku*, meaning "nine," and *ran*, meaning "orchid": "nine orchids."

藍堂英

Aido Hanabusa

Hanabusa means "petals of a flower." *Aido* means "indigo temple." In Japanese, the pronunciation of *Aido* is very close to the pronunciation of the English word *idol*.

架院暁

Kain Akatsuki

Akatsuki means "dawn" or "day-break." In *Kain*, *ka* is a base or support, while *in* denotes a building that has high fences around it, such as a temple or school.

早園瑠佳

Souen Ruka

In *Ruka*, the *ru* means "lapis lazuli" while the *ka* means "good-looking" or "beautiful." The *sou* in Ruka's surname, *Souen*, means "early," but this kanji also has an obscure meaning of "strong fragrance." The *en* means "garden."

一条拓麻

Ichijo Takuma

Ichijo can mean a "ray" or "streak." The kanji for *Takuma* is a combination of *taku*, meaning "to cultivate" and *ma*, which is the kanji for *asa*, meaning "hemp" or "flax," a plant with blue flowers.

支葵千里

Shiki Senri

Shiki's last name is a combination of *shi*, meaning "to support" and *ki*, meaning "mallow"—a flowering plant with pink or white blossoms. The *ri* in *Senri* is a traditional Japanese unit of measure for distance, and one *ri* is about 2.44 miles. *Senri* means "1,000 *ri*."

夜刈十牙

Yagari Toga

Yagari is a combination of *ya*, meaning "night," and *gari*, meaning "to harvest." *Toga* means "ten fangs."

一条麻遠，一翁

Ichijo Asato, aka "Ichio"

Ichijo can mean a "ray" or "streak." *Asato*'s first name is comprised of *asa*, meaning "hemp" or "flax," and *tou*, meaning "far off." His nickname is *ichi*, or "one," combined with *ou*, which can be used as an honorific when referring to an older man.

若葉沙頼

Wakaba Sayori

Yori's full name is Sayori Wakaba. *Wakaba* means "young leaves." Her given name, *Sayori*, is a combination of *sa*, meaning "sand," and *yori*, meaning "trust."

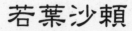

星煉

Seiren

Sei means "star" and *ren* means "to smelt" or "refine." *Ren* is also the same kanji used in *rengoku*, or "purgatory."

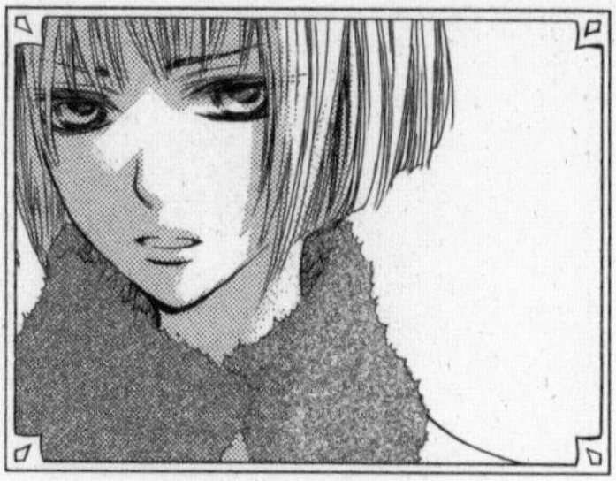

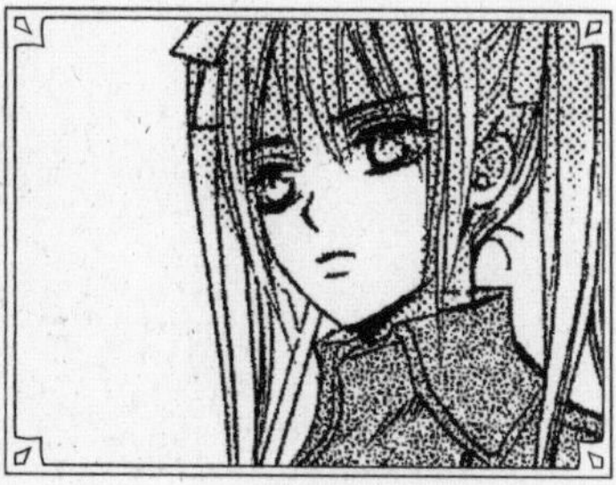

遠矢莉磨

Toya Rima

Toya means a "far-reaching arrow." Rima's first name is a combination of *ri*, or "jasmine," and *ma*, which signifies enhancement by wearing away, such as by polishing or scouring.

紅まり亜

Kurenai Maria

Kurenai means "crimson." The kanji for the last *a* in Maria's first name is the same that is used in "Asia."

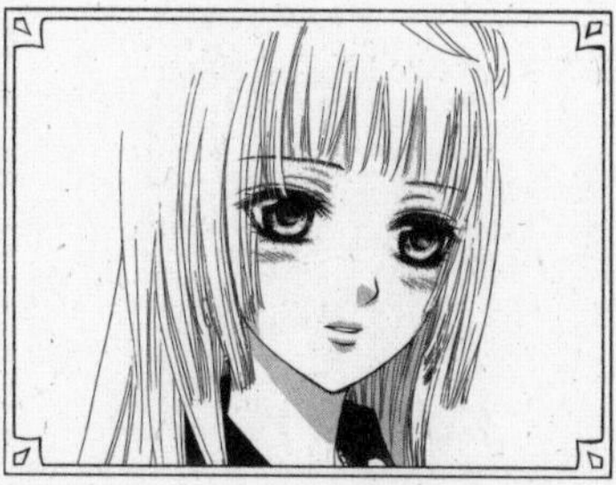

錐生壱縷
Kiryu Ichiru
Ichi is the old-fashioned way of writing "one," and *ru* means "thread."

緋桜閑, 狂咲姫
Hio Shizuka, Kuruizaki-hime
Shizuka means "calm and quiet." In Shizuka's family name, *hi* is "scarlet," and *ou* is "cherry blossoms." Shizuka Hio is also referred to as the "Kuruizaki-hime." *Kuruizaki* means "flowers blooming out of season," and *hime* means "princess."

藍堂月子
Aido Tsukiko
Aido means "indigo temple." *Tsukiko* means "moon child."

白蕗更

Shirabuki Sara

Shira is "white," and *buki* is "butterbur," a plant with white flowers. *Sara* means "renew."

黒主灰閻

Cross Kaien

Cross, or *Kurosu*, means "black master." Kaien is a combination of *kai*, meaning "ashes," and *en*, meaning "village gate." The kanji for *en* is also used for Enma, the ruler of the Underworld in Buddhist mythology.

玖蘭李土

Kuran Rido

Kuran means "nine orchids." In *Rido*, *ri* means "plum" and *do* means "earth."

玖蘭樹里

Kuran Juri

Kuran means "nine orchids." In her first name, *ju* means "tree" and a *ri* is a traditional Japanese unit of measure for distance. The kanji for *ri* is the same as in Senri's name.

玖蘭悠

Kuran Haruka

Kuran means "nine orchids." *Haruka* means "distant" or "remote."

鷹宮海斗

Takamiya Kaito

Taka means "hawk" and *miya* means "imperial palace" or "shrine." *Kai* is "sea" and *to* means "to measure" or "grid."

菖藤依砂也

Shoto Isaya

Sho means "Siberian Iris" and *to* is "wisteria." The *I* in *Isaya* means "to rely on," while the *sa* means "sand." *Ya* is a suffix used for emphasis.

橙茉

Toma

In the family name *Toma, to* means "seville orange" and *ma* means "jasmine flower."

Terms

-sama: The suffix *sama* is used in formal address for someone who ranks higher in the social hierarchy. The vampires call their leader "Kaname-sama" only when they are among their own kind.

Matsuri Hino burst onto the manga scene with her series *Kono Yume ga Sametara* (When This Dream Is Over), which was published in *LaLa DX* magazine. Hino was a manga artist a mere nine months after she decided to become one.

With the success of her popular series *Captive Hearts* and *MeruPuri*, Hino has established herself as a major player in the world of shojo manga. *Vampire Knight* is currently serialized in *LaLa* magazine.

Hino enjoys creative activities and has commented that she would have been either an architect or an apprentice to traditional Japanese craft masters if she had not become a manga artist.

VAMPIRE KNIGHT
Vol. 13
Shojo Beat Edition

GN
Hino

STORY AND ART BY
MATSURI HINO

Adaptation/Nancy Thistlethwaite
Translation/Tetsuichiro Miyaki
Touch-up Art & Lettering/Rina Mapa
Graphic Design/Amy Martin
Editor/Nancy Thistlethwaite

Vampire Knight by Matsuri Hino © Matsuri Hino 2010. All rights reserved.
First published in Japan in 2010 by HAKUSENSHA, Inc., Tokyo. English
language translation rights arranged with HAKUSENSHA, Inc., Tokyo.

The rights of the author(s) of the work(s) in this publication to be so identified
have been asserted in accordance with the Copyright, Designs and Patents
Act 1988. A CIP catalogue record for this book is available from the British
Library.

The stories, characters and incidents mentioned in this publication are
entirely fictional.

Printed in Canada

Published by VIZ Media, LLC
P.O. Box 77010
San Francisco, CA 94107

10 9 8 7 6 5 4 3 2 1
First printing, October 2011

www.viz.com

www.shojobeat.com